Globalization strategy in the hotel industry

Globalization Strategy in the Hotel Industry looks at the recent expansion of multinational hotel companies and the challenges they face in the international arena. The highly competitive global environment presents many problems as the hotel sector is tied in closely with other industries in the service sector, with real estate, with other forms of investment, employment patterns and different cultural management systems.

This book looks at the particular characteristics of the hotel industry and uses three regional analyses to reveal a variety of problems facing hotel groups today. It describes the current climate of America, Europe and South East Asia, particularly Hong Kong, talking to key managers and using case studies and extracts to show the differences in these three areas.

The final section takes an issues-based approach to explore the various strategic responses different companies have employed. It covers topics such as human resources, cooperation and competition, business failure and regeneration, business ecosystems, relating all these issues in international business to the particular dynamics of the hotel industry.

Using illustrations, extracts, interviews and key statistics throughout, this book provides a good reference to the way the international hotel industry works today for students and professionals alike.

Frank M. Go is Head and Professor of the Department of Hotel and Tourism Management at Hong Kong Polytechnic University. **Ray Pine** is an Associate Professor in Hotel Management, also at Hong Kong Polytechnic University.

Globalization strategy in the hotel industry

Frank M. Go and Ray Pine

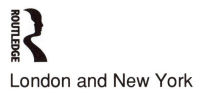

London and New York

First published 1995
by Routledge
11 New Fetter Lane, London EC4P 4EE

Simultaneously published in the USA and Canada
by Routledge
29 West 35th Street, New York, NY 10001

© 1995 Frank M. Go

Typeset in Baskerville by LaserScript, Mitcham, Surrey
Printed and bound in Great Britain by
T.J. Press (Padstow) Ltd, Padstow, Cornwall

British Library Cataloguing in Publication Data
A catalogue record for this book is available from the British Library

Library of Congress Cataloging in Publication Data
Go, Frank M.
  Globalization strategy in the hotel industry/Frank M. Go and
  Ray Pine.
  p. cm.
  Includes bibliographical references and index.
  1. Hotels – Planning. 2. Hotel management. I. Pine, Ray.
II. Title.
TX911.3.P46G64 1994   94-43129
338.4'764794 – dc20   CIP

ISBN 0-415-10322-3 (hbk)
ISBN 0-415-10323-1 (pbk)

FRANK: *To Frasquita, Justin and Niels for being there*
RAY: *To my old and new families*

Contents

List of figures   ix
List of boxes   x
List of tables   xi
List of contributors   xiii
Foreword   xiv
Preface   xvi
Acknowledgements   xix

Part I Introduction and general trends in the hotel industry

1 Introduction to globalization   3
2 The international hotel industry   25
3 Appraising the global competitive environment   50

Part II Strategic environment of the global hotel industry

4 Understanding the structural dynamics of the American hotel
    industry   97
5 Expanding in a barrier-free Europe   129
6 Sustaining the competitiveness of Hong Kong's hotel industry   168

**Part III Responses to strategic developments in the global
hotel industry**

7 Capitalizing on human resources strategy for competitive advantage 201
8 Reversing the cycle of failure through organizational renewal   235
9 Implementing globalization strategies   269
10 Competing and cooperating in the changing tourism channel
    system   306
11 Evolving towards a business ecosystem   327
12 Charting a new course into the twenty-first century   360

Notes   375
Bibliography   383
Index   404

Figures

1.1 Alternative corporate orientations to international hotel
    marketing   6
1.2 A flow diagram for creating value-added processes that lead to
    competitive advantage in the hotel industry   19
2.1 Significant strategic relationships   36
3.1 A matter of time and money   74
3.2 Product/market blending   79
3.3 The hotel market from a benefit segmentation perspective   80
4.1 Forces driving hotel industry competition   98
4.2 Segmentation strategy in the hotel industry   103
7.1 Policy regarding pay increases for hourly employees   211
7.2 Hourly pay compared to that of competitors   212
7.3 Benefit packages for hourly employees   213
7.4 Incentive bonus programmes   214
8.1 The cycle of failure   239
8.2 The cycle of quality service   255
9.1 Globalization of the hotel industry   271
9.2 Globalization and competitive bench-marking   273
9.3 Corporate-level strategy options   277
9.4 Globalization drivers   281
11.1 The relationship between leisure, recreation and tourism   331
12.1 'Switching gears' along the globalizing continuum   371

Boxes

1.1 Focus on independent hotels   15
6.1 Hotel developments associated with Hong Kong Airport
     Railway   173
7.1 Summary of Ritz-Carlton approach to service quality   231

Tables

2.1   The value chain concept applied to the hotel industry   35

2.2   Business travellers' expectations of de luxe hotel stay   37

2.3   Growth of voluntary hotel chain consortia 1991–1992   40

2.4   Total affiliation cost for a 200-room, mid-rate hotel over a ten-year period   41

3.1   Annual growth rate of international tourism receipts compared to selected trade commodities, GDP in OECD countries, and total world export, 1975–1986   51

3.2   Typology of competitive scenarios in the service sector   56

3.3   Variation in marketing orientation across different service industries   57

3.4   Average annual growth rates of real per capita income   58

3.5   US tourism to Europe 1950–1985   63

3.6   Sources of demand for hotel accommodation   69

3.7   Leisure hours   73

3.8   Average number of vacation days   73

3.9   Market segmentation in the hotel industry   81

3.10   Weekend pleasure travel segments and their attitudes to overnight accommodations selection   83

4.1   Major hotel company takeovers 1989–1990   99

4.2   Changes in the US lodging industry's size and structure 1948–1977   100

4.3   The US lodging industry's size and capacity 1928–1984   101

4.4   Source and disposition of the US hotel industry dollar in 1989   116

4.5   Goals, critical success factors and measures   119

4.6   CSFs most frequently mentioned by respondents   120

5.1   EEA versus NAFTA   130

5.2   International tourist arrivals in Europe 1970–1992   131

5.3   International tourism receipts in Europe 1970–1992   131

5.4   Leading tourism markets for Europe 1991   132

5.5   Trends in the capacity of hotels and similar establishments in Europe – 1986–1991   136

5.6 Top ten largest Europe-based hotel chains   153
5.7 EC concentration of room stock, 1990   154
5.8 Rating scale for transnational hotel expansion   156
6.1 Hotel supply situation 1993–1995   170
6.2 Visitor arrivals in Hong Kong, by nationality 1985–1993   176
6.3 Average nights spent in Hong Kong, by major market areas
     1985–1992   177
6.4 Visitor spending pattern 1992   177
6.5 World trade in commercial services 1991   178
6.6 Composition of exports of services at market prices of 1991   180
6.7 The main indigenous hotel companies in Hong Kong   180
7.1 Importance of goals   206
7.2 Importance of critical success factors   207
7.3 Importance of measures for monitoring critical success factors   207
7.4 Importance of strategic policies in personnel management   209
7.5 Importance of training activities   209
7.6 Methods used to hire hourly workers   210
7.7 Motivation of various employee groups   213
7.8 A comparison of the proportion of expatriates in different
     situations   224
7.9 Proportion of expatriate hotel managers in different levels of
     management   224
8.1 Four stages of service firm competitiveness   252
8.2 Characteristics of innovative leaders   260
9.1 Marketing taxonomy   296
11.1 Five levels of customer relationships   334

Contributors

Sarah-Jane Dawson, Pannel Kerr Forster Associates, UK. Joint author of Chapter 5.

Frank M. Go, Hong Kong Polytechnic University. Joint author of Chapters 5, 6, 7 and 10.

Ray Pine, Hong Kong Polytechnic University. Joint author of Chapters 6 and 7.

Paul Williams, Hong Kong Polytechnic University. Joint author of Chapter 10.

Ricky Yu, Hong Kong Polytechnic University. Joint author of Chapters 6 and 7.

Dov Zohar, Technion Israel Institute of Technology. Joint author of Chapter 7.

Foreword

The genesis of the present book, for which I am very pleased to write the foreword, may be found, to some extent, in the Congress theme for the Annual International Hotel Association's (IHA) Annual Congress held in Dublin, Ireland, 25–31 October 1987: 'Strategies for the 21st Century'.

The 1987 IHA Congress findings reiterated the idea that the world today faces a period of profound change. In keeping with these predictions the impact of the 'post-industrial era' through a wave of more advanced automation and computerization is revolutionizing, particularly, the developed world and, among other things, affecting the ratio of labour to capital in most production processes.

Changes in demographics and employment are in turn creating a revolution of sorts within the travel, hotel and related industries. Work in the future will be more complex, based more strongly on computer applications, and require a higher level of skills. At the same time, new substitute products are competing with traditional hotels for – in certain markets shrinking – business and leisure travel budgets.

Shifts in the demographics of countries in Europe, the Americas, and the Asia–Pacific region are altering the travel market to a significant extent, perhaps most profoundly in Europe. However, as a recent IHA research report concluded, 'Europe's travel industry is still treating seniors as a fringe market and lags behind North America in effective promotional policies.'

Achieving a competitive edge through better cooperative relationships as a means to compete more effectively has been corroborated by research conducted on Europe's Senior Travel Market for conferences co-organized by the International Hotel Association and the European Travel Commission in November 1992 and October 1993. Based on this study's recommendations and the findings of *Globalization Strategy in the Hotel Industry*, I wholeheartedly encourage hoteliers to seek opportunities, where appropriate, for greater cooperation between themselves and their partners in the National Tourism Organizations, sector organizations in the travel and tourism industry and other constituents, for example, in what might be called the 'welfare industry', to reach the expanding senior travel market more effectively.

The future of the International Hotel Industry, indeed the membership of the IHA comprising through its National Associations over 300,000 hotels in 142 countries worldwide, is inextricably intertwined with the changes brought about by the globalization of the market place.

The hotels the IHA represents comprise *all* types of accommodation from luxury, and city-centre business-based to resorts and hotels.

Some of the trends *Globalization Strategy in the Hotel Industry* identifies may affect business hotels more than resort properties. Other trends noted in the book may be more relevant to chain-affiliated hotels than independently operated hotels.

But despite the many differences there may be between hotel types and hotels in the different world regions, all share a salient characteristic. In a fiercely competitive environment they have to render quality service to survive.

Accordingly, *Globalization Strategy in the Hotel Industry* focuses, in essence, on the adding of value to services rendered, to guests and employees, as the best defence to global competition for hotel chains and independent hotels alike. At the same time, the book recognizes the importance to hotels of establishing a global presence either through physical expansion or exploiting existing international referral consortia.

To be successful during the 1990s and into the twenty-first century will require managers who are able to anticipate and understand the global market implications on the hotel industry. Furthermore, they will have to be able to formulate and implement a globalization strategy in the hotel industry.

Globalization Strategy in the Hotel Industry is an idea whose time has come. An idea which can help managers shape the future, respectively, of the hotel industry, hotels, the communities in which they operate and, lest we forget, their own destiny. I strongly recommend the book to operators, both in hotel chains and independent hotels, members of related industry sector associations, suppliers to the hotel industry, students on a wide range of diploma, degree and postgraduate hospitality and tourism management courses and those with a general interest in the evolution of the international hotel industry.

Christiane Clech,
Secretary-General, International Hotel Association,
July 1994.

Preface

The idea for this book arose from a dawning realization that the hotel industry is becoming increasingly drawn into the global market. And that the 'global corporation' as an organizational form may be attractive to only a few of the largest hotel companies. In addition, of late, the concept of the geocentric corporation has been called into question, especially in terms of its ability to deal with local conditions. Nevertheless, contemporary key issues for most hotel companies are how to organize, integrate, and manage their activities in order to respond to global competition, and how to modify approaches to suit local application.

This realization built in increments from a number of stimuli. First, attendance at the 1987 International Hotel Association (IHA) Congress in Dublin led to an awareness that the hotel business around the world is changing in fundamental ways. Second, the Economist Intelligence Unit commissioned Frank Go in 1988 to conduct a study of the 'Competitive strategies in the international hotel industry'. This work led to further awareness that the hotel industry at the end of the twentieth century is increasingly the subject of global, as opposed to local, competition. The study results also indicated that providing value is a top priority for hoteliers. Third, one year later the IHA commissioned Frank Go to conduct a study into human resources management in relation to the competitive advantage of hotel corporations. These study findings were presented at the IHA Human Resource Forum in Strasbourg, France in 1989.

From these origins, and through teaching and further research, we have attempted to seek an answer to the question: 'What are the implications of global competition for the hotel industry?' Or more specifically, 'What should be the intended direction and the competencies hotel companies must master to create and sustain a competitive advantage?'

Most of the current writing and thinking about global business follows either a 'generic strategy' approach or an 'organizational alignment' approach. These approaches developed independently of one another and cultivated their own biases. In particular, the alignment approach emphasizes organizational structure and environment, and tends to neglect strategic positioning.

Conversely, the competitive strategy approach focuses on competitive advantage but neglects organizational attributes. We have attempted in this book to explore the intersection of these two perspectives, specifically by investigating whether organizational and operational issues, when linked with business strategy, are a source for cultivating the capabilities and competencies through which competitive advantage may be sustained.

This approach is called 'globalization strategy', to denote the 'boundary-less' mindset, to paraphrase GE's Jack Welch, which hoteliers will require to enable them to face the pressures of global competition. In the broadest sense, globalization strategy expresses the ability to 'switch gears' across geographies; to work with customers and suppliers; to learn on an ongoing basis; and, to think and act cross-functionally. The main purpose of a globalization strategy is to create and sustain value for all constituents thereby improving competitiveness.

In this regard, the move towards unified markets in Europe (EFTA), North America (NAFTA), and South-East Asia (ASEAN), provides examples that regional management and marketing are highly likely to become more desirable and practical. Furthermore, the mounting public pressure to preserve the environment is an important example of why hoteliers should pay greater attention to local conditions and to developing their ability to 'switch gears' along the 'globalization' continuum, ranging from local, to regional, and to global, so that competitiveness in specific geographic arenas can be improved.

At the same time, globalization strategy is especially relevant as an evolving logic to respond to intensifying worldwide competition which drives customers' demands for value and leaves hoteliers little room for error. Value-adding service within hotels hinges on staff attitudes. The study findings reported in Chapter 7 indicate that whilst hotel managers espouse the view that employee attitude is the most critical factor to achieving guest satisfaction, there is a gap between this and their operating norms in that regard. We hope that this work will contribute in some small way to bringing this gap to light so that hoteliers realize that the correct attitude must start at the top.

Another observation we wish to share is that the leading hotel companies do not necessarily succeed because they apply the principles of 'war-like' competition. Rather, through cooperative relationships they initiate partnerships which create and sustain prosperous professional and host communities.

In this regard, we have tried to emphasize the important role hotels can play in the host community. Hotels make important impressions on the economic stability and employment creation in the host communities in which they operate. They determine, to a significant extent, what types of tourism will evolve in host destinations, as hotels, together with 'attractions', form the foundation of almost any community's tourism industry. The ability to think ahead and to pro-act, by designing and developing hotels that are 'appropriate' and 'environmentally responsible' in selected locales, are becoming hallmarks of professionalism, and set guidelines for leadership and survival in the broadest sense.

Judging by the best practices that are featured in the present book, there appears to be a gradual shift in the hotel industry from an era marked by the sole concern for building 'room-night volume' to an era characterized by value-based performance. As the shift towards value-based performance evolves, the ideas contained in *Globalization Strategy in the Hotel Industry*, particularly the logic which combines the intent for global reach with the need for local adaptability, will become more evident and important. And so will the imperative for training and management education to enhance competencies and capabilities which sustain competitiveness.

Frank M. Go and Ray Pine,
October 1994.

Acknowledgements

Many people have contributed to the development of this book.

A debt is owed to the individuals who co-authored some chapters: Sarah-Jane Dawson, Ricky Yu, Dov Zohar and Paul Williams.

Thanks go to the following who reviewed parts of the manuscript: Ewout Th. Cassee, the Hague Hotelschool, the Netherlands; Irene Herremans, the Faculty of Management, University of Calgary, Canada; Luiz Moutinho, University of Wales, Cardiff; Celik Parkan, City University of Hong Kong; H. Leo Theuns, University of Tilburg.

Thanks also to Stephen Hiemstra of Purdue University, Ruud Reuland, the Hague Hotelschool, and Catherine Woodhouse of Holiday Inns Worldwide for their help during the project's research stage.

Gratitude is also expressed to those who provided intellectual stimulation during years past: Jan G. Lambooy and Jozef H.J.P. Tettero, both at the University of Amsterdam; J.R. Brent Ritchie and Dean P. Michael Maher, both at the University of Calgary; Maurits C. Tideman, Consultant, the Netherlands; Anthony G. Marshall, Florida International University; Donald E. Hawkins, George Washington University.

We are also indebted to the many business, association and media executives who provided information and interpretations about their companies or the hotel industry which are incorporated into the book: Linda Chun Adams, Director of Marketing, Pan Pacific Hotels & Resorts; Daniel S.Y. Bong, Director, Regal Hotels International Holdings Ltd; Frances Brown, Editor, *Tourism Management*; Ann Checkley, Director Environmental Affairs, Canadian Pacific Hotels & Resorts; Brian Deeson, President & CEO, Century International Hotels; Edwin D. Fuller, Senior Vice-President and Managing Director, Marriott Lodging International; Jean-Marie Leclercq, General Manager, Hotel Nikko, Hong Kong; Mac Ma, Executive Director, New World Hotels International Limited; Peter Moore, UK Managing Director, Center Parcs; Kenneth Mullins, Senior Vice-President, Park Lane Hotels International; Nicola Pogson, Director of Industry Services of the International Hotel Association; Onno Poortier, President, Peninsula Group; Robert Riley, Managing Director, Mandarin Oriental

Hotels; Robin Spearman, Chairman, IHA Human Resources Committee; Behrouz A. Tamdjidi, Regional Vice-President Operations, Inter-Continental Hotels; Larry M.K. Tchou, Vice-President Hyatt Hotels and Resorts, Asia; Glenn Withiam, Executive Editor, *The Cornell HRA Quarterly*; Dick Vollenga, Co-Chairman, IHA Human Resources Committee; and, Manuel Woo, Executive Director, Hong Kong Hotels Association.

In addition, we are especially grateful to Jeanette Chan, Margaret Choy, Cecelia Tong and Ricky Yu whose tireless efforts and patience were instrumental in turning the many notes into a comprehensible text, and to Alice To for attending to the correspondence for permissions. Also Martha Wong, Elisa Wong, Bartholomew Leung, Neville Yu and Chris Cheung of Hong Kong Polytechnic University for their painstaking work in the production of the illustrations used in some of the figures presented in the book.

Last but not least, we would like to give our sincere thanks to the Routledge editorial and production team involved with this book. In particular Francesca Weaver and Laura Large whose help and encouragement enabled the manuscript to progress to its final stage, and Sally Close, Alan Fidler and Ann Southgate who then took the manuscript through to the production of the book itself.

Whilst acknowledging the great help from these sources, we retain personal responsibility for the book and any of its errors.

Part I

Introduction and general trends in the hotel industry

Chapter 1

Introduction to globalization*

The adjective 'globalization' in this book's title is relevant because both the domestic and global environments are intrinsic characteristics of modern industry in that a growing number of local businesses are being drawn into the global arena for two general reasons. First, the weakening of growth opportunities in 'slow-growth' industrialized economies is 'pushing' firms to expand abroad. Second, corporations that have their home base in the industrialized economies are being 'pulled' into rapidly expanding foreign markets by growth opportunities, that were triggered by conditions such as:

(a) The emergence of new business centres throughout the world, in particular in the Middle and Far East, and the competition between the newly industrialized countries (NICs) to become the leading commercial and financial centres resulted in a hotel construction boom and a big development opportunity for international hotel companies.

(b) Government incentives which encouraged many hotel corporations to expand their activities in selected countries. For instance the Spanish government's encouragement and support of tourism helped turn the country into one of the world's major mass-tourism destinations. Currently, the government of Turkey offers incentives to lure local and foreign investors to develop tourist facilities there (Baki 1990: 61–62). Conversely, governments also play a significant role in restricting the growth of international tourism. A wide variety of barriers to travel may be found around the world: restraining the flow of persons; administrative delays that hinder licensing, for example to start the construction or operation of a hotel; and discrimination against national flag carriers.

(c) The emerging multinational infrastructure. Most expansion of international trade and manufacturing around the world implies an increase in corporate travel, which in turn requires a growing market for hotel accommodation to facilitate business travel (Dicken 1986: 88). The presence of transnational hotels facilitates international tourism especially to and in developing countries (Ajami 1988; McQueen 1989: 287). For example, service networks comprised of hotel corporations, transportation and credit card companies made possible rapid increases in traffic from North America to Europe, from northern Europe to the Mediterranean, and on a more limited scale to more distant locations such as Kenya, Thailand, and the Caribbean. These service networks were sometimes following and in other instances leading customers (Heskett 1986).

The case at the end of this chapter gives an example of how one hotel company, Inter-Continental, has progressed through its own 'globalization' process.

INTERNATIONALIZATION ORIENTATIONS

The premise of strategic management is for the organization to adapt continuously to its changing environment so that it will survive and, better yet, succeed (Dev and Olsen 1989; West and Olsen 1989). This notion applies both to domestic hospitality firms and the multinational firm. The environment decision-makers select for their organization to operate in, and the attitude or orientation towards the selected business environment results in five possible orientations to international business. Firms may or may not choose to go through a learning curve changing from one orientation to another over time. Each orientation suggests a particular corporate culture, organizational goals, strategies, and structure.

(a) Little or no interest in operating abroad. The domestic market satisfies their expansion needs and foreign operations are often viewed as complicated and risky. Perlmutter (1967) identified four distinctive orientations associated with successive phases in the evolution of the internationalization process of firms.

(b) Ethnocentrism or home-country orientation. Some firms view foreign operations as an 'appendix' to domestic operations. An organization with this orientation tends to build its hotels in foreign markets that are most like the home country. Usually, firms who fit in this category will not conduct extensive market research or adapt promotional activities to respond to foreign markets. Canada, a foreign country but near and similar to the United States, remains a favourite international market for American international firms to expand to.

(c) Polycentrism or host-country orientation. Some firms establish in each foreign or overseas market. Often these subsidiaries are managed by nationals, and marketing activities are planned and administered on a country-by-country basis.

(d) Regiocentrism or regional orientation. Certain firms gear their operations to a particular continental region, such as North America, which incorporates the United States and Canada, countries with similar economies and cultures. The regional orientation affords firms opportunities to pursue market segments that cross national boundaries and potential scale economies.

(e) Geocentrism or global orientation. Some firms view the world market as their oyster. Levitt (1983a) is a strong advocate of firms offering globally standardized products that are advanced, functional, reliable, and low-priced and of the opinion that only companies that pursue this global approach will be successful in the long-term. However, the global marketing approach as advocated by Levitt may be less desirable for tourism and hospitality marketing because of the societal and cultural differences between nations. The global strategy advocated by Levitt which has a standardizing impact must be combined with a sensitivity for local customs and culture (Ziff-Levine 1990), so as to avoid uniformity among mankind. Later in this chapter, 'globalization strategy' will be introduced, which among other things seeks to make possible the globalization of tourism whilst preserving the very cultures that it makes accessible (Ave 1993).

The alternative corporate orientations to international hotel marketing are illustrated in Figure 1.1.

Rise of the multinational corporation

No matter what their country of origin, modern multinational firms share three common characteristics:

(a) They appeared quite suddenly in the 1880s and 1890s in Western Europe, the United States, and somewhat later in Japan.
(b) They were established and continued to grow in industries with similar technologies of production.
(c) They expanded their activities in much the same manner (Chandler 1986: 31).

The emergence of multinational corporations (MNCs) in tourism has contributed significantly to more effective operations, the efficient utilization of resources and the growing globalization of the economy in the 1990s. But the involvement of MNCs in tourism has also given rise to myriad challenges at the host nation level.

MNCs have been subject to a lot of attention attributable to their size, power, and impact on the economic, social, cultural, and political environment of host societies around the world. Fieldhouse (1986: 17) identified four central responses to the MNC phenomenon in the literature since the late 1960s: (a) those of popular alarmists; (b) theorists hostile to international capitalism; (c) applied economists, and (d) specialists in the theory of the firm. In surveying the aforementioned four central responses however, he found that one central theme seemed to emerge, namely:

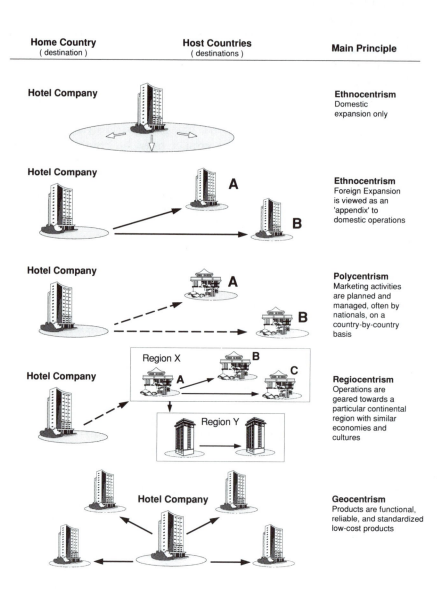

Home Country (destination)	Host Countries (destinations)	Main Principle
Hotel Company		**Ethnocentrism** Domestic expansion only
Hotel Company	A B	**Ethnocentrism** Foreign Expansion is viewed as an 'appendix' to domestic operations
Hotel Company	A B	**Polycentrism** Marketing activities are planned and managed, often by nationals, on a country-by-country basis
Hotel Company	Region X A B C Region Y	**Regiocentrism** Operations are geared towards a particular continental region with similar economies and cultures
	Hotel Company	**Geocentrism** Products are functional, reliable, and standardized low-cost products

Figure 1.1 Alternative corporate orientations to international hotel marketing

Source: Based on Y. Wind *et al.*, 'Guidelines for Developing International Marketing Strategies', *Journal of Marketing*, 37 (April), 1973

that while most early writers tended to accept the alleged universality of the MNC as a form of capitalism, many also asserting that its effects were harmful to both home and host countries, by the later 1970s both assumptions were in serious doubt.

(Fieldhouse 1986: 17)

Jafari observes a parallel development in the literature pertaining to MNCs, especially as regards tourism in developing nations:

First came those [publications] which urge the developing countries to attract international tourism in order to expedite their process of development. Then came awareness of publications which hypothesised or attempted to document that tourism far from contributing, actually retards the process and also generates much unwanted socio-economic costs. Finally came those perspectives which acknowledged both the touristic prospects and problems and suggested ways to maximise the positive and minimise the negative.

(Jafari 1988: 289)

Two issues seem relevant and significant to the potential involvement of transnational hotel corporations in the tourism industry in a host society. First is the development role, if any, that these MNCs can play in the industry and host nation. The second corollary issue pertains to the way in which a particular nation views MNCs and the package of policy instruments it formulates to ensure that their participation is compatible with overall goals of economic development (United Nations 1982: 2). The latter process is heavily influenced by whether a nation is a net contributor or a net recipient of the resources that are being reallocated by the TNCs (Weekly and Aggarwal 1987: 316).

Character of the multinational firm

The MNC is essentially a multi-plant firm whose operations transcend national boundaries and may be defined as 'an enterprise which owns and controls income generating assets in more than one country' (Fieldhouse 1986). The primary goal of MNCs has been to achieve long-term profits and one of the surest ways to attain and maintain this goal has been to reduce unit costs (Chandler 1986: 31). MNCs share many common characteristics, but the following managerial features are particularly relevant to our discussion:

(1) A multinational corporation is an integrated worldwide business system. Such integration is evidenced through resource transfers, that is, movement of capital, technology, and managerial personnel between parent and affiliates and among affiliates themselves which

allows the MNC to acquire materials and produce component parts wherever it is most advantageous to do so.

(2) MNCs are ultimately controlled by a single managerial authority (typically the top management group of the parent company) which makes the key, strategic decisions relating to the operations of the parent firm and all its affiliates. Such centralisation of management is imperative for achieving and maintaining worldwide integration and for attaining the basic objective of profit maximisation for the multinational enterprise as a whole;

(3) Managers of MNCs, especially the central management group, are presumed to possess a 'global perspective'. This means that the top managers regard the entire world as the relevant frame-of-reference for making the kinds of resource acquisition, focus of production, and market decisions.

(Weekly and Aggarwal 1987: 310–311)

The expansion of multinational hotel corporations in the 1970s and 1980s may be explained by Dunning's paradigm (1981) whose model of international production asserts that the extent, pattern, and growth of value-added activities undertaken by multinational firms outside their national boundaries is dependent on the value of and interaction between three main variables: (a) ownership-specific advantages of multinational firms, (b) location-specific advantages of countries, (c) market internalization or coordinating advantages.

Ownership-specific advantages

The concept of ownership advantage refers to the competitive advantage of multinational corporations over other firms (either domestic or foreign) in the country in which they are producing and typically arises from the MNCs ownership and ability to combine geographically dispersed activities.

Several factors in particular contribute to the competitive or ownership advantage of MNCs in the hotel industry:

(a) The provision of high quality services, including such attributes as design, comfort, performance, efficiency, degree of professionalism, and attitude towards customers. The hotel firm's trademark guarantees a certain desired quality level providing a significant competitive advantage on a firm, especially where customers are consuming the service in an unfamiliar environment.

(b) The ability of international hotel chains to enter new markets faster and easier due to a set of intangible assets and logistical skills that they can provide to any newly associated hotel at a lower cost than (potential) new entries into the hotel business.

(c) Their managerial and organizational expertise allow for technically superior methods of production in the day-to-day production, control, and maintenance of hotels. Their ability to invest in training hotel staff allows for the recruitment and retaining of better staff by offering better promotional prospects over other firms (Dunning and McQueen 1982a: 83–84).

(d) The availability of a global travel reservation system is generally also perceived by international travellers as beneficial and a means to facilitate the booking process (UNCTC 1988: 429).

Starting with the take-over of Inter-Continental by Grand Metropolitan in August 1981 and Hilton International by Ladbroke in September 1987, mergers and acquisitions have increased in frequency and magnitude to the point where they are perhaps the most crucial trends with the largest impact on the structure of the international hotel industry.

Scale economies coupled with the need to have hotel facilities in key markets around the world, have been, in part, cause for recent mergers and acquisitions. In December 1988, Inter-Continental was sold by Grand Metropolitan to The Saison Group, an international retailing, hotel and property conglomerate based in Tokyo. The Saison Group holds a 100 per cent controlling interest in Inter-Continental Hotels. Foreign direct investment by Asian multinationals has changed the international hotel industry's 'game rules' because the new entrants behave strategically differently. In particular, they focus more on the long-term than Western corporations. Furthermore, the 'injection' of Asian investments and management of international hotels implies that the international hotel industry is no longer limited to firms based in the USA and Europe.

In addition to economies of scale that may apply to hotel corporations, large multinational hotel firms have other advantages. For instance, they may obtain supplies more cheaply than small firms because of available discounts. As a result of their bargaining power when implementing international advertising campaigns, they may be able to negotiate lower marketing costs. And because of their resources they may be able to attract and retain quality staff. International hotel chains tend to operate properties larger than their domestic rivals. Their size affords them the opportunity to profit from differential factor costs, the international specialization of value-adding activities, and the economies of management arising from their ability to move people between the different parts of the same organization.

There appears to be a trend towards mega-organizations, events, and attractions in tourism to exploit scale economies and other benefits (Ritchie and Yangzhou 1987; Middleton 1988; Wheatcroft 1990; Holloway 1989: 125–126). As this trend evolves, the involvement of multinational hotel firms in mega-attractions and resorts will be inevitable because of the high levels of capital investment, expertise, and international marketing presence required in today's market. The theme parks of Disney Productions and

Universal Studios provide evidence of this trend in the entertainment sector. And the mega-resorts developed by the Hyatt Corporation point towards potential polarization in the resort industry with mega-resorts on the one end of the continuum and boutique resorts on the other.

Technologies typical of service industries are primarily skill-and experience-oriented and intensive, requiring considerable organization and management capabilities (UNCTC 1988: 429). The 'personality intensity' (Normann 1984: 10) of hotel services is significant in that the quality supplied to customers is, in large measure, the result of how the host performs in a specific situation. Hence, hotel organizations are very dependent on social innovation to mobilize human energy and skills thereby enhancing quality and cost efficiency.

Multinational hotel firms with headquarters in the United States, Europe, and Japan typically enjoy a competitive advantage over their rivals in the host country because of their favoured access to their domestic markets, their knowledge of what these respective customers want, and through collaboration with airlines and tour operators often based in the same locale. Consequently, TNCs active in the hotel industry tend to attract a certain clientele and therefore influence the type of tourism in a particular destination (United Nations 1982: 81).

Location-specific advantages

Hotel corporations that possess the competitive advantages described in the preceding section have a choice of where they engage their value-adding activities. Several variables determine whether the multinational hotel firm will become involved in a country by establishing a facility. They are broadly similar to those facing firms in other economic sectors, for example: the size and growth of demand; the policy of the host government towards foreign enterprise; and the general political, social, and economic stability of the country (McQueen 1989: 288; Go *et al.* 1990: 299–300). Last but not least location is critical in that it determines both the destination and the hotel's position within the destination. Typically, city centre hotels cater to the business traveller and resorts tend to attract pleasure travellers. However, these distinctions are becoming increasingly blurred because resort hotels attract a growing number of conventions and meetings. And, on the other hand, city centre hotels, which cater primarily to business-persons on weekdays attempt to appeal to the leisure market during weekends through discounted room rates (Witt *et al.* 1991: 24).

The siting of hotels in resort areas depends to a great extent on the location of the scenery, climate, and amenities desired by visitors. In addition to these general reasons, several very specific factors (UNCTC 1988: 423) influence the location of MNCs active in tourism services, such as:

(a) Being close to markets of significant size or assured of convenient access at reasonable transportation fares.
(b) Having the organizational capability to adapt products so that these coincide with the local infrastructure.
(c) Being able to employ key human resources at reasonable wages.
(d) Having access to suppliers who produce a wide variety of goods and services that are required for the operation of hotels.

Whatever explanation is applicable to individual hotels they tend not to be uniformly distributed in geographical space. However, it is possible to identify a pattern of recognizable location-specific hotel clusters which may be dispersed through a metropolitan area, and can be grouped according to specific categories (Ashworth and Tunbridge 1990: 64).

Internalization advantages

Since it is difficult in the diverse travel and tourism market to organize efficient intermediate product markets, there is a strong incentive for hotel firms to internalize these markets. Internalization is typically exercised through the acquiring of control over resources either through ownership of equity capital or through contracts (Dunning and McQueen 1982a: 83). Through the internalization process multinational firms create their own internal markets, which on the one hand increases their power and on the other hand increases their efficiency in the allocation of resources (Dunning and McQueen 1982a: 83; Litteljohn 1985).

The internalization of market transactions varies according to the type of service being exchanged and the market conditions in the host countries. In general however, the propensity to establish joint ventures or non-equity arrangements in the services sector has been greater than in the manufacturing sector. A major reason that the entry mode of MNCs in the hotel industry has primarily involved joint ventures or non-equity agreements can be traced to the possibility of codifying and controlling the key competitive advantages of such service firms in a management contract or franchising agreement (UNCTC 1988: 437).

Advantages that are especially relevant to explaining MNC internalization activities include:

- the seller's need to protect quality of intermediate or final products;
- the reassurance of buyer uncertainty about the nature of the product sold through branding; and,
- the avoidance of negotiations costs and government intervention.

Despite the significance of licensing and contracting in the services sector, foreign direct investment (FDI) has been a concern to the governments of many nations, especially those of developing countries.

Foreign direct investment

The economic development potential that MNCs may unleash should be a strong argument for developing countries to foster foreign direct investment (FDI). However, a major problem is that service industries and tourism in particular were, up to recently, not perceived by most authorities in industrialized and developing nations to make a positive contribution to the international balance of trade (Normann 1984: 6).

Worldwide investment by MNCs has undergone dramatic change, spurred on by the revolution in communications and technology and the growing importance of the service industries in the economy. The growing significance of the service sector is attested to by negotiations on international trade in services that were held as part of the 100-nation Uruguay Round of trade talks, begun in 1986 and scheduled to adjourn by the end of 1990 (Segal 1988).

The conditions under which multinational service companies establish business affiliates around the world is central to the negotiations, as many developing countries are worried that their own infant service industries will be driven out of business by entering transnationals. This has been a strong argument for developing countries to build up their own service industries. Meanwhile, the newly democratized economies of Central and Eastern Europe have recognized that linkages between the service sector and other sectors of the economy, including manufacturing and agriculture, are desirable and that transnational corporations operating in tourism can play a vital role in the creation of employment, output growth, and development. Franck (1990), for example, examined how investments by transnational corporations are turning tourism into a services sector of growing importance in Central and Eastern European economies. Specifically, Franck makes reference to five important economic effects attributed to tourism – namely, the balance of payments effects; the equalizing effect (that is, surpluses in tourism equalize deficits in the balance of payments and vice versa); the effect on employment; the multiplier effect; and the net product effect, which refers to the production of goods and services in the host country itself, leading eventually to a rise in national wealth (Franck 1990: 333).

Tourism is a major factor in the generation of hard currency for many nation-states, and may be used by governments to reduce the national debt or the balance of payments without losing nonrenewable resources (Edgell 1985; Mathieson and Wall 1982). Multinational firms are heavily involved in transnational transactions that affect balance of payments and have frequently been linked to problems, such as causing or aggravating balance of payments deficits (Weekly and Aggarwal 1987: 317).

MANAGING FOR GLOBAL EFFECTIVENESS

In relation to the hotel industry, globalization is popularly understood as a process designed to establish worldwide a hotel company's presence. Globalization is commonly perceived to have a standardizing impact in that products and institutions originally offered domestically appear on a worldwide scale. Within this contextual framework, transnational hotel corporations based in North America, Europe and Asia invest abroad, consolidate, introduce brand marketing practices and seek affiliation with global distribution systems. In the 1980s, the global corporation began to emerge as a new organizational form. Accordingly, there was speculation that corporations such as Holiday Inns, ACCOR and Hilton International might come to dominate the competitive behaviour in the hotel sector globally.

The global corporation operates essentially without the constraints of national borders or cultural traditions within the host country. It seeks to compete in any high-potential market on earth (Levitt 1983a). The global corporation is a consequence of several mega-forces that have shaped the world economy in the 1980s, including: the cumulative effect of information technology; the rise of worldwide media; the ease of long-haul travel; the development of capital markets with their ability to shift resources rapidly in response to new opportunities; the development and application of technology that seeks the simultaneous pursuit of high quality and low-cost in both the product and the production process; and a clear recognition of the potential for mass markets and global brands.

The development of the global organization in the late 1970s and 1980s was aided by regional integration and the geographical diversification of corporate activity. It led to a geocentric strategy in which the various operations of the global corporation were geared to a common goal and coordinated by a central plan.

However, the concept of the global corporation – in particular its penetration of 'foreign' markets and need to be competitive when building and operating hotels across borders – is being increasingly questioned. Global corporations, especially those involved in the hotel industry, have increasingly to accept the need to adapt their strategies to meet the particular socio-cultural, economic and environmental needs at the local level. Therefore, at the beginning of the 1990s, one of the central issues for many hotel corporations is how to organize, integrate, and manage their activities to respond to the simultaneous need for a sense of global strategic intent and a sense of localized focus and competitiveness that deals with local conditions, specifically the culture, traditions, and values of the host community. Globalization as a process to establish the worldwide presence of a hotel chain may be a widely understood phenomenon, but it masks to a certain extent other important dimensions of the same phenomenon.

One such dimension of the globalization thrust relates to the rising importance of international trade and developments, such as the Single European market, which have increasing effects on the domestic hotel industry of individual countries. For example, domestic hoteliers have to compete with foreign corporations which have penetrated their 'home turf' or risk surrendering a share of what had been considered 'domestic' markets. This aspect of globalization expresses the ease with which the world's best competitors can enter almost any market at any time. In other words, the globalization of the hotel industry has increased the competitive pressures by bringing more entrants into the domestic market. It also exerts a strong influence on consumer expectations and options. In that sense the performance of domestic hotels is greatly affected by the high and consistent service levels and brand-names of hotel chains with world-wide operations. This perspective of globalization implies that domestic hotel managers need to ask whether their operations are comparable to the world leaders as opposed to the domestic or multi-domestic leaders in the hotel industry. The idea of bench-marking against the best in the business is important in every aspect of hotel operation from purchasing to customer service. When bench-marking the best in the business, managers will have to seek knowledge outside the familiar domestic environment, to ensure effective innovation, skills development, build relationships, and create and sustain competitiveness. In this regard, the gathering of information and innovative ideas across borders may be understood as a process involving the globalization of know-how (Bardaracco 1991).

A third dimension of globalization relates to the blurring of the 'domestic'/'foreign' distinction in the market. The rise of global competition impacts the manufacturing, mining and agricultural sectors of national economies and therefore affects national tourism and domestic hotels (Go and Ritchie 1990). On another level, there is a set of global industries, including financial, banking and telecommunications (Mowlana and Smith 1990), that are affecting the operation and control of specific sectors in the domestic travel industry system, including domestic hotels. For example, the 'silent' revolution of information technology is causing hotel companies to adjust their strategies to compete successfully in the emerging marketplace through global distribution systems (GDS). The latter make improved yield management available to hoteliers. Yield management broadly means maximizing occupancy rates, and matching variations in demand on a seasonal and weekly basis to different pricing structures in order to maximize revenue. At the time, global distribution systems seemed to place large hotel chains in a position to exploit the new technology faster than smaller rivals. However, the use of global distribution systems, confounding most forecasts, is narrowing economies of scale in distribution, not expanding them. In particular, referral consortia are making it possible for independent hoteliers to reach customers worldwide under a global brand-name through GDS. Therefore, global-ization strategy has become an option to independent hoteliers, through referral consortia which employ GDS.

Up to now, knowledge about the home market was sufficient to survive. On another level, technical knowledge was often considered to be more important than the management of information. This is no longer the case, because to design and sustain a competitive advantage, hoteliers will have to think about and resolve problems in new ways, which requires a different mindset (Ohmae 1982: 4). Consequently, the key task of hotel managers should be the creation of innovative responses and formulae that fit to new situations and actively adapting the organization to the changes of the outside world (Cassee 1983: xv).

The experience of independent hotelier Jean-Marie Leclercq holds important insights for hoteliers who are keen to generate new answers and formulae to face the global competition (see Box 1.1). First, by thinking outwardly and taking cultural differences seriously hoteliers can become more sensitive to customers' needs. In this regard there is, for example, a significant difference between the expectations of Japanese and American guests, which must be understood before culturally sensitive service can be rendered appropriately (Ziff-Levine 1990). Second, by fostering an appreciation for how differently and equally well things get done in other parts of the world, hoteliers can build effective responses to local demands. As Leclercq's experience demonstrates, there are solutions to be found outside the familiar, conventional boundaries of one's home country. Third, global knowledge is a must today, not only to better understand the needs and tastes of international travellers, but because recent years have seen an acceleration of a shift towards interdependence among the world's economies. The implications for hoteliers are profound and the response will require leadership of the highest order.

BOX 1.1 FOCUS ON INDEPENDENT HOTELS: A PERSONAL PERSPECTIVE

At present, the 'split' between independently – and corporately – controlled hotel operations is changing, due to the inevitable trend towards consolidation. Today's global business environment requires organizations with adequate resources, in particular management talent and financing, to take on the most complicated tasks that are out of reach for smaller hotels. However, independent hotels that cannot hope to compete in terms of size have three main options to survive: they can affiliate with a large referral consortium, engage in niche marketing, or do both. With a travel market thriving on seg-mentation there are real opportunities for the independent hotel (which is still the backbone of the hotel industry) to develop location-specific and type-specific facilities and services.

As competition in the hotel industry shifts from the local to the global level, the resulting challenges, including increasing competition, rising customer expectations, and breakthroughs in service delivery, are affecting hotel chains and independent hoteliers alike. Though 'globalization' was an unknown entity in 1966, the global market offered an astute independent French hotelier big opportunities as the following example illustrates.

Back then, Jean-Marie Leclercq, a 31-year-old manager of a 200-room independent hotel in Paris, faced keen competition for American tourists who had 'discovered' the 'city of lights':

> At the time, [says Leclercq] I thought how can I ever be successful if I act like all other hoteliers? I knew I had to be shrewd to gain a competitive edge and squeezed my mind for ideas. Then I remembered an article which I had read in a business journal which mentioned that the Japanese economy was expanding at a phenomenal rate and the people of that faraway country were becoming wealthier. From my lessons I remembered that Japan was an island. Putting these pieces of information together I reasoned that the Japanese who had the money and were interested would at some stage travel overseas to visit other countries, including my own. After contemplating how I could attract the Japanese traveller, I came up with a sales programme, which to my delight worked beautifully.

Leclercq built a reputation in his native Paris for his ability to cater to the demanding Japanese travel market. His success in catering to the Japanese travel market led to his becoming the general manager of the Nikko Hotel de Paris, a subsidiary of Japan Airlines' hotel division. Via Sydney, Australia, where he opened the new Nikko hotel, Leclercq made his way to Hong Kong in 1992, to become actively involved in a local energy conservation programme as the general manager of the Nikko Hotel Hong Kong (see Chapter 6).

In recognition of the fundamental nature of this development, *Globalization Strategy in the Hotel Industry* attempts to present the globalization phenomenon as a totally pervasive aspect of the marketplace rather than a separate issue for independent and chain hoteliers alike.

The present book concentrates on issues of strategic importance and tries to deal with the formulation and implementation of policies which contribute to the global effectiveness of hotel organizations. Globalization strategy in the hotel industry represents the logic by which hoteliers, both independents and chains, intend to effectively compete in a global market, to become world-class competitors. Specifically, globalization strategy consists of a set of coordinated decisions in several key areas. In particular, it challenges hoteliers to combine a global strategic perspective with the pragmatism local policy implementation requires. Therefore, an effective globalization strategy is not synonymous with the effective management of a hotel chain which operates on a worldwide basis. Many independent hoteliers have been able to build reputations as world-class competitors, as attested to for example by *Hotels'* (magazine) Annual Award to the Independent Hotelier of the year. In building and implementing a globalization strategy the following factors deserve special attention:

- understanding how the global market has changed the rules of competition;
- anticipating the general strategies of the world's best hotel companies;
- comprehending how to build a worldwide presence, either by establishing a physical presence, or exploiting existing networks, or both;
- acknowledging people power as the organization's most important asset to develop global competitiveness 'from the inside out';
- making the profitable delivery of customer value the organization's key concern and;
- developing the leadership, relationships, and skills to adapt to continual 'waves' of change and innovation.

Regardless of whether they represent hotel chains or independently operated hotels, managers who implement a globalization strategy accept the challenge to compete with the world's best through the effective delivery of value-adding service into the twenty-first century.

PURPOSE AND ORGANIZATION OF THE BOOK

Globalization Strategy in the Hotel Industry has two key objectives. The first objective is to address the broad international dimensions of the hotel industry. The international arena within which the hotel industry operates is frequently turbulent, highly competitive and sometimes hostile. There is a clear relationship between economic, political, legal, social, and cultural factors and the hotel industry's performance. In this context *Globalization Strategy in the Hotel Industry* introduces the evolving global market and the structural dynamics of the hotel industry in the United States of America and its impact on the reforms of the hotel industry in Europe and Asia.

The second objective is to examine the potential application of managerial concepts by providing a framework for identifying, analysing and making decisions regarding selected key problems and issues in the hotel industry. Various problem-solving tools are introduced in an attempt to develop managers' abilities in solving human resource and operational problems in the hotel industry.

This text is distinctive from others in the field because of its unifying theme of achieving and sustaining a competitive advantage in response to global market pressures through creating value-adding service. It attempts to give continuity to the analysis of key developments in the hotel industry by linking practical business examples to theoretical principles. Wherever possible chapters use real-life business examples to illustrate major points. In addition, every chapter contains a case which discusses an issue or development within a particular hotel company to stimulate reader interest. Chapters also contain either a reading or an additional case to provide the viewpoints of internationally known executives. These viewpoints serve to supplement and clarify the material being discussed. Each chapter concludes with a list of study questions to help the reader to synthesize the range of material presented in the chapter.

The framework developed in this text for the creation of value-added processes that lead to competitive advantage in the hotel industry is presented in Figure 1.2.

As the model implies, hotel corporations can only compete effectively when they succeed in creating an environment in which employees want to perform well and are able to perform well. The model's arrows show the cross-influences at work in determining the window of strategic opportunity. Delivering value-added service in the hotel industry shall depend increasingly on the application of technology as a complement to human service. Responding swiftly and smoothly to market shifts requires the building and sustaining of an organizational structure that focuses its energies and resources on continuous improvement and maintaining relationships in the network. The transnational corporation model introduced by Bartlett and Ghoshal (1989) creates important opportunities for gaining and sustaining competitive advantage to maintain relationships with customers and suppliers. It also enables managers to build superior execution in a volatile environment, because the transnational model is based on the network concept which guarantees speed and flexibility in execution.

The material within *Globalization Strategy in the Hotel Industry* comprises empirical findings, evidence from the literature, and observations relating to past developments, current trends and practices. The book contains twelve chapters which are divided into three parts.

Part I provides a general introduction to the text along with relevant industry and general trends. Chapter 1 introduces and explains the concept of globalization within the hotel industry, including a review of the importance of multinational corporations, as well as providing this structural description of the book's contents. Chapter 2 deals with various characteristics of the hotel industry to provide the context within which later discussions are set. Chapter 3 examines how the rate of change in the

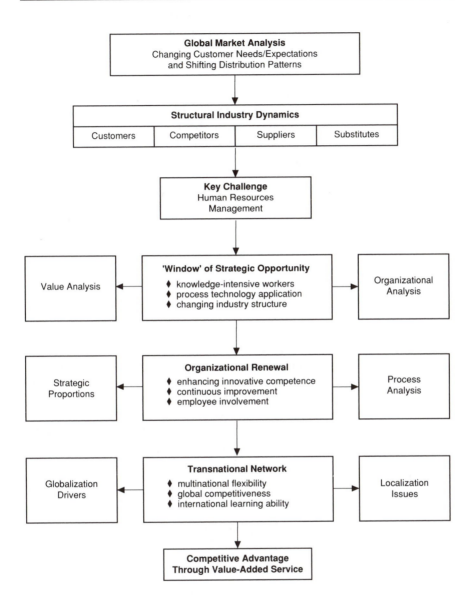

Figure 1.2 A flow diagram for creating value-added processes that lead to competitive advantage in the hotel industry

marketplace has clearly outstripped the speed at which conventionally organized hotel corporations are able to respond. It looks at fundamental issues such as the dichotomy between the emerging globalization and fragmentation of the market, and rising environmental concerns requiring hotel managers to make hard choices.

Part II contains chapters which provide the strategic environment background of hotel industries around the world. Thus, Chapter 4 explores the trend towards greater concentration in the US hotel industry through mergers, acquisitions and joint ventures. The changing structure has lead to excess capacity and greater competitive pressures, not only for customers but for employees as well. Chapter 5 provides a situational analysis of the impact global change has had on Europe's major centres where the hotel industry is concentrated. It discusses emerging trends with regard to product development, branding, equity investments, and the way in which hotels are financed. Chapter 6 focuses on the determining reasons for the hegemony of Hong Kong's hotel industry and its changing role as a regional centre to supply hotel development and management expertise to Asia's rapidly expanding economies.

Part III then looks at solutions available to handle the various strategic developments in the hotel industry. Chapter 7 identifies 'superior service' and 'employee attitude' as the critical success factors in the hotel industry and indicates that hotel managers should communicate the importance of these factors in their organizations, measure them, and reward staff who meet them. Chapter 8 pinpoints leadership as the key to organizational renewal and culture, which in turn are prerequisites to transform hotels from an 'available for service' attitude to a mindset determined to deliver 'world-class service'. Chapter 9 diagnoses the potential for global strategy, competitive conditions, the hotel organizational capability to respond to global competitiveness, local market needs, and international learning to stimulate worldwide innovation. Chapter 10 explains how the hotel industry's traditional roles are being redefined within the travel and tourism distribution channel and the emerging need for networking to foster cooperative relationships. Chapter 11 expands on the idea of creating cooperative networks in the hotel industry by introducing the business-ecosystem and the transnational model as the key means to successfully adapt to continual waves of change and innovation. Chapter 12 concludes the book with a summary of the major challenges and opportunities into the twenty-first century.

CONCLUSION

The globalization of the hotel industry has several significant strategic implications in that it:

- increases competitive pressures by bringing more entrants into the market;
- increases the complexity of doing business, from learning to find and manage employees with a diverse background in different countries to designing and delivering products uniquely suited for separate national markets;
- requires new knowledge – that is, knowledge beyond what is known and deemed to be necessary knowledge to successfully cater to foreign visitors, for example.

Global competition forces hotel companies to create and sustain a competitive advantage, through adjusting to a buyers' market by reducing costs while maintaining service quality levels. Competitive advantage is to a large extent based on the ability to create new answers to new situations in a dynamic environment. Traditionally, hotel managers have faced change rather reluctantly and think they may be making the necessary changes when in actual fact they are rearranging things through actions like reorganizations. To continue with old ways in the global environment is a blueprint for potential disaster. Consequently, there is a growing need in hotel firms for management education and organizational learning to translate a desired globalization strategic orientation into an actual management process.

CASE: INTER-CONTINENTAL HOTELS CORPORATION – A PIONEER OF GLOBAL GROWTH

Company Profile

Inter-Continental Hotels is a leading international hotel company operating 111 hotels in 47 countries around the world. Of these, 93 are five-star, luxury properties under the Inter-Continental brand. To complement the Inter-Continental product and satisfy the requirement for high quality, moderately priced accommodation, Inter-Continental established Forum Hotels International in 1972 of which there are now 18 in Europe, the Middle East, North America, Latin America and Asia.

Over the past 40 years, Inter-Continental has achieved a reputation for providing a consistently high, personalized service in luxury hotels situated in prime locations around the world, making it a recognized name among international business and leisure travellers. With an experienced, international staff of more than 40,000 people and unparalleled geographic coverage, Inter-Continental Hotels has become a truly global company.

Founded in 1946 by Pan American World Airlines, Inter-Continental's early expansion developed along Pan Am's routes into Latin America and then throughout the world. In 1981, the company was acquired by Grand

Metropolitan. The combined group of Grand Metropolitan, Inter-Continental and Forum Hotels was reorganized to produce a group of quality hotels which exemplified the established identity of the Inter-Continental and Forum brands. During this period, 21 Grand Metropolitan hotels were added to the group and included several landmark properties.

In December 1988, Inter-Continental was sold by Grand Metropolitan to The Saison Group, an international retailing, hotel and property conglomerate based in Tokyo. Saison now has a 100 per cent controlling interest in Inter-Continental Hotels.

The history of a pioneering hotel company

Taking off with Pan Am in 1946

Inter-Continental Hotels Corporation was founded in 1946 by Pan American World Airlines, following America's encouragement of investment by US companies in Latin America after the Second World War. The airline was approached by the US State Department as the logical company to undertake a hotel investment programme because of its already established network of air routes and its long-time business relations with Latin American countries.

Unlike other hotel companies that established themselves in the more conventional business and leisure destinations of their home markets, Inter-Continental (as its name suggests) was a pioneer from the start, setting out to establish hotels along Pan Am routes in South America and the Caribbean. Here hotels were built to offer not only superior hospitality, but also a safe haven in places that were, at times, far from stable. The first hotel to open was the Grande in Belem, Brazil. Under the lively chairmanship of Lucius Bloomer, creator and Chief Executive of Park Avenue's Waldorf Astoria Hotel, management agreements were entered into for the Victoria Plaza Hotel in Montevideo and the Hotel Carrera in Santiago, Chile, followed shortly thereafter by the Hotel Tamanaco in Caracas and hotels in Bogota, Maracaibo, Mexico City and Havana.

First into Africa and the Middle East

Over the next two decades, Inter-Continental's horizons broadened dramatically. Entry into the Middle East was spearheaded by the Phoenicia Inter-Continental Beirut which opened in 1961 and established Inter-Continental's leading position in the region.

Today Inter-Continental's commitment to the Middle East remains unparalleled with 15 hotels in 13 cities, including 5 hotels and palace hotels in Saudi Arabia. A new hotel opened in Jeddah in 1992 and two resort hotels are under construction in Hurghada and Luxor, Egypt, due to open in 1994.

The same pioneering development was evident in Africa where Inter-Continental was the first international hotel company to open a hotel – the Ducor Inter-Continental in Monrovia, Liberia in 1961, followed by the Ivoire Inter-Continental Abidjan. Growth coincided with independence in many countries where new national governments were keen to enlist the services of a professional, global hotel company.

Building strong European foundations

The 1960s saw a period of rapid expansion, particularly in Europe, with hotels opening in London, Paris and most major European business destinations. Europe rapidly became a hub of Inter-Continental activity.

Ahead of its time, Inter-Continental was looking into Eastern Europe. In 1964, an agreement was negotiated for a hotel in Zagreb, Yugoslavia. For nearly 20 years, Inter-Continental was the only quality hotel chain in Eastern Europe offering 11 city centre hotels in Hungary, Yugoslavia, Romania, Poland and Czechoslovakia. In November 1991, the historic Hotel Metropol reopened in Moscow, a symbol of Inter-Continental's ability to realize the most challenging opportunities and restore a magnificent landmark to the city.

Europe remains very much at the heart of Inter-Continental's global map with 47 of the total 109 properties located in 19 European countries. A new 1,007-room Forum Hotel in Berlin was added to the portfolio in May 1992 to complement Inter-Continental's two existing five-star properties in the city. In October the company took over the running of another city centre property in Geneva, the Forum Hotel Geneve. There was a flying start to 1993, with the signing of contracts to manage the Hotel Inter-Continental Leipzig, the Churchill Inter-Continental London and the Terrace Inter-Continental Adelaide.

Enter North America and the landmark hotels

The success story continued into the 1970s as Inter-Continental gained a substantial foothold in North America and attained a phenomenal increase in its global hotel portfolio. Recently Inter-Continental opened hotels in Canada, in Toronto and Montreal; and the new Hotel Inter-Continental Los Angeles opened in November 1992.

During the 1980s, landmark hotels with a stature, a tradition and often a name all of their own, were successfully included in the chain. Because the Inter-Continental name has always been associated with high quality hotels (never operating inns or three-star properties under the same brand), the Willard Inter-Continental in Washington, the Mark Hopkins Inter-Continental in Paris, the Amstel Inter-Continental Amsterdam and the

Carlton Inter-Continental in Cannes all benefit from being part of the chain and in turn give it prestige.

Focus on Asia following a pioneering tradition

In 1991, Inter-Continental opened the striking, space-age Yokohama Grand Inter-Continental. Rising majestically above the Bay of Tokyo, the hotel represents Inter-Continental's ability to reflect the culture and character of the cities in which it operates and deliver a 'local' experience with a five-star service.

With the assistance and encouragement of The Saison Group, Inter-Continental is undertaking major expansion throughout Asia. The first hotel opened in Jakarta in 1960 and today Inter-Continental is established in 11 major Asian business and leisure destinations with hotels in Singapore, Bali and Surabaya due to open over the next three years. Inter-Continental has also signed a management agreement to operate the Terrace Inter-Continental Adelaide from March 1993.

Under the flagship of the Yokohama Grand Inter-Continental, the company is moving into Asia in the footsteps of its pioneering tradition to create hotels that are indigenous, international and uniquely Inter-Continental.

STUDY QUESTIONS

1 Describe the following orientations which a hotel firm may have towards international expansion; ethnocentrism; polycentrism; regiocentrism; geocentrism.
2 Do any of the above orientations best fit the development of Inter-Continental, or do different ones apply at different stages of that company's expansion?
3 What positive contributions has the emergence of MNCs made to tourism?
4 What problems could be attributed to MNCs in relation to tourism?
5 Briefly describe the ownership advantages which MNCs have over other firms.
6 Discuss the advantages of internalization over internationalization.
7 Discuss the links between MNCs and FDI.
8 What does globalization mean in relation to the hotel industry?
9 What factors deserve special attention in the building of a globalization strategy?
10 Discuss strategic implications of globalization in the hotel industry.

Chapter 2

The international hotel industry

The hotel industry is far from uniform, there are significant differences between hotel corporations. Almost every hotel corporation should have a different perspective which depends on the company being primarily a real estate owner and operator (e.g. Forte), primarily interested in management opportunities (e.g. Hyatt), or primarily interested in franchise opportunities (e.g. Choice Hotels International). A hotel company's perspective has a significant influence on its strategy, type of development targets, and how it responds to new market needs.

This chapter recognizes the growing importance of hotel chains, and specifically the multinational corporation in terms of its ability to create and sustain a competitive advantage from conceiving of new ways to deliver value-adding service. (The rest of the book attempts to provide relevant information which could be implemented in the strategic marketing process in order to adapt the hotel corporation to the changing business environment on which it depends for its survival.)

The case at the end of this chapter provides a comparison of the different growth strategies of Forte Hotels and Choice Hotels. The reading, by William S. Watson of Best Western, presents views on the changing role of research in the hotel industry.

THE HOTEL INDUSTRY

In any major field of human endeavour, there seems to be a fundamental urge among people to understand how ideas developed, to provide insights into what keeps things running smoothly and to shed light on the impact of certain phenomena. The hotel industry is no exception. The definition of a hotel as used by industry practitioners and laymen alike is imprecise. In this book the hotel industry has been defined as a set of 'lodging firms, including motels, in competition, and producing goods and services of a like function and nature'. Thus, to the extent that hotels cater to pleasure travellers, they can be considered to be, for instance, in competition with supplementary accommodation comprised of seasonal lodging facilities that are geared only to the needs of holiday and leisure related travellers. Go and Welch (1991) have divided accommodation into two types: commercial and supplementary. The commercial category is quite straightforward, and includes hotels in all locations, including resorts, as well as establishments such as motels, boarding or guest houses, and hostels. The supplementary category has several sub-groups and includes accommodation of commercial, social and non-commercial natures. One group would be holiday camps, holiday villages, sanatoria and spas, youth hostels, mountain cabins, villas, apartments and rooms for rent where such facilities are used almost exclusively for travellers and holiday-makers. A second group would be those types of accommodation which are not permanently used for travellers but which may be converted to such use on a seasonal basis, for example, student hostels or university dormitories.

Yet another group would consist of second homes, interval ownership of resort condominiums and apartments, facilities used by their owners or permanent occupants for holiday and recreation but which can also be made available to other persons on a rental exchange, cost sharing or hospitality basis. There is also a group which includes bed and breakfast accommodation, which is of a residential nature but which is occasionally made available to others on an exchange or cost sharing basis. (Go and Welch 1991: 125)

The hotel industry is a sub-sector of the travel and tourism sector, which, in turn, is one of the most rapidly expanding fields in the service sector. Tourism consists of two elements:

- a dynamic element, spatial movement (travel); and
- a static element, namely the temporary visit at one or more destinations for reasons of observation, recreation, meeting people or for other reasons.

According to the World Travel and Tourism Council (WTTC), travel and tourism has become the leading economic contributor to the world and national economies in terms of gross output, value added, capital investment, employment, and tax contributions. But travel and tourism are far from being recognized as such in most countries around the world.

Because it caters to the accommodation needs of the 'away from home market', the hotel industry is of central importance to the development of travel and tourism. The evolution and performance of the contemporary hotel industry has been shaped by a set of economic characteristics which may be summarized as follows:

(a) It is a labour intensive industry with an emphasis on personal service. To provide quality service employees have to be properly trained, motivated and supervised. Though it is costly, training is a necessity because the 'moments of truths' or the impressions, both positive and negative, an employee makes on the guest have a direct influence on whether the guest will return.

(b) It is an extremely competitive industry. The consequences of overbuilding and excess capacity have produced intense competition. In addition, the globalization process has increased the number of 'players' in the hotel industry and significantly increased competition in many markets.

(c) It is an industry which is extremely sensitive to fluctuations in demand. Hotels offer a perishable product. The number of rooms rented tends to vary from weekdays to weekends and from season to season. Hotels serve both business and pleasure travellers. This implies that forces outside the control of management that affect travel usually have an impact on hotel performance. For example, the Gulf War had a devastating impact on the travel industry and the hotel business in many countries. The curtailing of business travel and entertainment during a recessionary period typically has adverse effects on the expenditures on hotel room, food and beverage expenditures and therefore hotel profitability. In general, a stable and expanding economy tends to influence hotel performance positively. Conversely, rising inflation causes expenses for labour, energy, and construction to increase and profit margins to erode, especially when the hotel is unable to raise room rates proportionately due to prevailing market conditions.

(d) It is a very capital intensive industry. The average cost of building a hotel exceeds US$100,000 per room in many markets and much more in areas where real estate is more expensive.

There were, according to estimates by the World Tourism Organization, 11.3 million rooms worldwide in hotels and similar establishments in 1991, up 11 per cent from 1987 when the world's total room stock amounted to 10.1 million. The hotel industry has a marked concentration in Europe and the Americas, which had 44.7 and 38.5 per cent of the world's hotel rooms in 1991 respectively. The East Asia Pacific region had slightly less than 11.3 per cent, with the balance spread over Africa, Latin America and the Caribbean. From a revenue generating perspective, the hotel industry is even more concentrated. A 1985 estimate by the Marriott Corporation, for example, placed the combined lodging revenues for the USA, Europe, and Far East in the luxury, moderate, budget and quality markets at US$53 billion, of which US$41 billion or 77 per cent arose in the USA. More recently, Inter-Continental Hotels estimated that the luxury hotel market alone, in which it competes, accounts for global sales worth over US$40 billion annually.

Strategy

The most relevant goals to the hotel industry in the 1990s are profitability and growth. In order to achieve their goals hotel corporations have to formulate and implement strategies. Strategy, the qualifier in the title of this book, is a key determinant of business performance and is, at least to some degree, subject to managerial influence. Strategy is a relevant concept in the discussion because hotel companies are continuously faced with uncertainties and complexities and need to adjust their behaviour to compete (Ansoff 1987). Hotel strategy and structure are inextricably intertwined because pricing decisions, new product introductions, and advertising campaigns require operational and administrative support. To ensure rapid response in an unpredictable environment, marketing, operations, human resources, and administration should be closely coupled organizationally (Ansoff 1987: 25).

In order to achieve profitability, hoteliers have to operate their property in a manner which will yield maximum revenues at the lowest possible costs. Specifically, they can attempt to increase sales by expanding the market size, by increasing the local market share (especially with regard to restaurant sales), by improving productivity through decreasing costs, adjusting the sales mix, or a combination of all of these variables.

To meet the objective of increasing sales, hoteliers will typically try to accomplish the highest room occupancy at the optimal average daily room rate. Most commonly, for the 'average' hotel, market penetration is probably the most important strategy available. Successful market penetration relies on more effective and efficient utilization of available resources. Overall the most critical element is to have a clearly defined business with a distinctive image serving the needs of a specific market segment. Many of the benefits of market penetration relate to the size of the hotel and degree of market domination. A large share of the market acts as a buffer during downturns in the economy when customers might rely on larger, better known, more reliable hotels. It also provides a power-base from which to deal with suppliers, travel agents, tourist groups, and other business contacts. Nevertheless, size is dependent upon the market served. Even the small hotel can use market penetration to build a share in fewer, more narrowly defined markets (Moutinho 1989: 141).

Under today's market conditions it is very difficult, and at times even near impossible, to rely solely on a market penetration strategy because this strategy builds on existing needs whilst growth in the existing markets is slowing, and on existing products in an oversupplied market.

In their struggle for market share hoteliers therefore have little choice but to place greater emphasis on other means of developing demand more effectively and efficiently. In an environment marked by intense competition, it is essential that hoteliers pursue a market development strategy which seeks to attract market segments, which the hotel did not concentrate on in the past. Such a strategy may either attempt to attract new types of customers in addition to traditional ones, or may resolve to replace the hotel's past market segment appeal.

Hotels derive the bulk of their demand from individuals and groups who originate both in domestic and international markets. They travel for leisure and business purposes from their usual habitat to a particular destination. Hotel guests are not the same. In particular, international travellers tend to have tastes, preferences, buying habits, and spending budgets that are likely to be very different from those of domestic travellers. International tourists are defined as visitors from abroad staying at least 24 hours but not more than one year in the country visited, and the purpose of the trip may be classified under one of the following headings: (a) pleasure, recreation, holiday, sport; (b) business, visiting friends and relatives, missions, meeting, conference, health, studies, religion (Chadwick 1987: 48).

Origins of oversupply

In the current competitive environment it is becoming more and more difficult for hotel companies to expand. In particular, hotel companies located in Europe and North America face conditions that are much different from those during the 1980s. The majority of markets in America and Western Europe are oversupplied and assets are under-performing, due to the slow growth rate in demand. How did the hotel industry get into a situation of overbuilding?

Research conducted in the United States by Arbel and Woods (1990) indicates that the hotel industry started on a construction binge in the mid-1970s because, alone among most industries, it could borrow money at almost no cost. In some cases during the 1974–1988 period, hotel companies could even borrow money at negative interest rates. In other words, hotel companies were in effect paid to borrow money. Taxes and inflation combined to give hotel builders an easy ride in financing new properties.

> While all borrowers benefit from tax advantages and from borrowing money at low rates during inflationary periods, the hotel business is particularly effective in the inflation hitch-hiking game.
>
> (Arbel and Woods 1990)

After analysing 500 leading companies in all industry groups, Arbel and Woods found that, while many companies in other industries benefited from a low cost of debt due to inflation and tax credits for interest payments, hotels achieved the lowest effective costs among virtually all industries.

The researchers offered several reasons for low debt costs in the hotel industry:

(a) 'The industry is capital intensive.'

(b) 'The industry's real estate component provides excellent guarantees and collateral for loans that lenders perceive as inflation resistant', thus enabling hotels to borrow at relatively low rates.

(c) The industry is highly leveraged, borrowing more than any other industry except airlines, real estate and banks.

(d) Hotel companies usually have longer-term debt than most companies, enabling them to take better advantage of the full impact of inflation.

(e) 'Hotels are perceived to be highly effective in adjusting room rates to the general price inflation. This characteristic of the industry is the most critical in its ability to hitchhike on inflation.'

(Arbel and Woods 1990)

Their study findings disclose startling results in measuring the effective cost of debt:

(a) In the 15 years from 1974 to 1988, the average effective cost of debt for the hotel industry as a whole was minus 0.8 per cent with a low of minus 8.03 per cent in 1980.

(b) The average effective cost of debt for the nine years from 1974 to 1982 was an amazing minus 3.9 per cent, also with the 1980 low of minus 8.03 per cent. This means that the hotel industry was paid on average about 4 per cent a year to use other people's money.

(c) The average effective cost of debt from 1983 to 1988 was 3.9 per cent with a low of 2.24 per cent in 1984.

While both large and small hotel companies benefited, the debt costs for small firms were substantially higher because generally they pay higher interest rates, their tax rates typically are lower and they usually borrow for shorter terms. Inflation was high enough to create this anomaly of low capital costs for hotels. But over the long run, bargain basement financing did not provide a free ride for the hotel industry. 'In retrospect, it is pretty obvious that rapid overbuilding throughout the industry is one by-product of the free money that hotels have been offered over this period' (Arbel and Woods 1990). The coincidence of these events brought into public view the inherently troubled condition of the hotel industry.

The focus of European investments on diversification of brand products emphasizing mid-scale hotels could well result in an overbuilding of the markets in Europe during the 1990s, similar to the oversupply in the US in the 1980s when tax law stimulated excess construction.

GROWTH AVENUES

Whilst objectives set the performance levels which hoteliers seek to achieve, strategies provide the direction and guide the process of developing hotel organizations in their quest of capitalizing on new opportunities. Whichever strategy a hotel decides to apply, it is significantly determined by the marketing objectives, the target market, and market conditions.

In today's highly uncertain environment, hoteliers are attempting to achieve growth through, amongst other things, adjustments in the hotel product mix, developing new products and ceasing provision of, or modifying existing hotel products; segmentation; consolidation and internationalization.

Product strategies

Distinguishing characteristics which set hotels apart from other types of 'public accommodation' generally centre around the extent of facilities, services, and amenities available to guests. The primary product the lodging industry offers for sale is the guest room, which can be measured in terms of capacity and sales in much the same way seats are in the airline industry. Other hotel services may include restaurant seats and meeting rooms.

The findings of the *Hotels of the Future* study released by the International Hotel Association (IHA) in 1988 indicate that there appear to be three main emerging patterns with regard to the evolving hotel product. First, changing demographic and social patterns have resulted in customers having higher expectations in terms of standards. Hoteliers have to take these customer expectations into account in order to provide the appropriate kind of product and level of quality service. Second, hoteliers are attempting to provide enhanced value for money by reducing costs, for example by eliminating non-room facilities and public facilities in so far as this is possible. This trend is likely to lead to greater product specialization and the supply of more 'do-it-yourself' type of facilities. For example, Residence Inn, acquired by the Marriott Corporation in 1987, has become the leading extended stay product in the US lodging market and reflects the trend to 'do-it-yourself' facilities. Third, hotel and similar facilities are being better designed in terms of aesthetics, guest comfort and operational efficiency. The aforementioned IHA (1988) *Hotels of the Future* study indicates that the various 'hotel products' are evolving along the following broad scenarios:

Hotel bedrooms

Hotel bedrooms are becoming more functional. There is a trend towards rooms that offer full office facilities, television sets that provide a wide range of functions (including check-out), the provision of communication both within and outside the hotel, and a wide range of entertainment. The trend towards non-smoking rooms or sections can be anticipated to continue.

Hotel restaurants

In part, due to competition from restaurants in the vicinity of hotels and the need for quick service and leisure dining, hotel restaurants will become more specialized. Specialized theme restaurants with a brand-name are commonly found in hotels, as well as foodservice outlets offering a range of services from take-away foods to home catering. At the same time, in the US many hotels are successfully letting restaurant space to brand-name franchise systems.

Hotel conference rooms

Conference rooms in hotels are increasingly being purpose designed and built. These conference facilities incorporate first-rate audio-visual equipment, air purification, ventilation and lighting systems, and ergonomically designed chairs into their design.

Hotel health centres

Although the provision of the leisure/health centres may not be financially viable, their availability is widening because they support the sale of bedroom accommodation.

In general, the issue of environmentally friendly hotel products will become more important and certain hotel companies, such as Inter-Continental and Canadian Hotels and Resorts, have provided important leadership in this area. For example, to maintain the ecological balance, both companies have adopted throughout their hotels energy saving and recycling procedures to preserve the precious environment.

Segmentation

Market segmentation has developed rapidly in recent years. Hotel companies such as ACCOR operate a wide range of different and clearly defined products ranging from a luxury product (Sofitel), midscale product (Novotel), economy product (Ibis) and a basic product (Formule 1). Within the same hotel property hoteliers are offering different products under a distinct brand-name. And executive floors, such as the Sheraton Towers, designed primarily as a means to attract the business executive, have become common in many luxury hotel chains.

FINANCE

Financial considerations are increasingly driving hotel investment. Specifically, as the *Hotels of the Future* survey indicated, that from a private sector perspective:

(a) In some key city-centre locations, real estate values are tending to drive the investment and capital value, rather than these being justified on potential income streams; indeed some investors have entered the market to realize a short- or medium-term capital gain as distinct from being involved long term in hotel operation.

(b) Some international transactions have been driven by exchange rates favourable to the investor; this has serious implications for valuation purposes.

(c) Hotels are often perceived as enhancing a mixed use complex, and in some cases investors in the complex will therefore accept a lower than usual rate of return for the hotel.

The public sector is interested in hotel investment because it can make a contribution to government policy in terms of the creation of employment (both direct and indirect jobs in, for example, support industries; the improvement of the environment (through for example the regeneration of inner cities and the enhancement of social amenities); the generation of hard currency; and the multiplier effect of tourist earnings on the local community.

At present, innovative financing approaches involving individual investors or owners are achieving success throughout Europe and the US – for example, time ownership, condominium-hotels and fractional ownership of vacation properties, are increasing the degree of competition faced by the hotel sector.

CONSOLIDATION

As organizational entities, hotels are not identical and are commonly classified in several ways, e.g. according to type, location, size, standard and level of service, ownership, and chain affiliation, if any. The hotel industry is comprised of a large number of independent hotels and a relatively small group of hotel chains (defined as hotel companies with two or more properties).

An increasingly uncertain market environment has resulted in the need for competent hotel management. This circumstance has led to the growth of hotel chains because hotel chains offer important advantages over independently operated hotels. First, within hotel chains, ownership and management tend to be two distinct and separate functions. Second, most hotel chains offer their affiliated properties a recognizable brand-name, a central reservations system, a product of consistent quality in many locations, training and staff development, and professional marketing, sales and advertising support, designed to increase market share. Third, because of their larger size and financial 'clout' hotel chains have found it traditionally easier to obtain financing than independently owned and operated hotels.

COMPETITIVE ADVANTAGE

In order to acquire profits or ownership of another firm, hotel organizations must compete in the market. Competition is a process of responding to a new force and a method of reaching a new equilibrium.

According to Bain, who was cited by de Jong (1985: 73), three elements determine the market structure in particular, namely: (a) the level of industry concentration; (b) the entry conditions or barriers to the industry in question; and (c) product differentiation, and lead to the theory of competitive advantage.

Creating and sustaining a competitive advantage will involve making decisions about trade-offs that are the keys to the hotel corporation's success and survival in the 1990s. In building competitiveness, the hotel corporation has several potential sources of competitive advantage from which it can choose: (a) exploiting national differences for the resources used and products offered; (b) scale economies; (c) scope economies; and (d) geographical dispersion through the dispersion of its network (Horsburgh 1991: 32).

The theory of competitive advantage offers an important perspective on business strategy that facilitates analysis of the competitive environment. The key factors for success of different industries lie in different production functions at distinct positions throughout the 'value chain' (Porter 1990). The way in which one activity within the value chain is performed affects the cost or effectiveness of other activities. The key factors for successful value creation to gain market share and profitability for different types of companies fall at distinct points along the stream of functional activities as shown in Table 2.1 that starts with the acquisition of real estate and the search for hotel financing and ends with guest service.

Value

In the 1990s 'value' has become the marketer's watchword. Value is what customers are demanding. Value is somewhat of an elusive concept which brings together key attributes, in particular the right combination of quality, need, expectation, and price. Consumers use perceived value as the means to select, retain or reject suppliers. As the basis for differentiating between competing suppliers and because of its effect on consumer behaviour, value is important (Stephens *et al.* 1987: 5). From conceiving of new approaches to routine activities hoteliers can create value and gain competitive advantage (Porter 1990: 40). Activities vary in importance to competitive advantage in different industries, and can vary from segment to segment in a particular industry. The expectations of value typically also vary from market segment to market segment. The general process of attracting specific travel market segments to build hotel occupancy at the

Table 2.1 The value chain concept applied to the hotel industry

Upstream	Key function	Specimen firms	Corporate example(s)
1	Real estate acquisition and financing	Hotel owner/developer Institutional lender Syndications Hotel operating firms Government	VMS; Prudential Realty
2	Facility design and construction	Hotel developer	Marriott Corporation
3	Franchising	Franchiser/franchisee	Choice Hotels
4	Operations management	Management contract companies	Hilton International
5	Human resources management	Hotel operations firm	Hyatt Hotels & Resorts
6	Marketing/sales	Hotel operations firm Hotel sales Representatives	Forte Hotels; Supranational Hotels
7	Reservations and referrals	Hotel operations firm Hotel referral system Computer reservation system	Holiday Inns; Best Western; Galileo
8	Administration control	Hotel operations Firm/owner	Meridien/ Air France
9	Guest service	Hotel operations firm	Novotel

Downstream

Source: Adapted from K. Ohmae, *The Mind of the Strategist: Business Planning for Competitive Advantage*, New York, Plenum, 1982, p. 47. Reproduced with permission of McGraw-Hill, Inc.

highest possible average daily rate, by providing a differentiating value than competitors at a lower cost in a particular destination is illustrated in Figure 2.1.

The Marriott Corporation has maintained its status as a premier growth company essentially by providing outstanding value to customers and shareholders, and by being responsive to the needs of current and potential employees. It follows a simple formula by delivering outstanding customer value:

We listen to them, and supply superior services and products to meet their needs. We use market research to identify needs, and to design and deliver products which satisfy them. Then we support those products with friendly and efficient customer service.

(Marriott 1988: 3)

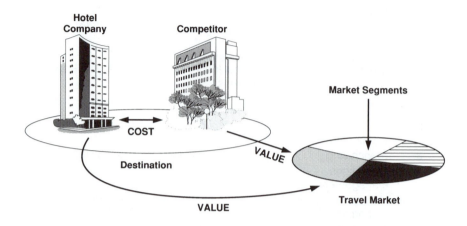

Figure 2.1 Significant strategic relationships

Source: Loosely after K. Ohmae, *The Mind of the Strategist: Business Planning for Competitive Advantage*, New York, Plenum, 1982, p. 92. Reproduced with permission of McGraw-Hill, Inc.

Four Seasons Hotels and Resorts is another corporation that aims to provide its clients with value-adding service for hassle-free stays. In 1991, the company commissioned Goldfarb Consultants to conduct a study among more than 500 business travellers who had averaged 20 business trips and 41 nights in luxury hotels over the past year. The main study findings confirm the importance of value-adding service rendering in de luxe hotels. The study findings identify guests expectations and clearly show that clients rank consistent, reliable service much higher than paying a low price (see Table 2.2). It is this ability to deliver an exceptional level of service consistently that Four Seasons guests depend on. Busy executives consider Four Seasons good value because they know that the services and facilities they need will be available when they want them; this lets them concentrate on their business, making their trip more productive and profitable.

Business formats

Beside acquisitions, mergers, and joint ventures, hotel chains generally expand on the basis of one or a combination of three main operating formats: management contracting, franchising and hotel consortia. The various business formats in the international hospitality industry have been

Table 2.2 Business travellers' expectations of de luxe hotel stay

	Rank
1 No hassle check-in/check out	9.3
2 Consistent reliable service	8.9
3 Good value	7.8
4 Allows me to be productive	7.7
5 Lets me travel light	7.6
6 24-hour room service	7.5
7 Has a concierge	6.5
8 Welcome gifts	5.8
9 Low price	4.7

Source: Four Seasons Hotels & Resorts, Impressions (1992) April, p. 4

Note: Survey respondents include more than 500 business travellers who are accustomed to pay at least US$175.00 per night for a hotel room. The rating scale is from ten ('extremely important') to one ('not important')

detailed elsewhere (Jones and Pizam 1993) and are therefore discussed in broad terms only.

Hotel ownership vs management contract

In the hotel industry, hotel ownership may be approached, as a business activity which is separate from the hotel operations management activity or from the marketing and reservations function, through a hotel franchise or referral system. In contrast to the UK where hotel companies own hotel property, the major US hotel companies, such as Hilton, Hyatt, and Marriott have become primarily management companies with hotel ownership being a distinct and separate function from managing hotels. Companies that are in the business of hotel ownership focus on the acquisition of real estate and the ability to enhance their assets by making informed judgements in the areas of project feasibility, project financing, and financial control in cooperation with a management contract company. For example, Prudential Realty and VMS Management Companies of Chicago are the first and second largest hotel owners in America, both using more than ten different management contract companies to operate their respective hotel properties (Hotels and Restaurants International 1987).

Because low-quality staff will cause costs to rise and affect business performance negatively, the recruitment, development, and management of human resources is critical to hotel operations management companies. Since wage and salary levels vary little among hotel companies, the ability to recruit appropriate workers, and train and retain them, essentially determines each hotel company's performance and, therefore, its attractiveness to hotel owners who seek profit and asset enhancement.

According to the IHA (1988) *Hotels of the Future* study, there are several salient trends that characterize the evolution of management contracts:

(a) Owners are increasingly requesting a performance clause in the management contract as a basis for the remuneration of the operator, and to provide a minimum level of financial performance which the operator must achieve and beneath which the owner can terminate the contract. A difficulty which has emerged is to find a workable basis equitable to owner and manager alike.

(b) The trend is towards a shorter time-frame for management contracts from the traditional 20- to 25-year period, with regular periodical reviews in the latter years.

(c) Owners want to have the ability to terminate a contract on sale of the property and particularly in mature valuable real estate locations, offer vacant possessions, but may need to share any uplift in the sale price with the operator.

(d) Given the increasing likelihood of hotel company acquisitions and mergers, owners are wary of the possibility of finding themselves in a contractual arrangement with a company different from the original.

(e) Owners now expect management companies to accept some element of the investment risk, either by direct investment, or by some form of 'standback' until the hotel has produced a certain minimum level of cashflow that is sufficient to service its loan funding.

A more recent IHA study (1993) indicates that today's owners are increasingly profit motivated and more selective when appointing management. Furthermore, it affirmed that management contracts are an essential part of the structure of the hotel industry. In particular, the survey indicated that during 1991, a year in which the hotel industry witnessed a dramatic downturn, corporate brands such as Hilton, Inter-Continental, Ramada, Meridien and Holiday Inn outperformed lower profile operators who rely on the appeal of each individual property.

Franchise

In the hotel franchising business, the development of the franchise network is the crucial factor. Since each additional property in the hotel chain is financed by the franchisee who also pays both a franchise fee and royalties (and is responsible for his property's staff development), the parent company or franchiser is able to spread the high fixed cost of the franchise reservations network over a larger number of franchisees.

A critical mass of franchisees allows the franchiser to maintain training and advertising departments, functions in which independent hoteliers seldom excel. Last, but not least, each additional franchised hotel exposes the franchiser's brand-name in a new geographic market, creating the potential to build referral business for other hotels in the system. Holiday Inns is the hotel company whose expansion is primarily based on franchising. Within the context of more widespread market segmentation and branding, franchising represents significant potential to both the franchiser and franchisee, particularly for modest sized units.

The franchise system affords smaller hotel operators advantages that are not accessible to independent hoteliers. With the spread of franchising it is likely that certain franchisees, who have established a portfolio of franchised properties, may break away and develop their own brand-name operation.

In the constant search for growth avenues certain corporations are exploring the switch from a management contract strategy to a franchise strategy. For example, the Marriott Corporation's most valuable asset – its brand-name – recently enabled it to turn to franchising. The company had expanded during the 1980s by building hotels, selling them to investors, and collecting fees for managing the hotels that carried the Marriott name. During the 1980s Marriott's profits grew at a 20 per cent rate annually until its strategy was derailed by an oversupply of hotels, a collapsed real estate market, and a lingering recession. In 1993 Marriott franchised 27 per cent of its hotels worldwide and intends to increase that to more than 50 per cent by 1997. The further diversification into franchising enables Marriott to extend its brand-name; increase its profits by an estimated 25 per cent, but at the risk of a loss of quality. However, now that Marriott has entered the franchising field, other hotel corporations which thus far have spurned it, such as Hyatt, have indicated they will also commence franchising development (Rice 1993) that is likely to have major consequences.

Hotel consortia

The growing importance of 'branding' and the increase in competition has left independent hoteliers and smaller second-tier hotel chains little choice but to seek affiliation. As a consequence consortia have grown rapidly between 1991 and 1992 (Table 2.3).

Consortia, such as Best Western International, offer independent hoteliers membership affiliation in a centralized organization which affords them the opportunity to remain independent whilst benefiting from the marketing, financial and educational services offered.

The brainchild of M.K. Guertin, a California motel owner, Best Western International was established in 1946 when lodging chains were non-

Table 2.3 Growth of voluntary hotel chain consortia 1991–1992

Company	Rooms added	Total rooms
1 Utell	60,000	1,360,000
2 SRS Hotels Steigenberger	60,000	1,360,000
3 Supranational Hotels	5,832	123,000
4 Leading Hotels of the World	3,049	73,049
5 Concorde Hotels Group	2,677	15,800
6 ILA Chateaux & Hotels	2,110	16,902
7 Associated Luxury Hotels	2,077	26,202
8 Preferred Hotels Worldwide	1,500	26,754
9 TOP International Hotels	1,000	20,500
10 Relais & Chateaux	1,000	13,000

Source: *Hotels*, 1993 Annual Survey

existent. Guertin reasoned that success in the lodging industry could be developed through referral of business and cooperation among a large number of property owners who set and maintained high standards of guest service. Guertin toured other properties, choosing motels that were in his opinion clean, comfortable and reasonably priced, and recommended these to his guests. In turn, other property owners referred their guests to Guertin's motel. During the 1950s the loosely knit organization grew from 50 to 492 properties. Recognizing the need for a common marketing identity, the brand-name 'Western Motels, Inc.', was adopted.

Today, there are numerous other consortia chains that are based on the ideas which Guertin espoused. But they offer independent hotels two additional advantages: access to the worldwide market through global distribution systems and specialization in niche markets. For example, Leading Hotels of the World and Preferred Hotels Worldwide represent de luxe hotels around the world. And Relais and Chateaux represent small-scale heritage inns.

Consortia members pay a membership fee for their affiliation. For example, Best Western, a non-profit membership association, operates on a cost–recovery basis. A recent independent study conducted by consultants Stephen Rushmore, President of Hospitality Valuation Services in Mineola, New York, projected the total affiliation costs for a representative hotel, over a ten-year period. Using common assumptions for occupancy, average rate, and the published fees, dues and other charges, the total costs for seven major hotel chains were calculated. Rushmore's study findings are shown in Table 2.4.

Table 2.4 Total affiliation cost for a 200-room, mid-rate hotel over a ten-year period

Company	Affiliation cost ($)	Total cost as percentage of total room revenue
Days Inn	3,539,366	8.1
Ramada	3,329,877	7.6
Howard Johnson	3,173,885	7.2
Holiday Inns	2,793,501	6.4
Compri Hotels	2,658,401	6.1
Quality Inns	2,465,854	5.6
Best Western International	533,774	1.2

Source: Stephen Rushmore, Hospitality Valuation Services, Mineola, New York, n.d.

CASE: FORTE HOTELS AND CHOICE HOTELS – A COMPARISON OF GROWTH STRATEGIES

Forte Hotels and Choice Hotels International both compete in the accommodation market. But the companies are in a different league. The differences between these two hotel corporations offer important insights into the hotel industry and illustrate the complexity of competitive strategies in the international hotel business. Their stories are also apt metaphors for some of the forces that will be sweeping the global hotel industry into the twenty-first century.

Forte, previously Trusthouse Forte, is the United Kingdom's market leader in its three core businesses – hotels, restaurants and contract catering. The success of Trusthouse Forte can be ascribed in particular to the merger between Forte Holdings and Trust Houses Limited of 1970 which has been the key to the growth of the company. The acquisition of the majority shareholding in California-based Travelodge International and Gardner Merchant (its contract catering subsidiary), entry into mainland Europe in 1973, and the subsequent acquisition of 35 Strand hotels from J. Lyons & Company in Britain and of the Knott Hotels Corporation in the US made it one of the leading hospitality companies internationally. In 1990 Forte purchased 43 Crest hotels.

Forte owns many of its properties, a position in contrast with the typical American hotel chain which is essentially a management company with little or no equity in its properties, operating on a fee basis. As the owner and operator of hotels Forte can make its own decisions without having to consider the influences from absentee owners. Up to recently, the lack of a global brand image to compare with Hilton, Holiday Inns and Sheraton had been perceived as one of Forte's major weaknesses. Competitors operating under distinct hotel brands were successful in taking market share from Forte's hotels. Consequently, it was imperative for Forte to adapt to change in the market. In 1991 it introduced new hotel brands and adopted a new group name, Forte plc, which could be more easily associated with the company's brands throughout the world.

The Forte hotel portfolio is structured into three brands: Forte Travelodge providing roadside budget accommodation; Forte Posthouse, a UK chain of modern hotels; and Forte Crest, a chain of high-quality modern business hotels. The Forte hotel collections bring together a range of individual properties each with its own name, style, and character catering to a specific market segment: Forte Heritage – a collection of character hotels throughout the British Isles, ranging from historic coaching inns to elegant town houses, renowned for their traditional and friendly hospitality, excellent menus and local ales; Forte Grand – a collection of first-class international hotels offering traditional European standards of comfort, style and service; and the exclusive portfolio comprised of de luxe properties, each of which is an internationally renowned name in its own right, such as the Grosvenor House in London, the Hotel Plaza Athenee in Paris, and The Ritz in Madrid.

The Forte Hotels' brands and collections are backed by the Fortress reservations facility which provides computerized links with individual hotels and is served by mainframe computers at Aylesbury in the UK and Kansas State in the USA.

Due, in part, to Forte's preference for freehold hotel property ownership international expansion has progressed slowly. Major operators such as ACCOR, Bass, Choice International, Hilton, Marriott, and Ramada are all expanding substantially in Europe and have placed pressure on Forte to make considerable growth overseas one of the company's priorities.

Choice Hotels International introduced product differentiation on a grand scale into the hotel industry in 1981. With nearly 2,800 hotels in 26 countries, and headquarters in Washington, DC, Choice Hotels International is the world's largest franchise hotel company. Formerly named Quality International, Choice Hotels International pioneered the application of branding in the US hotel industry by chance. When the company's Chief Executive Officer went shopping for jogging shoes in 1981 and found 106 styles to choose from, he came up with a concept that spread throughout the hotel industry in North America. The implementation of hotel branding within Choice Hotels International resulted in four brands: Sleep Inns, Comfort Inns and Suites, Quality Inns and Suites, and Clarion Hotels, Resorts, and Suites.

In 1990 Choice's parent company, Manor Care, a major owner and operator of nursing homes throughout the USA, acquired 615 Econo Lodges, 85 Friendship Inns and 148 Rodeway Inns.

The contrasts with Forte are telling. Choice's franchise system enables it to expand very rapidly internationally through master franchise agreements within specified geographic areas.

In terms of structure Choice can remain a lean organization as franchise systems maintain control through agreements which detail the quality specifications that the franchisee has to maintain to preserve the franchise integrity. Hence, the decision as to what organizational structure is desirable to obtain optimal business performance is one that the franchisee has to make (rather than Choice as the franchiser).

As major funding sources more and more frequently require chain affiliation as a condition of financing, independent hotels will find themselves under pressure to acquire a brand-name and affiliation with an international reservation system. Consequently, Choice Hotels International can only see its portfolio of properties multiply. It has become one of the global hotel industry leaders with 2,502 hotels worldwide in 1992.

It is tempting to assess Forte's hotel owner/operator strategy as antiquated and ill-equipped to match competitors such as Choice which have applied innovative franchising techniques to conquer the global market. But this would be misleading. Their respective positions reflect both strategic choices and intentions. However, their future performance depends on how well each can adapt to the changing environment. If Forte succeeds in its intention of building its key brands to serve growing markets it has excellent prospects for continued expansion. Conversely, Choice's growth strategy hinges on its ability to ensure consistent product quality by seeking strategic alliances with appropriate business partners.

READING: THE NEW RESEARCH RESPONSIBILITY: EMERGING NEEDS FROM THE HOTEL INDUSTRY PERSPECTIVE

by William S. Watson, Senior Vice-President – Best Western Worldwide Marketing at the Travel and Tourism Research Association's Annual Meeting, 14 June 1993

I have some very real concerns about the historic role of research in the hotel industry and some real hope for its application in the future. At its most basic level, there are only two things we need from research in the hotel industry. And while those two things are distinctively different, they are equally critical to our success.

The first thing we need is information that answers questions from the hotel development perspective such as: Should I build a hotel and, if so, should I build it here? Can I make a profit by doing so? What type of hotel is needed? How many rooms? What ancillary facilities?

Obviously, this information is critical, not only to hotel operators and managers but also to bankers and developers. A tangential need to that, of course, is re-positioning or switching chains.

However, once a hotel is developed or re-positioned in the marketplace our research needs to change. We must begin to consider the second type of research which is related to the ongoing profitable marketing of the property.

Given the setback the hotel industry suffered in the 1980s – when the supply of newly built rooms far exceeded the demand for them – one can only speculate about the market research and the manner in which it was interpreted to develop the prognosis for that era.

But before I share my thoughts about the use of research and the prognosis for the next era, I want to make some general remarks about the nature of the hotel industry within the context of the entire travel industry, particularly for those not intimately involved in hotels.

The nature of the hotel industry

We are a peculiar industry. Our origins go back at least as far as that spectacular overbooking problem in Bethlehem, probably earlier. While there have been some extreme changes in the quality of our product – and more recently the technology supporting it – there are still many aspects of the industry that have hardly changed in almost 2,000 years. Perhaps the most obvious is overbooking.

The other thing that has not changed is the position of the general manager. They still share some of the unique attributes of dictators or princes of small kingdoms. Seriously, however, it is the structure of ownership within the hotel industry that sets it aside from much of the rest of the travel industry.

There are often conflicting needs, objectives, and tactics between property owners or managers and chain management. Another distinguishing feature of the hotel industry is that although we share customers with other sectors of travel, there are fundamental differences in what attracts customers to their hotel of choice.

It is not simply a matter of picking a room with a bed and bath. It is investing in an experience. It encompasses style and quality. It involves food and beverage, and entertainment. It involves all the senses and goes far beyond the basic requirement of simply being there – which is more than the requirement for an airline flight for getting somewhere, or a car rental for getting somewhere.

Obviously, consumers stay at a hotel for a multitude of reasons far exceeding the basic reasons for using just about any other travel industry segment. To mention a few, they may live permanently in a hotel or be there for an extended period – obviously it may be for business or leisure. Perhaps a meeting or convention, or a reunion. They may not really be staying at the hotel at all, but attending a function. Or just using hotel facilities such as one of the retail outlets – food and beverage, nightclub, or bar.

The reasons to use the hotel product go far beyond the simple need of 2,000 years ago – the need for a room safe from the night and from the elements. In short, today's hotel industry is as much an experiential purchase as it is a travel commodity.

The changing role of research

With the unique differences of the hotel industry as a segment of the overall travel industry in mind, let's explore some of the more recent changes and my concerns with the role of research.

Over the years, I believe the hotel industry has lagged seriously behind other industries in terms of research and planning.

Earlier, I touched briefly on the overbuilding virus that infected the hotel industry in the 1970s and 1980s. At the time we saw somewhat cursory reviews of new development opportunities which, unfortunately, didn't examine the complete picture.

I remember one example: in Stamford, Connecticut, there was one very successful Marriott property operating at virtually 100 per cent capacity. It was a booming market with major companies relocating from all over. Some research companies involved with the hospitality industry persuaded a number of chains and developers that there was an immense opportunity for one more hotel in Stamford. This hot opportunity was grasped quickly and a number of new properties were built in that area.

The rest of the story is obvious – and predictable. The recession began and left a lot of hotels with a lot of empty rooms chasing too few customers and carrying huge debt – a number of them now bankrupt.

Now perhaps we can't blame the researchers for not forecasting the essential nature of recessions. The fact remains, however, that someone should have been looking at competitive activities and doing some worst-case scenario planning.

During that same period, we witnessed major marketing decisions being made throughout the industry based on no more research than the gut feelings of hoteliers who had little background in professional marketing or selling. In part, those decisions were being made because solid data was difficult to obtain on customers, indeed, on the industry itself.

But things started to change. For example, when I arrived at Best Western about a year ago, I was delighted to find an abundance of customer information and an active marketing research team. We had fallen into a different trap, however. We had the data, but we hadn't worked to take full advantage of it.

That is changing at Best Western, as I think it must change throughout the industry. Those changes are happening now.

A number of fundamental driving forces have caused the hotel industry to change its view of research and information. Some of these are obvious and are based on 20/20 hindsight. Others are the result of more recent events.

(a) The experience of the overbuilding of the 1980s.
(b) Major changes in marketing and reservations automation, creating new sources of data.
(c) Some very smart research companies, like Smith Travel Research and DKS, that have developed industry-wide systems for tracking rate and occupancy and customer trends and preferences.
(d) We have woken up to the need to listen to the customer.

Marketing automation is sweeping the industry

In the last half dozen years or so, marketing automation has swept through the hotel industry. We now have reservations systems that track guest information which allow us to:

(a) Accurately manage rooms.
(b) Provide accurate, immediate inventory access to descriptive data from which to sell.
(c) Link up with more and more electronic sources of booking with travel agents and other distribution channels. (In fact, reservations from third-party sources are beginning to rival our reservations made by phone.)

These central systems are also becoming linked at the property-management system level so that any user of the system can access various types of data according to their needs. And, most importantly, all information on all guests, no matter how they book, is being captured.

Think about the marketing implications of having that much information available so quickly. It's complex and it's never been available before. We are all struggling to learn how to make full use of it.

This flow of information is causing some restructuring in our industry. The automation of marketing needs and reservations needs is becoming a utility. New alliances are being formed between chains to address the need for reducing the cost of reservations transactions and information, while still allowing for competitive and individual uses of that information.

I believe we are combining these new trends with the lessons we learned from the 1980s.

New professionals are coming into the industry and they are spurring a new awareness of our needs. There is an increasing demand for systems and quantitative data to better manage in the hotel industry.

So where does that put us today?

The hotel industry is a smarter industry. We now have business systems to measure our progress and activities and, equally as important, to help us plan.

Nearly all of us now belong to systems like Smith Travel Research, and DKS can actually look at competing rates and occupancies in different market areas and compare customer perceptions of competing chains. Most of us either are developing or have developed new reservations and marketing automation systems either singly or in alliances, the key differentiating factor between us being how we use the data that comes from those systems and services to make the best competitive decision.

And lastly, we have learned the lesson that researching, testing, and planning are more important – and more critical to both survival and success – today than ever before in our history.

These changes in technology I've been outlining have occurred literally in the last few years and, of course, are generating more changes of their own. Rapid changes on the systems side require rapid changes in our research and planning needs.

Rapid changes in research, planning needs

I think it is almost a given that operating a hotel requires specific, creative and – especially today – customer service-oriented attitudes. The 2,000-year history of the industry, coupled with several hundred more years of hotel school training, has created a stream of qualified people capable of operating good hotels.

But I think we must now go a step beyond that. We now recognize the need for more professional marketing management.

We are in an industry where rooms at today's dollars are essentially selling below those of ten years ago. We are a financially strapped industry, recovering from the severe period, operating in lean organizational structures with enormous pressures to make today's bottom line. As marketers, we are inundated by data.

Marketers are generally willing to make some intuitive leaps. Indeed, the creative aspects of our character tends to be critical in that regard, but we need just enough information to make reasonable decisions.

Arthur Hays Sulzburger recognized that fact more than 40 years ago when he said: 'Obviously, man's judgment cannot be better than the information on which he has based it.'

As marketers, our judgement cannot be better than the information on which we have based that judgement. And – the extension of Sulzburger's thought – we must let our judgement move beyond the obvious interpretation and learn to make use of what we have learned.

Researchers must put less emphasis on data and more on the interpretation of data. They must work towards turning data into usable information. In other words, researchers need to integrate research data with other information and understand the client business – whether it is a separate business or part of the same organization. They must determine what areas are critical to the business and the best way to provide measurement for that. Researchers must stop thinking about data and reports and work with us to solve the marketing problems before us.

Collecting data for its own value is like collecting stamps. It's a nice hobby but it doesn't deliver the mail.

Research has to be relevant. Providing isolated facts – such as the fact that travel agents on the average arrange 30 corporate meetings a year – is not very meaningful without applying it to other relevant facts. For example, if you know the number of travel agents who book these corporate meetings, then you have more complete information. If we can also identify the types of travel agents who book these meetings and the types of hotel product they are looking for, then we are beginning to turn data into useful marketing info. With that information, we can begin to apply some real marketing logic.

Researchers generally don't think in marketing terms, but rather in terms of numbers – collecting data.

Researchers working in the hotel industry must learn to relate measurements that are industry standards, industry language. Let's all start talking about room nights rather than person trip or bed nights, for example.

Researchers must also address some of the other common areas, as well, such as how information is presented. Graphs must be clear and well labelled. Research jargon should be avoided, sourcing statistics from syndicated research versus original research needs to be clearly shown.

The time lag in statistics is another very real concern for a marketer. Frankly, seeing 17-month-old statistics has little relevance to my needs or the market conditions today – the conditions in which I'm making marketing decisions. And in that regard, the volume of data which comes out to marketers is often poorly packaged. In today's world few of us have the luxury of time to wade through books and pages and pages of data. We need succinct summaries expressed in usable terms.

We are addressing these issues specifically at Best Western International. The research function is now a planning function with research as a supportive adjunct. We still collect the data, but now we seek to apply it creatively and plan with it.

I have turned our research and planning department into an integral part of the marketing team working in a matrix-like context.

The hotel industry is an old industry. But its greatest and most rapid changes have come in the last half-dozen years. In the industry, we accept that we must deliver the service product and the physical product that today's customer demands. And we must do it in an environment of the most extreme competition in our industry's long history.

If we are to succeed, we must know what those demands are. That's the old, basic research responsibility. Then we must use that research to plan.

The new research responsibility is to guide us in that planning, to allow us to avoid the mistakes of the last decade and bring this industry back to profitability.

STUDY QUESTIONS

1 Describe the economic characteristics of the contemporary hotel industry.
2 Why do hotel companies need to formulate and implement strategies?
3 Discuss factors which have made it difficult for hotel companies based in Europe and North America to expand.
4 What 'product strategies' have been identified by the IHA *Hotels of the Future* study?
5 Discuss 'competitive advantage' in relation to the hotel industry.
6 Compare and contrast hotel ownership, management contracting and franchising.
7 Outline the benefits of consortia membership and discuss which type of hotel company might derive most benefit from such membership.
8 Discuss the different approach to expansion adopted by Forte Hotels and Choice Hotels International.
9 Which company, Forte or Choice, is better positioned to enact extensive globalization?
10 Discuss the changing role of research in the hotel industry.

Appraising the global competitive environment

Information technology is at the core of today's economy, and the purpose of Chapter 3 is to pinpoint in particular how the new information technologies are changing the demand, altering long-standing relationships, and creating new forms of competition overnight. For example, the launch of global distribution systems (GDS) has created the potential concentration of the dispersed hotel demand. Specifically, the consolidation within the travel agency business and the linking of worldwide affiliates through computer networks allow individuals and companies to benefit from substantial price reductions through the 'bulk buying' of hotel rooms.

On the other hand, the new information architecture is creating fundamentally different relationships between producers and buyers. In particular, sophisticated computerized programs will facilitate the direct booking process between buyer and supplier and increasingly result in the bypassing of intermediaries in the channel system.

Poon (1989) provides a concise comparison of the 'Old Tourism' of the 1950s, 1960s and 1970s with the 'New Tourism' of the future. The 'Old Tourism' is characterized by large volume, standardized and rigidly packaged holidays, hotels and tourists. The characteristics of 'New Tourism' are flexibility and segmentation, providing a more personalized or individual tourism experience. It also involves a high level of integration in organization and management within the tourist industry, largely made possible by a greater utilization of modern information technology, described by Poon (1989: 97) as 'a vital pillar of the new tourism'.

The case at the end of the chapter looks at the way Harrah's Casinos has found a most useful way of employing database marketing. The reading, by Clive Jones of Economic Research Associates, gives a broader view of the importance of database marketing.

THE END OF MASS MARKETING

The growing interaction between science and technology, on the one hand, and industry, transport and communications, on the other, are factors that enhanced the standardization of products, a vital component of mass production (Teichova 1986: 365). During the first half of the twentieth century, mass market economies evolved first in the USA, then in Europe, and later in Japan. The mass market economy, coupled with the primary goal of business to achieve profit, favoured the creation and growth of transnational corporations which reduced unit costs and expanded share in domestic and foreign markets.

Thirty 'Glorious Years' (1945–1974) brought a phase of unparalleled economic prosperity based on the Bretton Woods system: a gold-backed, dollar-based series of exchange rates. The Bretton Woods agreement set the stage for an economic boom. Improvements in transportation infrastructure and mass communications, combined with aggressive development policies of nation-states, doubled worldwide trade in goods and services in real terms between 1965 and 1985 (Segal 1988: 35).

The energy crisis triggered by the oil embargo of 1973 heralded a decade of uncertainty and chaos. Between 1975 and 1986 the annual gross domestic product (GDP) growth rate of industrialized nations dropped to 2.9 per cent from 5 per cent over the 1960–1973 period. Significantly, international tourism receipts rose at an average annual rate of 5.4 per cent between 1975 and 1986, displaying the fastest growth rate among world trade commodities and in relation to the gross domestic product in OECD countries, and total world export, as shown in Table 3.1.

The improvement in living standards in most industrialized countries provided the impetus for the growth of tourism and the demand for hotel accommodation. The explosive growth of business and pleasure travel during the post-Second World War era is partially the result of the economic growth triggered by the rise of the service sector which in turn has been the product of several interrelated processes (Gershuny and Miles 1983).

Table 3.1 Annual growth rate of international tourism receipts compared to selected trade commodities, GDP in OECD countries, and total world export, 1975–1986

	Annual growth rate (%)
International tourism receipts	5.4
Gross domestic product in OECD	2.9
Total world export	3.5
World export of agricultural products	2.5
World export of minerals	3.2
World export of manufactured goods	3.6

Source: Government of Canada (1988c) *The Challenges in Tourism Product Development*, Ottawa: Tourism Canada (May)

First, the increasing geographical specialization that characterized the industrial era had the effect not only of stimulating trade but also of generating new opportunities for employment and investment in the service sector. Second, the market for many basic manufactured goods had become saturated, leaving consumers free to spend a larger proportion of their incomes on leisure and personal services. Finally, a large number of jobs were created in the public sector of industrial economies where gross domestic product from services has reached more than 60 per cent (Price and Blair 1989: 12).

A combination of technological developments, economic changes, and social dynamics is transforming the texture of the marketplace. A new generation of dominating motives among consumers, different from traditional values, is becoming evident. While these changes affect many institutions, they have special implications on business, in that the new consumer motives shape the expectations of clients, employees, managers, shareholders, and the public at large.

The application of micro-electronic technology in general and the computer in particular has played an especially important role in the transformation from the mass market to a fragmented market. Given the appropriate knowledge and equipment, marketing strategies today can be based on databases. Companies that have shifted from mass media to direct marketing have been able to reduce the number of advertising dollars that were spent ineffectively in the mass media or abandon them altogether. They are able, through the application of database marketing, to deal with the buyer on a one-to-one basis as opposed to a collection of buyers.

Though mass marketing is still widely practised, mass markets and mass media abound, and image building and product awareness advertising are still important, there is no denying that the marketplace is changing profoundly. The shift towards the 'age of the individual' in marketing is driven by the proliferation of micro-processing technology. The application of computers has made it feasible to build a desired relationship with individual customers. However, as relationship marketing is moving to the forefront of strategic thinking (Rapp and Collins 1992: 5), a turn-around in marketing thinking is required which recognizes that 'a database is only a means to an end. The end is direct contact, dialogue, and involvement with the individual prospect or customer leading to increased sales and brand loyalty' (Rapp and Collins 1992: 6).

The observation that the 'back office' (database administration) holds in effect the key to the 'individualization' of the customer service process implies that this function contributes importantly to a company's ability to attain a potential competitive advantage. Another implication, based on the premise that customer satisfaction is the keystone of business success, is that the delivery of satisfactory 'front line' service depends on the quality of products and service supplied by the 'back office'. Based on these observations, we can deduct that 'a company's ability to meet its external customer needs depends directly on how well it satisfies the needs of these internal customers' (Pfau *et al.* 1991: 9).

The emergence of the 'internal customer' illustrates a significant development that is taking place in business. It is the emerging notion that it does no longer make sense to think in 'either/or' terms in service businesses. As the application of information systems is moving beyond the simple automation of routine tasks and the provision of support for decision-making, the role of the 'back office' in relation to the 'front line' will take on a new shape. Information systems may be used, for example, in the education of both customers and service providers and in drawing the customer more and more into self-help or 'self-service' processes. Thus, instead of emphasizing the effectiveness of the front line in relation to 'the moment of truth',[1] which is about the ways a customer meets the company, managers ought to examine both the 'front line' capabilities in relation to the 'back office' capabilities to explore how traditionally separate functions can be shaped into new patterns that improve customer service.

The emergence of the idea of the 'internal customer' has become accepted as one of a 'chain of customers' (Schonberger 1990). Because the lack of close attention to internal supplier–customer relationships can jeopardize 'buyer' satisfaction, companies have to ensure that all 'customers' are satisfied, both within and outside the firm. Companies are beginning to develop 'customer' relationships with their internal functional units through internal marketing (Wasmer and Bruner 1991), with buyers, with suppliers, with business partners, and sometimes with competitors. The re-configuration of the market logic, which abandons the 'conventional wisdom' about the market, is especially relevant to hotels because hotel demand is a derived demand. This implies that the most penetrating market analysis and the most imaginative marketing applications are worth little unless hotel executives take full account of key environmental demand trends that both influence and are influenced by manufacturing and service businesses. Any hotel company that wants to survive has to understand the shifts in demand that are most vividly demonstrated in the travel market by:

(a) Information technologies that are increasingly blurring the boundaries between demand and supply, especially in the services sector where the customer plays an increasingly important role in the production process, i.e., if producers make the effort to educate customers.

(b) The concentration of demand through global distribution systems (GDS). The GDS is changing the supplier–buyer relationship and permitting alternative linkages between buyers and vendors, and therefore spawning new roles for travel agents, distributors, and linkages with customers.

(c) The emergence of the 'global customer'. Instant worldwide news reporting through, for example, the Cable News Network (CNN) has resulted in consumers around the world who know the same things at the same time. The increasing homogenization of customer needs worldwide has spawned a global lifestyle and raised consumer expectations for ever faster and better service and higher levels of product quality at lower cost. Within the quality service context, consumers rate hotels not only with hotels but other types of businesses serve also as bench-marks to assess the level of hotel service. Systematically in industry after industry, power is shifting from sellers to buyers, because the latter have easy access to information and more choices in that there are more multinational companies competing across borders for the favour of the consumer.

(d) The new market opportunities that are being created through market fragmentation. Unlike the mass market, each segment of the fragmented market demands the 'undivided' attention of the producer. For example,

- Higher income professional people who are constantly under pressure in the workplace seek to combine business travel with short getaway trips. For this segment, a rewarding experience, rather than the expense involved, is the determining success factor and the key to customer loyalty.

- Though the bulk of hotel demand is still concentrated in the Western industrialized markets, the Pacific Rim markets offer excellent prospects for growth. Rising numbers of visitors from Asian markets will pose a challenge in the service delivery process in that hotel personnel in, for example, Western countries may not be familiar with Asian cultures and languages and vice versa. Hall (1994) provides a very useful overview of tourism in these markets.

- Dual career households may have more discretionary income, but obtaining the maximum benefits from leisure time has become more important because finding mutually convenient leisure time periods is more complex and often results in compromises.

- Rising environmental concerns have triggered greater demand among certain customers for 'green' products and services. The increasing urbanization of the world's population is likely to support the trend for a better quality of life and the consumers' search for open spaces, clean air, and clean beaches and oceans, and at the same time, the realization of self and inner-values.

- The ageing of a growing number of consumers in industrialized countries has placed greater importance on comfort, safety, and health concerns. Other distinctive market segments include the 'baby boomers' who are looking for new experiences. At the same time, the variance between high-income and low-income earners in industrialized countries is widening, suggesting a growing differentiation between products geared to the high and low ends of the market. However, despite the market diversity, all segments demand value for money.

The new marketplace realities will spell the demise of mass marketing and deeply affect hotel corporations, either favourably or unfavourably. It calls for a marketing approach that emphasizes relationships and which is dramatically different from the traditional producer-led, brand-oriented marketing practised by the majority of international hotel corporations. Customers are less loyal to specific brands, because in a dynamic environment their needs and preferences are shifting continuously and so are product offerings. The convergence of forces that are changing the market leaves hotel executives with little choice but to develop a new way of strategic thinking in order to survive.[2] The remainder of this chapter will examine a range of areas which provide pointers about these forces which are changing the market, such as the economics of substitution, developments in the technological environment, the globalization and fragmentation of the travel market, and quality considerations.

THE ECONOMICS OF SUBSTITUTION

The market boundaries are constantly shifting due to economic inducements and the changing awareness customers have of the possible substitutes and the degree of substitutability of the product or service alternatives for satisfying their needs. Substitutes-in-use are especially relevant to the international hotel industry. For example, when addressing the commercial travel market (customer groups) it will become evident that a businessman's need for communication with a client (customer needs) may be satisfied by a combination of the facsimile machine and the postal and telecommunications network (applied technology). Similarly, in the pleasure segment of the market, a recreational trip may range from the mass produced package tour 'sold off the rack' in the retail travel agency to the custom-designed dream experience for the select few (Kotler 1984). In the latter case new holography technology could potentially pose a future threat to the pleasure travel market in that it will have the capability to simulate dream experiences.[3]

New technologies will not only have a profound effect on the way hotels communicate (Moutinho 1989: 141) but will increasingly provide consumers with alternatives to help solve their daily problems. The matrix designed by Tettero and Viehoff (1990: 33–35) depicted in Table 3.2 forms an effective departure point for the analysis of substitute options and alternative choices from a demand-side perspective in the services sector. In order to understand to what extent and degree substitutability in use

Table 3.2 Typology of competitive scenarios in the service sector

Substitute options	Alternative choices		
The possibility to choose substitutes in the form of other services, including convenience services and products	*The degree to which barriers to entry exist*		
	1 High	*2 Modest*	*3 Low*
	respectively the possibility to choose between alternative suppliers		
	1 Small	*2 Medium*	*3 Great*
1 Small	– Specialist medical services – Global distribution systems (GDS)	– Dentistry services – International services	– Architectural services – Retail services
2 Modest	– Music schools – Higher education	– Accountancy services – Air passenger transportation	– Savings and loans – Hotel and convention facilities
3 Great	– Postal services – Translation services	– Taxi – International cargo services – Theatre performances	– Tour operator services – Cinema (movies) – Restaurants (food services) – Cleaning services

Source: J.H.J.P. Tettero and J.H.R.M. Viehoff (1990) *Marketing voor dienstverlenende organisaties*, Beleid & uitvoering, Deventer: Kluwer Bedrijfswebenschappen, p. 36

and application, which goes beyond substitutes in kind (Day 1990: 92), affects hotel corporations it therefore seems appropriate to examine hotel services in relation to other service alternatives that could satisfy similar market needs. Tettero and Viehoff's (1990: 36) service sector typology comprised of three categories:

(a) Knowledge, and expertise related services: including health care services, research and development, education and training, engineering services etc. A number of the aforementioned service suppliers may be able to raise their price without much consumer resistance depending on the level of professional expertise and competition between suppliers.
(b) Facilitating services such as commercial banking, air transportation, postal services, insurance, cable television services, etc. Due to the substantial capital investments, infrastructure, and knowledge required, the number of suppliers in this category tends to be limited. Most of the services in this category can only be profitably rendered when a large group of (potential) consumers is present.

(c) Convenience services, including all services which consumers purchase because they prefer third parties to perform a particular task. The services in this category (including entertainment, hotel and restaurant services, advertising) can often be performed by the consumer and are especially vulnerable to substitution. The extent of rivalry among convenience service firms tends to be strong, which typically results in significant price competition.

Because the potential substitution, both 'in kind' and 'in-use', forms an immediate threat, it is imperative that hotel corporations demonstrate a marketing orientation. How marketing oriented are hotel firms compared to other firms in other service sectors? A survey conducted by Parasuraman *et al.* (1983) studied 323 service firms. The survey revealed that the average marketing orientation score across all service firms was 3.71 on a scale of 1 to 5. Hotels had a below average score of 3.68, as shown in Table 3.3. Although this score does not necessarily mean a 'failing' grade for hotels, it does point out that there is adequate room for service firms in general and hotel firms in particular to improve their marketing orientation.

Gross domestic product

The growth in travel is inextricably linked to gross domestic product (GDP) growth in general, and growth of per capita income in particular.

Table 3.3 Variation in marketing orientation across different service industries

Industry type	Number of firms surveyed	Percentage of firms surveyed	Average marketing orientation score
Personal services	9	3	4.16
Business services	54	17	4.10
Miscellaneous services	22	17	4.02
Repair services	17	5	3.88
Construction	18	6	3.76
Transportation	27	9	3.76
Hotels and lodging places	28	9	3.68
Brokerage firms	30	9	3.52
Banking	73	23	3.46
Recreation	18	6	3.41
Non-bank credit agencies	22	7	3.32
All industries combined	323	100	3.71

Source: A. Parasuraman, L.L. Berry and V.A. Zeithaml (1983) 'Service Firms Need Marketing Skills', *Business Horizons* 26(6): 29. Copyright © 1983 by the Foundation for the School of Business at Indiana University. Used with permission

Note: Percentages do not add up to exacly 100 due to rounding off. Average scores are on a 1 to 5 marketing orientation scale

In this regard, the speed with which Japan caught up with and overtook European countries is striking: the annual growth rate of per capita income in Japan in the 1960s averaged 9.1 per cent.

Between the end of the 1950s and the beginning of the 1970s, the average annual growth rates of real per capita income in all countries that are members of the Organization for Economic Cooperation and Development (OECD) combined measured 3.9 per cent. This annual growth rate tapered off to 2.2 per cent between 1970 and 1980, while the world recession between 1980 and 1984 resulted in nothing short of an international economic crisis with an annual growth rate of 1.1 per cent (Table 3.4).

An analysis in terms of rising and falling elasticities, and saturation regarding the basic structure of consumer expenditures, can be used to distinguish a hierarchy of consumer preferences. These consumer preferences tend to shift away from 'necessity goods' due to the saturation of demand for these products in developed countries. As a result of technological innovations, advanced production processes, and fierce competition, the variety of goods and services available for consumption will continue to expand.

However, increases in income do not imply equal increases of all expenditures. Elfring's (1989) findings indicate that demand for goods and services relating to recreation is expanding, partly as a result of more leisure time for the population of industrialized countries. This finding is significant because it signals that future market needs might differ from the historical market needs, which in the hotel industry were chiefly perceived to be related to the business travel market.[4]

Travel expenditures

Personal travel accounts for two-thirds of the almost US$2 trillion of travel and tourism sales, while business and government account for the

Table 3.4 Average annual growth rates of real per capita income

	1960–1969	1970–1979	1980–1984
Total OECD	3.9	2.2	1.1
Japan	9.1	3.2	3.0
Total developing countries	3.1	3.1	0.0
Africa	2.2	0.8	−2.5
Asia	3.6	3.8	2.3
Latin America	2.6	2.9	−2.6

Source: OECD (1989) National and International Tourism Statistics, 1974–1985, Paris: Organization for Economic Cooperation and Development. © OECD, 1989. Reproduced by permission of OECD

remaining third. Personal sales of nearly $1.3 trillion represented a significant portion (11 per cent) of global consumer spending in 1987 (WEFA n.d.: 2). These figures approximate WTO data which indicate that in 1988 international tourists spent about US$195 billion, an increase of 22.5 per cent over the previous year (Government of Canada 1989a: 2).

Projections made by Edwards (1988: 12) indicate that total tourism expenditures could increase between 1988 and 1999 from US$200 billion to more than $300 billion. Nine countries – Japan, the US, the UK, Saudi Arabia, France, Italy, Canada, the Netherlands and Germany – might generate travel expenditures by 1999 in the order of $164 billion, at constant 1985 prices and exchange rates. The same study (Edwards 1988: 15) indicates that the number of nights abroad, worldwide, will rise from an estimated US$3 billion in 1988 to US$4.9 billion in 1999 – a 63 per cent increase.

Buckley *et al.* (1989) point out the significance of the rapid growth rate of Japan's overseas tourism relative to other major originator markets. In 1986 Japanese international tourism expenditures were 35 per cent of the level for Germany, 42 per cent of the level for the USA, and 81 per cent of the level for the UK.[5]

In most major non-Communist countries, travel is the third largest consumer expenditure after food and housing (WEFA n.d.), for example:

(a) The typical American household spends $3,900 per year on travel in the United States and abroad, almost as much as it spends on private health care or on food, beverages and tobacco combined, and twice as much as it spends on clothing.
(b) Consumers in the UK spend about the same on housing and about one-fourth as much on clothing as they spend on travel.
(c) In space-scarce Japan, consumers spend only 25 per cent more on housing than they spend on world travel. However, the amount spent on travel is still twice as much as on clothing or on furniture and household equipment combined, including appliances and electronics.
(d) European households spend in total almost 40 per cent more on worldwide personal travel than North and South American households do, and American households spend, in total, over 60 per cent more on worldwide personal travel than their Asian and African counterparts combined.

These findings on personal consumption expenditures reveal the relative importance consumers attach to travel and tourism. Furthermore, though there are differences between world regions, the findings demonstrate that travel and tourism demand (and, by extension, hotel demand) is concentrated in the industrialized nations.

What is important to note is that relatively high tourist expenditures do not necessarily translate into a high number of nights spent abroad, and it is the number of such nights which is an indicator of expenditure going to hotels. For example, despite Japan's fast growth as measured in tourist expenditures in 1986 relative to the industrialized Western nations, it lagged considerably behind Germany, the UK, the USA, and France in terms of the number of nights spent abroad by Japanese travellers. This may be due in part to the relatively high per capita expenditure of Japanese tourists and their usually short length of stay in foreign countries. The very significant position of European countries with regard to nights spent abroad in 1986 is predicted by Edwards (1988) to become a dominant position by 1999. By that year it is projected that Switzerland, Austria, and the Netherlands will be ranked 4, 5 and 6 respectively, with Germany, the United Kingdom, and the United States remaining in the first three places (Edwards 1988: 6).

Relative price changes

Ease of mobility, cost of transportation and changing consumer tastes and preferences have a synergistic effect and determine the aggregate effect on the demand of international travel in a given outbound market area. Fluctuations in the economy such as exchange rates, inflation rates and transportation costs affect travel patterns and hotels catering to international markets significantly (Arbel and Geller 1983).

Edwards (1987) indicates that shifts of exchange rates tend to be more important in the short term, while in the longer term differences between rates of inflation and the declining costs of air travel are of greater significance. Relative price changes often affect travel shares most, not in the year in which they take place, but mainly from one year to three years later – due partly to the fact that holiday decisions are usually taken well in advance, and partly because it takes time for an area to earn a reputation for being relatively cheap or relatively expensive.

The effect of a 5 per cent rise in the cost of holidays in one destination compared with competitive destinations is, usually, to depress the market share of that destination by between 10 per cent and 17.5 per cent. If relative costs rise more sharply by, for example, 20 per cent, market share can be expected to drop by between 30 and 40 per cent. Typically these effects take about three years to work through in full (Edwards 1987).

THE TECHNOLOGICAL ENVIRONMENT

Historically, new technology has been developed with the goal of improving productivity and lowering the cost of production. This trend is likely to continue, as new innovations and technologies are combined with those of the Industrial Revolution. For managers, it will be important to envision the type and degree of change and to take steps, within international hotel corporations, to anticipate such change. In the technological environment, the speed of new transportation modes and advances of information technologies are especially relevant to the international hotel industry.

Hotel executives will have no control over the developments that will take place in the transportation sector, although transportation technology advances will have significant consequences for the hotel industry. In contrast, hotel industry leaders who embrace new information technology by actively participating in the technology planning process will be able to identify new uses of technologies and manage them for improved competitive advantage.

As the focus of research shifts from creating technology that improves hotel business efficiency to identifying innovative technology applications that will enhance the guest experience, hotel executives have to gain an in-depth understanding of the key attributes of customers, competitors, and the strengths and weaknesses of the company. Only by understanding the market will the hotel executive be able to determine business needs and the potential use of technology.

Transportation

Technological advances, especially in transportation, have influenced the development and maturation of the physical means through which passengers and goods are moved. The demand for hotel accommodation over the past two centuries has been greatly influenced by developments in transportation. The modern hotel evolved from the caravan era along oriental trade routes to the hostelry located on coach trails to the railway hotel. Automobile travel in the twentieth century led to the creation of the motel, while air transportation resulted in the demand for hotels near airports and in far-flung resort and business centres.

Similarly, a decline in demand for a particular transportation mode or a shift in spatial travel patterns can have massive consequences for international hotel firms, in particular with regard to accommodation demand. The availability of substitute products such as faster and more frequently available transportation means or advanced telecommunications, which enable people to return to their homes on the day of their trip departure or to place a 'conference' telephone call, may cause a potential drain on hotel industry room nights (Rushmore 1983: 1–9).

First revolution

In the eighteenth century the Industrial Revolution led to a massive migration of the British population away from rural areas to industrial cities. This migratory development had a two-pronged result: first, workers became aware of the attraction of their rural surroundings in stark contrast with the dark and polluted cities; second, factory work, however monotonous, led to higher wages and a population demanding more goods and services (Holloway 1989: 25). The opening of the Liverpool and Manchester Railway in England in 1830 heralded the advent of the railway (Hodgson 1987: 4). Riding on the wave of the Industrial Revolution of steam and steel, the revolution of pleasure travel occurred in Great Britain with the introduction of the organized tour in 1841 when Thomas Cook set the wheels in motion leading to modern tourism (McIntosh and Goeldner 1990: 30).

Thomas Cook & Son took full advantage of steam transport technology by initiating a 'revolution' in tourism. By 1855, Cook had extended his enterprise to the Continent where he organized the first 'inclusive tour' to the Paris Exhibition of that year (Holloway 1989: 26), and by 1890 the Britain-based enterprise operated fifteen steamers on the Nile river and a hotel in Luxor, Egypt (Turner and Ash 1975: 57–59). These accomplishments turned Thomas Cook & Son into one of the first transnational tourism companies in the world.

Second revolution

A burst of motor car related innovations occurred between 1870 and 1890 which initiated an automobile industry developed primarily by the French who can be credited with the first significant production of automobiles (Stewart 1989: 103). The period between 1890 and 1920 was characterized by the growth of national markets, national corporations and steady progression and technology changes. The assembly-manufactured automobile first introduced in the USA by Henry Ford in 1914 (Stewart 1989: 104) caused the second tourism revolution, and the tourism phenomenon began to lose its rather elitist image. For example, Hugill (1985: 436) chronicled how automobiles revolutionized the travel habits of Americans in the first two decades of the twentieth century from a 'class to mass' activity. The growing popularity of the automobile caused the steady decline of the railways both in Europe and in America.

Improvements in transportation infrastructure, especially the US Interstate Highway system put in place through the Federal Aid Highway Act, turned tourism into a popular pastime. With the construction of highways, Americans packed their belongings and families into the car and headed for vacations in places that were becoming increasingly accessible by interstate highways. Roadside tourist courts and motels flourished.

Third revolution

Before the 1930s the use of aeroplanes was largely confined to the military, mail carriage and the exploration of new frontiers by few, because air travel was too unreliable and costly for the travelling public at large. In the early 1930s, a new generation of piston-engine aircraft was offering faster, more comfortable commercial service. But only in the period of economic reconstruction following the Second World War did demand for air transportation rise as a result of intermodal competition, which resulted in price competition. In Europe this caused, among other factors, the search for cheaper methods of air transport and led to the creation of a charter airline community (Gialloreto 1988: 16).

The third tourism revolution commenced in the late 1950s when trains and ships began to lose a growing number of passengers to the airline industry. By 1952, the first commercial jet could fly three times the speed of the traditional propeller craft. Jet air travel was introduced on selected routes and characterized by several incremental innovations in terms of engines used, aeroplane designs and related technology (Stewart 1989: 110). In 1959, the Boeing 707 was placed into regular transatlantic service and reduced travelling time across the Atlantic from up to 16 to 6.5 hours (Sampson 1984: 139). Table 3.5 indicates how jet transportation acted as a substitute for ocean-liner transportation across the Atlantic. Consequently, from 1961–1969 the demand for air transportation tripled, while demand for ocean-liner transportation declined by 46.6 per cent. From 1969–1985 air transportation across the North Atlantic rose by 170.7 per cent and effectively put an end to the era of transatlantic luxury liner travel (Tideman 1987). Along with transatlantic air transportation came the phenomenon of mass travel by air charter which generated mass tourism demand to 'new' destinations, like North Africa, as early as 1963 (Theuns 1985).

Fourth revolution

The re-emergence of rail technology in Western Europe and Japan is leading to a 'transportation revolution as radical as any since the introduction of civilian jets in the 1950s: A Great New Railway Age'. Since the

Table 3.5 US tourism in Europe 1950–1985

	Number of passengers (000s)		Transportation fares in US$		Trip duration in days	
	Air	Sea	Air	Sea	Air	Sea
1950	100	200	647	593	50	71
1954	200	220	640	620	43	68
1961	620	206	630	700	36	65
1969	2,253	110	407	675	28	59
1985	6,100	–	300	–	20	–

Source: Dr M.C. Tideman (1987) '25 Jaar Hotellerie in Nederland', farewell lecture presented at the Hotelschool, the Hague (June)

introduction of the TGV (*train à grande vitesse* or 'high speed train') in France in 1981, a growing railroad network offers passengers streamlined, swift, and comfortable inter-city transportation at more economical fares than the airlines.

A recent study revealed that,

> the expected diversion of potential air traffic to surface transport will be noticeable when the total train trip time is similar to the total air trip time. For instance, for a given sector, if the total air trip time is equivalent to the total train trip time . . . then the expected diversion of potential air traffic to surface transport facilities could be of the order of 50 percent.[6]
>
> (Airbus Industries 1991)

The same study indicates that high-speed rail will be successfully applied as an alternative to air transportation in the North European 'area bounded by Paris, London, Amsterdam, the Ruhr and Frankfurt'. The availability of fast, reliable, and economical surface transportation is expected to help propel the 'harmonisation' of trade in the European Community and 'bind peripheral countries like Greece and Portugal closer to the rest of Europe' (Sullivan 1989: 46).

The implications of high-speed rail travel are mixed. On the one hand, it should revive inner-city hotels, especially those located near railway stations that are part of the high-speed rail network. However, there is a chance that high-speed rail travel may make resort destinations less attractive, because the system facilitates access and may encourage 'over-crowding'. For example, in 1964 the resort town of Atami in Japan was connected with Tokyo by a high-speed rail link reducing travel time from three hours to 50 minutes.

> Developers built hotels and restaurants; geishas flocked to the area. But tourism slacked off five years after the shinkansen's (bullet train) arrival. Perhaps the romance of going away for the weekend was lost in a place you could reach in 50 minutes.
>
> (Mabry 1989: 48)

As higher standards of luxury are introduced by the high-speed railways, hotel corporations may lose some meeting and conference business to the railways. For instance, the German Federation Railways high-speed Inter-City Express (ICE) offers passengers conference rooms on board, as well as a restaurant and bistro, while *en route* for example from Hamburg to Basel (Transport 1991: 9).

Telecommunications

Innovations in telecommunications are laying the foundation for an international information highway system that will eventually wire the world into a more or less integrated communications network. Developments in telecommunications are vital to the service sector (Price and Blair 1989: 114) because they have the potential to change the way people work, learn, shop and the way they are entertained and cared for in terms of social, legal, medical and travel services.

Will tele-conferencing capabilities improve to an extent where tele-communications will offer a substitute product for business travel? Or will tele-conferencing serve as a supplementary product to face-to-face meetings because of the ongoing need for human interaction in an increasingly complex and global society? At present no specific patterns have emerged to answer these questions. In general, technological advances have been affirmatively beneficial to the development of leisure activities in society, especially with respect to home entertainment. Broadcasting technology has contributed to tourism by encouraging greater awareness of place. Czinkota *et al.* (1989: 632) view international (tele)communications as the great 'equalizer' of the future, because it involves the transmission of news and information about lifestyles, products and ideas.

Evidence of rapid technological change is pervasive. It has changed the nature of competition in all industries, and the trend towards the concentration of demand through the use of information has become increasingly evident. For example, the introduction of information systems, in particular the global distribution systems (GDS), allows airlines to dominate the distribution system almost completely. The silent revolution caused by GDS is changing the international tourism infrastructure (Mowlana and Smith 1990: 315) and extending information flows well beyond the traditional travel and tourism boundaries.

Due to information technologies, work is becoming increasingly detached from place and operations from their central headquarters. Telecommunications networks, spanning the globe with bursts of data speeding thousands of kilometres, mean the breakup of old geographic habits and locations. Bell (1988) observes 'a change of extraordinary historical and sociological importance – the change in the nature of markets from "places" to "networks"'.

The new information and decision technologies have revolutionized society and tourism. The latter has become a complex global process based, in part, on decision technologies. The new technologies link the tourism infrastructure with the telecommunications sector and transnational banking, in particular airline reservation systems and non-bank credit cards (Mowlana and Smith 1990: 317).

However, while the market is becoming increasingly fragmented in terms of customers' tastes and preferences, Lickorish (1987) refers to a 'mini-mass market' which is simultaneously becoming more concentrated. The increasing vertical economic concentration in the airline industry through the introduction of GDS has proved an almost irresistible invitation for hotel affiliation because of the patronage these systems can generate through channel of distribution intermediaries like travel agents. At present, the majority of hotel corporations lack the technology and/or the necessary knowledge to participate in state-of-the-art reservation, sales, and marketing systems required to meet the service expectations of travellers, or their travel agents, using conventional technology. In a world that consists of complex relationships with a variety of organizations, hotel corporations require alliances with various types of markets and firms to help them achieve their long-term objectives. Recent examples of the convergence of airline GDS with hotel reservation systems include: (a) Speed Travel Destination Management Company's Hotel Reservation Systems launched in March 1990, and (b) the expansion of Steigenberger Reservation Service (SRS) to a marketing consortium of 1,000 to 2,000 hotels of all categories by the mid-1990s. SRS's new Trust II reservation system connects member hotels, largely independent, as opposed to chain-affiliated hotels, with SRS reservation offices in 30 countries, airline reservation systems, and large travel offices. Through its compatibility with Sabre, PARS, Apollo, Amadeus, and Galileo, Trust II can manage the flow of as many as 2,280 transactions per minute and stores 56,000 International Association of Travel Agents (IATA) addresses (Smith 1991: 185–187).

AUTOMATION

The trend towards higher levels of automation will increase as mechanical and information technologies are combined and computer and micro-processors become smaller, more powerful and less expensive (Makridakis 1990: 269).

The elimination of many manual factory jobs may take place in the 1990s due to the introduction of robotics in the workplace.[7] Office and service jobs, on the other hand, will increase – but only for those who are prepared to increase their technical efficiency. Automation in the form of robots, supercopiers, and information networks are anticipated to replace, during the 1990s, many of the low-skilled and semi-skilled jobs prevalent in the economy of the 1980s. As automation increases more free time should be available to the average worker, accelerating the trend towards more leisure activities such as sports, entertainment and vacation travel (Makridakis 1990).

Potentially negative aspects include the replacement of skilled and semi-skilled workers in the labour force. The application of technology instead of labour would imply the loss of income for certain groups in society and contribute to the growing difference between high- and low-income earners. Observable in most advanced industrialized societies, this trend suggests a growing differentiation between hotel products geared to the high and low ends of the market spectrum.

GLOBALIZATION OF THE TRAVEL MARKET

The swift rise of Japan to second place in terms of gross national product among industrial powers, the advent of the unified European market and 'free-trade' between the USA and Canada (and potentially Mexico), has resulted in what Ohmae (1986) refers to as the 'Triad' comprised of three main trading blocs: Europe, Japan and North America. The emergence of the 'Triad' has led to increasing tensions and may result in serious obstacles in particular protectionist trade barriers. Since international trade and tourism are intertwined and the growth of international tourism depends primarily on the free movement of people, there is a need to reduce barriers to international travel, including restrictions on passports, visas, currency controls and travel allowance restrictions. Edgell (1990: 55) notes that more than 100 countries have some form of travel allowance restrictions, which can only be removed through multilateral negotiations between the governments of nation-states. Since its inception in 1947, the General Agreement on Tariffs and Trade (GATT) has engaged in seven rounds of negotiation. The GATT concluded its Uruguay Round of Negotiations in December with the controversial question of the desirability of including trade in services within the scope of the Agreement or in a separate agreement to be known as (GATS) the General Agreement on Trade in Services (Cobbs 1991: 213).

The evaporation of trade barriers in Europe in 1993 will boost the European Community's GNP considerably, lower prices, and create jobs. The Cecchini study of the European Community (EC) (Government of Canada 1989b: 5) was probably too optimistic in forecasting an increase in GNP of the EC by 5 per cent, a decline of prices by 5 per cent, and an increase in employment of 2 million new jobs. But GNP is anticipated to advance in the 1990s at a faster rate than the 2.8 per cent the EC averaged between 1985 and 1988. This could increase travel expenditures to about 4 per cent or even more per year. Total travel expenditures are expected to increase to 5 or 6 per cent per year. The EC long-haul market is expected to be the fastest growth segment in the next decade, increasing shares from 10 per cent in 1989 to 20 per cent by 2000 (Government of Canada 1989c). However, besides Canada and the US, there will be many destinations aggressively competing for this business.[8]

With the labour force in industrialized countries ageing and a growing number of young, unemployed people in developing countries, there is likely to be an upsurge in migration. Transnational corporate investments in developing countries and labour from developing countries imported by, for example, some European countries, Canada and the USA have hardly made a dent. The reason for this may be that present permanent emigration rates are small compared with the rates of inter-continental migration from Europe in the eighteenth and nineteenth centuries.

A World Bank forecast indicates that if 700,000 immigrants a year were admitted to the major host countries from low-income countries, less than 2 per cent of the projected growth in population in these countries between 1982 and 2000 would have emigrated. But the evolving new labour market is likely to result in a global workforce by the end of the 1990s. As personnel policies and practices become more standardized due to the dual forces of companies responding to global labour markets and governments negotiating trade agreements (Johnston 1991: 121), employers will increasingly reach across borders to find the skills they need.

The increasing homogenization of customer needs and lifestyles, the nature of the international hotel industry's macro-environment, which demands a worldwide presence, and the development of computerized reservation networks has led to a global market.

> Telecommunications, television and international travel have laid the groundwork for a 'global lifestyle', especially in the metropolitan cities of industrialised countries. The film and television media deliver the same images throughout the global village. [Air] travel opens the avenues of exchange which has resulted in a 'globalized' market comprised of groups of consumers in large metropolitan areas, like New York, Stockholm, and Milan who may show more similarities than consumers in Manhattan and the Bronx in New York itself.
>
> (Naisbitt and Aburdene 1990: 118–120)

The trend towards globalization in the services sector follows the precedent set by manufacturers who produce their standardized products and sell them under a brand-name on a worldwide basis to reap economies of scale. The Japanese corporations have been particularly successful in exploiting global markets by being very customer-oriented, as Levitt (1983a) observes.

The major international hotel corporations pursue global markets with standardized branded products. Where international travel is extensive, for example in Europe, a global brand can have a substantial advantage in that the brand impacts upon country visitors through advertising and distribution outlets (Aaker 1991: 265). They may be aware of the brand because of the marketing and distribution activities that the international hotel corporations carry out in the visitors' home country as part of the value chain activities that are usually tied to the travel generating markets. Due to the service nature of the hotel product, the 'production' and service delivery have to take place in the traveller's destination.

Day (1990: 91) has observed that 'when markets are globalizing then regional distinctions become important'. In this regard, it should be observed that there are pitfalls and traps in an approach that overlooks cultural and regional differences but there is danger as well in assuming too much similarity.[9] Specifically, the more homogeneous consumers' lifestyles become, the more steadfastly they are likely to cling to deeper values and treasure the traditions that spring from within (Naisbitt and Aburdene 1990: 120).

Furthermore, the needs and preferences of customers around the globe will simultaneously become more universal and more specialized. Clear-cut differences are likely to remain from country to country, but international corporations shall satisfy them with adjustments to standardized products and services. The homogeneity and specialization paradox will allow greater diversity, distinctiveness, and uniqueness in customer preferences (Hickman and Silva 1987: 102). Akin to this last observation, it should be noted that globalization is not 'an all or nothing proposition as far as branding is concerned, [but that it] can involve some elements of the brands – the name, the symbol, the slogan, the perceived quality, or the associations – it need not involve all of them' (Aaker 1991: 268).

For example, the golfing 'boom' represents a global market opportunity for hotel corporations that is constrained by the problem of building enough golf courses to accommodate players. While the world's golfing population has doubled, the number of golf courses has increased by only 16 per cent.[10]

The characteristics of the lodging markets of North America and world-wide hotels are fairly similar (see Table 3.6). Some 36.6 per cent of hotel reservations are made directly by the client. Travel agents and tour operators account for 27.8 per cent and reservation systems for 24.9 per cent of indirect hotel reservations. The highest percentage of direct reservations is made in Europe, the lowest percentage in this category may be found in Latin America and the Caribbean, where the contribution to advance hotel reservations is most pronounced at 36.6 per cent, the highest of all world regions.

THE QUEST FOR QUALITY

Quality is acquiring a new meaning both in the manufacturing and service sectors. The push for quality has been driven by the development and introduction of the transistor, satellites, jet aircraft in the 1950s, and the

Table 3.6 Sources of demand for hotel accommodation (percentages)

Purpose of Visit	Worldwide	Africa and Middle East	Asia and Pacific	North America	Western Europe	Latin America
Business	55.2	57.9	47.8	58.1	57.7	48.5
Leisure	34.4	23.8	43.2	33.6	31.6	45.9
Undefined	10.4	18.3	9.0	8.3	11.0	5.6

Source: Horwath and Horwath (1987) *Worldwide Hotel Industry*

emergence of Japan as an economic 'superpower'. These technological innovations caused geographic distance to become less relevant and the world to become a global marketplace through better and faster communication systems. In turn, better communication systems have resulted in the rapid diffusion of innovations, wherever they may have been invented in the world.

New technology is forcing a revolution in quality innovation and customer service improvement, especially within TNCs which compete with one another and domestic companies on the basis of quality, low cost, and speedy delivery of the product. For example, in the photographic trade, it used to take several days to have one's film developed and printed. Today this same process can take less than one hour. Similar quality improvements have been made in other fields. The instigator or driving force behind the quality revolution has been Japan, where industrialists applied the techniques of quality assurance under the guidance of two Americans, W. Edwards Deming and J.M. Juran, who could not find an audience at home in the post-war era (Dobyns and Crawford-Mason 1991: 80).

Japan's clear vision to produce low-cost, quality products increased the global competition among European, American and Japanese TNCs. It also generated Japanese products, such as cars and electronic household goods, that were perceived by many Americans and Europeans to be of superior quality. 'In the 1980s companies in Europe [and in America] began to realise that their only way of surviving in business was to pay much greater attention to quality. In many markets, quality has already become the competitive edge' (Anon. 1992a: 5).

The quality revolution has placed more power in the hands of customers, who have a greater choice of products to select from than ever before. As a consequence, continuous quality improvement has become a matter of survival for all companies.

Globalization increases the complexity of doing business in that hotel companies have to be able to cater to the tastes of foreign guests and manage employees in foreign (host) countries and from diverse cultural backgrounds in the home country. At a strategic level the global market requires hotel companies to redefine their market and the ways of defining and accomplishing work (Moutinho 1989: 139).[11]

FRAGMENTATION OF THE TRAVEL MARKET

Slowing population growth rates in developed nations due to a declining fertility rate, the deferred rate of marriage and rising divorce rates have led to a decline in the industrialized nations' share of total world population. Therefore population growth may become a national priority given the fact that in Western European countries the population is shrinking (Czinkota *et al.* 1989: 631).[12]

The once-accepted authority and influence of family, religion and political institutions are being replaced by emancipation, a concern for ecology and a growing interest in well-being, health and lifelong learning. The international hotel industry will be the potential beneficiary of these trends in increasingly diverse lifestyles if it manages to adapt to 'demographic and social shifts (that) are occurring which will dramatically transform the level and nature of tourism' (Ritchie 1991: 152).

For the international hotel industry, some of the more significant demographic changes have included the ageing of the population in the industrialized countries, the reduction in the household size, and a decline in the leisure time of people who possess the bulk of discretionary income.

(a) Young professionals constitute a major travel market in developed countries where existing attitudes have made the two-income household accepted practice. Typically, in the 25–44 age group, this segment tends to be better educated and more widely travelled than previous generations, and they place a high priority on travel as a means of broadening personal experience. This category of traveller is affluent, status conscious and brand loyal, though time constraints will tend to shorten trip duration and increase trip frequencies.

(b) The growing older segment of the population includes a significant segment with retirement savings and relatively high disposable incomes for leisure travel. This segment is also healthier and more mobile than previous generations and better educated. According to the US Bureau of Labor Statistics, for example, the median income for US households headed by individuals aged 55–64 is about 8 per cent above the average national level of discretionary income. Viant (1993) provides a detailed appraisal of this 'elderly' travel market from a European perspective. With both time and income available, older consumers are more inclined to travel than ever before, and also tend to stay in the better class of accommodation when they do so.

(c) The family vacation remains a vital element in leisure travel, and the peak summer months, despite attempts by many destinations to spread the peak, remain of central importance. Vacations tend to be more activity oriented, however, and as major markets such as the USA amend their school years towards longer school years, the nature of this market may also change (Go and Welch 1991: 11).

Ageing population

As a result of the increase in life expectancy, a larger share of travellers will consist of older people who are healthy enough, have a secure income, and fewer family responsibilities. Though population growth in Europe is close to zero and the propensity for travel already high, the demand for travel and, therefore, for hotel services can be anticipated to increase as a function of an ageing population. For example, in Europe, 20.1 per cent of the population was over 65 in 1980; by the year 2025 that figure will have risen to 29.2 per cent. Taking into consideration those aged between 55 and 65, the number of Europeans who will be part of the 'mature market' by 2000 will be about 100 million.

The average life expectancy in Europe in 1980 was 72.2 versus 57.3 for the rest of the world. By the year 2000 the average world life expectancy is anticipated to have risen to 65.3 and in Europe to 75.4 (ILO 1989: 73). The ageing population, especially in Europe and North America, forms a large and affluent potential travel and leisure market. A larger share of tourists will consist of older people. So far, attention in industrialized nations has focused largely on the pressures the growing group of elderly will place on pensions and health care. But in fact the changes to come will range from where seniors will live, where they will eat, and what foods they will consume: a market with enormous opportunity for the lodging industry. Developers are beginning to investigate this relatively new but rapidly expanding market segment, i.e., the growing need for senior citizen housing. Increasing demands from the ageing population provide opportunities for private retirement centres, including the new lifecare centre concept, which has excellent growth potential well into the twenty-first century.

Household size reduction

The trend away from marriage and low population growth implies that Western society will be increasingly influenced, and in certain countries perhaps dominated, by households consisting of singles or couples. Smaller households with fewer children will mean changing spending patterns, more dollars to spend on themselves, and potentially greater mobility to devote to travel and leisure activities. Hotel corporations shall have to be responsive to, for example, the consumers' concerns for their physical fitness and state of mind.

Discretionary income in relation to time

Conventional wisdom held that the long working hours of the nineteenth century would decline due to the automation of the workplace and the influence of unions, and that as a consequence discretionary or leisure time would increase for the average worker.

Instead, the reverse seems to be happening. In America, for example, one survey shows that:

> From 1973 through 1985, the number of leisure hours available to most Americans dropped from 26.2 hours to 17.7 hours a week, a loss of 8.5

hours every week, or one hour and 12 minutes a day ... Taken together, the number of hours the average American spends at work each week has increased from 40.6 in 1973 to a current 48.8, a rise of 8.2 hours a week or one hour and 10 minutes a day. One key reason for the dramatic shifts in working hours and leisure time can be found in the increasing number of women who are working, now up to an estimated 56 percent of all adult women. That means that both spouses are spending more time at work and have less time left for leisure. Another is that the country has shifted radically away from blue-collar production to white-collar service jobs. Blue-collar hours have remained steady or declined, while white-collar hours of work have risen.

(Harris 1987: 17–19)

Other studies (see Tables 3.7 and 3.8) indicate typical leisure hours per week and number of vacation days per year in a range of western countries.

Affluent US consumers with plenty of discretionary income must choose from a great number of goods and services and lack the time to use them.

Table 3.7 Leisure hours (average person per week)

Country	Hours
The Netherlands	31
Denmark	28
Canada	27
United Kingdom	25
Finland/United States	24
Austria/Japan/Switzerland	23
Norway	22

Source: Survey Research Centre, University of Maryland

Table 3.8 Average number of vacation days

Country	Vacation days
West Germany	30
Italy	25
Great Britain	24
France	21
Spain	21
United States	12

Source: Federation of German Employees Association

A similar pattern in discretionary income and time appears to be shaping in Western Europe, if one can extrapolate the findings of a study done by researchers in the Netherlands to other countries in the European Community. This study goes so far as to postulate that the way in which consumers allocate their discretionary time and money can be used to segment the market. Accordingly, Lakatos and Van Kralingen (1985) suggest a new order of segmentation based on time and money, as diagrammed in Figure 3.1. The central theme in their new segmentation thinking is the availability of discretionary time in relation to discretionary money. On this basis they typify four market segments:

(a) Segment A: Consumers with 'much time' and 'insufficient amounts of money'.
(b) Segment B: Consumers with 'much time' and 'lots of money'.
(c) Segment C: Consumers with 'insufficient amounts of time' and 'money'.
(d) Segment D: Consumers with 'insufficient amounts of time' and 'lots of money'.

Though this segmentation approach could no doubt be refined, it does result in insights into the fragmentation of the marketplace in an industrialized economy and offers a rough division of the four proposed segments. For example, in segment 'A', one could use university students as an example of a category with plenty of time, but often insufficient discretionary money. In segment 'B', wealthy, older consumers come to mind. Segment 'C' would be dominated by the 'youth' and the 'unemployed'. Finally, in segment 'D' one could identify fast-track professionals, who have high incomes but limited amounts of leisure time.

Consumers in segment 'D' ('insufficient amounts of time' and 'lots of discretionary income') represent the market segment that is of most

	Budget conscious	Luxury prone
Discretionary time	**A** Lack of money Much time	**B** Much time Lots of money
Time constrained	**C** Lack of money Lack of time	**D** Lack of time Lots of money

Figure 3.1 A matter of time and money

Source: Adapted from P.A.M. Lakatos and R.M. Van Kralingen, *Naar 1990 Een Kwestie van Tijd en Geld*, Amsterdam: Elsevier, 1985

interest to the travel and hotel industries. However, the consumers in this segment are under increasing pressure and lack of time, at least if one compares this segment to society as a whole. For example, research findings in America showed that the population in general 'seems to feel worn out' by the demands of work, family and personal achievement (*The New York Times* 1988).

The growing demands on the personal time of individual consumers requires greater sensitivity on the part of producers to develop 'time-saving' services that coincide with the individual demands of travellers, based on their economic and socio-cultural background. In general, the international hotel industry has been slow to catch up with this important trend.

Rising environmental concerns

Greater interest in nature and the protection of the environment are part of shifting value structures and lifestyles in society. A recent study conducted by the Stanford Research Institute described the reassessment and redefinition of the meaning of life, its goals and quality as the greatest intellectual revolution since the Renaissance.[13]

For a growing number of consumers in the industrialized world, quality of life issues have become as important as standard of living issues, because the former are perceived to affect their well-being. The present intellectual revolution in society affects the hotel resort market in particular. On the one hand, rising urbanization of the world populations will increase the demand for scenic beauty and nature. On the other hand, millions of consumers will put increasing pressure on policy-makers and business leaders to preserve the environment. For example, Aderhold (1992) reports on the growing sensitivity to environmental matters among Germans on vacation. Specifically, he indicates that the percentage of German holiday-makers who noticed problems relating to the environment during their holidays has doubled between 1985 and 1988.

Adverse environmental effects can have particularly negative consequences for resort areas and their hotel trade. One study, for example, describes how the eutrophication of the Adriatic Sea and the subsequent negative publicity led to general tourist dissatisfaction. The crisis affected the hotel operators 'with the highest standards, who had made the most effort to attract foreign tourists' to a greater extent (with a decline estimated at between 50 per cent and 60 per cent) than the boarding houses with loyal clients (Becheri 1991: 229).

The present concern for sustainable development and environmental preservation poses questions for tourism developers and hotel and resort managers about the values which are afforded the tourism environment. During the European Year of Tourism in 1990, a conference was held in

Scheveningen, the Netherlands, which focused on the future of Europe's old resorts. The conference addressed many vital issues, such as:

(a) How long a life is there for the Costas of Spain and new resort regions like Languedoc-Roussillon in France, the Portuguese Algarve, the coastal developments on the Adriatic and Mediterranean?
(b) Will the deteriorating quality of sea water, air pollution, and growing change affect future demand and satisfaction?
(c) Can international programmes by the European Community, the United Nations, Blue Flag and other schemes help preserve the environment?
(d) By which mechanisms and means – financial, organizational, etc. – can the commercial sector, tourist industries and government interests link up, so as to secure a viable future for our resorts?

The issues raised at Europe's resort Conference[14] signal that at least the Conference organizers corroborate the priorities and guidelines identified at the First International Assembly of Tourism Experts in Washington, DC in 1990, the 'recognition that there are finite limitations to tourism development, in terms of both physical and social carrying capacity of destinations' (Ritchie 1991: 151).

The 'environment' has become a megaforce that will influence the type of products the market is likely to want in the future. The growing number of consumers who care about the environment implies that the international hotel industry has to be concerned about environmental matters. It can demonstrate a genuine concern for the environment by investigating how hotel facilities can contribute in a positive way to resort areas, either through marketing or product changes.

IMPLICATIONS OF SHIFTING DEMAND

Travelling abroad for pleasure purposes by large numbers of people is a relatively modern occurrence, dating from the early nineteenth century. Increased awareness of the outer world in particular led to an increased readiness among the more educated groups in society to migrate temporarily or even on a permanent basis (Cohen 1972: 197).

Travel demand is a function of the propensity of the individual to travel and the reciprocal of the resistance of the link between origin and destination, which may be expressed as:

Demand = f (Propensity/resistance)

Propensity is a person's predisposition to travel based on such factors as psychographic profile, travel motivation and socio-economic status (McIntosh and Goeldner 1990: 256–258).

Resistance relates to the relative attractiveness of various destinations and is inversely related to demand. The resistance factor is a function of several factors including economic distance, involving time and cost to reach a destination, the cost of tourist services at the destination, the quality of service at the destination, seasonality, and the effectiveness of advertising and promotion.

At present, there are a number of significant travel demand shifts taking place that will affect the hotel industry, including:

(a) A potential, substantial discontinuity (Crouch and Shaw 1990: 18) of international travel flows due to the dramatic changes taking place in Central and Eastern Europe and the Asia–Pacific Rim region. Increasing numbers of visitors from new markets will pose a challenge for destinations. For example, Asian visitors tend to be uncomfortable in a completely foreign setting. This recognition has implications for food service, language ability of service staff and so on.
(b) The populations of the industrial countries where the vast majority of international travellers are ageing and families are getting smaller on average. The contemporary urban household often consists of two income earners, including professional individuals whose jobs generally involve longer hours in a high pressure environment (Lakatos and Van Kralingen 1985; Gibbs 1989).
(c) Demanding customers. Greater affluence, higher levels of education and more sophistication place new demands on traditional travel activities including those involving attractions, events, shopping and dining. Constant renovation of facilities and upgrading of service to ensure quality are 'musts'. Upscale consumers are searching for new experiences, including themed tours, cruising and all-inclusive resorts.

The shifts in demand have implications for business travel, pleasure travel, personal travel, and international travel. Market segmentation in the hotel industry has generally taken place along the dimensions of main target markets such as corporate travellers, group travellers, conference groups, aircrews and leisure travellers. Each segment typically has its own specific requirements. One now identifies visitor needs and interests as fundamental to a continuing research process necessary to better understand visitor market segments and their motivations and behaviours.

Business travel

Travel for business embraces trips to attend meetings and conventions, smaller corporate gatherings, and commercial sales visits. Business travellers are more likely to stay in hotels, and corporate travel demand tends to be more stable and not as price-sensitive as non-business travel. The business travel market has the following subsegments:

(a) The independent corporate travel market: business travellers are more likely to visit larger cities. Corporate travel demand tends to be less seasonal and not as price-sensitive as pleasure travel. The largest portion of business-oriented lodging demand stems from travellers who are visiting clients. The former's choice of destination will be determined by the nature of their business.

(b) The business group travel market: travellers associated with meetings and conventions are more important in terms of the expenditures they generate in a host community than their numbers indicate. Meetings and conventions typically result in considerable sums spent on banquet and meeting rooms facilities, guest rooms, and food service. In some cases conference traffic can be scheduled to occupy a hotel during off-peak periods. The most popular destinations for conference trips vary according to factors such as budget, trip purpose, and the taste of the target audience. Organized groups staying in hotels for purposes of attending a conference, convention, or meeting require efficient group check-in and check-out services and comfortable and acoustically-sound meeting room and support facilities.

(c) Industrial travel: airline and flight cabin crews require accommodation while on stopovers at or near an airport location. This industrial market segment is usually the subject of a low room rate/high volume crew contract for specific airlines. Due to tight flight schedules, airline crews have different needs from those of the corporate traveller, such as 24-hour food and beverage operations and complete room blackout (Lewis and Chambers 1989: 242).

Pleasure travel

The pleasure travel market is the largest segment comprised of persons taking both the typical one- or two-week vacations and shorter weekend trips. The predominant form of transportation pleasure travellers use is the family car; air transportation ranks a distant second. Pleasure travellers are more likely than other travellers to share rooms or avoid hotels, e.g., by staying with friends and relatives. The pleasure market is price sensitive and therefore easily affected by economic conditions. Furthermore, the pleasure travel industry faces competition from non-travel entertainment for both consumers' leisure time and discretionary income. In addition, factors such as fuel shortages, transportation workers' strikes, and poor weather may have direct effects on the discretionary travel decision. The pleasure travel market has several subsegments such as the package tour, free independent travellers (FIT), the resort segment, the senior segment, the singles segment, the teenage segment, the eco-tourism and adventure tour segment (Rosenfeld 1986). Due to earlier observed demographic and lifestyle changes there is a premium on segmentation to lure discretionary travellers to specific tourism products.

D'Amore (1985) suggests a purposeful product/market blending as depicted in Figure 3.2 including vacation markets, business travel, mini-vacations, weekend outings, meetings and conventions, and greater local and regional use to achieve greater utilization of facilities and resources.[15]

Market segmentation

The concept of market segmentation – that is, the process of breaking down the heterogeneous tourism market into relatively homogeneous segments – has proved to be an effective marketing method in an increasingly competitive environment, and is used by both profit-oriented and non-profit organizations (Smith and Beik 1982).

Four commonly used bases for segmenting consumer markets are geographic segmentation, demographic segmentation, behaviour-related segmentation, and psychographic segmentation. These segmentation bases can make a significant contribution to the effective execution of marketing strategies provided they are significantly relevant to differences in buying behaviour (Kotler 1980b: 297; Lewis and Chambers 1989: 208).

Visitor markets have been segmented based on seasonal benefits (Calantone and Johas 1984), distance travelled (Etzel and Woodside 1982), vacation preferences and magazine readership (Crask 1981), decision-making processes (Raaij and Francken 1984), age (Jobes 1984), and motivation (Dann 1981; Snepenger 1987; Pearce and Caltabiano

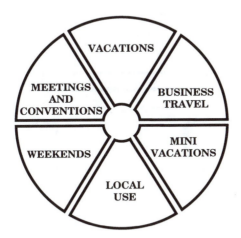

Figure 3.2 Product/market blending

Source: L.J. D'Amore, 'A Third Generation of Tourism Thinking Towards a Creative Conspiracy', *Business Quarterly*, summer, 1985. Reprinted by permission of *Business Quarterly*, published by the Western Business School, The University of Western Ontario, Canada

1983). Specifically, the hotel market is often segmented according to three perspectives:

(a) Product segmentation which explores the choice of specific features in a hotel and the kinds of facilities and services most desired during the guest stay.
(b) Geographic segmentation which examines where guests originate and the destinations they travel to.
(c) Benefit segmentation which looks at travel motives and particular experiences people are searching for.

Market segmentation is basic to understanding hotel industry design, marketing and operations management. Subsegments of hotel demand may include the following factors: (a) fluctuations in demand: by day, by month; (b) single versus double room occupancy; (c) length of stay; (d) needs/preferences for meeting space, restaurants and recreational amenities; (e) price sensitivity; (f) extent of repeat patronage; (g) specific sources of room demand both from within and outside the geographic market area.

A typical profile for different hotel market segments suggesting travel motives are depicted in Figure 3.3. A wide range of demand characteristics exist between the main segments and sometimes variations occur within a given segment. An example of market segmentation in the hotel industry is provided in Table 3.9.

A study conducted for Marriott Hotels & Resorts (1986) revealed that people in the USA are increasingly taking short pleasure trips: 73 per cent of pleasure trips during 1986 were of one to three days; 59 per cent of those

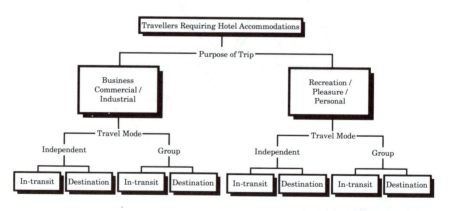

Figure 3.3 The hotel market from a benefit segmentation perspective

Source: Laventhol and Horwath/The Urban Land Institute, Washington, DC *Hotel/Motel Development*, 1984, p. 19

trips were taken on weekends; 28 per cent said they are taking more weekend trips than two or three years ago.

Personal needs, many lifestyles-driven, influence preferences for shorter trips: 79 per cent of Americans agree travelling helps them get away from everyday routines; 77 per cent agree one of the nice things about going away is seeing new sights. Men rated relaxation as the second most

Table 3.9 Market segmentation in the hotel industry

Main target market characteristics	*Specific requirements*
Corporate travellers	
Travelling/working away from the normal place of work, invariably travel business services, such as expenses, are reimbursed, at least in part.	– Guaranteed reservations; – Rapid check in/check out; – International direct dial phones, facsimile transmission, secretarial and translation services, study-style bedrooms.
Group travellers	
Organized groups of leisure travellers or holiday-makers in transit or based in a particular location as part of a single or multi-destination trip.	– Group check in and check out; – Leisure facilities; – Assembly areas; – Courier points.
Conference groups	
Organized groups staying in hotels for the purposes of attending a conference, convention, meeting.	– Group check in and check out; – Meeting rooms and support seminar or course facilities, whether staged in the hotel or not.
Leisure travellers	
People travelling for non-work purposes and paying for their own accommodation; in some cases these are 'off-duty' corporate travellers sometimes accompanied by a spouse.	– Leisure facilities; – Value for money; – Food and beverage facilities; – Local information and booking services; – Entertainment.
Aircrews	
Airline and flight cabin crews requiring accommodation while on stopover at or near an airport location; usually the subject of a low price/high volume crew contract for specific airlines.	– 24-hour operations; – Leisure facilities; – Room blackout.

Source: Coopers and Lybrand Associates, and Jonathon Rounce (1987) 'International Hotel Product Branding: Segmenting the Marketplace', *Travel and Tourism Analyst*, February

frequently cited reason for taking weekend pleasure trips behind getting away; women rated relaxation fourth behind getting away, visiting family and having fun.

Americans are not impulsive regarding travel: 67 per cent of Americans who travel on weekends plan their weekend pleasure trips at least two to three weeks in advance; 86 per cent who take long trips (of four days or more) plan them at least two to three weeks in advance; 23 per cent of 55–64 year olds plan their weekend pleasure trips no more than a few days in advance, making them the most impulsive group. The majority of Americans select lodging as the most preferred accommodation for weekend trips: 62 per cent of Americans select hotels, motels or resorts as the type of accommodation they most prefer for weekend trips; 12 per cent choose to stay with family or friends; the remainder select campgrounds, cruise ships and small inns. Four out of ten Americans are price/value shoppers when planning weekend pleasure trips: Americans would spend over $300 on average for weekend pleasure trips; Southerners would spend the most for these trips ($332) while those in the North Central portion of the USA would spend the least ($287); Americans aged 18–24 would spend the most for weekend pleasure trips ($387) and those age 65 and over would spend the least ($256).

At the same time, low gasoline prices accelerated this trend by en-couraging more weekend driving trips. Marriott Corporation tapped this market segment with tremendous pent-up demand and opportunity for growth – the weekend traveller, representing an estimated $6 billion market in revenues. The company's approach diverged from segmentation practices in the lodging industry in that its focus is on lifestyle rather than accommodation style to lure what appears to be an expansive 'new' market. The Marriott survey found that five key factors were considered by travellers in making a decision on accommodations: (a) luxury/entertainment features, such as health clubs and fine restaurants; (b) location and convenience; (c) basics, such as a clean safe room; (d) budget and cost, and; (e) family orientation. Given the relative importance of each of these factors to the consumer decision-making process, four segments of Americans were ident-ified having differing attitudes in their selection of overnight accommo-dations for weekend pleasure travel: the 'All Amenities Fun Traveller', the 'All Amenities Visiting Traveller', the 'Makes No Difference Traveller', and the 'Budget Traveller', as described in Table 3.10.

Challenges and choices

In a global marketing environment, existing and potential markets present the international hotel industry with important challenges. The long-term success of the international hotel industry resides in its executives' capacity and willingness to:

Table 3.10 Weekend pleasure travel segments and their attitudes to overnight accommodations selection

(a) *The 'All Amenities Fun Traveller'*
This group seeks luxury and full amenities and wants night life and cultural activities nearby. Price and family orientation are unimportant to this group, which comprises 19 per cent of the population.

(b) *The 'All Amenities Visiting Traveller'*
Luxury is also important to this group, made up of 26 per cent of the population, as are activities, but location of accommodation has to be convenient and near friends or family.

(c) *The 'Makes No Difference Traveller'*
This group, consisting of 12 per cent of the population, is unconcerned with any of the factors such as price, activities, or amenities, when making their destination decision.

(d) *The 'Budget Traveller'*
This is the largest of the four groups, consisting of 42 per cent of the population. A clean, safe room at a reasonable price is more important to this group than are amenities or location.

Source: Marriott Hotels and Resorts 1986

(a) adapt the existing hotel product to changes in the demands of the global and local markets, in particular as far as value for money is concerned relative to substitutes-in-use;
(b) align to the greatest extent possible the existing and future hotel product with the integrated telecommunications and transportation networks;
(c) enhance product and service process quality while lowering costs, using leading global corporations as bench-marks;
(d) assess new niche and speciality market opportunities, which have themselves become global markets (for example, the golf market), as opposed to monitoring and serving the mass market;
(e) build the organizational capability to respond quicker and more effectively throughout the distribution chain.

In order to meet these challenges, international hotel corporations will have to make strategic choices. Making the 'right' strategic choices in the present turbulent marketing environment may be likened to 'mission impossible' in that the rate of change and the complexity of commercial transactions can easily turn today's great business opportunity into tomorrow's threat.

Day (1990: 6) identified four areas in which corporations have to make strategic choices in order to set their direction:

(a) Arena: the markets to serve and customer segments to target.
(b) Advantage: the positioning theme that differentiates the business from competitors.
(c) Access: the communication and distribution channels used to reach the market;
(d) Activities: the appropriate scale and scope of activities to be performed.

The selection of target segments in the international hotel industry seems clear, because business travellers to most hoteliers represent the bulk and most profitable part of the market. However, since most large urban hotels cater to the business market, this logic might be misguided. Currently, hotel corporations serve the broad travel market with different products or limit their coverage to a single segment.

The building of competitive advantage 'is a positioning theme that sets a business apart from its rivals in ways that are meaningful to the target customers' (Day 1990: 9). The most successful positioning themes are based on enhanced quality, lower cost, and greater responsiveness to customers. Gaining access to a dispersed travel market is critical in the hotel industry and so therefore is the choice of the distribution channel, especially because information technologies are spawning new distribution linkages with customers. In order to add optimal value to products and processes, hotel corporations shall have to make choices regarding what activities to engage in. Rather than offering restaurant service(s) as a given, for example, the hotel executive will have to determine if the restaurant department is likely to make a positive contribution to the competitive advantage of the company.

CONCLUSION

Shifting markets and world-class competition require hotel businesses to change. On the demand side, the main variables that are most relevant to the survival and growth of international hotel corporations are: (a) the fragmentation of the mass market, combined with the increasing inter-nationalization of the business travel market, and pleasure travel market has resulted in a much more diverse hotel market; (b) the slow growth of demand in industrialized countries has caused expansion opportunities in the 'home' markets of hotel corporations to weaken and has had a 'push' effect on their foreign expansion; (c) the emerging concentration of demand through global distribution systems (GDS) will most likely make it a central force in shaping the access channels.

The present heterogeneous market is only unified by a single factor: customers who demand quality and value for their money. It could be argued that it is no longer possible for any hotel company to understand the entire travel market, leading to the end of mass marketing and the placing of increasing importance on market segmentation. The emergence of the notion that the market consists of a 'chain of customers' both within and outside the firm, and the growing importance of direct involvement with the individual buyer, implies that relationship marketing is moving to the forefront of strategic thinking.

Therefore, gaining and sustaining a competitive advantage is very likely to be increasingly a function of how well a hotel corporation can manage its relationships with competitors, suppliers and customers in the value chain.

CASE: HARRAH'S CASINOS – APPLICATION OF SOPHISTICATED DATABASE MARKETING

One of the most surprising yet logical places for sophisticated database marketing to niche markets is the casino industry. Faced with fierce competition for the best customers, the smartest casinos have been leaders in building a database and using it for direct marketing and customer communication.

Harrah's core marketing strategy is to foster and then cater to a relatively small group of dedicated gamblers by building brand loyalty. The company uses various strategies including a proprietary database marketing system and casino hosts whose sole responsibility is to develop relationships with regular gamblers.

The key to building a database is Harrah's Gold Card. When presented at a gaming table or inserted into gambling machines, the Gold Card records how much an individual spends in the casino. To encourage use of the card, gamblers earn bonus points towards non-gambling amenities and find it easier to cash cheques in the casino. Each cardholder's gaming patterns are statistically analysed to determine the expected house win from each customer. The customer is then graded as to the type and value of complementaries that the casino can afford to offer.

Casinos want to know everything – your age, birthdate, and anniversary, how often you come to gamble, what you play, where you like to stay, how you travel to the casino, what your budget is. They even want to know about your cars, pets, and favourite sports. With this information, casinos devise specific promotions for different customer segments and individual customers within the database. The databases also tell the casinos where their customers come from and how they travel. By analysing which zip zones have the most customers, the casino can get a better fix on where advertising should be concentrated and where charter bus service can be most productive.

READING: APPLICATIONS OF DATABASE MARKETING IN THE TOURISM INDUSTRY

by Clive B. Jones, Senior Vice-President, Economics Research Associates

The conventional ways of looking at consumer behaviour – especially in tourism and leisure – are becoming outdated. No longer (if they ever were) are the purchasing habits of the leisure customer predictable by labelling a group as a segment of the market and describing it with average characteristics. More and more, marketers are turning to tailored and targeted marketing to individuals. This is now possible through new technology with sophisticated database management systems and immense amounts of historical and purchased information (lists) on individual preferences and purchase behaviour. This trend is particularly appropriate for tourism marketing, since there is a world of paradoxes in leisure behaviour. Sameness and diversity and security and risk-taking seem side by side. Some accountants sky dive; people eat at McDonald's for lunch and a four-star restaurant for dinner; take luxury BMWs to the self-service petrol pump; trade a large investment portfolio through a discount broker; visit Hawaii and never go in the ocean. Leisure lifestyles, in particular, are inconsistent, contradictory, and individual.

This multi-profile customer is difficult to motivate by traditional institutional means. The 1990s and beyond belong to the individual. Destination marketing and leisure product development must adjust to this new environment (see table).

Means turning away from	And turning towards
Mass marketing ⟶	**Direct customer communications**
– Socio-economic groups	– Customer databases
– Media placement	– Telemarketing/targeted messages
– One-way communication	– Building customer relationships

Adjusting to the new marketing environment

In the effervescent tourism environment of the 1980s, as long as you came up with a saleable product, let enough people know about it, and had an adequate distribution system, things worked out just fine. That is hardly the case now. The difficulties of the 1990s have exposed the impoverishment of yesterday's beliefs; the sheer futility and astonishing waste of conventional tourism advertising is clear to anyone with eyes to see. The news is out, and there is no going back. But that does not mean everyone is jumping on the bandwagon – far from it, in fact.

The challenge of database marketing for tourism is strategic. The economics of large scale production favours large firms with strong brand identities. The economics of customer information favours a generation of smaller, flexible firms with healthy firm-to-customer relationships. Japan Travel Bureau has recognized this and departed from a centralized organization structure to form literally hundreds of individual 'companies'. Investment in big brands with broad appeal is yesterday's solution, useful in the shallow communications environment of broadcasting. The future lies with firms who can use the new two-way channels of communication to create customer based relationships, reaching across a whole range of travel, leisure, and financial services products and resting on honest and intelligent dialogue.

Whenever database marketing has been done correctly, its belief system has been validated. Here are the major tenets:

- Past consumer behaviour is the best predictor of future behaviour.
- A purchase is simply one event in a customer's file. To figure a customer's true worth you have to calculate lifetime value.
- Customers are more important than non-customers.
- Certain customers are more important than other customers.
- Customers are likely to share certain characteristics.

An example of the changing nature of travel marketing and the need to adjust is illustrated by Cathay Pacific Airways' considerations in its decision to appoint an advertising agency for its HK$250 million (US$32.3 million) account. Because the airline is totally committed to customer satisfaction it is more interested in locating a marketing consultancy than in simply engaging an advertising agency. It requires a company which understands both database management and direct marketing. Essential components of global marketing strategies now include the management of database operations, direct marketing, and other media activities, in addition to the usual advertising campaigns.

Applications of database marketing in accommodations

In the mid-1980s, hotel chains such as Marriott, Holiday Inn, Radisson, and Hyatt jumped on the airline bandwagon with their own frequent-traveller programmes.

Marriott's 5-million-member Honored Guest Program now requires the efforts and attentions of around 200 full-time staff – ranging from systems designers to customer service personnel – to maintain it. Marriott's vice-president-database marketing Lynn Roach has no doubts the money is well spent. 'We regard our program as an asset which enables superior customer understanding.' 'We can carve out market segments of several hundred thousand at a time. It also allows us to test-market initiatives and be more responsive. Evaluated behavior before and after enrolment shows that post-enrolment business increases by 60 percent.'

While most programmes are similar in principle, they vary in design according to the marketing objectives and market position of the particular properties. 'Our members are primarily interested in additional hotel service features during their stay rather than price factors. So our program tends toward room upgrades and benefits such as late check-outs', states Sheraton. Westin's programme follows much the same theory. Their documentation states 'guests are interested in immediate tangible benefits during their hotel stays'. On the other hand, Ramada has identified that its guests primarily check into Ramada properties for price reasons. Consequently, the rewards of the programme revolve around escalating discounts.

The Days Inns organization gears itself to a wide marketing base. The system has organized a range of offerings which, in addition to business travellers, also specifically targets senior citizens, sports teams, teachers and US government or military employees. September Days, the club for seniors, offers senior-oriented features (primarily discounts on a range of other travel-related products, such as auto rental or insurance). Days Inns' School Days is targeted entirely to teachers.

The growing sophistication and responsiveness of database marketing allows chains to roll out continuously evolving programmes. If business in resort properties is down, then the immediate impact of offering double points or special discounts can quickly be assessed. In order to boost sales at city properties, a particular section of the membership might be enticed with a special offer of free theatre tickets or special hotel services.

Recently, ten of ITT's Sheraton hotels in Hawaii forecasted low occupancy for the months April, May, and June. The traditional approach to that would have been to increase advertising in Sunday travel sections. Instead, Sheraton mailed a targeted offer to 650,000 people who might travel to Hawaii and the Sheraton Hotel Company gained $3 million in revenue for its ten hotels in Hawaii for the April, May, June period. The mailing cost Sheraton about $200,000. Bob Cotter, formerly Senior Vice-President of marketing for ITT Sheraton, comments: 'The interesting thing is, we looked at the buyers again and are convinced now that we could do it again, but instead of mailing 650,000 pieces, we could mail between 200,000 and 300,000 with 90 per cent results.'

A new $70 million reservation system provides Sheraton with the market information it requires to understand its customer base and do database marketing. Sheraton's database marketing programme is interactive, in that customers can respond directly to the company. It is also affordable in that messages can be printed and distributed by mail. The database marketing programme incorporates 600,000 members of the Sheraton Club International (SCI) frequent-stay programme, who receive a $5\frac{1}{2}$ by $8\frac{1}{2}$ inch publication every month called *Update*. Sheraton's letter notifies them of the month's specials and encourages them to call the programme's dedicated 800 number to make a reservation.

As this example illustrates new technology makes it possible, and highly desirable, for hotel companies to dialogue directly with their customers and stay ahead of the competition.

General applications of database marketing

Develop private media

Private media help companies avoid the clutter of mass media and make their communications more targeted and response-oriented. An effective database-driven private medium is:

(a) owned and managed exclusively by the database owner;
(b) considered of great interest and value by the people who tune into it;
(c) interactive – meaning that those same people have a way to respond to the database owner directly through the channel; and
(d) affordable, which usually means it is printed and distributed via the mail. In addition to informing or educating, it must also get a response.

ITT Sheraton is one of the new breed of marketers creating such vehicles. The 600,000 members of the Sheraton Club International (SCI) frequent-stay program, receive a $5\frac{1}{2}$ by $8\frac{1}{2}$ inch publication every month called *Update*. This adletter notifies them of the month's specials, encouraging them to call the programme's dedicated 800 number to make a reservation. What sets ITT Sheraton's letter apart from many others is that it gives customized messages as well as member account information. If members have accumulated enough points to earn a bonus discount, they may see a related message. If it is their birthday month, it wishes them a happy birthday. Special deals in locations known to be of interest to a member are offered.

Support complementary travel distribution channels

In the conventional travel distribution environment, travel agents and tour operators control access to customer information. The travel product supplier (destination, hotel, attraction) probably knows a portion of the customer's transaction history but does not have any detailed information on the traveller's priorities and characteristics. The agent, not the supplier, owns the relationship with the customer. In this environment, the supplier is vulnerable to changes in the travel agency sales force, and the agency does not get any targeted customer support from the suppliers.

The Caribbean cruise business is typical of many in which independent agents jealously block the supplier's access to the customer. Traditionally, therefore, advertising and PR have been the only direct communication channels between cruise lines and their customers. Recently cruise lines have begun to build database systems that offer such value to travel agents that they are willing to provide the names and addresses of frequent cruise takers in exchange for centrally managed direct promotion of the agency.

Improve marketing productivity

Marketing is a notoriously inefficient activity, mainly because it is difficult to account for results. Database marketing improves marketing's productivity in three ways. First, we can link expenditures to results. We can know whether an individual received a communication and whether he or she responded and purchased our product. We can measure room-nights won not just ad impressions counted. Marketing programmes can be refined by a process of test and retest at the individual level. Second, database marketing can identify and reach profitable market niches too small to be served by mass-marketing methods. This is particularly useful for tourism marketing. Specific high spending activity participants (ecotourists, divers, archaeology buffs) who travel internationally can be targeted for direct individualized promotion. Finally, database marketing makes possible a shift in product development strategy: from producing generic tourism products and services to tailoring market driven products for particular customers.

Summary

An increase in targeted marketing requires an increase in customer data. In the future, those who have not taken advantage of what computer technology can offer to reach *individual customers*, will be at a competitive disadvantage.

Who are the customers?

1 *The visitors themselves*
   (a) Those on an existing database and those added when they contact a tourism organization.
   (b) Past visitors on whom data can be obtained.
   (c) Non-visitors whose travel habits and characteristics indicate they could be future visitors.

2 *Those that influence the visitors*
   (a) Travel agents and tour operators. The Australian Tourism Commission's
        Tourtrax database is an excellent example of this for North America.
   (b) Association meeting planners, clubs, corporations, and specialized
        tour operators. ERA has developed an extensive database of North
        American, European and Asian meeting planners as part of its
        METROPOLL and INTERPOLL surveys.
   (c) Transportation suppliers, including airlines, train operators, cruise
        lines, and automobile associations.
   (d) Hotel chains, car rental companies and other travel industry services.

Leaders in the tourism industry speak about the customer as king. So it is
particularly important to view database marketing through the eyes of each
of these customers – providing them with what they want, when and where
they want it.

To reach these customers, develop databases that identify existing visitors,
customers like existing visitors, people who visit nearby areas, and visitors
who are looking for products we want to develop. To find people like
existing visitors, gather information about existing visitors that can be used
to identify databases of persons with similar characteristics. For example,
get information on product ownership and brand loyalties, affinity group
and club membership, readership patterns, business and occupation profile,
etc. This information is much more useful than the typical data obtained
in travel surveys because it identifies likely databases that will contain new,
high prospect customers.

As a practical example, ERA recently analysed the market for a new
resort in Hawaii. We were asked to examine how to reach new customers in
what is generally agreed to be a weak market. As part of this study, we
conducted an extensive survey of all resort property owners in Hawaii to
determine if there were common database characteristics. The analysis
showed a surprising amount of commonality. However, this commonality
was not in the traditional measures of demographics, or travel and activity
characteristics. Rather, it was in how and when they accumulated their
wealth, level of entrepreneurship, membership in interest groups and
industry associations, and preferred media. These results led to entirely
new prospect lists and marketing channels for reaching like customers.

Does it pay off?

AT&T was a late arrival in the credit-card business when it introduced its
Universal Card in the spring of 1990. But it burst on the scene with a
significant advantage – a proprietary database marketing system gleaned
from its telephone customers covering tens of millions of prospective
cardholders. Using these data, AT&T was able to fine-tune both the credit

A COMPARISON OF TOURISM MARKETING APPROACHES

Mass marketing	Database marketing
Market identification	
Segmentation marketers measure demographic and psychographic profiles. They group together individuals with similar profiles, and treat them as if they were identical. Advertising communications are designed for the mean of the target group.	Interactive marketers use actual behaviour to identify customers and prospects and statistical models to assess their value. Each customer can receive a customized offering. Advertising uses information on the individual customer. Private media reinforces customer loyalty.
Promotion	
Image advertising through television and magazines. Promotional offers such as free-standing newspaper inserts are delivered indiscriminately to homes defined by geodemographics.	Direct marketing is integrated into the advertising programme. Promotions are tailored to an individual's past behaviour, and are selectively delivered to that consumer.
Pricing	
Price discrimination depends on customer self-selection.	Pricing is based on individual price sensitivity.
Sales management	
Customer data resides with the travel agent and tour operator.	Sales management of the tourism supplier has access to customer files.
New products	
Tourism product development is supply driven.	New tourism products and services are market driven.
Monitoring	
Market share, sales and profit are the indirect monitoring tools. Audience surveys measure a hoped for level of awareness but not purchase behaviour.	Traditional measures are supplemented by tracking purchase behaviour and measures of success in retaining customers.

line it offered each applicant and the incentives it presented each one to encourage use of the card.

AT&T's high-tech marketing paid off big time. Within three months, more than a million new cardholders had already charged more than $500 million on their new Universal cards. By the end of the year, charges were totalling $1 billion per month, according to an AT&T spokesperson. That was an unprecedented head start in a highly saturated market and grati-fying proof that the effort to build and maintain a marketing database can be absolutely worth while.

Tom Peters, the noted co-author of *In Search of Excellence*, adds his voice to the rising chorus with a nationally syndicated column headlined, 'Marketing is out, databases are in.'

STUDY QUESTIONS

1 Explain the causes of post-Second World War growth in tourism and demand for hotel accommodation.
2 Discuss the differences between mass and fragmented travel markets.
3 Explain the term 'internal customers' in a hotel and discuss their significance.
4 What are 'global customers', and what significance do they have for hotel companies?
5 What are the key technologies which allow fragmented markets to be efficiently and effectively targeted by travel and hotel companies?
6 Discuss key factors in the economics of substitution in relation to the hotel industry.
7 Discuss major developments in the technological environment which have had a major impact on the travel and hotel industries.
8 How could an international hotel company benefit from a similar idea to the Harrah's Gold Card?
9 Outline the general applications of database marketing in the travel and hotel industry.
10 Discuss the ways that hotel companies can make profitable applications of database marketing.

Part II

Strategic environment of the global hotel industry

Chapter 4

Understanding the structural dynamics of the American hotel industry

Traditionally, American hotel corporations served domestic markets in which competition was limited, at least by today's standards. Until the mid-1980s, the hotel industry seemed to have a lot going for it: building sites in many countries were readily available, construction and development were affordable, and unskilled labour was rather abundant. As the hotel industry entered the 1990s, conditions changed significantly. It appears that the 'golden rules' of rapid physical growth to build critical mass and the hiring of 'cheap labour' have been exploited to the fullest.

Chapter 4 analyses the hotel industry according to Porter's (1980) general structural model (Figure 4.1) comprised of the following five forces:

- industry competition;
- the threat of new entrants;
- the bargaining power of buyers;
- the threat of substitute products;
- the bargaining power of suppliers.

This model is used to gain an insight into the evolving structure of the American hotel industry and its expansion overseas which is expected to have a chain reaction, forcing market reforms to varying degrees, initially in Europe and in other world regions. In this chapter the terms 'lodging' and 'hotels' will be used interchangeably.

There are two cases at the end of this chapter. The first looks at the Carlson Hospitality Group as a typical example of growth by diversification in the US domestic market, followed only recently by international expansion. The second case features Marriott as an example of a US hotel company which has found success from its rapid and relatively extensive international expansion.

HOTEL INDUSTRY RIVALRY

Rivalry among existing competitors is one of the most important factors in

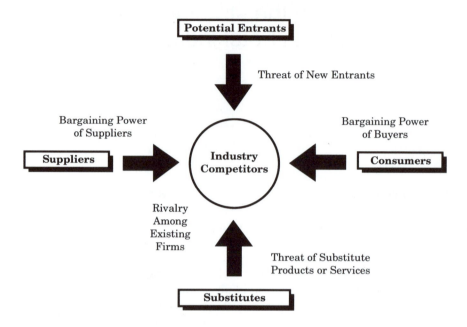

Figure 4.1 Forces driving hotel industry competition

Source: Based on M.E. Porter, *Competitive Strategy*, New York, The Free Press, 1980, p. 4

the US lodging industry. Rivalry 'occurs because one or more competitors either feels the pressure or sees the opportunity to improve position' (Porter 1980: 17), in an environment characterized by variables such as:

(a) underperforming assets, while most markets are oversupplied;
(b) tax law restriction of financial incentives for owners and developers;
(c) a relatively low inflation rate (making new projects harder to 'pencil out');
(d) more cautious lenders and investors;
(e) difficulty in establishing product differentiation;
(f) the considerable investment in building, renovating, and high fixed cost;
(g) the high level of exit barriers stemming from issues such as specialized assets, for instance hotel facilities' design and construction make it difficult to use hotels for residential and commercial (office) purposes. (Lattin 1987; Reichel 1986)

The aforementioned variables have led to heightened competition and subsequently to a greater degree of concentration, primarily through acqui-sition such as Ramada's acquisition of Rodeway Inns International, and the

Table 4.1 Major hotel company takeovers 1989–1990

Company (date)	Value	Seller	Buyer
Swissotel (Pending)	Estimated $328 million	Swissair, Switzerland	Aoki Corp., Japan
Embassy Hotels (Pending)	£202 million	Allied-Lyons plc, UK	Jarvis Hotels Ltd, UK
Holiday Inns (February '90)	$2.2 billion	Holiday Corp.	Bass plc, UK
Norfolk Capital (February '90)	Estimated £160 million (Norfolk shares for 5 Queens Moat)	Norfolk Capital, UK	Queens Moat Houses plc, UK
Ramada Inc. (December '89)	$530 million	Ramada Inc., USA	New World Development Co. Ltd, Hong Kong (in turn sold 1/3 interest for $180 million to Prime Motor Inns Inc., USA*
Friendship Inns (December '89)	(not disclosed)	Friendship Inns Int., USA	Econo Lodges, USA
Pickett Suite Hotels (December '89)	(not disclosed)	Pickett Suite Hotels, USA	Guest Quarters Suite Hotels, USA, subsidiary of Beacon Hotel Corp., USA
Days Inns (November '89)	$765 million	Days Inns, USA	Tollman–Hundley Hotels, USA
Thistle Hotels (November '89)	£645 million	Scottish & Newcastle Breweries, UK	Mount Charlotte, UK
Park Inns International (July '89)	(not disclosed)	Park Inns International, USA	EIE International, Japan
Regal 8 Inns (March '89)	$91 million	Regal 8 Inns, USA	Tollman–Hundley, USA
Aircoa Cos. (February '89)	$50.15 million	Aircoa Cos., USA	Regal Hotels (Holdings) Ltd, Hong Kong

Source: *Hotels*, July 1990, p. 50

Note: *In the first half of 1991 Prime Motor Inns had sold 65 per cent of Ramada and Howard Johnson Franchise systems to Blackstone Capital partners

UK-based Bass plc. In 1989, Bass acquired the 38 hotels in Canada then belonging to Scott's Hospitality Inc. By the turn of that same year, Bass had also absorbed the hotel division of the Holiday Corporation, thereby adding to the overseas Holiday Inns it already owned, the 1,268 franchise hotels in North America and the management of a further 121 hotels. Despite divesting 43 of its Crest Hotels chain in the UK to Trusthouse Forte, Bass was thus the world's largest hotel operator at the beginning of the 1990s. Major hotel company takeovers for 1989–1990 are listed in Table 4.1.

THREAT OF NEW ENTRANTS

Porter defines an industry as the group of firms manufacturing products of a like nature (1980: 5) and contends that industries which offer relatively high rates of return generally attract new entrants. The motives of the new entrants may differ: for example, some will wish to diversify, others may want to add new capacity. Whatever their motive is, new entrants in an industry usually increase competition. The threat of new entrants to an industry depends on the barriers to entry and the reaction to new entrants from established competitors. Six major barriers to entry in the hotel industry – economies of scale; product differentiation; capital requirements; location; experience-curve effects; and legislation – will be examined from a general perspective and in relation to the hotel chain industry.

Economies of scale

Vernon (1966) and Kindleberger (1969) found that proprietary production techniques enabled firms to utilize technology in production to generate better or less expensive products than those produced by their competitors. The operation of a production facility that attains lower costs per unit at large levels of output is referred to as 'economies of scale'. Economies of scale are typically classified in three categories. The first category addresses the principle that construction costs per unit of plant

Table 4.2 Changes in the US lodging industry's size and structure 1948–1977

Number of hotels	1948	1977	Average annual increase (%)
300+ guest rooms	255,399	398,292	1.5
100–299	390,996	710,992	2.1
50–99	335,222	377,886	0.4
25–49	285,852	260,435	(0.3)
Under 25	194,890	157,215	0.9

Source: G. Witham (1985) 'The evolution of the hospitality industry', The Cornell HRA Quarterly, 26(1): 41. Copyright © Cornell University. Used by permission. All rights reserved

Note: Includes only year-round establishments

capacity should decrease as plant size increases. From the change in composition of accommodation in North America, it is evident that the hotel industry has increased plant size. For example, in 1948 only 44 per cent of US hotel rooms were in establishments of 100 or more rooms. By 1977 this figure had risen to 58 per cent and was closer to 62 per cent by mid-1985 (Table 4.2).

The annual growth in hotel and motel room inventory has been only 1.3 per cent since 1928, most of it concentrated in larger hotel establishments (Table 4.3). Through economies of scale, lodging facilities with fewer than 50 rooms are being gradually 'phased' or forced out of business, particularly in seasonal markets where profit margins do not support additional investments (Government of Canada 1984: 5). Independent hotels, by their very nature tend to be smaller in size. The bulk of independents lies in smaller properties, fully 56 per cent of all independents have less than 150 rooms and are usually family owned and operated (Laventhol and Horwath 1987).

The second economy of scale category is based on the principle that operating costs per unit of output should decrease as plant size increases. However, the opposite seemed to have been the case in the US hotel industry. The changing structure of the industry had a two-fold effect: hotels became larger and increasingly complex due, in part, to the offering of additional services demanded by guests. This resulted in a more than doubling in the number of full- and part-time employees in the US lodging industry between 1948 and 1983. The hours worked annually per occupied room rose by nearly 40 per cent in the 35-year period (Lesure 1985: 72).

The third area in which potential economies of scale may be achieved regards non-manufacturing cost elements, including marketing, national branding, distribution, administration, central purchasing and new product development (Porter 1980: 203). The 'non-manufacturing cost' category,

Table 4.3 The US lodging industry's size and capacity 1928–1984

	1 May		
	1928	*1984*	*Average annual increase (%)*
Establishments	25,950	53,600	1.3
Rooms	1,521,000	2,714,000	1.0
Estimated value (millions)	$5,024	$91,600	5.3
Employees	576,000	1,194,800	1.3
Annual sales (millions)	$1,315	$33,367	5.9

in particular, has been exploited by American hotel chains which offer the travelling public highly standardized accommodation, both in price and quality level. Although admittedly standardization has drawbacks, this approach has one major advantage: a higher probability of consistent product quality.

During the 1960s and 1970s the US lodging industry experienced a switch from independently owned and operated hotels to properties with a chain affiliation. By 1979, the balance of power between independent and chain properties had shifted to 60 per cent in the latter's favour. Due to the benefits chain operations offer, notably nationwide advertising and an (inter)national reservations and referral network, Wyckoff and Sasser (1981: 27) postulate that the trend towards hotel and motel chain affiliation will continue in the future.

Product differentiation

One limit to economies of scale and potential lower costs to incumbents identified by Porter (1980: 16) is the trade-off with other potentially valuable barriers to entry such as product differentiation (for example, scale may work against product image or responsive service). Product differentiation is a marketing strategy designed to make two or more products look different from each other and from competitors' products and offer variety to buyers. Differentiation can come about through advertising, from value-added features (e.g., quick hotel check in procedures), and from actual product differences such as outstanding service or a superior location due to close proximity to the city's financial centre, a feature businessmen would value (Kotler 1980b: 293). Product differentiation was introduced in the hotel industry when Robert Hazard became chief executive of Quality Inns, an organization primarily in the business of franchising hotels and motels. The Quality Inns chain had a wide variety of franchisees with diverse properties. The result was a blurred consumer image with mixed expectations and a high risk factor (Lewis and Chambers 1989: 205). To solve his business problem, Hazard applied product differentiation, an idea which he had come about by chance.[1]

Essentially driven by growing consumer sophistication and demand, intensive competition of various chains, and a better understanding of what the public wants, the hotel industry has followed Quality International's lead and committed itself to supplying an ever-widening spectrum of varied new product lines. Today's contemporary hotels, designed to please almost every taste and income level, are as rich in variety as in location, and quite a departure from an era marked by sameness and complacency, when downtown hotels, highway motels and resorts virtually monopolized the lodging industry. However, despite the variety of product offerings, two clear patterns seem to be emerging.

One is to provide higher quality including service and improved leisure and other facilities. The second is to provide enhanced value for money by reducing or eliminating non-room facilities and public areas so far as possible, which in turn implies that more 'do-it-yourself' facilities will be supplied, particularly in bedrooms. 'Long-stay' service apartments will become more popular in city centre locations. The specialist hotel is destined to become the growth hotel of the future.

(Horwath and Horwath 1988: 15)

The segmentation phenomenon has been further stimulated by recognition of the increased marketing potential of a brand- or trade-name. By establishing a brand- or trade-name, the international hotel firm possesses a marketing advantage in that it may be able to attract additional customers due to name recognition, and a reputation for high quality products, good service, or value relative to competitors' products (Vernon 1966; Cave 1971). More recently, the power of brands has been analysed by Aaker (1991) in relation to building product differentiation and developing sustainable competitive advantage.[2] Product segmentation in the international hotel industry has developed rapidly in recent years, along certain

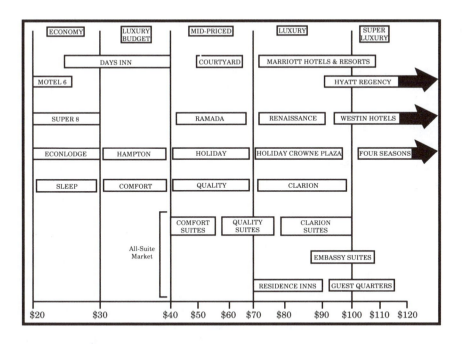

Figure 4.2 Segmentation strategy in the hotel industry

Source: Choice Hotels

guidelines such as price and level of provision and facilities. Hotel companies sometimes offer a number of different and clearly defined products.
Some hoteliers are investigating the possibility of establishing different
products within the same unit. Product branding is likely to become more
focused and reflect increasing levels of segmentation (Horwath and
Horwath 1988: 16–17). An example of segmentation within Choice Hotels
is illustrated in Figure 4.2.

Growth is desirable for all businesses, and it is imperative for publicly
held hotel companies. But after the construction boom in the 1980s many
companies found expansion increasingly difficult, simple geographical
limitations being one of the reasons for this slowdown. With many high
quality sites occupied by existing hotels, appropriate new sites were becoming more difficult to locate. By launching new chains and new product
lines, hotel companies have created a new vehicle for growth. If the
mid-price market is full in a given location, Quality International can
franchise a budget-price Comfort Inn; Ramada can develop an upscale
Renaissance. When Marriott had developed the prime sites for its existing
brand of hotel, its newly reduced service Courtyard could be located in
many additional areas.[3]

The multiplicity of hotel services contributes to the complexity of management, not only because it extends the scale of the problems but also
because each service can and does interact with others. The level of service
offered by hotels is generally reflected in their pricing structure and
classification. A typical classification is the one used by Choice Hotels (see
Figure 4.2) which broadly identifies five classifications: super luxury;
luxury; mid-priced; luxury budget; and economy.

Capital requirements

The need to invest large amounts of capital to enter an industry may prove
a significant barrier to entry. The amount of investment necessary to enter
the hotel business in the US has increased dramatically over the years,
particularly due to escalating real estate and construction costs. Large
expenditures for advertising to compete with multi-unit operations also
pose a capital-based barrier to entry. However, sophisticated financing
schemes are more readily available for major developments in or near
urban centres. Major changes in the financing of hotel facilities have
occurred in the past decade. Rather than owning hotel assets, American
hotel chain organizations have selected to expand primarily through franchising, management contracts and partial ownership such as master limited
partnerships, traded separately on the stock exchange.

Primary sources of hotel financing include institutional lenders, institutions acting as intermediaries, syndications, developers, hotel operating
companies, brokers and mortgage bankers acting as intermediaries, and

government (ULI 1984: 80). Smaller- and medium-sized lodging operations have historically experienced difficulty in borrowing funds, whether for new projects, refinancing, or for the expansion and upgrading of existing facilities. On the other hand, sophisticated financing schemes are more readily available for major hotel developments in primary urban centres (Government of Canada 1984: 6). Real estate traditionally has been labelled a 'boom and bust' industry, a cyclical business which fluctuates with money markets and the overall health of the economy. In the late 1960s investors discouraged with the 'bear' stock market turned to the real estate investment trusts (REITs), a 'mutual fund of real estate loans', which provided small investors with an easy vehicle to invest in real estate. Through REITs, commercial banks, savings and loans associations, and other lending institutions were under pressure to push high risk/high return commercial real estate construction and mortgage loans in an effort to boost earnings. Consequently, the construction of apartments, condominiums, hotels and motels surged ahead of demand in most parts of the US. The subsequent overbuilding in the hotel field was aggravated by several factors such as: (a) the energy crisis, which became apparent in late 1973, reducing travel and transient accommodation market potential; (b) an increase in construction costs causing significant cost overruns; (c) soaring interest rates which reduced project profitability; and (d) the impact of the recession which withered consumer confidence and demand for real estate projects of all sorts. In this hostile environment, construction and mortgage lenders found themselves owners of, rather than lenders to, hotel properties (Sasser and Banks 1975: 5).

Up to the mid-1970s, hotel and motel financing had been viewed as high risk but with tremendous upside potential. It was an orderly, standardized process that matched developers with investors and lenders. The problems experienced by lenders changed all that. The financing process became more fluid and complex. For example, by 1980 the loan-to-value percentages went below 75 per cent, call provisions became common, front end fees were frequently charged, life insurance firms reduced their participation because of real estate portfolios heavily weighted with hotel projects, and international investors entered the financing market, especially with regard to mixed use property developments that include hotels (ULI 1984: 79–80).

In case of property construction, the owner must obtain interim financing, but would not be awarded same unless long-term financing had been previously arranged (Wyckoff and Sasser 1981: vii). In America, for the first half of 1987, sales of public hotel partnerships increased 35 per cent to US$231.3 million. Limited partnerships in real estate have been popular for many years in the US, but until recently, the properties usually involved office or apartment buildings. Hotels represent a relatively new type of publicly traded limited partnership sold through US brokers. Although they have little liquidity, hotel limited partnerships can yield a 100 per cent return of capital after seven to 12 years. Like other forms of real estate, hotel investments offer a long-term hedge against inflation, along with accelerated depreciation rates and mortgage interest deductions that raise the average yields from 10 per cent to 12 per cent annually. Unlike office building and apartment building owners burdened by long-term leases, hotel operators can raise room rates when inflation 'hits'. It takes longer to raise office building or apartment rents. However, in contrast to other real estate developments, hotels are more difficult to change into other high yield use.

In the past, hotel property and buildings were usually owned by individuals or families. Typically, they thought of their hotel in terms of real estate and were often not fully aware how to maximize the hotel's profitability through management techniques. The early chain owners, like Sheraton's Henderson, were (real estate) investment oriented (ULI 1984: 7). Over the past 10 to 15 years, there has been a significant change in the ownership of hotels worldwide. The Hyatt Corporation was among the first modern lodging chains to take advantage of dividing the 'operating functions' from a hotel's real estate by establishing one company to hold the real estate inherent in hotels and a separate management company to deal with hotel operations. With the tendency to construct and operate larger properties, which require larger investments, today's majors in the US have found it more profitable to expand through management contracts, selling off the hotel's real estate to investors, usually an institutional insurance or financial company or a number of companies, like pension funds, manufacturing, communications, and transportation companies, which typically employ an industry expert to help control their hotel investment.

Recently, laws and high interest rates have made local US investors more cautious, but as the value of the dollar declined in 1986 about 20 to 30 per cent against most foreign currencies over 1985/1986, offshore investors gained a renewed interest in US real estate, and became a powerful new source of long term money for US hotel development (Motel/Hotel Insider 1986). Funding is coming from all over the world, but originates in particular in Europe, the Middle East, Hong Kong and Japan. For instance, Japanese investment in US real estate in 1988 was $16.54 billion, of which $3.57 billion was in hotels. By the end of 1989, Japanese real estate investments in the US had shrunk to $14.77 billion, but hotel investments increased to $4.16 billion (Hara and Eyster 1990: 98). They point to the appreciation of land prices in Japan as an indirect but essential factor to explain Japanese real estate investments in the United States. Other reasons for the increase in Japanese investment in hotels include (Salomon Brothers 1990: 6–7):

(a) the excess borrowing capacity and excess of available capital;
(b) the lack of alternative investment opportunities in Japan;
(c) favourable exchange rate factors;
(d) the Asian travel boom.

While international hotel corporations have established a foothold in the US, American firms considered leaders in hotel management (Porter 1990: 240) have become increasingly involved in exporting their expertise to other nations (Lattin 1987: 12).

Location

As Porter (1990: 19) observes: 'Competitive advantage is created and sustained through a highly localised process. Differences in national economic structures, values, cultures, and institutions, and histories contribute profoundly to competitive success.' Since, within this context, the need for lodging is generally a derived demand, location *vis-à-vis* proximity and convenience to tourist destinations or points of business activity are critical considerations in the lodging business. Another issue related to the location decision is the local competitive climate and the balance of supply and demand in the marketplace in which the hotel is located. Commonly, five categories of location may be distinguished: city centre, airport, suburban, highway, and resort locations (Wyckoff and Sasser 1981: xxiv).

City centre

City centre hotels continue to play a vital role in communities as a business, political, and social centres. Typically, city centre hotels consist of high-rise buildings with attached or covered parking, and vary in terms of numbers of guest rooms, ranges of facilities and amenities, depending on their market orientation and pricing level. Many hotel projects have acted as a catalyst for multi-use real estate development and contributed to the enhancement of neighbourhoods in many urban areas in North America and Europe.

City centre hotels typically attract commercial and convention business – the ratio for the top 100 city centre performing hotels as listed by *Lodging Hospitality* magazine is 74 per cent to 26 per cent at rates to support their high costs. Half of the 100 top performing city centre hotels are located in eight US cities: San Francisco with 11 properties, Washington, DC with ten, Boston had seven, and six each in New York and Los Angeles, four each in New Orleans and Houston, and three in Chicago. The top performers in the city centre category tend to be older (16 per cent of city centre properties are 50 years or older) than properties in other categories. Occupancy in city centre properties in the top 400 declined from 70 per cent in 1986 to 69 per cent in 1987. But sales per room increased from $33,333 to $42,764, a 28 per cent increase (*Lodging Hospitality* 1988: 50).

Suburban and airport locations

Suburban and airport hotels consist of low to mid-rise buildings with surface parking, interior corridors, recreational amenities, and meeting and banquet rooms. These properties typically offer better price values, including lower rates, lower food and beverage charges, free parking, better security, convenient location near suburban offices and more public facilities and amenities than downtown hotels of the same rate class. The top 100-performing suburban properties increased their occupancy from 70 to 76 per cent. This resulted in an increase in total sales per room from $28,640 in 1986 to $34,740 in 1987 – a rise of 21.3 per cent. This performance should be compared to the performance of suburban properties across the US which dropped from 65 per cent in 1986 to 64 per cent in 1987, causing sales to decline from $20,557 in 1986 to $19,934 in 1987. The characteristic 70 per cent of the top performing suburban properties have in common is their chain or referral affiliation. Also these properties tend to be very dependent on commercial business, accounting for 75 per cent and 25 per cent leisure (*Lodging Hospitality* 1988: 62).

Highway locations

Highway motels are typically low-rise structures with surface parking, exterior corridors, some food and beverage outlets, minimal meeting space, and possibly a pool. The top performing highway locations showed a 79 per cent occupancy in 1987, up from 70 per cent. This compares with 64 per cent in 1987, up from 62 per cent in 1986 for all highway hotels (*Lodging Hospitality* 1988: 68).

Total sales per room for top performing highway properties in 1987 amounted to $25,232, up from $24,162 in 1986. This performance should be compared to the performance of all highway hotels with total sales per room decreasing from $14,262 in 1986 to $13,405 in 1987. An important characteristic of highway motels is that almost all of these establishments belong to a referral system and 61 per cent are franchised facilities (*Lodging Hospitality* 1988: 68).

Resort locations

Resort hotels are typically located outside urban areas, since these facilities are highly dependent on natural and/or man-made amenities to attract tourists. With resorts catering mainly to the pleasure market, a broader variety of recreational, food and beverage, meeting and banquet outlets are commonly available. Because of their relative isolation, resorts must create the majority of their demand through their own marketing efforts to build an image and awareness for their destination as a whole. Independent establishments dominate the top 100 performing resorts, depending on social rather than corporate or convention business. The average customer mix is, respectively, 64 per cent leisure guests and 36 per cent commercial business. There appears to be a considerable degree of concentration in resorts, with Florida, California, Hawaii, and Arizona accounting for more than 50 per cent of the top performing establishments in this category (*Lodging Hospitality* 1988: 56).

Experience-curve effects

The principle function of hotel managers is to produce the best possible return from the available space in their property's guest rooms, restaurant seats, and meeting rooms. The key features likely to cause managers performance problems in producing the best possible return from available space include:

(a) the labour intensive nature of the industry, especially in upscale hotels;
(b) the perishable nature of the product requiring 'immediate' sale;
(c) the simultaneous nature of production and consumption, which make it impossible to separate the consumer from the production process;
(d) the heterogeneous nature of the product, which makes it difficult to maintain consistent service levels; and
(e) the demands of seasonality on profitability, labour and product quality.

In many instances there is a significant gap between the way hotels are managed and the way these facilities ought to be managed in order to perform in a profitable manner, due to low labour productivity, unhealthy ratio of equity/debt in financing hotel projects, and a 'fire-fighting' approach to coping with the demands of the establishment which can only be undertaken to the neglect of other areas of management practice, notably personnel training, marketing, and finance.[4] Typically, the key deficiency in independent operations, lies in the area of effectively managing the service concept, ensuring quality of service, and understanding when and where the guest consumes the product (Bateson 1989: 8). These are aspects mastered only by a select number of hotel chain systems, and independent hoteliers with a long-standing reputation. Meanwhile, it has become increasingly difficult to hire and retain service workers because of labour shortages (Koepp 1987: 28–34).

Experience-curve effects are cost advantages gained over time as a company's knowledge accumulates and the total number of units produced increases. When firms in an industry have gained experience-curve cost reductions, new companies entering the industry will ordinarily have inherently higher costs than their established competitors. In order to manage change effectively, hotel managers will require more accurate sources of management information that go beyond the data traditionally provided by accounting systems, as these have proved to be inadequate. Therefore, it will be mandatory that hotel companies think about and pinpoint their executive data needs.

Legislation

By 1986, the American hotel industry was building new properties at a faster rate than at any time since the late 1950s. This situation was due to the US Economic Recovery Tax Act of 1981, which improved the outlook for hotel investment by shortening the life for depreciation and providing tax credits for rehabilitation of old properties. Declining interest rates also have improved the climate for hotel investments. However, despite a record number of 91,000 rooms added to inventory (a 3.5 per cent increase from 1985), occupancy actually rose slightly, up 0.7 per cent, for a year-end nationwide average of 64.9 per cent. The Tax Reform Act of 1986 has made it far less attractive to invest in hotels in the US. It is clear that provisions of the Act, in particular the lengthening of the depreciation period, the requirement that straight-line depreciation be used, the elimination of preferential capital gains treatments, and limitation on the ability to shelter salaries and other non-passive income with losses from passive investment, have limited commercial construction. As a result, the Act will force investors to make decisions based on a purely economic basis, rather than on artificial tax motivations. However, the Act will have a favourable impact on hotel management companies, for it will significantly reduce their corporate tax rates (ULI 1987: 6–7).

Both domestic and international hotel corporations have to analyse the shifting structure of the lodging industry in relation to the threat of new entrants. In this regard, many of the strategic issues are the same or similar for the domestic and international hotel corporation. But there is an important strategic aspect that is peculiar and relevant to the international hotel corporation, which revolves, in one way or another, around the idea that what an international hotel corporation does in one country affects what is going on in other countries; Porter (1987: 29) refers to this as 'the connectedness among country competition'.

For example, the slow growth in one country in combination with the influx of new entrants in that country will result in an increase in competition in the lodging industry, and in a hotel industry structure that is characterized by greater industry concentration and diversification. Faced with a 'discontinuous', i.e. 'a significant departure from the historical growth vector', as opposed to an 'incremental' change (a relatively small and logical departure from the past) (Ansoff 1987: 117–118), the domestic hotel firm will rather diversify, then internationalize, because 'internation-alization leads to the dual difficulties of penetrating a new country and offering a novel technology' (Ansoff 1987: 125–126). Given a scenario of discontinuity and the experience it has gained abroad, the international hotel corporation is more likely to be 'pushed' and 'pulled' to further internationalize to expand its portfolio, in that it has built transnational management expertise which domestic firms lack.

BARGAINING POWER OF BUYERS

One of the key challenges in the international hotel industry is to connect a very fragmented lodging sector with a dispersed marketplace. Within this context, Kaven (1974) has defined the (international) hotel firms' need to be identified in the marketplace as follows:

> hundreds of thousands of lodging establishments are seeking to gain identity with untold millions of potential customers covering the whole spectrum of incomes, interests, knowledge, sophistication, and needs; but few single establishments can afford the marketing costs.
>
> (Kaven 1974: 115)

As a consequence, single or independent hotels tend to be extremely vulnerable, while hotels operating within a chain or network tend to have access to the necessary capital, marketing expertise and technology neces-sary to survive.

In the international hotel industry, buyers include tour wholesalers, travel agent retailers and consumers. These buyers impact on the hotel industry by forcing down prices, demanding higher quality and greater variety of services, and playing competitors against one another – all at the expense of industry profitability. Buyers, sure that they can always find alternative hotel space, have used this knowledge to play one hotel firm against another (for example, when meeting planners of a company or association negotiate to hold their conference at a particular hotel).

Similarly, wholesalers, travel agencies and tour brokers account for about one-third of the room nights consumed annually in the United States (Brewton 1987: 12). The needs of travel organizations who resell the hotel rooms they buy are different from those of the user. Although consumers are expected to continue to play the starring role, Leven (1982) suggests that hotels have become more removed from their clientele, that client decisions are largely controlled by more than just the individual user, and that the 'gap' between supplier and consumer will continue to widen. Channels of distribution in the hotel business refers to the path by which a firm or guests execute a reservation to use a facility (Leven 1982). It covers all activities designed to bring the travel product to where the demand is; such activities are generally performed by producers and commercial enterprises. An important feature of the travel product is its complexity – or the variety of services it comprises – and the complementary nature or interdependence existing between the various services. The features of travel services in combination with the complex nature of travel marketing make it desirable to use intermediaries or indirect channels.

Direct channels still exist and are chiefly concerned with the sales function at the individual hotel level whereby sales representatives concentrate on (a) maintaining sales contacts with channel intermediaries; (b) maintaining sales contact with community organizations; and (c) following leads furnished by other sources (Kaven 1974: 116). However, indirect channels of distribution have become increasingly important to represent the hotel firm in multiple markets of origin. In this regard Bitner and Booms (1982) analysis of structural, motivational and change-related data of the distribution system indicates that travel agents will retain their roles as the primary distribution intermediary for airline and lodging services. Another intermediary is the tour packagers and wholesalers who generally coordinate and promote the development of package tours. The primary advantage for producers is that wholesalers tend to purchase services in bulk and, importantly, in advance, allowing producers to anticipate sales volume. Hotel representatives, another intermediary, act as sales and reservation agents for a number of non-competing hotels such as resorts and are frequently used by foreign hotels selling to consumers in the industrialized travel markets. Other types of intermediaries include association executives, corporate travel offices, and incentive travel firms through which hotels can attempt to influence when, where and how consumers travel. In other words, they control to some degree how much business an individual airline, cruiseline, or hotel may get (Bitner and Booms 1982). Among the trends Kaven (1974: 119–120) cites that will have a major effect on the distribution of hotel services is the increasing horizontal concentration with an increasing number of hotel rooms coming under the management, control, and ownership of brand-name organizations.

THREAT OF SUBSTITUTE PRODUCTS

The third major competitive force is pressure from substitute products. Substitutes limit the potential return of an industry by placing a ceiling on the prices a firm can charge. The more attractive the price–quality alternative offered by substitutes, the less the industry sells, and the lower the industry's profitability. Recently, competition has come from other industries with offerings that can potentially replace the need for hotel rooms, such as:

(a) More frequent and faster jet travel which enables busy consumers to schedule one-day round-trip flights to their destination.

(b) A whole array of accommodation substitutes with the potential to drain pleasure market 'room nights' from the hotel industry have come on the market, such as resort time shares, condominiums, second homes, recreational vehicles, camping grounds, and cruise lines. The cruise line business in particular may be seen to be competing directly with the hotel and resort industry for the recreation segment of the tourism market both in the US and in Caribbean destinations. One estimate (Hall and Braithwait 1990: 339) puts the number of people who took a cruise vacation in 1990 at five million.

(c) Travel abroad opportunities let American consumers spend their dollars in foreign destinations and possibly foreign (owned) hotels.

(d) Price elasticity of demand (i.e. the responsiveness of demand to a change in price) has caused many consumers, particularly those not on expense accounts (e.g., holiday-makers), to seek lodging substitutes and/or shorten their length of stay at hotels.

BARGAINING POWER OF SUPPLIERS

Suppliers to an industry can drive down profitability by raising prices or reducing the quality of goods sold to the industry – squeezing profits when the industry is unable to pass along cost increases to consumers through raising prices. Two types of hotel industry supply will be considered: (a) technology and (b) labour.

Technology

As the demands of change evolve, so do the business means and methods to cope. Technology is one tool that – when properly applied – can help companies to build their competitiveness. Leading airline, banking, whole-sale and retail distribution businesses have been using technology successfully to facilitate the change management process and at times gain a competitive advantage.

The lodging industry is often considered a technology laggard and will continue to be slow in technology assimilation unless it overcomes two main barriers: (a) lack of management understanding, and (b) uncertainty among technology buyers about the effectiveness of technology investments (AH&MA 1989: 3–4). At the same time the American Hotel and Motel Association study identifies several forces that will press the industry to implement technology, specifically:

Over 64 percent of the lodging executives surveyed believe 'improving the quality of guest stay' will continue to be the most important driving force of technology innovation. Given a changing industry structure and more demanding guests, lodging executives who were surveyed cite four areas specifically as the most important strategic opportunities for technology investment: 'Reservation systems' (51 percent), 'Sales/Marketing Information Systems' (40 percent); 'Property Management Systems' (42 percent) and 'Yield Management Systems' (34 percent).

(AH&MA 1989: 4)

The four areas identified by executives as strategic opportunities for technology investment have either an internal or external focus. Marketing information systems, property management systems, yield management systems, monitoring energy saving systems, and point of sale systems, for example, are strategic systems that directly affect the quality of guest service and productivity. They have an *internal focus* because they address the needs and uses of information to support the business operation and internal control.

Global distribution systems (GDS) on the other hand – the central depository of sales and marketing information and the critical means to form business partnerships through an integrated network – have a decidedly *external focus*. Since very important customer information is gathered during the time when reservations are made, American lodging executives consider reservation systems to represent the highest ranked strategic opportunity in the early 1990s (AH&MA 1989: 13).

For the hotel industry the vital feature to monitor is that, while GDS are airline led and dominated, the customer is increasingly able to reserve hotel space as well as many other features of his or her travel arrangements in addition to the airline seats which are the starting point for most travel transactions. Hotels within large national markets and across frontiers run the risk of losing business if they do not feature on these megasystems.

The major GDS may well consolidate into perhaps two or three dominant international systems by the mid-1990s, and indeed this consolidation process has already begun. How these groupings might in reality develop is not a subject for this study, but the implications for the international hotel industry clearly are, and are likely to be very far-reaching.

Hotels have little practical choice but to ensure that they feature on these systems, though how the choice of system is made and how many systems a given hotel company needs to participate in remains unclear. These issues will only be resolved once a clearer picture emerges of which systems will succeed and how they will be positioned in the international marketplace.

It does seem clear, however, that the costs to hotels will be very significant, and could well result in an all-round rise in hotel room rates. Therefore, hotel managers would be well advised to calculate exactly what the costs of such reservations will be to them before they sign any agreement. Go and Welch (1991: 117–18) have identified how the hotel industry stands to gain some significant benefits from the mega GDS. First, much improved yield management techniques will be available via the GDS, as opposed to yield management systems currently in existence that are strictly internal in scope. Yield management broadly means maximizing occupancy rates, and matching variations in demand on a seasonal and weekly basis to different pricing structures in order to maximize revenue. Use of new reservation technologies can help to set targets for the number of rooms that can be sold at a given set of prices on different days of the week and/or seasons of the year. Such parameters can be built into the GDS and can be used to manage capacity by influencing the decision to purchase at the point of sale.

'Sell through' techniques are part of this process. These are means whereby the day-to-day judgement of staff can be supplanted by set criteria within a GDS to influence the nature of bookings that a given hotel will accept. For example, if there is to be a major trade fair in a city, the GDS can be instructed not to accept bookings for less than the duration of the fair if it is known in advance that the hotel stock in the city will be more or less full during that week. Equally, it may be known that certain nights of the week are typically full in a given hotel while others are less well patronized. The GDS can be instructed to deal with this imbalance by price variations.

One of the areas where GDS will find it more difficult to replace skilled staff will be in the role of the hotel booking agent, such as are found at most major airports, for example. The late release of rooms, or the necessity to manage room availability to cater for flight delays and the unexpected, is a difficult area for GDS. The hotel booking agent who puts a lot of business in one hotel or group of hotels will normally cultivate close personal relationships with the hotel front desk staff. In return for loyalty, the hotel will tend to help out the agent when rooms are needed at peak times, or late bookings have to be made.

The impacts of GDS on the international hotel industry will vary. Broadly, the bigger the company the greater the potential benefit. The major international groups will be better able to afford the investment necessary to bring their own systems up to a standard which permits them to interface with the GDS than smaller, less well off groups. In return, the majors will be able to develop a better, directly manageable source of detailed knowledge on their clients, will be able to manage their yields much more tightly, and should achieve the lion's share of advance reservations from foreign clients before their local, often independent rivals.

By the same token, the weakest and most vulnerable part of the hotel industry in the area of GDS development will be the independent property. The hotels most vulnerable would seem to be the smaller, independent properties whose business comes, to a significant degree, through sales and travel agents overseas or a long way from their local markets. In most cases the investment required to link into a large number of the major systems may be beyond the small unit. If they cannot place themselves in front of their national or international clients at the point of sale they will obviously be at risk of losing a substantial slice of their business.

A detailed knowledge of their current markets and a reasonable appreciation of unexploited potential is likely to give hotels the basis on which to define what sort of GDS linkages they need, and this in turn will give a clear indication of the investment costs involved. While not all hotels will then be able to implement all these aspects, at least some rational decisions will be possible. Fundamental decisions will have to be made here about distant sales representation and those that cannot afford to be in the most important GDS in these markets will almost certainly lose market share.

Labour

The hotel industry is not only people-oriented, it is people-dependent as well. An important ingredient of a satisfying visitor experience which must be present for success is a well-trained labour force (Kaiser and Helber 1978: 200). By any measure, the lodging industry is relatively labour-intensive. Labour costs in the US, including wages and related expenses, consume more than 30 per cent of revenues (Table 4.4) and although the average earnings per employee are low, revenues per employee are low as well (Wyckoff and Sasser 1981: ix–xi).[5] The great variety of types and levels of workers required in a hotel operation, who by many guests are perceived as the product (Bateson 1989: 10), complicate labour force management and intensify the need for quality control. However, by definition, it is impossible for a service firm to perform 100 per cent successfully all the time (Bateson 1989: 11).

Table 4.4 Source and disposition of the US hotel industry dollar (hotels and motels) in 1989

Revenue		Expenses	
Total revenue	100.0%	Total expenses	100.0%
Rooms	61.9	Salaries, benefits and meals	32.7
Food (including other income)	23.1	Operating expenses	24.9
Beverage	7.2	Cost of sales	9.2
Telephone	2.2	Energy costs	4.0
Other operated departments	3.0	All taxes	3.9
Rentals and other income	2.6	Insurance, rent, interests, depreciation, amortization, other additional/deletions	25.3

Source: PKF (1990) *Trends in the Hotel Industry* (USA Edition), Houston, Texas: Pannell, Kerr, Forster Worldwide, p. 41

Unlike labour in other sectors, such as transportation (the Teamsters and unions in the airlines), the hotel and restaurant industry's labour force is organized locally (Wyckoff and Sasser 1981: xii). It is estimated that 12 per cent of the hotel and restaurant industry's labour force is unionized, compared to an estimated 20 per cent of the US workforce (Lane and van Hartesvelt 1983: 126).

During the 1960s and 1970s, the US 'baby-boom' population crowded the labour pool with young people, helping industries like lodging that depend on 'unskilled' and semi-skilled labour. But the 'baby boom' turned into a 'baby bust' in the 1980s and resulted in the following: (a) fewer entry-level workers; (b) lower unemployment rates; (c) a burgeoning job market competing to hire immigrants; and (d) wage increases.

Currently, the hotel industry is experiencing a shortage of labour despite the influx of new immigrants from Latin America and Asia. The shortage is 'due to the decline in birth rates which began in the early 1960s' (Hiemstra 1988: 1). Consequently, fewer younger people are available and those who are have high career expectations. This scenario will lead to problems, especially for service sectors which have traditionally relied on young, low-wage workers to fill entry-level positions.

In particular, Hiemstra's study findings (1988: 1–2) indicate that:

The number of men in the 16–25 age group is expected to drop by a total of 6 per cent by the year 2000, which represents a decline of 0.4 per cent per year. The number of females in this age group in the workforce is expected to remain almost exactly the same – the decline in birth rates is expected to be offset by the continued increase in the proportion of females in the workforce. The shortfall in the overall workforce is not expected to be offset by older workers. While the number of older people is increasing as life expectancy increases, people are retiring earlier and leaving the workforce. The number of men age 55 or older in the work-force is projected to remain about constant over the 1986–2000 period (decline 0.1 per cent annually). However, the number of women is expected to increase slightly, 0.7 per cent annually. Of course, even after retirement, some of these people may be available for part-time work in the industry.

The lodging industry must adapt to the shifting population and begin to approach heretofore largely untapped sources of labour.[6] The lodging manpower report (Hiemstra 1988) concludes that it seems anomalous that the labour shortage exists while unemployment prevails.

The image of the hotel industry is not perceived as being attractive in many countries and therefore is low on the list of those wishing to develop careers and also low on the list of those wishing to re-train from other industries.

(Horwath and Horwath 1988: 23)

Therefore, American lodging corporations that plan to penetrate the European market should be aware that they will not escape the human resource problems encountered domestically. Across Europe, for example, the international hotel industry faces the following persistent human resource problems, detailed in an industry survey conducted by the European Institute of Education and Social Policy (EIESP 1991: 13–15):

(a) Recruiting workers is an increasing problem for employers. Educational programmes and formal training courses are often ill-adapted to the industry's needs, which further aggravates the growing problem of recruiting enough, as well as qualified, workers to meet its needs.
(b) Retention continues to be a problem as many organizations experience high labour turnover. The causes of high turnover vary, but they include the following: poor compensation, inadequate training, lack of career path options, lack of management or organizational support, poor working conditions, and the poor social status ascribed to many entry-level positions.[7]
(c) The industry's image in offering attractive career opportunities is often negative. Subject to cultural and organizational stereotypes, the public, industry workers, and career counsellors generally have a negative image of the industry. This poor image is reinforced by the causes mentioned in point (b) above, as well as by the industry's lack of involvement in education and training initiatives in both private and public sectors.
(d) Training and education of personnel is often inadequate, and many companies are uncertain about the potential benefits and costs of training activities. 'Too many companies still feel that the cost of sending employees on exchanges, or "stages", abroad is too high in staff time and disruptive to daily routine.'
(e) Existing management and supervisory skills are generally weak and contribute to the problems mentioned above. To a large extent, many tourism and hospitality companies are captives of their past since their organizations negatively influenced managers' abilities to develop appropriate responses to changing environmental forces.

To make matters more complex, changes in the business environment are also changing job requirements at management, supervisory, and front-line levels.

STRATEGIC OPPORTUNITIES FOR IMPROVEMENT

Since the purpose of any business is ultimately 'to create and keep a customer', hotel companies have to produce services that consumers 'want and value at prices and under conditions that are reasonably attractive to those offered by others to a proportion of customers large enough to make those prices and conditions possible' (Levitt 1983b: 5–6).

To provide services that customers value, hotel corporations require information about customer wants. But are hotel managers generally getting the information they need to measure customer satisfaction? Several studies suggest that they may not. One way to pinpoint a company's information needs is through 'Critical Success Factors' (CSF) analysis (Geller 1985: 77).

Table 4.5 Goals, critical success factors (CSFs), and measures

Glossary

Goals
Broad, overall aims of the organization; the end points an organization hopes to reach.

Critical success factors
The areas in which good performance is necessary to ensure attainment of the goals; the few key areas where *things must go right* for success (thus, performance in these areas should be continually measured).

Measures
Indicators or pieces of information that help monitor performance in a key area; some measures are 'hard' (objective), others are 'soft' (subjective).

Some examples

Goals	Critical success factors	Measures
Market share	Good service	Ratio of repeat business Occupancy Informal feedback
	Employee morale and loyalty	Turnover Absenteeism Informal feedback
Financial stability	Image in financial markets	Price/earnings ratio Share price
	Profitability	Earnings per share Gross operating profit Cost trends Cash flow
	Strength of management team	Turnover Division profit Rate of promotion Informal feedback
Owner satisfaction	Adequate cash flow	Occupancy, sales Gross operating profit Department profit

Table 4.6 CSFs most frequently mentioned by respondents

Critical success factor	Number of responses	Rank
Employee attitude	25	1
Guest satisfaction (service)	21	2
Superior product (physical plant)	19	3
Superior location	11	4
Maximize revenue	8	5
Cost control	8	5
Increase market share	6	6
Increase customer price–value perception	5	7
Achieve market segmentation	4	8

Source: A.N. Geller (1985) 'Tracking the Critical Success Factors for Hotel Companies', *The Cornell HRA Quarterly*, 25 (4): 80. Copyright © Cornell University. Used by permission. All rights reserved

In any business situation, a handful of critical success factors tends to determine the outcome. Therefore, the CSFs represent variables that have to go 'right' in order for the company to achieve its objectives. Typical hotel industry goals, based on a sample of US firms, include profitability, growth, and greater market share (Geller 1984: 15–22). To monitor the CSFs, management has to identify measures. The relationship between goals and CSFs as well as performance measures has been illustrated in Table 4.5.

In conducting a research study to determine what information American hotel executives require to gauge their performance, the list of common goals which Geller (1984) generated contained few surprises. However, the results of the CSFs analysis appeared less predictable (Table 4.6) in that 'employee attitude' was leading the list.

Thus according to the sample of hotel executives surveyed, hotel corporations have to cultivate a proper employee attitude to achieve their goals, which Geller interpreted as follows: 'It is not so surprising that employee attitude is on the list – the hotel industry has always viewed itself as a people business – but it is surprising that employee attitude leads the list, and by so large a margin' (Geller 1985: 80).

When combining the goals and CSFs most frequently mentioned by respondents, the executives of the sample hotel companies demonstrated a high interest in 'best management', 'employee morale', and 'employee attitude', which all have a human resources connotation. The second most significant CSF 'guest satisfaction' (service) bears an important relationship to employee attitude.

Interestingly, Geller (1984: 25) discovered that executive information systems in hotels that are directly relevant to the top two CSFs were weakest in the areas of human resources and marketing.

When viewing the hotel business within Porter's framework (1985) as a complex transformation system, comprised of a supply system providing the inputs and a user system taking its outputs, it appears that the value chain of hotel companies, at least those in Geller's sample, tends to be weakest in the most vital areas, i.e., in the activities (human resources and marketing) that are most likely to give hotel companies a competitive advantage.

Both the human resources and marketing processes can be managed to create a more consistent, high-quality performance. A process model proposed by Ishikawa (1985) and Crosby (1979) comprised of (a) outputs, (b) activities, (c) inputs, and (d) performance standards can be applied to find ways of ensuring that customers feel that they are obtaining value for the money (Band 1991: 61–64).

Poor design of the business process has been cited as the cause of at least 80 per cent of output problems (Band 1991: 64). By analysing the business process in a particular hotel operation, managers can identify the *cause* factors within a process within the business system and come up with ways to improve the effectiveness and efficiency of the process. In the context of hotel companies, the major concern with regard to continuous process improvement will be to balance the impersonal but productive use of technology with the human touch of personalized service. Providing superior customer service to guests takes a thorough understanding of guest characteristics and a well-coordinated series of service activities as the following example illustrates.

For example, the Hyatt Hotels Corporation based in Chicago caters primarily to the business travel market. Adding value to the experience of business travellers requires the examination of the current state of business travel. It is Hyatt's goal (output) to come as close as possible to offering its customers a 'hassle-free' business travel experience.

To understand the business travel experience (the activities), Hyatt commissioned a major study involving in-depth interviews with business travellers, and taped diaries on which business travellers recorded their most stressful moments. Specifically, the study had three objectives:

The first was to take a look at what was wrong with business travel – to identify and correct the pet peeves, [including] towels that are too small, telephone cords that don't extend from the bed to the desk, and . . . theft-proof coat hangers. In the second part of the study . . . we looked at how business travel affects some lifestyle issues – specifically nutrition, separation from family, and stress. The impact of technology on business travel [was the third factor the study explored]. There are only two kinds of technological advances that are relevant to Hyatt: those that make business travel unnecessary, and those that make business travel easier.

(Townsend 1990: 46–47)

One of the stressful, non-value adding activities travellers face most often in a hotel is the waiting in line to either check-in or check-out. To reach its goal (to eliminate any hassle for the guests), Hyatt plans to change the method (input) it currently uses – the conventional front desk – to allow guests to enter and exit their hotels through an alternate process.

By applying technology, in particular a magnetic card reader on the door lock of guest rooms, the Hyatt Corporation intends to eliminate guests standing in line in the future (performance standard). Coincidentally, the adding of value to the business travel experience would also result in the elimination of many front-desk employees and presumably help to increase productivity.

The Hyatt example illustrates that problem-solving in the hotel industry requires a consumer-orientation and a broad perspective. Thus, a potential obstacle to effective strategic hotel marketing has been the tendency of many hotel executives to view their problems and potential solutions within the context of the hotel industry rather than the service sector.

By broadening the 'corpus of knowledge', through forward thinking, and by focusing on the potential application of technology in service operations, there appear to be three strategic opportunities that are of deciding importance for hotel corporations to gain a competitive advantage, or at least to understand the hotel industry in a competitive context.

First and foremost is the challenge to deliver quality customer service to a diverse market. Customers are simultaneously becoming more sophisticated and demanding, especially as far as receiving 'value for money' is concerned. The application of process technology to add value to customers' experiences has implications for the employees who operate within the process and the relationships between internal hotel departments which will have to become more integrated in order to be effective. The level of competency and sophistication of hotel employees requires that their training and skill levels have to match the more complex and demanding tasks to be performed. Thus, the hotel industry is likely to become more 'knowledge-intensive' and 'personality-intensive'. Therefore,

education and training are seen as the cornerstones of future success in hotel keeping. . . . Education is not just within hotels and hotel colleges, it starts with educating the public and career advisors that hotels are worthwhile in terms of successful long term employment. Then there is the need for adequate and professional education and training tailored to the needs of each category with hoteliers playing a significant role in liaison with education. . . . The resources that need to be devoted to human resources need to be increased and must be viewed as worth-while long term investment in the future.

(Horwath and Horwath 1988: 24–25)

Second, the shrinking labour pool presents both a challenge and an opportunity to explore potential alternative processes of service delivery to seek productivity improvement and possible new labour sources. Though technology should not replace the human touch, there are important opportunities for technology to complement human service to enhance the service delivery process.

Third, the changing structure of the international hotel industry is likely to benefit some operators and threaten the survival of others. The dual forces of consolidation on the one hand and convergence on the other have resulted in (a) the percentage increase of the hotel chain brand affiliated properties, and (b) the greater segmentation of the market (in response to market fragmentation) and the growth in the number of corporate chain hotel brands. Given the changing industry structure and heightened levels of competition, international hotel corporations are likely to seek opportunities, both domestically and internationally, with possible partners in the business channel who have mutual interests.

CONCLUSION

The American hotel industry is facing major challenges. Assets are under-performing and most markets oversupplied. The concentration of hotel corporations due to mergers and acquisitions has favoured the growth and profitability of international hotel brands over a collection of local hotel products. Foreign direct investment, especially by Asian corporations, has intensified the level of competition and changed the 'game rules' because the Japanese corporations behave strategically differently, more long term than Western companies.

The automation issue and GDS in particular is causing increasing concern for hotel companies that want to be part of the new technology develop-ments. At the same time, hotel firms view themselves as pawns in what is essentially an airline industry game. As global distribution systems, GDS mean a loss of independence for hotel firms as it becomes increasingly clear that GDS are driving the hospitality business. Consequently, hotel corporations face several strategic imperatives to improve their informa-tion knowledge and techniques. The impact of computer technology, including global computer reservations systems, will prove central to the international travel industry, including hotel operations in the 1990s and beyond.

The labour shortage exerts pressure on the management because em-ployee skills form the foundation for service delivery, the critical success factor in hotel corporations. Put differently, the hotel industry is a business of human relationships, because none of the capital investments and facilities can produce a return on investment unless the hotel's employees please the guests.

Given that a hotel has the capital, location, and business expertise but cannot deliver the 'value-added' product due to a shortage of labour, the major problem from a competitive perspective facing the hotel industry is human resources. Consequently, the present dearth of trained labour is considered the most critical problem hotel corporations face.

CASE: CARLSON HOSPITALITY GROUP – DIVERSIFICATION, GROWTH AND GLOBALIZATION

Starting in 1938, with nothing but an idea, a mail drop and $50 of borrowed capital, entrepreneur Curtis L. Carlson founded the Gold Bond Stamp Company in his home city of Minneapolis, Minnesota. His trading stamp concept to stimulate sales for food stores proved to be an idea which was right for the times and it swept the nation in a wave of dramatic growth.

From this base the company expanded for four decades at an annual compounded growth rate of 33 per cent. Early diversification led to related motivation, incentive and consumer marketing industries, the foundation of today's Carlson Marketing Group, Inc. and Carlson Promotion Group.

In 1962 the company expanded into the hotel business with the purchase of the original Radisson Hotel in downtown Minneapolis. This move was the genesis of Carlson Companies' hospitality businesses which today encompass more than 160 major hotels spreading around the world and two large restaurant chains across North America. In addition to Radisson Hotels, Colony Hotels and Resorts and Country Hospitality Inns and Suites, Carlson's Hospitality Group includes TGI Friday's and Country Kitchen restaurants.

In the early 1970s, Carlson Companies became involved in real estate development and property management with the establishment of Carlson Properties. Today, these operations, which include Carlson Properties and Carlson Real Estate Company, have been combined under the Carlson Investment Group. They include a portfolio of real estate holdings throughout North America and several real estate developments.

Numerous acquisitions and extensive expansion of retail and wholesale travel companies during the past several years have resulted in today's Carlson Travel Group being the largest retail travel organization in North America. Carlson Travel Group today encompasses Ask Mr Foster travel agencies in the United States; P. Lawson Travel, the most important travel company in Canada; Cartan Tours, Inc., a de luxe group travel organization, and Firstours.

Today, Carlson Companies, Inc., is one of America's largest privately held corporations. Despite its international scope and extensive diversification, Carlson Companies remains committed to the principles upon which it was founded – entrepreneurial initiative, goal setting, excellence of performance with the objective of being the best in each of its businesses.

The history of Carlson Companies is a dramatic, though not unique, illustration of the American free enterprise system at work. Mixed feelings about expanding abroad when the domestic market is so vast has been an important factor keeping Radisson Hotels and many other American hotel corporations from taking, earlier on, an aggressive international posture. The majority of American hotel corporations prefer the domestic market over foreign markets, as the former is perceived as safer and simpler. However, due to the effects of globalization of the economy, American hotel companies are pulled into the international market because of excellent opportunities for development abroad and pushed due to the overbuilt US hotel industry.

Juergen Bartels, President of Carlson Hospitality Group, Inc. is leading the way in the globalization of the American hotel industry. 'The front lines of the battles for guests are not just Atlanta or Boston but also Bombay, Jakarta, and Shanghai' (Bartels 1993).

CASE: MARRIOTT – POISED FOR GLOBAL EXPANSION THROUGH PROFITABLE PARTNERSHIPS

Whilst American hotel corporations operated very cautiously in the early 1990s due to the crashed US hotel and real estate markets and decreasing cash flows, the Marriott Corporation announced that 1993 had the potential of being the biggest year in its corporate history, at least in terms of international expansion.

Edwin Fuller, senior vice-president and managing director of Marriott Lodging International, a division of Marriott Hotels, Resorts and Suites based in Washington DC, announced that since the beginning of 1993 Marriott had:

(a) acquired the 349-room Duna Hotel in Budapest, Hungary, in a joint venture with GiroCredit Bank of Austria;
(b) announced two management contracts for a 270-room resort on the Red Sea at Hurghada, Egypt, and for a 505-room hotel in Kuala Lumpur, Malaysia;
(c) opened two hotels: the 235-room de luxe J.W. Marriott hotel in Dubai and a 260-room hotel in Leeds, England;
(d) begun construction on a 439-room de luxe hotel in Jakarta, Indonesia and on a 333-room hotel in Paris;

(e) signed a contract to manage the National Hotel in Moscow following its refurbishment; and

(f) negotiated contracts to manage a resort in Aruba and a hotel in Puerto Rico, respectively.

Marriott embarked on its accelerated globalization programme in 1990 when Fuller was charged with the responsibility of positioning the company's hotels and resorts in markets outside the US. 'Our goal is to have at least 100 properties outside the US by the year 2002. We intend to reach this objective through management contracts, joint venture agreements or franchise arrangements.' Presently, Marriott has 17 hotels in Britain and nine in Continental Europe.

Marriott's development goals include first establishing a de luxe presence in gateway cities, major commercial centres and established resort destinations as the company's sales and marketing programmes are geared towards customers who use these types of hotels. Once firmly established, Marriott will pursue other opportunities in secondary cities by using products that are smaller and simplified such as the Courtyard brand.

To put Marriott's plans into perspective, it is helpful to consider that the company opened its 100th property in Maui, Hawaii in 1980. At that time, there were just two Marriott hotels outside the US, in Barbados and Amsterdam.

In the intervening years, Marriott concentrated on building an irrefutably strong position in the US and learning how to navigate and adjust its operations to the needs of a variety of national customs and cultures. No upstart company, Marriott was founded in 1927 by the late J. Willard Marriott with quality and value as the guiding principles. The key to understanding the strength and professionalism of the US$8.7 billion Marriott Corporation is an overview of its wide range of business enterprises. Today, Marriott employs more than 200,000 people in 3,800 units including hotels, timesharing operations, restaurants, contract food and beverage facilities, merchandise concessions, child-care facilities and golf courses. The hotel division represents more than half of Marriott's 1992 turnover.

Marriott is primarily a management company, hired by owners to manage their hotel property. However, owners monitor the performance against the final result – the bottom line, because they want to enhance their property value. Marriott has earned, on average, a revenue share premium of 15 per cent, largely due to its state-of-the art Revenue Management System which is similar to the Computerized Reservation Systems perfected by the airlines.

Marriott's MARSHA reservation system maximizes revenues based on effective forecasting. It gives sales offices immediate access to total hotel inventory and its Demand Forecasting System (DFS) effectively manages this inventory. DFS can forecast demand for 90 days, and recommend specific room rental strategies to maximize revenue from customers. According to a survey conducted by the Graycon Group, which was sponsored by 13 of the 20 largest US-based global hotel chains, it costs Marriott's international partners up to US$3.00 less for a Marriott reservation than for any of the other large hotel chains. Marriott's central reservations contribution to hotel occupancy is 29.6 per cent – the highest of the upscale hotel chains.

The Honored Guest Awards (HGA) Program is another Marriott activity that boost the company's performance in that it contributes 30–35 per cent of Marriott's room nights. It rewards loyal Marriott customers with free accommodations at luxury hotels and resorts around the world. During each Marriott stay, members earn 'points' which may be redeemed later for travel awards such as a four-day cruise, a free vacation at a Marriott golf school, or the 200,000-point award that includes a week in any Marriott Hotel or Resort, plus two round-trip coach airline tickets on any of six airlines and a car rental. The Sydney Marriott in Australia, owned by Mirvac Hotels of New South Wales, obtains about 10 per cent of its business through the Honored Guest Award Program. Marriott's HGA programme with its 5 million customer names, has a strong appeal on the company's travel industry partners who have access to the HGA mailing list.

Last but not least, Marriott's above average performance is based in great measure on its ability to attract hardworking, outgoing employees who understand the need to please the customer through Total Quality Management (TQM). TQM is a management process being practised by enlightened companies around the world. It urges employees (associates, as Marriott calls them) to use their own ingenuity to please guests. At workshops, associates learn that they must take care of a customer, regardless of what it takes. The meetings are attended by everyone in the hotel, from the dishwasher to the general manager to discuss how service, systems and physical plant can be improved.

Marriott calls TQM 'Bottom-Up Management'. The front line (of associates) must do what is needed to satisfy the customer, or the hotel has failed its entire mission. Marriott's trainers understand that the same specific actions cannot be taught to all the Marriott hotels' employees worldwide. There has to be an awareness of local cultures and customs so that the Marriott philosophy of associates personally taking care of guests can be properly blended with the folkways of each country.

Marriott is counting on strategic alliances with foreign partners to facilitate its development in overseas markets which are often dramatically different from the US environment. For example, in Indonesia the Marriott Corporation has a joint venture with Duta Anggada, a real estate development company, to develop and finance up to seven hotels on a long-term agreement, including the 439-room Marriott in Jakarta.

In the UK Marriott's partner is Scott's Hotels with whom it has a master franchise and development agreement. Scott's is a 20-year old company that has 15 hotels, all of which were converted to the Marriott name and systems.

STUDY QUESTIONS

1 With reference to Porter's general structural model, discuss hotel industry rivalry.
2 Discuss 'economies of scale' in relation to the hotel industry.
3 Explain 'product differentiation' and show its application in the hotel industry.
4 Do you agree with the contention that large amounts of capital are needed to enter, or expand in, the hotel industry? Explain your answer.
5 List and describe the different categories of 'buyers' in the international hotel industry.
6 With reference to either technology or labour, discuss the bargaining powers of suppliers over hotels.
7 What strategic opportunities for improvement are available to hotel companies?
8 What advantages do you think are gained by Carlson Hospitality Group hotels as a consequence of being part of that large and diversified group of companies.
9 Discuss the way that the Marriott Corporation achieved its globalization goal.
10 What advantages does Marriott gain from its MARSHA reservation system?

Chapter 5

Expanding in a barrier-free Europe*

This chapter starts with an appraisal of the European tourism and economic context, examining trends that are of particular relevance to a business as international as the hotel sector. This examination acts as a backdrop to the Pannell Kerr Forster Associates' EuroCity Survey on the hotel markets in individual European cities which is used to provide a descriptive summary of the current situation in major European cities.

It is clear that the structure of Europe's economy has changed in the past decade and is altering the role of a number of cities, and the business mix of hotels, to a considerable extent. Finally, a review of the prospects for hotel expansion in Europe is presented. The reform of the European hotel industry in the 1990s, in part, is a response to the changes that are occurring as the Single European market takes shape. It also follows, in part, developments in the US hotel industry, in particular with regard to product development, branding, equity investments, and the way in which hotels are financed.

The case at the end of the chapter looks at the global growth of the French-based Groupe ACCOR. The reading gives the views of Michael Hirst, Former Chairman and Chief Executive Officer of Hilton International, on profitability versus risk.

EUROPE AND TOURISM

With less than 3 per cent of the world's land and less than 10 per cent of its population, Europe plays a disproportionately large role in the world's economy. The European Economic Area (EEA) which came into force on 1 January 1994 is one-sixth of the area of the North American Free Trade Area (NAFTA), comprised of Canada, the United States and Mexico, but surpasses it in population, gross domestic product, imports and exports (Table 5.1). The EEA consists of the combined European Free Trade Association (EFTA): Austria, Finland, Norway, Sweden, and Iceland, and the European Economic Community (EEC): Belgium, Denmark, France,

Germany, Greece, Italy, Ireland, Luxembourg, the Netherlands, Portugal, Spain, and the United Kingdom.

While NAFTA is geographically almost five times bigger than the EEA, the latter has 372 million consumers against 360 million in NAFTA. And the EEA, whose members overall send more than half of their exports to each other, will cover US$1.67 trillion in imports and US$1.61 trillion in exports against US$715 billion and US$624 billion respectively, in NAFTA. The EEA is also bigger than the Association of South-East Asian Nations (ASEAN), which groups together Thailand, Singapore, Indonesia, the Philippines, Malaysia and Brunei, and has set a 15-year timetable for implementing its own trading zone, the ASEAN Free Trade Area (AFTA).

Europe also has the world's biggest single tourism market and as such has tremendous importance to the international travel and hotel industry. The growth in international demand for stays in Europe for the period 1975–1984 averaged nearly 6 per cent per year. However, since 1981 there has been a gradual decline in the rate of growth, interrupted by sharp short-term fluctuations, while demand for other regional destinations, especially in the Caribbean, East Asia and the Pacific, has grown more rapidly. The trend data in Tables 5.2 and 5.3 indicate that the growth in international tourism receipts in Europe has surpassed the growth of arrivals by international tourists between 1970 and 1992.

Preliminary statistics from the World Tourism Organization (WTO: 1993) indicate that the arrivals by inbound international tourists to Europe in 1993 totalled 96.5 million or 59.3 per cent of the total world arrivals by international tourists. International tourism receipts for 1992 amounted to US$153.8 billion, or 51.89 per cent of the world total. From a geographic perspective, international tourist demand for Europe tends to be unequally distributed. Western Europe commands the lion's share with about 113 million international tourist arrivals, Southern Europe ranks second with 88 million international tourist arrivals, Eastern and Central

Table 5.1 EEA versus NAFTA

	EEA	*NAFTA*
Population	372 million	360 million
GDP	7,501 billion (US$)	6,770 billion (US$)
Land area	3.6 million sq km	21.3 million sq km
Imports	1,679.5 billion (US$)	715 billion (US$)
Exports	1,615.9 billion (US$)	624 billion (US$)
Exports per person	3,878 (US$)	1,683 (US$)
Trade balance	−63.6 billion (US$)	−91 billion (US$)

Table 5.2 International tourist arrivals in Europe 1970–1992

Years	World (000s)	Change (%)	Europe (000s)	Change (%)	Share of Europe in world total (%)
1970	165,787	–	113,000	–	68.16
1975	222,290	34.08	153,859	36.16	69.22
1980	287,771	29.45	189,830	23.83	65.97
1985	329,636	14.54	214,264	12.87	65.00
1986	340,808	3.38	218,320	1.89	64.06
1987	366,758	7.61	233,623	7.01	63.70
1988	393,865	7.39	243,020	4.02	61.70
1989	427,884	8.63	270,548	11.33	63.23
1990	455,594	6.47	284,178	5.04	62.38
1991	455,100	−0.11	277,904	−2.21	61.06
1992	475,580	4.50	287,529	3.46	60.46

Source: World Tourism Organization (WTO 1993)

Table 5.3 International tourism receipts in Europe 1970–1992

Years	World (US$m)	Change (%)	Europe (US$m)	Change (%)	Share of Europe in world total (%)
1970	17,900	–	11,096	–	61.99
1975	40,702	127.38	26,130	135.49	64.20
1980	102,008	150.62	61,654	135.95	60.44
1985	115,424	13.15	61,181	−0.77	53.01
1986	139,811	21.12	77,028	25.90	55.09
1987	171,577	22.72	96,428	25.19	56.20
1988	197,743	15.25	107,121	11.09	54.17
1989	210,837	6.62	110,021	2.71	52.18
1990	255,074	20.98	139,253	26.57	54.59
1991	261,070	2.35	138,234	−0.73	52.95
1992	278,705	6.75	147,205	6.49	52.82

Source: World Tourism Organization (WTO 1993)

Europe are third with 50 million international tourist arrivals, and Northern Europe is last with about 25 million international tourist arrivals. However, when one considers receipts rather than arrivals, Northern Europe would be ranked third and Eastern and Central Europe ranked last. Germany is Europe's largest tourism market and accounted for 18.33 per cent of its tourist arrivals market share in 1991. The proportionate share of the other nine leading tourism markets for Europe is shown in Table 5.4.

Table 5.4 Leading tourism markets for Europe 1991

Rank	Origin	Tourist arrivals 1991 (000s)	Market share % of total arrivals in Europe	Average annual growth rate (%) 1985–91
1	Germany	50,960	18.33	3.97
2	UK	26,272	9.45	3.41
3	Italy	17,120	6.16	8.59
4	France	15,717	5.65	2.73
5	Netherlands	13,956	5.02	2.55
6	Scandinavia	12,727	4.58	3.44
7	Belgium	12,063	4.34	12.09
8	USA	11,034	3.97	−8.49
9	Switzerland	10,054	3.61	4.42
10	Spain	9,545	3.34	10.92
Sub-total (1–10)		179,448	64.57	3.52
Total Europe		277,904	100.00	10.36

Source: World Tourism Organization (WTO 1993)

In the early 1990s, the world looked towards Europe as 'the market of the future'. After all, the former Eastern Bloc nations were opening their borders to worldwide business, and Europe was getting prepared to become a single market. The formation of the Single Market called for open trade, a consistent currency exchange rate, and a tight fiscal policy that required low levels of inflation, government deficits and debt. The primary objective of the Single Market, comprised of 12 member states, is to create a trading area of over 360 million potential customers characterized by the freedom of movement for people, goods, services, and capital. This development is especially significant for the tourism industry which depends for its prosperity on the free movement of people and capital. It will stimulate the European economy by increasing competition and reducing cost and prices.

If the Single Market has contributed to tourism expansion it has been very limited to date. The preliminary WTO data for 1993 indicate that European tourism resembles a mixed picture with generally slow expansion in the major mature destinations. There are a number of factors that have influenced the growth of travel and tourism demand of late. Perhaps the most important development has been the uncertainties of societal change in Europe. For example, the high rate of unemployment in Western Europe (especially in France and the United Kingdom), and the high cost of Germany's reunification (estimated at nearly US$100 billion per year), are acting as impediments on travel demand.

Among other envisaged changes and developments, which will also influence the growth and patterns of travel demand in Europe are:

(a) The increase in Europe's senior population. In 1990, seniors represented 20 per cent of the European travel market. The availability of leisure time and disposable income, especially amongst Europe's senior consumers has led to a 10 per cent increase in travel between 1988 and 1991 and is presently approaching 200 million trips annually (Clech 1993: 135).

(b) Newly emerging travel markets. Especially in Europe's southern countries, the propensity to travel is likely to increase as a consequence of economic growth and a more pronounced European orientation of their populations in terms of lifestyles.

(c) The combined effect of Single Market measures, including fiscal, regulatory harmonization and air travel liberalization. These measures will increase air travel and tourism generally in Europe.

(d) The mounting public concern over growing threats to the environment. Europeans are increasingly interested in buying products and holidays from companies that are perceived to manage limited resources in a sustainable manner.

(e) The European Monetary System, through the Exchange Rate Mechanism (ERM), will help limit the volatility in exchange rate patterns, but nevertheless variations in EC currencies can be expected to influence tourist flows between countries with strong and weak currencies.

(f) The broadening of intra-regional travel later this decade, predominantly by Western European travellers visiting Eastern European countries once the infrastructure in these countries has improved.

The following trends appear to be the most salient in influencing the supply side of Europe's tourism industry during the 1990s:

(a) Large corporations are increasingly orienting their strategic conduct towards greater internationalization, cooperation and concentration. Due to a growing number of international companies entering domestic markets, the competition in these markets is anticipated to heat up and cause smaller companies to become more specialized by catering to niche markets.

(b) International travel is being facilitated by the shrinking distance–time matrix because of the availability of high-speed trains connecting densely populated centres throughout Europe and the abandonment of border formalities.

(c) The congestion of transportation infrastructure – especially, airport, traffic control systems, and highways – will place great pressure on existing facilities, and is expected to limit the expansion of travel and tourism potential into the twenty-first century.

(d) The construction of the requisite tourism infrastructure in Eastern European countries, which will cause the overall tourism supply to expand (PBC 1990).

In summary, the development of tourism in Europe in the 1990s will depend on the evolution of a series of variables. However, the expansion of tourism in Europe is inextricably intertwined with and dependent on the growth of gross domestic product (GDP). The expansion of GDP hinges on the (un)employment rate of domestic economies. Four countries, Germany, France, the UK, and Italy account for nearly 70 per cent of Europe's GDP and 60 per cent of Europe's population. The restructuring of industry in Europe's 'big four', has led to a scenario that has been referred to as 'long-term' unemployment (Walsh 1994). In the first quarter of 1994 the following unemployment rates were recorded for Italy (11.7 per cent), France (12 per cent), Germany (8.1 per cent in the west and 15.4 per cent in the east), and the UK (9 per cent) (Walsh 1994).

However, it should be noted that the unemployment data present averages and that Europe is comprised of a mixed picture with places that range from more to less prosperous. The wide range in prosperity amongst places is confirmed by the following trend analysis of European cities.

HOTEL TRENDS IN MAJOR EUROPEAN CITIES

The following section is based on Pannell Kerr Forster Associates' EuroCity Survey report, a questionnaire-led survey of the quality hotel market in 25 major European cities. Hotels in Europe's major cities performed poorly in 1991 due, for the most part, to the Gulf War. Though hoteliers hoped for improved results in 1992 the EuroCity Survey findings indicate that only around half of the cities managed to record a higher occupancy in 1992 than in 1991. Whilst some cities benefited from the return of tourists during 1992, notably Athens and Istanbul, other cities were prey to a deteriorating national and international economic climate, resulting in a decline in demand for hotel accommodation. Though the performance across the cities analysed varied, the average occupancy for the overall sample was 63.6 per cent – marginally above 1991 levels.

In absolute terms, there was a 13.2 per cent increase in the number of room nights from the USA and Canada, representing 17.2 per cent of total room nights. This increase could well have been greater had it not been for the presidential elections held in November 1992. This event deterred many Americans from travelling abroad. An upsurge in demand from Japan and the Middle East was also experienced, although together these countries only represented 9.6 per cent of total room nights. European travellers generated 62.5 per cent of the room nights sold in 1992 which made the European travel market the most significant source of demand for hoteliers.

Of the 25 cities analysed, 15 recorded a daily rooms revenue yield below 1991 levels when expressed in Deutschmarks. The overall sample recorded a daily revenue yield of Deutschmarks (DM) 146.53, some 3 per cent below the 1991 level. The decrease in rooms yield was due to an erosion in the average daily room rate and a fall in rooms occupancy. Hotels in the Paris sample achieved the highest rooms revenue yield at DM378.78. The most dramatic decline in rooms revenue yield was experienced by hotels in the Helsinki sample, which decreased 23.3 per cent.

Increasing price competition in many markets was reflected in the shift away from the higher rated segments. Compared to 1991, there was a 15.1 per cent drop in the number of rooms sold at full rate for the total sample. Incentive travel made a comeback in 1992 and rose 15.7 per cent in absolute terms in comparison with the previous year. In response to pressure on the average rate, there was a general realignment of tariffs to reflect market conditions. Although average discounting fell by 2.6 per cent, net tariffs declined by around 7.3 per cent when expressed in Deutschmarks.

With the general decline in rooms sales performance thus affecting profitability, Europe's hoteliers will need to look towards improved cost controls in order to optimize profitability. This has been a priority for many hoteliers, as is illustrated by the 4.3 per cent decline in the number of staff employed in the hotels that were surveyed in 1992 compared to the previous year.

OVERVIEW OF EUROPEAN CITIES

The structure of Europe's economy has changed significantly in the last two decades and with it the economic importance of European cities. European cities that depend on heavy industry and manufacturing are, by and large, in decline because these centres are unable to compete with the newly industrializing countries and their abundant cheap labour. Those cities which have been able to develop their economy by attracting high technology-based industries, often in combination with expansion in the financial service and other service sectors, have experienced real growth.

The capacity of hotels and similar establishments in Europe has risen from 4.7 million rooms in 1987 to 5.1 million rooms in 1991, an 8.5 per cent increase according to WTO data. Over the 1986–1991 period, the regional distribution of capacity of hotels and similar establishments re-mained fairly stable. Perhaps with the exception of East/Central Europe where the number of rooms declined, and Southern Europe where the number of rooms showed a slight increase over the same period (Table 5.5).

As Goodall (1989: 78) has indicated the forms of tourist accommodation in Europe can be placed in different categories ranging from commercial to non-commercial, and from serviced to self-catering. Facilities that fall outside the hotel category are beginning to impact on hotels due to the

Table 5.5 Trends in the capacity of hotels and similar establishments in Europe – 1986–1991

Sub-regions	1987	1988	1989	1990	1991
Total Europe	4,774,696	4,954,511	5,046,584	4,986,629	5,057,598
(%)	100%	100%	100%	100%	100%
East/Central	392,239	414,123	427,439	310,544	299,779
(%)	8.21%	8.36%	8.47%	6.23%	5.93%
Northern	725,680	807,659	810,440	819,149	826,006
(%)	15.20%	16.30%	16.06%	16.43%	16.33%
Southern	1,997,183	2,049,452	2,093,839	2,139,782	2,192,982
(%)	41.83%	41.37%	41.49%	42.91%	43.36%
Western	1,626,217	1,648,295	1,680,801	1,685,764	1,710,316
(%)	34.06%	33.27%	33.30%	33.80%	33.82%
Israel	33,377	34,982	34,065	31,390	28,515
(%)	0.70%	0.70%	0.68%	0.63%	0.56%

Source: World Tourism Organization (WTO 1993)

trend amongst European consumers towards the substitution of self-catering tourist accommodations for commercial hotel accommodation.

The following overview of the hotel industry in selected major cities of Europe presents the findings of Pannell Kerr Forster Associates' EuroCity Survey 1993; the data should be viewed with caution as in some cases sample sizes are small and may not be representative of the situation in the city as a whole. In this presentation of the survey results, cities are listed by country and each country is grouped into one of four geographical sectors as follows: Western Europe, Scandinavia, Eastern Europe, and Southern Europe. The results for Western Europe dominate the presentation, which is inevitable as most hotel activity occurs where there is the highest blend of domestic population and industrial and economic activity.

WESTERN EUROPE

Western Europe – the United Kingdom

London

After the slump in tourist visitation during 1991, London experienced a marked improvement in visitor numbers. The number of overseas visitors increased by just over 10 per cent to 10 million, whilst domestic visitation remained static at 7 million. Visitors from North America to the UK showed an upturn of around 18 per cent over 1991. The North American market remains a key source of demand for quality hotels in London, representing 27.6 per cent of guests. Visitors from the European continent represent 22.9 per cent of total guests. A new initiative has been launched to revitalize London's tourism appeal. London Forum, funded by both the public and the private sector, is aiming to attract the affluent first-time visitor to London, both from the USA and the UK. Although hoteliers are not likely to benefit from this promotion in 1993, on a longer term basis increased visitation to London is expected.

The 39 properties that responded to the survey and comprise its sample represent 77 per cent of the rooms of the 51 quality hotels which operate a total of 12,764 rooms. The hotels in the sample registered an average room occupancy of 67.7 per cent in 1992, up from 64.2 per cent in 1991. Average room rates decreased to £102.76 from £106.05 in 1991.

Birmingham

Birmingham has been undergoing a period of major change as the city moves away from its traditional industrial base towards a new infrastructure and economy. Initiatives, taken by both the public and private sector, have enjoyed a great deal of success. The present recession, however, has slowed the transformation and it may be some time before the metamorphosis is complete. In 1992 when UK hoteliers continued to trade under difficult circumstances, hoteliers in Birmingham's quality hotels, representing 1,215 rooms, fared relatively well compared to 1991. Room occupancy averaged 52.5 per cent – up 1.7 per cent over 1991 – and the average rate increased by 1.7 per cent to £52.26. The growing diversity of the local economy and Birmingham's central location have helped in generating hotel demand. One of the problems Birmingham has to overcome is its low profile as a tourist destination, thus constraining weekend demand for accommodation. The potential increase in quality hotel supply, notably hotel developments in Brindley Place, Heartlands and Great Charles Street, would add around 700 new rooms and present a threat in the medium term to established hoteliers.

Edinburgh

Whilst Edinburgh did not escape the recent economic recession, its effects have not been as pronounced as in the south-east of England. The opening of the Edinburgh International Congress Centre (EICC) in the summer of 1995 will offer state-of-the art meeting and exhibition space. Linked with the proposed EICC is the development of adjacent land for commercial use. Standard Life has already committed itself to 300,000 square metres of space and other companies are expected to follow once economic conditions improve. These developments are likely to generate additional need for hotel development. It is anticipated that the EICC will generate demand for accommodation in the quieter months for Edinburgh, thus reducing the effects of peaks and troughs in demand. ACCOR have submitted proposals for the development of three hotels: Ibis, Novotel and Sofitel on an adjacent site.

The quality hotel supply in Edinburgh is comprised of nine hotels with a total of 1,583 rooms. Seven hotels participated in the sample, representing 73 per cent of the city's total quality hotel supply. The sample of hotels in Edinburgh recorded 67.2 per cent occupancy, broadly unchanged from the previous year.

Manchester

When the UK economy makes a full recovery, Manchester will be well positioned to take advantage of an upturn in commercial activity and expand its base of office floor space. Very little vacant space exists at the present time. New developments in Manchester include the opening of the Metrolink, the cross city tramway, and the opening in 1993 of the second terminal at Manchester Airport, which expanded its maximum capacity to 18 million passengers a year. The Airport has turned Manchester into a gateway and enhanced the city's profile internationally.

The four properties that responded to the survey represent 73 per cent of Manchester's six quality hotels, which combined operate a total of 1,506 rooms. The hotels in the sample registered an average room occupancy of 58.9 per cent in 1992, up from 57.9 per cent in 1991. Average room rates decreased to £49.37 from £52.19 in 1991.

Western Europe – Germany

Berlin

Though the German government seat is still in Bonn, Berlin has been attracting the attention of major international hotel chains. In 1993, there were 12 hotels with a total of 4,387 rooms that form Berlin's quality accommodation supply. But only nine hotels were analysed in the sample. Several hotels in former East Berlin that were previously operated by InterHotels AG are presently operated by national and international hotel chains. For example, Maritim Hotels currently lease the Grand Hotel and the Metropol, whilst the operation of the 1,006-room StadtBerlin has been taken over by Inter-Continental hotels under the Forum brand-name. Room occupancy levels declined in 1992 by 12.8 percentage points to 61.7 per cent. The decline reflects the impact of the costs of unification, estimated at around DM150 million a year for the next ten years. These costs, combined with the recession, have slowed the unification process and Germany remains a divided country in terms of 'haves and have nots'. The travel market became increasingly price sensitive during 1992 and the sample hotels experienced a 32 per cent reduction in full rate business. Though 1992 saw a small increase in average achieved room rate, the substantial fall off in demand resulted in an overall decline in rooms yield of over 13 per cent. Berlin's market is predominantly domestic in nature; German visitors and European visitors represent 59 per cent and 21 per cent of the city's total hotel demand.

Although the current state of the economy and the cost of re-unification are limiting factors to rapid development, prospects for Berlin in the long-term are positive. There continues to be a high level of interest on behalf of hotel companies to establish a presence in Berlin. As part of its development of the Potsdamer Platz, Sony is considering the redevelopment of the former Esplanade Hotel. There are also plans to redevelop the former Adlon Hotel and the Unter den Linden Hotel, and Four Seasons has scheduled to open a 212-room hotel in 1996.

Frankfurt

As one of the leading financial and banking centres of Europe, Frankfurt continues to attract a high level of international visitation and has, to date, been less impacted by the recession than other cities in Germany. Whilst no decision has been reached on the establishment and location of the Eurofed Bank, Frankfurt, as the headquarters of the highly influential Bundesbank, is likely to play a pivotal role in the movement towards economic and monetary union in the EC. This should continue to underpin the strength of commercial demand in the city. Frankfurt Airport, already one of Europe's leading hub airports, will expand. The new passenger terminal was scheduled to open in October 1994 and a new InterCity Express (ICE) fast train is scheduled to commence service at the terminal in 1997. The Messe will develop a purpose built congress centre adjacent to its existing fairground halls. The main hall of the congress centre will have capacity for 2,300 people. The centre will be a multi-component of a development housing a 523-room hotel and an office block of some 20,000 square metres.

The quality hotel supply in Frankfurt is comprised of eleven hotels with a total of 4,795 rooms. Nine hotels participated in the sample, representing 84 per cent of the city's total quality hotel supply. During 1992, Frankfurt's sample hotels recorded 67.2 per cent occupancy, a decline of 1.8 per cent. The average room rate dropped from DM215.49 in 1991 to DM213.77 in 1992. Overall the hotels located in the vicinity of the airport outperformed those located in the city centre.

Munich

Munich continues to prosper, in spite of uncertainty regarding the present state of the German economy. Fears had been expressed that Munich's location might be such that it would not benefit from the surge of investment that was expected to take place in the five new federal states in eastern Germany. In reality, Munich has not experienced any significant adverse effects. Rather, new opportunities have arisen to strengthen economic links with Austria and the Czech and Slovak Republics. The problem presently facing Munich is the lack of space for commercial and residential development. As a result, there has been a strong trend for new companies to locate in the suburbs of the city. The development of the airport in Erding has resulted in the highest rate of commercial development occurring in the north of the city. As a result there are four hotels in the area around the new airport.

The quality hotel supply in Munich is comprised of 17 hotels with a total of 4,555 rooms. Of these the 352-room Maritim hotel opened in 1992 and was therefore not included in the survey. Ten hotels participated in the survey, representing 73 per cent of the city's total quality hotel supply. In 1992, Munich's hotels in the sample recorded 70.4 per cent occupancy, up from 66.6 per cent in 1991. The average room rate dropped from DM200.04 in 1991 to DM197.07 in 1992.

Western Europe – France

Paris

Paris is one of the world's major tourist destinations. The completion of the Channel Tunnel will further promote tourism to Paris. The number of tourist arrivals in 1991 was impacted by the Gulf crisis, although there was evidence of foreign tourists returning to the city during the summer of 1992. Paris hotels benefit from the city's excellent transportation network. The two TGV (*train à grande vitesse*) routes operating from Paris to Marseilles, Grenoble and Montpellier, and Tours, Rennes and Nantes, respectively, were linked in early 1992 by an interconnecting station at Massy, to the south of Paris. This station, along with the new TGV stations planned at Roissy and La Defense, will provide direct links between Paris and the Channel Tunnel, the Belgian border and the rest of France.

The Palais des Congres is currently extending its facilities, including the addition of a new amphitheatre. The construction of an International Conference Centre on Quai Branly, close to the Eiffel Tower, is scheduled for completion in 1995. This development is expected to increase demand for hotel accommodation in the city. Tourism levels are growing again after the 1991 slump and Paris continues to be the most popular venue for international conventions in Western Europe. Paris is also the leading venue for international fairs and trade shows. Several major hotels opened in Paris in 1992 – for example, the 400-room Hyatt Regency near the Charles de Gaulle Airport and the 240-room Quality Hotel. Meanwhile, the Marriott Corporation is planning to open a 400-room hotel to the south-east of the city at Bercy, while Four Seasons plans a 205-room property at Porte Maillot.

Western Europe – Italy

Milan

Milan, located at the heart of one of the most highly industrialized areas in Italy, has potential to further develop its economic and tourism base in the longer term. In the short term, however, the city's potential is somewhat less certain, primarily on account of the recent scandals which have affected a number of prominent civic leaders in both public and private organizations. At present, supply of office space is anticipated to exceed demand. Milan's fairgrounds are currently operating at peak periods. There are plans to move the main fairground to the outskirts of the city and three sites are under consideration, the most popular being Pero, north-west of the city centre.

The 98-room Four Seasons Hotel opened in March 1993 and the 200-room Ramada Hotel opened in the autumn of 1993. This increase in quality accommodation, combined with the poor political and economic situation in the country, is likely to have a detrimental effect on the overall performance of quality hotels.

The nine properties that responded to the survey and comprise its sample represent 92 per cent of the rooms of the 11 quality hotels which operate a total of 2,648 rooms (not including the Four Seasons Hotel and Ramada Hotel which both opened in 1993 and therefore could not be included in the survey). The hotels in the sample registered an average room occupancy of 51.7 per cent in 1992, down from 58.3 per cent in 1991. Average room rates decreased to Lit 221,981, from Lit 223,087 in 1991.

Rome

Rome is one of the major tourist destinations in Europe, including historical attractions, architecture, entertainment, shopping facilities, and the Vatican which attracts both individual visitors and group tours. As the capital city of Italy, Rome is also a major commercial centre attracting both domestic and international business visitors. Rome has become cheaper to North American visitors because of the devaluation of the lira, and hotels are expecting to profit accordingly. The importance of Rome as a tourist and business destination, and the restriction on increasing hotel supply, at least in central Rome, imply good future prospects for the quality hotels. However, it has to be recognized that the impact of both internal and external political events, together with exchange rate movements, results in fluctuations in hotel performance. The immediate future is somewhat dependent on how quickly the politicians resolve the present crisis and tackle the underlying problems of the economy.

Western Europe – the Netherlands

Amsterdam

Amsterdam is the largest city of the Netherlands and the country's major commercial centre. Though The Hague is the capital of the Netherlands and Rotterdam a major port and industrial centre, Amsterdam, because of its tourist appeal, has attracted the greatest interest from hotel developers.

Over recent years, the first-class hotel sector in Amsterdam experienced a significant demand growth as a result of increases in both commercial and tourist activity. However, in 1991 the market declined both in terms of annual room occupancy and (in real terms) average room rate. This decline in performance resulted from a simultaneous fall in demand, due in 1992 to the slow down of the Dutch economy with GDP growing by only 1.7 per cent, compared to 2 per cent in 1991, and an increase in the supply of quality hotels such as the 230-room Jolly Carlton Hotel, the 247-room SAS Royal Hotel, and the 166-room Hotel Grand Amsterdam. This expanded the supply in Amsterdam's quality hotels in 1992 to 4,393 rooms. The recovery of hotel occupancy in 1992 was primarily due to the staging of one-off events such as the Aids congress in July 1992 and the Floriade flower festival which attracted a substantial number of holiday-makers to Amsterdam.

Western Europe – Belgium

Brussels

Brussels is often referred to as Europe's capital. The city's economic base has shifted from an emphasis on industry to, at present, the service sector. The presence of the European Commission, and more than 1,000 headquarters offices of international associations and multinational companies in Brussels, creates a constant stream of commercial visitation to the city. Though hotels in Brussels have not escaped the influences of recession currently impacting other European cities, its effects have been cushioned by the large number of visitors associated with the European Commission. Presently the number of rooms operated by 25 quality hotels amounts to

5,378. The Brussels sample comprised 16 hotels. In recent years Brussels has experienced a great deal of hotel development. In 1993 two quality hotels opened: the 269-room Conrad Hotel and a 100-room hotel operated by the Finnish chain Arctia. In 1994, the Meridien group opened a hotel at the Carrefour de l'Europe.

The presence of the EC in Brussels continues to have an overwhelming impact on the nationality of guests at sampled hotels. European nationals accounted for 65 per cent of rooms demand in 1992, compared to 61.1 per cent in 1991. The additions to Brussels' room supply has impacted hotel performance. Room occupancy in 1992 was 64.6 per cent compared to 65.6 per cent the previous year. The average room rate in 1992 was BFr 3,810 down from BFr 3,915 in 1991. However, the importance of Brussels as the administrative capital of the EC, and the increasing number of countries set to join the Community will almost certainly bring about an increase in the number of visitors to the city.

Western Europe – Switzerland

Geneva

Geneva owes its cosmopolitan character to the presence of about 100 international organizations that are represented in the city. The presence of so many international organizations has led to Geneva being perceived as a large city (it is often referred to along with London and Paris), when in truth it is very small by comparison. Geneva is also an important financial centre of international standing; however, it is anticipated that the city is in danger of losing its importance on the international scene because of Switzerland's decision not to enter the European Community. This will have a detrimental effect on Geneva with major international conferences going to other cities. Swissair has moved more flights from Geneva to Zurich and this will have a negative impact on Geneva's hotels. The ten properties that responded to the survey sample represent 80 per cent of the rooms of the 13 quality hotels which operate a total of 2,635 rooms. These properties registered an average room occupancy of 54.5 per cent in 1992, from 57.5 in 1991. Average room rates fell from SFr 283 in 1991 to SFr 280 in 1992, a decline of 5.1 per cent in real terms. The recent increases in supply brought about by the opening of the Holiday Inn Plaza in 1989 and the Movenpick Radisson in 1990 have still not been absorbed. Geneva is oversupplied in terms of quality accommodation, but it continues to achieve the second highest average room rate amongst the 25 cities surveyed.

Zurich

Zurich remains one of the world's leading financial centres, despite reforms to the laws governing share structures and banking secrecy. However, it is widely feared that Switzerland's decision not to enter the European Community is having a detrimental effect on the capital markets in Zurich. Brokers are warning that a quick decision is needed to bring Switzerland in line with the rest of Europe and to maintain Zurich's importance at a time of intense competition from Frankfurt and London. Historically, the well-established 'traditional' hotels continue to perform well on account of their reputation and their location in the city centre. Over the last two decades, new hotels have been developed in less prestigious locations on the periphery of the city, away from the important banking and finance districts. Due to a lack of office space and high real estate prices in the city centre, much of the new commercial development is taking place in the peripheral area of Zurich.

Western Europe – Austria

Vienna

In Vienna the market for hotel accommodation has been traditionally reliant upon the North American market. This left Vienna vulnerable to changes in the exchange rates, terrorist threats and the price of airfares. However, the opening up of Central and Eastern Europe has diminished this dependence, and has resulted in increased demand from many other sources. In particular the development of a 'tourism triangle' between Prague, Budapest and Vienna has been of significant benefit to the hotel industry. Much of this new tourism activity is at the budget end of Vienna's hotel market and has therefore had a limited impact on the performance of the quality hotels. However, Vienna's increasing importance as the banking and investment centre for Eastern Europe is increasing, and is likely to result in more international visitation in the full rate and corporate discount segment.

The political changes throughout Eastern Europe in the past few years have shifted Vienna, and indeed all of Austria, back towards the centre of Europe. It is anticipated that Vienna will develop as a business hub for Eastern Europe. Presently, over US$700 million has already been committed to the expansion of Shwechat international airport.

SCANDINAVIA

Scandinavia – Finland

Helsinki

In recent years commercial demand has become of increasing importance to the Helsinki hotel market. The Helsinki City Tourist Office estimates that 68 per cent of guests at accommodation establishments in Helsinki in 1992 were in the city for business purposes compared to 48 per cent in 1985. In recent years the ferries, which are in effect floating hotels, operating between Sweden and Finland have begun to compete in the meetings and conference market. Where previously it was often necessary to overnight in Helsinki before connecting with a flight to the Commonwealth of Independent States, the improvement in air links from many European cities to destinations in the former Soviet Union has made this less necessary. The additions of the hotel room supply in 1991 and 1992 have compounded the difficulties for the quality hotels in Helsinki.

The quality hotel supply in Helsinki is comprised of nine hotels. But the 462-room Grand Marina hotel opened in February 1992 and was not included in the survey, which therefore concerned eight hotels with a total of 2,390 rooms. Helsinki's sample hotels occupancy plummeted from 55.1 per cent in 1991 to 51.0 per cent in 1992, a decline of 4.1 percentage points. The average room rate dropped to Fmk469.88 in 1992 from Fmk496.79 in 1991. Market conditions in the short term will be difficult. But the recent devaluation of the Finnish markka will offer Finland the opportunity to promote itself as a more competitive tourist and conference destination. In the longer term the opening up of the Baltic States, particularly Estonia, is likely to create a new source of business for Helsinki's hotels.

Scandinavia – Norway

Oslo

The recent economic difficulties and additions to rooms supply resulted in a year of competitive trading for hoteliers in Oslo. Partly due to the high level of indirect taxes, Oslo is often perceived as an expensive destination, and this has reduced the city's ability to attract individual and group leisure travellers, resulting in a high dependency on domestic demand. However, steps have been taken to counteract this situation and in January 1993 Oslo Promotions commenced operations. This organization combines the role of tourist board, by selling its services to the city council, with that of marketing the city abroad. In addition it is also responsible for attracting international congresses to the city, and is reported to have secured a number of future events. The Spectrum Centre, which opened at the end of 1989, is a multi-purpose venue with the capacity to accommodate over 8,000 delegates for congresses, exhibitions, sporting events and trade fairs. Norway hosted the winter Olympics in 1994, and the Olympics committee arranged for seven passenger ships to be docked in Oslo harbour for the duration of the Games to cope with accommodation demand.

Scandinavia – Sweden

Stockholm

Stockholm's current recession, forecast to continue until the mid-1990s, is suppressing domestic demand for quality hotels. The recent airline de-regulation in Sweden has resulted in an increase in the number of airlines operating in Sweden. Due to the increased level of competition among the airlines, fare prices have been reduced between 10 and 40 per cent. The reduction in airfares, together with the recent devaluation of the Swedish krona, has reduced the cost of visiting Sweden by as much as 20 per cent. The Swedish Tourist Board ceased operation at the end of 1992 and has been replaced by One Stop Sweden.

The potential to promote Stockholm as an international conference venue, together with its relatively reduced cost as a tourist destination, provides the only note of optimism for hoteliers in the city at the present time.

EASTERN EUROPE

Eastern Europe – Hungary

Budapest

In Budapest the first results in the privatization process by the Hungarian State Property Agency (SPA) occurred in December 1992, with the partial privatization of the Danubius Hotel and Spa Company which operates the Hilton, Ramada, Gellert and Thermal Hotels. During 1993 the Duna Intercontinental Hotel was sold to Marriott Hotels and Resorts. This was the second hotel to be managed directly by an international hotel manage-ment company in the city, the first being the Kempinski which opened in 1992. Further hotel sales are expected. ACCOR secured a stake in the Pannonia Hotel and Catering Company, which manages 14 hotels in Budapest including the Atrium Hyatt, Penta and Novotel hotels. The 13 quality hotels in the survey sample operate a total of 4,621 rooms. These properties registered an average room occupancy of 62.5 per cent in 1992, a decline of 1.9 per cent compared to 1991. Average room rates increased by 6.2 per cent, to US$64.40 in 1992 from US$62.50 in 1991. Budapest, being an attractive city (it is often referred to as the Paris of central Europe), should continue to attract large numbers of tourists and overseas business visitors. A boost in international visitation is anticipated in 1996 when Budapest is scheduled to host the World Exposition (EXPO).

Eastern Europe – Czech Republic

Prague

In Prague there has been considerable interest in both the renovation of existing hotels and the development of new hotels since the introduction of joint venture legislation. However, many hotel projects are likely to remain uncertain until the process of restitution is complete.

Prague is presently the capital of the newly created Czech Republic and its future will be influenced by developments in the country. Following the elections in 1992, the Czech Republic has a democratic conservative coalition while in Slovakia the Movements for a Democratic Slovakia won the majority vote. Although the task of building a successful market economy is great, it is widely felt that the Czech Republic will achieve this sooner than Slovakia. Prague, being the capital, is the main beneficiary of investment interest from abroad and increased commercial activity.

Eastern Europe – Poland

Warsaw

In Warsaw a number of international hotel companies are investigating new development opportunities. However, it appears that the city could sustain any substantial supply increases at this time. Poland was the first East European country to shake off the constraints of communism and embark on tough economic reforms. The growth potential and perceived stability of Poland has not gone unnoticed, with the climate for private investment expected to improve. To date, the largest single project is Fiat's US$2 billion commitment to manufacture small cars in Poland. This project has led to investments by some of Fiat's traditional suppliers.

SOUTHERN EUROPE

Southern Europe – Greece

Athens

In Athens there are six hotels which, when combined, number 1,877 rooms and comprise the city's quality hotel supply. Occupancy levels at the sample hotels increased to 70.1 per cent in 1992. Revenue per available room or the rooms yield, increased by 43 per cent in 1992 compared to the previous year. The growth in rooms yield was underpinned by the return to more normal levels of tourist visitation, after the downturn following the Gulf War.

The 1992 opening of the Athens concert hall, which can be used for both cultural events and conferences, has improved the city's attractiveness as a conference centre. A metro system is under construction, partly in response to Athen's traffic and pollution problems. The Greek government has recently launched a multi-million dollar urban renewal plan to transform the city centre into an 'archaeological park'.

The government plans to build a purpose-built convention centre and a new airport at Sparta, just outside of the city. Athens' requisite features of a leading tourist destination and the centre of Greece's commercial activity seem to assure the local hotel industry of the prospect of good occupancy levels.

Southern Europe – Turkey

Istanbul

There are various initiatives under way to promote Istanbul as a conference and tourist destination. Istanbul's hoteliers are working with the tourism ministry to promote the city as a leisure destination. The 'Irresistanbul' campaign is being promoted throughout Europe. Furthermore, hoteliers are supporting the mayor in his efforts to secure funding to convert a sports centre into a congress centre for 5,000 delegates. In 1992 the 627-room Conrad Hotel and the 305-room Movenpick Hotel opened. In 1993 the 400-room Penta Hotel and the 360-room Hyatt Regency opened. The recent hotel additions have made the Istanbul market more competitive but allows the city to attract more conference and incentive business.

The seven properties that responded to the survey sample represent 81 per cent of the rooms of the 12 quality hotels which operate a total of 4,188 rooms. These properties registered an average room occupancy of 62.7 per cent in 1992, up from 49.6 per cent in 1991. Average room rates increased to US$66.28 from US$52.21 in 1991.

Southern Europe – Portugal

Lisbon

Lisbon experienced a considerable increase in its hotel room supply in 1992. Though not all of the new additions are in direct competition with the quality hotels, they do, however, offer a lower price alternative to the group and tour market. Portugal experienced lower economic growth in 1992 compared to 1991 but is still the fastest growing European economy. The Portuguese government has been successful in attracting foreign investment to the country, particularly in and around Lisbon. Portugal has also been the recipient of European Community funds which are available to assist the EC's poorer states. This influx of funds is assisting in a more rapid modernization of the economy, closing the gap with other European countries.

There are 13 hotels in Lisbon that collectively form the city's quality hotel supply. The Pullman and Hotel Da Lapa opened in 1992 and were not included in the survey, which included responses from nine of the remaining hotels, representing 83 per cent of the quality room supply. These properties registered an average room occupancy of 59.1 per cent in 1992, down from 65.3 per cent in 1991. Average room rates increased to ESC15.983 from ESC13.789 in 1991.

Southern Europe – Spain

Madrid

With the growing strength of the peseta against other leading currencies, Spain in general, and Madrid in particular, became a more expensive destination for tourists during the 1980s. The recent devaluation should not only help tourism but also increase the competitiveness of Spanish industry in general. The recovery in occupancy in 1992, following the low levels attained in 1991, did not occur to the extent that had been hoped for and was widely predicted. Tariff levels for Madrid's quality hotels increased by just over 5 per cent over 1991. The city's five-star de luxe hotels in particular have published tariffs which rank among the most expensive in Europe. With these hotels continuing to achieve lower occupancy levels than the market as a whole, they are tending to offer more competitive rates in order to bolster occupancy. The price gap between the luxury hotels and the remaining quality hotels continues to erode.

The 11 properties that responded to the survey and comprise its sample represent 87 per cent of the rooms of the 14 quality hotels which operate a total of 4,677 rooms. The hotels in the sample registered an average room occupancy of 60.1 per cent in 1992, up from 57.8 per cent in 1991. Average room rates increased to 18,365 pesetas, a 7.8 per cent increase on 1991.

ENTRY AND EXPANSION STRATEGIES

The 1960s and 1970s saw a period of rapid expansion in Europe, with hotels opening in London, Paris, Amsterdam and most other major European business destinations. Europe rapidly became the hub of activity. American hotel chains, such as Holiday Inns, Hilton International, Inter-Continental, and Sheraton were able to apply their franchising and management contract system with hardly any opposition from local hoteliers. For example, Sheraton's European operations commenced under the leadership of John Kapioltas in 1968, who built the corporation's scope to expand not only across Europe but throughout the Middle East and Africa as well.

The hotel chain phenomenon, which originated in the USA, had been instrumental in the gradual concentration and internationalization of the hotel industry in America long before these trends became noticeable in Europe. The expansion of American hotel corporations overseas has had a chain reaction, forcing market reforms to varying degrees in Europe's hotel industry. In particular, the following key shifts characterized the evolution of the international hotel industry during the 1980s (Litteljohn and Beattie 1991).

First, the control over hotel companies, such as Holiday Inns, Hilton International, Inter-Continental, passed from American to British, and in the case of Inter-Continental to Japanese/Scandinavian ownership. Second, the emergence of the acquisition of hotel chains, for example, the take-over of Holiday Inns by Bass breweries and of Hilton International by Ladbroke. The acquisition of hotel chains was primarily motivated by companies that wished to diversify their portfolio in a bid, for instance in the case of Bass, to compensate for falling beer sales. Mergers and acquisitions became a means to hotel expansion and a supplement to 'organic growth' – that is, the addition of the number of units in the network that had characterized hotel chain development until the 1980s. One of the consequences of the European and Asian ownership of major hotel corporations resulted in a dilution of the hegemony of American hotel corporations; another is the greater concentration of hotel room stock in the United Kingdom. Third, there was a pronounced shift from a single brand strategy to a multi-tier brand strategy in Europe's hotel industry.

The latter development in particular will have major consequences for hotels in Europe, because branding is a central feature in making possible the strong expansion (Barge 1993: 123). A hotel brand can be defined by three imperatives necessary to establish and maintain its inte- grity by a 'standard set of internal and external specifications', performed 'consistently to appeal to selected target markets' (Slattery 1991: 23–24).

The Paris-based ACCOR group has been the leader in the development of multi-tier brands, essentially since its predecessor Novotel SIE acquired Jacques Borel International in 1983. Between 1983 to 1990, ACCOR began to broaden its portfolio of hotel brands. At present, its brand portfolio ranges from upscale hotels, under the Sofitel and Pullman brands respectively. These upscale, mid-size hotels primarily cater to the business clientele by providing high comfort and service in refined settings. The Novotel brand represents a 'three-star' hotel product catering to a clientele of business and leisure travellers. The Mercure–Altea brands offer a quality, service and comfort deeply rooted in the traditions and culture of the regions where these brands operate. The Ibis–Arcade brands represent a mid-range hotel product located in city centres, along major highways, in

business districts and near airports. The Formule 1 brand, which was introduced in 1985, offers functional, clean lodgings at low prices. To raise the
coherence of its brands further ACCOR will likely decide to merge several
of its brands within a particular 'star category'. For example, ACCOR will
start operating Sofitel and Pullman under a single brand in the near future.

Traditionally, the accommodation market in Europe had been characterized by many independents offering a wide range of tourist accommodation
from commercial to non-commercial, and from serviced to self-catering
(Goodall 1989: 78). Furthermore, due to its diverse collection of
nationalities, Europe has had many hotel chains or groups each with their
own national or regional brands – for instance, Mount Charlotte in the
United Kingdom, Van der Valk hotels in the Netherlands, Grupo Sol in
Spain, and Scandic throughout Scandinavia. Hotel groups such as the
Bass-owned Holiday Inns, Ladbroke's Hilton International, Trusthouse
Forte and ACCOR are true multinationals and perhaps the few examples
of companies that have initiated broad European representation. Each of
these companies recognized the expansion opportunities in Europe by
aggressively increasing its network of hotels (Turner 1990).

There are several factors that constrain the expansion of hotel chains
and especially the 'replication' of standard 'hotel formulas' in most
European countries.

The first such factor is the trend, particularly in urban areas, towards the
centralization of facilities. Though geographical patterns may appear to be
quite widespread, closer inspection will reveal that the bulk of provision is
rather concentrated in relatively few locations. For example, the majority
of hotel beds are typically concentrated in a few selected locations in the
city centre near the financial and business districts (Price and Blair 1989: 83).
In this context new hotel projects have to compete with other commercial
and residential developments for scarce space. In many European countries local planners give priority to the development of residential
accommodation over the building of hotel projects.

Second, because of a scarcity of space in many urban areas throughout
Europe hotel developers tend to encounter high land and development
costs which generally offer a lower initial return on investment than retail
or office developments. Furthermore, the planning and appeal procedure,
which hotel developers must endure, is often lengthy and expensive. In
addition, there tends to be the added cumulative interest on the cost of the
site, and the delay in realizing cash flow from the new development.

Third, throughout Europe the long heritage of hotel buildings from
Tudor manor houses to Georgian townhouses makes it near impossible to
standardize the 'external' specifications, such as the façade, of most hotel
brands, and by deduction therefore the internal specifications with respect
to the interior design, decor, etc. (Slattery 1991: 29).

Consequently, with the exception of budget hotels which for the most part expanded around the peripheries of most cities, because of cheaper land costs, most hotel chains have grown through acquiring existing hotels, converting older buildings into hotels, or the development of hotels that are part of a multi-purpose real estate project.

The conversion option has been used primarily by upscale corporations that are committed to restoring historic buildings to 'fit the fabric' of the host community. For example, Inter-Continental has renovated buildings that were once palaces, government establishments and coach houses, to the highest standards, whilst maintaining their original character and charm as much as possible. Usually situated in prime city centre locations, each hotel is distinctive. In addition to returning a valued landmark to the community, restorations have proved financially successful. For example, Le Grand Hotel Inter-Continental, built in 1862 and home to the famous Café de la Paix, recently completed a major US$50 million renovation programme.

There is a trend towards real estate development which combines residential, hotel, and recreational facilities; often also a cultural/heritage element to optimize cash flow by phasing the development. In this context, the residential component of the entire project can provide a quick return if sold at an early stage, but can often be expected to realize more if the hotel and the recreational facilities are already available (Bodlender 1986: 2).

Perhaps most important, multi-tier branding has become a vehicle to expand in places which were previously 'off-limits' due to one or more of the aforementioned obstacles. The implementation of a multi-product strategy, designed to attract clearly defined market segments through carefully planned brands, allows hotel groups to match the available space in selected geographical areas with specific hotel products. It enhances a corporation's opportunity to raise market share through a market penetration strategy by entering a larger number of distinct types of locations within countries (Litteljohn and Beattie 1991).

The introduction of basic hotel products, such as Formule 1, can be likened to mass-market consumer products offered by the automobile, electronics, and food and beverage industries. The budget market, according to ACCOR's estimates, is about twice as large as all other hotel categories combined. It is also growing much faster. Lower-priced hotels have begun to attract whole new market segments, who may have the time, but lack the financial means, to travel, such as retirees and young people on a budget. As cross-border trade and travel increases in the European Community and the tastes and expectations of its consumers become more uniform, the opportunities for branded hotel products, that have the required pan-European appeal, should flourish. By learning from the experiences of the consumer goods industry, from brands such as Coca-Cola, Ikea, Levi's, Mars bars, and McDonald's for example, hotel corporations will recognize that a transnational product will expand faster than a collection of local brands (Turner 1990; Slattery 1991).

As a result of the aforementioned market shifts, the hotel industry has become more competitive. In 1993, the five market leaders were ACCOR, Club Méditerranée, Forte, Hilton International, and the Sol Group (Table 5.6). However, many American and even Asian hotel companies, such as Nikko Hotels, complement these Europe-based 'majors'.

Therefore, there is growing pressure to develop a brand with pan-European appeal and representation. In response, major European and American hotel groups have begun to expand throughout Europe with a variety of products ranging from first class to budget motels in response to the segmentation that is taking place throughout the world (Turner 1990).

For example, Forte announced a branding programme in 1991, which the company saw as a prerequisite to the achievement of its corporate goals including the improvement of customer loyalty, guest satisfaction, profitability, and growth. Though the approaches of the main players, such as ACCOR and Forte may be different, the branding strategy of both companies

Table 5.6 Top ten largest Europe-based hotel chains

	Corporate chain headquarters	Rooms 1992 (1991)	Hotels 1992 (1991)
1	ACCOR Evry, France	238,990 (212,500)	2,098 (1,875)
2	Forte plc London, England	79,309 (76,330)	871 (853)
3	Club Méditerranée Paris, France	63,067 (66,269)	261 (269)
4	Hilton International Watford, Herts, England	52,979 (50,799)	160 (151)
5	Sol Group Spain	40,163 (40,150)	156 (150)
6	Inter-Continental Hotels* London	39,000 (37,052)	104 (95)
7	Société du Louvre Paris, France	27,427 (22,429)	398 (324)
8	Husa Hotels Group Barcelona, Spain	21,500 (21,300)	98 (105)
9	Meridien Hotels Paris, France	18,261 (19,412)	58 (58)
10	SAS/Sunwing Brussels	16,507 (14,235)	46 (40)

Source: *Hotels* (1993) July

Note: *Inter-Continental Hotels owned by a Japan-based parent company

aims at expanding throughout Europe. Furthermore, to counter the competitive threat, independent hoteliers will need to join a referral consortium to enable them to employ a brand image and create an identity in the market.

The consolidation of Europe's hotel industry, through a gradual concentration of room stock (Table 5.7), in combination with the emerging phenomenon of brand-names and along with changing business and travel patterns, has given rise to expansion opportunities to hotel groups which offer the 'appropriate' product. As it is essential for the major hotel chains to have pan-European representation, the major chains will likely either upgrade or expand existing hotels; develop new properties; acquire single properties or groups of properties; forge strategic alliances, or utilize a combination of these options (Turner 1990).

Any proposal to expand operations in another country must be evaluated on the basis of potential risks and return. When a hotel company expands in Europe, a market characterized by an industrial economy, one of the main concerns is generally the level of competition. Hotel corporations typically determine marketing opportunities in a foreign country by way of a four-step process – analysis of the general environment, determining market potential, forecasting sales and estimating, and weighing prospective profitability versus risks.

Table 5.7 EC concentration of room stock, 1990

Country	Total country room stock	Total quoted room stock	Quoted company concentration (%)
UK	5,000,000	117,695	23.5
France	518,000	93,638	18.1
Germany	335,000	33,475	10.0
Italy	920,000	16,051	1.7
Greece	191,000	1,911	1.0
Netherlands	50,180	10,236	20.4
Belgium	60,000	8,443	14.1
Spain	359,000	11,646	3.2
Portugal	30,400	3,961	13.0
Ireland	20,740	2,526	12.2
Luxembourg	10,000	1,155	11.6
Denmark	36,500	831	2.3
Total	7,530,820	301,558	4.0

Source: P. Slattery and S. Johnson (1990) *Quoted Hotel Companies: The World Markets*, London: Kleinwort Benson Securities, cited in Litteljohn and Beattie (1991) p. 7

Business environment analysis

Often intuitively understood by decision-makers in domestic markets, analysis of the business environment takes on a much more significant dimension in plotting international expansion. Such an analysis includes examining political, economic, and social aspects of the target country. There may actually be a hidden benefit to unfamiliarity with local conditions in that the 'outsider' may spot opportunities overlooked by domestic companies.

The rate of cultural change between their home market *vis-à-vis* their host market orientation is probably one of the most important factors to comprehend. Similarities in culture and language between the host market and the home market of hotel managers tend to facilitate the process of planning, development, managing and controlling hotels abroad.

Local conditions are especially relevant in Europe, because when it comes to culture, at least in practical terms, the Single Market is something of an illusion. The differences from region to region, and country to country, are real. There are, in some respects, similarities within the three broad ethnic groupings in Europe: the Anglo-Saxon/ Benelux/Scandinavian countries, the Germanic countries, and the Gallic countries. But even within these clusters, business and leisure differ from country to country by at least as much as they have in common. And lodged in diverse national heritages, these cultural differences are likely to persist for the foreseeable future. Olferman and Robbins (1987) raised the important question whether 'standardization or differentiation' should drive business due to the persistent distinctions between European cultures, thereby possibly more accurately meeting local customer expectations.

The idea of differentiation has been implemented by ACCOR's Mercure–Altea brands, for example. Both these hotel products have been adapted to respond to local market requirements. However, most of ACCOR's other hotel brands appear to be designed according to a standardized format to facilitate development and the building of brands with a pan-European appeal.

Physical proximity to origin markets is an important criterion in location decision-making, although more frequent and faster air transportation, and better communication systems via satellite and computer networks, has slightly reduced the significance of this factor.

Television reports about the civil war in Yugoslavia underscore how popular destinations can turn from 'boom to bust' almost overnight, due to political instability. This example underscores the importance of political stability as a prerequisite for a successful hotel venture. Because of the number of variables involved (including the investigation of a large number of sites), environmental analysis can be facilitated by the use of the screening methods in search for the appropriate site. Important screening criteria are listed in Table 5.8. Close relationships between the screening

Table 5.8 Rating scale for transnational hotel expansion

Screening criteria	National rating (1 – 10)	+ Weight	= Combined score
Political stability	———	——	———
Government attitude	———	——	———
Repatriation of capital	———	——	———
Repatriation of earnings	———	——	———
Investment incentives	———	——	———
Ownership restrictions	———	——	———
Controls on foreign managers	———	——	———
Taxation provision	———	——	———
Exchange rate	———	——	———
Per capita income	———	——	———
GNP	———	——	———
Prospect of economic growth	———	——	———
Rate of inflation	———	——	———
Size of market	———	——	———
Tourist number growth	———	——	———
Hotel occupancy rate	———	——	———
Hotel industry legislation	———	——	———
Hotel concentration	———	——	———
Tour operator activities	———	——	———
Attractions	———	——	———
Availability of necessary supplies	———	——	———
Cost of supplies	———	——	———
Labour costs	———	——	———
Total combined score	———	——	———

Source: Frank Go, Sung Soo Pyo, Muzaffer Uysal and Brian J. Mihalik (1990) 'Decision criteria for transnational hotel expansion', *Tourism Management*, 11(4): 297–304

criteria, the objective of the search, the cost effectiveness of the screening process and thoroughness are prerequisites for the success of the screen-based search. After the best candidate sites have been selected according to the sum of screening criteria scores, specific sites in the candidate countries can be researched in more detail.

Market potential

Demand analysis consists of identifying a market, market factors and estimating potential, which in turn is used to forecast revenues. Hotel corporations must gauge the size of potential markets in order to develop needed business projections. An important consideration is the gross national product of the major travel-generating countries and its anticipated growth. Another key dimension is the degree of development and competition in the host country. For example, Asian-based and American-based hotel corporations will face considerable competition in Europe from local operators. In general the marketplaces in Western Europe are more competitive than those of, for example, the countries in Eastern Europe. Between 1964 and 1985, Inter-Continental Hotels was virtually the only upscale hotel chain in Eastern Europe offering 11 city centre hotels in Hungary, the former Yugoslavia, Romania, Poland and the former Czechoslovakia. In 1991, Inter-Continental Hotels re-opened the historic Hotel Metropole in Moscow, and signed a contract to manage the Inter-Continental Hotel, Leipzig in the eastern part of Germany in 1993.

However, in Eastern Europe there is currently more market potential for mid-scale hotels that offer an all-purpose restaurant and lounge and conference rooms built to meet the needs of the local, and foreign business and leisure markets (Bell 1992).

Since hotel projects in foreign countries depend on domestic and international business, income and travel demand must be measured. Such data, like visitor arrivals, are therefore a crucial factor. But visitor arrival figures are not the only concern of decision-makers, they have to observe changing spending patterns as well. In this regard, the mid-range travel market that is, consumers who want something more than a budget or economy roadside hotel but at the same time are reluctant to pay £60–70 a night – is on the increase. Holiday Inn is one group that exploited the gap with its Garden Court product and Patio Hotels, which charge £40–50 a night. The company planned to open dozens of Garden Courts across Europe (Harper 1990).

The European scene has changed rapidly over the last few years and, as earlier discussed, will further evolve for a number of reasons. In terms of infrastructure, it seems clear that the economic heartland of Europe, running north–south, will remain strong, although there is a gradual shift that will, in time, allow for the growing strength of a united Germany. The changes in Eastern Europe are a significant new factor now for hotel development. As the EuroCity Survey indicated, the status of leading financial centres such as London, Paris, and Frankfurt is likely to be strengthened in a unified Europe, while Brussels should continue to serve as Europe's political capital and Amsterdam should maintain its geographical position as part of Europe's heartland. These cities and the major cities in the unified Germany will prove attractive to hotel companies as a point for expansion in Europe, sooner or later.

The Mediterranean sun-belt, running from Barcelona through to Milan and Trieste, is also set to increase in importance, particularly as a target of high technology firms, as their equivalents have done in California. Madrid and Lisbon will be less isolated as improvements in infrastructure are completed, and these two cities will see a buoyant demand for office and retail space as well as hotel investment opportunities. The major change to the European equation is the new axis in the East, between Budapest, Prague and Vienna, where long term opportunities are being anticipated in each of these major cities.

Another prime consideration in the expansion of hotels in Europe is its evolving transportation network. In Europe, the energy crises of the 1970s, combined with demographic changes, have altered lifestyles and caused governments and consumers to look increasingly to alternative public-oriented modes of passenger transportation. The deregulation of air transport, the opening of the Channel Tunnel between the UK and France in 1994, and the anticipated new European road and railway structures will certainly affect distribution links and travel patterns, and further the era of post-mobility adjustment (Van Doren 1981). Hotel managers require a firm understanding of transportation needs and costs because these factors will have a significant influence on hotel location decisions. The major airports best placed to serve a United Europe appear to be London, Paris, Amsterdam, Milan, Madrid, and Brussels, while Budapest's airport is showing signs of becoming the major airport location of Eastern Europe.

The very diversity of the European markets within a constantly changing Single Market creates exciting opportunities for the development network of hotels across Europe, but at the same time presents significant challenges and calls upon the need for a structured plan that is based on comprehensive research.

Information from government publications, trade journals and other secondary sources, such as the EuroCity Survey, in addition to interviews with travel industry representatives, government officials and other experienced professionals in the travel market under study, can be helpful in identifying potential markets and hotel sites.

To find the best potential markets for further analysis entails a series of steps which:

(a) determine basic needs – accommodation, convention, and exhibition space;
(b) establish the manner in which these needs are currently being met;
(c) select market indicators, e.g. occupancy rates, number of tourists, present and forecast volumes;
(d) estimate market potential from the chosen indicators;
(e) eliminate countries which do not meet the minimum criteria, such as economic growth, political risk, available labour;
(f) rank the remaining countries by potential;

(g) eliminate countries where trade or investment barriers prohibit profit-
     able market entry;
(h) select the most suitable countries for further analysis (Kahler 1983).

Forecasting sales

What percentage of industry-wide sales can the hotel corporation expect to
capture? To answer this question, the hotel corporation must conduct
some kind of forecast. The crucial factors in making the forecast are
competition, including the size, market share, facilities and service level,
and financial resources of major rivals and anticipated competitors, and
the strengths and weaknesses of the hotel corporation involved (how it will
measure up to the competition).

Forecasting sales is an extremely difficult and uncertain undertaking, as
has been illustrated in the last decade by the worldwide phenomena of
erratic exchange rates and political uncertainties including terrorism. For
example, in 1986 the European travel industry suffered one of its most
disappointing years on record as US tourists stayed at home, due to
terrorist threats, resulting in significant losses for hotel groups, and serious
balance of payment problems for Greece, a country especially reliant on
tourist receipts. In part because of erratically fluctuating exchange rates
and inflation, it has become more difficult for hotel corporations to develop
accurate sales projections and make hotel projects 'pencil out'.

Prospective profitability versus risks

When profitability of the project has been assessed, the hotel company
must weigh the prospective profits of entering the foreign market against
the risks involved. This last stage in the evaluation process tends to be the
most difficult, for there are no simple mathematical tools to guide decision-
makers in weighing the risks of international business.

Predicting economic trends is one thing, anticipating the political risks
of transnational investment can be more difficult. However, the hotel
company must estimate the possible entry profits. Such an evaluation
involves a forecast of the capital, facilities and personnel required. At this
stage the hotel company should determine the desirability of foreign
market entry – for example, through a joint venture approach. At this
stage, decisions are also typically made with regard to the time period
covered by the entry plan, the organizational method of entry and the
initial marketing mix.

Because of the way international investment characteristics, especially in
Eastern Europe and Russia, differ from those of domestic business, decision-
makers may need to consider investment theory, international economic
theory, and international monetary theory and risk (Lum and Graham

1984). Because at least two countries and economies are involved (the home country of the hotel company and the host country), the international investment analysis is more complicated than its domestic counterpart. Besides market share, revenue, cost structure, assets required, inflation, regulations and other factors that affect the investment's return, and interaction between countries and economies should be examined. The political, economic, and financial factors affecting the valuation of one currency in terms of another, as well as additional taxes – such as withholding taxes – affecting the return of profits to the investing country, should be considered (Lum and Graham 1984).

The most common used measures of investment are net present value (NPV) and internal rate of return (IRR) – NPV is the value of cash flows discounted at the firm's cost of capital; IRR is the discount rate at which the net present value of discounted cash flows is equal to zero (Lum and Graham 1984).

If the NPV is greater than zero or if the IRR is greater than the firm's cost of capital, the project is feasible. The NPV can be expressed as:

$$NPV = \sum_{t=0}^{n} (CFt)/(1 + k)^t$$

where CFt is the expected net cash flow at period t, k is the project's cost of capital and n is the anticipated life of the project; and when NPV=0, the value of k is the IRR (Bringham and Gapenski 1985).

Although no single method is generally used, k (the cost of capital in foreign currencies) can be approximated by a series of calculations based on local interest rates, local corporate income tax rates, the firm's cost of equity denominated in its home currency, a forecast of the anticipated devaluation rate and a debt-to-equity ratio (Lum and Graham 1984).

To incorporate political and economic risks – such as currency fluctuations and expropriation – which are encountered overseas, five possible methods can be considered:

(a) shortening the minimum payback period;
(b) raising the required rate of return of the investment;
(c) adjusting cash flows for the costs of risk reduction, e.g. charging a premium for overseas political risk insurance;
(d) adjusting cash flows to reflect the specific impact of a given risk;
(e) using certainty equivalents in place of expected cash flow (Shapiro 1982).

Since the value of a project is determined by the NPV of future cash flows back to the investor, the hotel management contract company, for example, should value only those cash flows that are, or can be, repatriated net of any transfer costs (such as taxes) (Shapiro 1982).

To analyse the cash flow of foreign investments of an American hotel corporation, five different aspects would be essential.

- *Local currency cash flows.* This process is equivalent to a US investor analysing an investment project in the USA. Although this analysis is worth while it does not provide the US investor with the full implication of the attractiveness of the investment.
- *US dollar operating cash flows.* The local currency cash flows are translated into US dollars at the forecast average or year-end exchange rates. These figures provide the US investor with an indication of the operating cash flow of the investment.
- *Fully translated US dollar cash flows.* It is necessary to examine the investment base in dollars as well as the annual operating cash flow by translating into dollars the assets and liabilities of the operation. The financial statements under the most economically appropriate method corresponding to the nature of the investment are analysed.
- *Dividend cash flows.* Dividends paid by the foreign operation are usually reduced by local withholding or remittance taxes. The dividend flows are further subject to US taxes and corresponding credit allowances. To generate an IRR for an international investment, based on the amount of funds invested in the country, dividend flow plus an estimated residual value can be used.
- *Combined cash flow.* A combined cash flow analysis involves translating local currency financial statements into dollars reduced by the net amount of repatriation taxes, including both withholding and US taxes. Discounting this combined cash flow by the cost of capital will yield a fairly representative NPV, and, if an IRR is calculated, will also be fairly representative of the real return (Lum and Graham 1984).

CONCLUSION

Almost half of the world's hotel establishment stock is situated in Europe.

The countries in Western Europe have market-based economies and a high standard of living compared to the rest of the world, and competition in its hotel industry is fierce.

Three major shifts changed the nature of the European hotel industry in the 1980s: the control over several major hotel chains passed from American to British, and to Asian ownership; the acquisition of hotel chains by 'companies with a wider industrial portfolio' (Litteljohn and Beattie 1991: 9); and the introduction of multi-brand hotel strategies.

To expand hotel corporations, equity sharing, management and franchise, or some other form of marketing agreement (such as the referral consortia), are used. The search for appropriate locations has been greatly enhanced by the availability of multi-brand portfolios which enables hotel corporations to match available sites with the 'right' product. For a greater return, various business environmental factors, market potential and capital budgeting should be studied. The ideal site, besides having a greater amount of NPV and a higher IRR, should have high scores in the screening criteria which encompass risk, incentives, foreign investment restrictions (if any), tax, market and the hotel industry growth rate.

CASE: ACCOR – A GLOBAL SCALE BUSINESS

The French Groupe ACCOR was established as the result of a merger in 1983 of the Novotel S.I.E.H. Hotel Group, founded by Paul Dubrule and Gérard Pélisson in 1967, and the catering and service voucher company of Jacques Borel International. In 1990 the Groupe ACCOR acquired Motel 6, the number one budget motel chain in the United States. And in 1991, the Groupe ACCOR became the majority shareholder with 69.7 per cent of the capital of the Compagnie des Wagons-Lits.

Since 1967, when they opened their first Novotel Hotel in Lille in Northern France, Paul Dubrule and Gérard Pélisson have worked in tandem. With the establishment of the Groupe ACCOR in 1983 they became the company's co-chairmen. Today, the ACCOR Group consists of six divisions.

The hotel division is comprised of 2,000 establishments; in 1992 about 100 new hotels were under construction. The catering division represents 6,000 restaurants, plus collective catering, and public catering units. The service voucher division holds a 52 per cent share of the world market. It sells service vouchers in a number of service sectors ranging from restaurant vouchers, to petrol, transport, health care and uniforms.

The railway division operates sleeping compartments on board trains for 7 million passengers each year, and railway restaurants which provides 1.2 million meals and 5.4 million in mini-bar sales. The tourism and business travel division is comprised of leisure hotels, tour operators, ground operators who are specialized in tourist reception services, and over 1,000 travel agencies. The car rental division operates the leading European network in its class with over 100,000 vehicles.

With a wide range of complementary activities, ACCOR has become the world's only comprehensive hospitality and tourism group, employing more than 144,000 employees around the globe.

In an interview with Michel Péron and Eric Charvet, faculty members of Groupe ESC Lyon, Lyon's Graduate School of Business, which follows, Gérard Pélisson, co-chairman of ACCOR analyses the reasons for the success of his company and underscores the importance of training for companies.[1]

How can you account for the success of the Groupe ACCOR?

I don't like the word 'success', no doubt because I am slightly superstitious, but above all because one never succeeds actually. Let us rather talk of our evolution. Numerous reasons can account for our evolution.

I'll mention three of them:

(a) The first reason lies in our strategy: we have always known how to target the growth markets in our sector of activity and how to adequately adjust offer to demand. To-day the budget hotel business represents our major axis of development. Both Western and Eastern Europe, without forgetting North America, make up a huge market. Since 1985, ACCOR has already built 150 'Formule 1' (as these ACCOR hotels are called) in France and opens a new one every week. Our objective is to have 1,000 'Formule 1' within the EEC by the year 2000. In the US, ACCOR led a successful takeover bid and acquired 540 hotels ('Motel 6') located in 42 states. We do not take it as a criticism to be called the McDonald's of the hotel business. We believe in budget hotels because young people whose financial means are meagre and retirees whose resources are limited, will nevertheless be moving around. Of course, this type of hotel business can only be profitable if our products are sophisticated enough and quite up to scratch. The 50 units we are opening every year must be technically well managed by properly trained teams.

(b) The second reason is the extremely rigorous management of our businesses. It is very easy, when building hotels or restaurants, to indulge oneself in showy but unprofitable investments. Unfortunately, in our field of business what is beautiful does not pay off. One has to make absolutely sure that people should get good value for their money and that there shouldn't be any budget overruns, while paying proper attention to the thousand aspects of day-to-day management.

(c) The third reason is ACCOR's dynamism. The dynamism of its employees is the key factor for the success of our Group. We open three hotels per week, we create one restaurant per day. We invest Fr3 billion a year (Fr9 billion last year [1990], exceptionally). We are a top-ranking French Group for all our products, i.e. either worldwide as regards vouchers or in Europe for the hotel business (Europe is the first 'issuer and receiver' as regards tourism worldwide) etc. . . . .

Is international development a priority in the Groupe ACCOR?

We lead the traditional hotel business in Europe, in the two star (Ibis) and three star (Novotel and Mercure) categories and we are world leader in the budget hotel business. We are currently seeking to strengthen our leadership in Europe, hence the closer links we have established with Compagnie des Wagons-Lits. Our international development remains our top priority. We thus intend to reinforce our position in Spain and Italy, and we are going to increase the number of our establishments in Germany and Great Britain. We are canvassing Eastern Europe for new business but we should not expect any positive results before at least ten years. However, we are already running six Novotels in Poland and others in Bulgaria and Hungary, one Sofitel in the centre of Moscow and we plan to open another one in Leningrad as well as Novotel in association with Aeroflot. But the budget hotel business, particularly well adapted to the Eastern European market and to European mass tourism will remain the mainstay of our development.

North America offers the same opportunities for the budget hotel business as South America does for vouchers and cafeteria-meals. We want to lead the hotel business in Asia (Thailand, Korea, Singapore, Vietnam) within ten years from now. We wish to diversify not only geographically but also in our three main sectors of activity (catering, services and tourism) by type of products without going outside our own business field. As regards catering, for instance we are running the whole gamut from LENOTRE (high-quality haute cuisine) to Pizza Del Arte (n° 1 in French pizzeria chains). As for services we are the uncontested specialists of restaurant vouchers in the world, an activity inherited from Jacques BOREL in 1982. In the field of tourism, we are present in Le Parc Astérix (a French theme park), and in the sector of cruising with Croisières PAQUET. We are developing vacation spots on the five continents and we are now embarking (with the creation of EPISODE, a tour operator) upon the development of tourist packages, short stays, etc. . . . .

ACCOR hires over 3,000 people a year. Is training of importance to you?

Motivating and training people represent two major stakes for our Group. To my mind, training is an essential element for the success of service companies. Training is the only way to ensure that people within a firm have the skills necessary to keep up the competitiveness of the latter and competitiveness helps keeping companies in good shape. We are recruiting people with some solid basic training completed by a permanent in-service training in our Group. We have an ACCOR Academy for the training of trainers, for managers who need some retraining, and also a number of highly specialised schools such as the LENOTRE School for pastry-making and freeze-dried cooking, a school for our 'Formule 1' and another one for 'Motel 6' managers'.

READING: PROSPECTIVE PROFITABILITY VERSUS RISK

by Michael Hirst, former Chairman and Chief Executive Officer of Hilton International and 1993 Corporate Hotelier of the World[2]

Hotel management is a specialized profession requiring specialist knowledge. The maximization of profit and return results from a considered and commercial approach to the development, funding structure, marketing and operation of each individual project.

Success or failure is determined right from the beginning. First, and many would say second and third, comes location. There remains absolutely no substitute for building an hotel in the right place for its intended market. Far too many current failures are due to poor appraisal of site and marketplace. Those hotel operators who realize the importance of location operate prime sites which retain their intrinsic value and attract clearly identifiable markets.

Hotel operators have to understand their marketplace and market segment and design a cost effective hotel with commensurate specification and facilities. More than ever before, today's hotel operators can only afford to construct and fit out a project at a cost relative to potential income. This can be clearly seen by the segmentation and different product offerings that have occurred from budget hotels through mid-market products to full service properties.

The number of bedrooms, size of conference and meeting rooms, food and beverage concepts, leisure facilities and the careful consideration given to space allocation in relation to the back of house areas will determine the eventual efficiency of the operation. Far too many hotels in difficulties today were conceived by owners, architects and designers totally unskilled in understanding market led design related to hotel operational needs. The appropriately designed properties and their profit ratios show the benefits of the involvement of professional ownership and operators.

Another essential success ingredient for ultimate profit is the creation of the financial structure and operating arrangement. Too many hotel developments and acquisitions have been driven by the availability of funding as opposed to demand led forces. The lack of well thought out projects through feasibility studies can spell eventual disaster. There are many reasons for sound hotel investment and many different profiles of current and potential investors. In many parts of the world government agencies still play a critical role, often pro-actively investing for job creation, better infrastructure provision, hard currency earnings and for general economic benefits. In the developed economies of Europe the rationale for almost any hotel project is strictly commercial. Developers seek added value for eventual development profit, whilst investors consider capital appreciation income flow and growth.

Generally, hotel operators internationally have regarded themselves as service providers as opposed to investors. The main aim of operators in hotel investment has been to secure the operating contract and their level of investment will relate to the considered importance of the location.

However, traditionally the UK hotel industry has grown through the combination of owner/operator being the same entity. This approach has meant, in the long run, the maximum return to the investor through operating profit and capital gain. Conversely, of course, the operator takes all the operating and capital risks.

Though it is true that many UK companies have turned to overseas investment to benefit from growing markets and still rising property values, there still remain good opportunities in the UK to develop profitable hotels with returns in years three and four, considerably in excess of debt service. A more common approach to investment structure in continental Europe is through the finance or property lease where the operator pays a fixed or variable rent to the developer or financial institution. Better still is a contingent lease, where levels of rent are geared to levels of performance. The main advantage of applying the lease to the operator is of course the avoidance of a significant outlay but the risk in this approach is the level of rent which can be minimized if a variable formula is adopted.

Well structured leases can be good for operator returns on investment, with good opportunities for a share in upside profits but there is always the risk of leasehold ownership without the benefits of capital growth. From a developer/investor point of view the return is predetermined, the capital value locked in and with a contingent rent the added benefit of profit sharing. This type of arrangement, that is the basis of a genuine partnership between the funder and operator, could derive maximum benefit from a successful hotel enterprise, if more often applied in the UK.

For many individual investors, hotel investment companies, hotels being developed in new areas and increasingly for distressed properties, the management contract remains the best method of operation to maximize hotel performance. The management company brings all its expertise together for a fee based on sales and profit, sometimes on a tiering formula. Branding, marketing, selling, reservations technology, purchasing power, human resources, training, technical service and business acumen all add value to the hotel performance. However, it is important to note that the level of management fees paid to the operator have less impact upon the viability of a project than the gearing of the financial structure used for its funding.

Management contracts can be very attractive from the risk point of view and with the right company will maximize profit potential and enhance property value. With increasing flexibility being built into arrangements, owners and operators can keep their operations available for changes to reflect the developing marketplace. Investors are now also able to influence business performance, if they wish, by more direct involvement in policy-making by regular communication with the management company. A recent Horwath consulting paper commissioned by the International Hotel Association concluded that there was a clear case for optimizing hotel performance through management contracts offered by experienced and well branded hotel companies. There is a growing trend amongst operators to make a minority investment in the owning company to secure a contract. Often this is treated by the operator as key money or a premium and written off in the early years of operation.

Finally, franchising has become a popular option for hotel expansion. It affords the owner the opportunity to manage a property directly within the confines of a brand, marketing and operational policies of a franchising system. Franchising offers the franchise company half price management fees with arguably the same resource and cost as a management agreement. Franchise systems may offer more locations than management contract networks, but the former also provide less quality and management control, which often leads to diffused service standards and poor property upkeep. Thus, franchising may represent a short-cut to branding for investors often ending in under-performance due to a lack of professional know-how.

In summary, there are many interesting options available for funding and operating an hotel project and each depends upon particular circumstances. The key is flexibility and a realistic approach to investment criteria, the operator's role and reward. However, some would argue that to obtain greater efficiency and operational flexibility from existing operations, operators will have to demonstrate more dedication and focus to meet well defined market needs.

STUDY QUESTIONS

1 Outline the factors which will influence the growth of and patterns of travel demand in Europe.
2 What trends are likely to be most influential on the supply side of Europe's tourism industry?
3 Attempt to account for possible differences in hotel supply and demand trends in each of the following European sectors: Western Europe; Scandinavia; Eastern Europe; Southern Europe.
4 Explain why there was a period of rapid expansion in hotel openings in the 1960s and 1970s.
5 Discuss the factors which constrain the expansion of hotel chains in most European countries.
6 Discuss the impact on hotel industry development of the many and varied cultures which exist in Europe.
7 Discuss the market potential for hotels in Europe.
8 What problems need to be addressed by hotel companies entering a foreign market?
9 What reasons can be given for the successful evolution of Groupe ACCOR?
10 Discuss the various ingredients required to achieve success and profitability in the hotel industry.

Chapter 6

Sustaining the competitiveness of Hong Kong's hotel industry*

This chapter examines the hotel industry in relation to the host community. It uses Hong Kong as a context to demonstrate the major contribution the hotel industry can make to develop tourism into a leading industry. It pinpoints the determining reasons for the present hegemony of the territory's hotel industry in Asia and reviews what leading hotel executives consider to be the main challenges that must be addressed to ensure the industry's future growth. The chapter concludes with a vision statement which imagines Hong Kong, into the twenty-first century, as Asia's centre of excellence for the export of hotel management and tourism development expertise to developing economies throughout the region. This vision will be enhanced by Hong Kong's proximity to the vast and rapidly expanding China market.

The case at the end of the chapter examines the way that the Hotel Nikko Hong Kong is contributing to environmental protection. The reading takes a wider view of the region as seen through the eyes of Hyatt International's Bernd Chorengel.

HOTEL SUPPLY OVERVIEW

Tourism is Hong Kong's second most important earner of foreign currencies. In 1992 nearly 7 million international visitors came to Hong Kong and spent US$ 6.2 billion (based on an exchange rate of US$1 = HK$7.8) which represents 6.5 per cent of the Territory's gross domestic product. By comparison, the textiles and garments industry earned US$12.2 billion. In addition, Hong Kong registered more than one million tourist arrivals from the People's Republic of China. The number of tourist arrivals in 1993 was 8.9 million, including both international visitors and arrivals from China (HKTA 1993).

The hotel industry in particular continues to expand, but it is difficult to enter the Hong Kong market, one of the world's best performing pieces of real estate, due to the extravagant development costs. The price of residential and commercial real estate rose 30 per cent in 1993. Property price increases have been the result of speculation and a shortage of residential quarters and offices to accommodate the workers Hong Kong needs to support its future development. Another drawback constitutes Hong Kong's double-digit inflation causing wages and hotel rates to rise alarmingly, and major concerns amongst Hong Kong's hoteliers. They face a changing tourist market, global competition, the 1997 issue, a saturated infrastructure, and other metropolitan centres in the region that vie to dominate Asia's hotel industry.

The hotel industry has the potential to add substantial value to its host community and vice versa. For example, the community's growth stimulates hotel performance; conversely, hotels contribute to the community's economic, social and cultural development. Within this context there is a significant symbiotic relationship, rarely emphasized, between hotels and the community in which they are located. However, this symbiosis warrants more attention as the competitiveness of tourist destinations will increasingly hinge on the close cooperation between the host community and its hotel industry.

In 1974, the Hong Kong Hotel Association (HKHA) had 30 member hotels with a total of 10,000 rooms. At the end of 1993, the HKHA had 80 members who offer 35,000 rooms. Hong Kong's hotel industry created direct employment opportunities for about 40,000 people (HKHA 1992). Hotels also generate substantial amounts of revenues for Hong Kong by attracting US$7.7 billion in tourist receipts in 1993. Tourists spent their dollars not only in hotels but throughout the community, resulting in an economic multiplier effect. Finally, hotels generate tax revenues through hotel room taxes and real estate taxes which benefit Hong Kong.

The hotel industry greatly benefits from the Territory's economic growth and stability and the support of complementary real estate developments such as office buildings, retail malls, entertainment facilities and a world-class convention centre. These real estate developments draw both commercial and pleasure travellers and help to create room demand.

Most of Hong Kong's hotel properties are located in major business districts which include Central and Tsimshatsui. An active property market and limited land supply continues to raise the price of land in the traditional tourist and shopping districts. The price of Grade A office rentals in the first quarter of 1994 was double the asking price in 1993. This steep increase in rentals offers some insights into why Hutchison Whampoa, owned by Hong Kong tycoon Li Ka-shing, intends to raze the landmark Hilton Hotel to build in its stead a high yield office tower. In January 1994, Hutchison Whampoa paid Hilton US$125 million to terminate the Hilton International's management contract. Despite the penalty Hutchison Whampoa is paying to cut short its contract with Hilton International, the former stands to generate a handsome profit after the present Hilton site has been redeveloped into a Grade A office block (Li 1994).

Table 6.1 Hotel supply situation 1993–1995

Location	Rooms	Location	Rooms
DE LUXE (ROOM RATES ABOVE US$205)		**TOURIST (ROOM RATES BELOW US$133)**	
Current hotels		**Current hotels**	
Conrad Hong Kong	Queensway 513	Bangkok Royal	Tsimshatsui 70
Furama Kempinski	Central 517	Century	Wanchai 506
Grand Hyatt Hong Kong	Wanchai 573	China Harbour View	Wanchai 316
Hong Kong Hilton	Central 750	China Merchants	Wanchai 285
Hyatt Regency Hong Kong	Tsimshatsui 723	Concourse	Mongkok 359
Island Shangri-La Hongkong	Central 565	Eastin Valley	Happy Valley 111
Kowloon Shangri-La	Tsimshatsui East 719	Eaton	Yaumatei 392
Mandarin Oriental	Central 542	Emerald	Wanchai 316
JW Marriott Hong Kong	Queensway 605	Evergreen Plaza Hong Kong	Wanchai 332
New World Harbour View	Wanchai 862	Fortuna	Yaumatei 187
Peninsula	Tsimshatsui 156	Grand Plaza	Quarry Bay 248
Regal Hongkong	Causeway Bay 425	Grand Tower	Mongkok 549
The Ritz-Carlton Hong Kong	Central 216	Guangdong	Tsimshatsui 245
Sheraton Hongkong	Tsimshatsui 791	Harbour	Wanchai 200
Victoria	Central 536	Harbour View Int'l House	Wanchai 320
		Imperial	Tsimshatsui 214
Current room supply	8,493	International	Tsimshatsui 89
Additional room supply due to hotel developments in 94/95		Kimberley	Tsimshatsui 496
		King's	Yaumatei 72
Peninsula Extension (4/94)	Tsimshatsui 150	Kowloon	Tsimshatsui 735
		Kowloon Panda	Tsuenwan 1,026
Reduction in room supply due to reconstruction of hotel into office building 94/95		Luk Kwok	Wanchai 198
		Majestic	Yaumatei 387
Hong Kong Hilton	Central 750	Metropole	Mongkok 487
		Miramar	Tsimshatsui 500
Total 1995 room supply	7,893	Nathan	Yaumatei 186

FIRST CLASS (ROOM RATES US$133–205)

Current hotels

Hotel	Location	Rooms
Ambassador	Tsimshatsui	313
The Charterhouse	Wanchai	237
City Garden	North Point	615
Excelsior	Causeway Bay	911
Gold Coast	Castle Peak Road	450
Holiday Inn Golden Mile	Tsimshatsui	594
Holiday Inn Crowne Plaza	Tsimshatsui East	593
Lee Gardens	Causeway Bay	660
New World	Tsimshatsui	543
Nikko Hong Kong	Tsimshatsui East	461
Omni The Hongkong	Tsimshatsui	709
Omni Marco Polo	Tsimshatsui	440
Omni Prince	Tsimshatsui	400
The Park Lane Hong Kong	Causeway Bay	815
Ramada Renaissance	Tsimshatsui	500
Regal Kowloon	Tsimshatsui East	592
Regent	Tsimshatsui	602
Royal Garden	Tsimshatsui East	420
Royal Pacific Hotel & Towers	Tsimshatsui	676
The Wharney Hotel	Wanchai	335
New Astor	Tsimshatsui	151
New Cathay	Causeway Bay	225
New Harbour	Wanchai	173
Newton Hong Kong	North Point	362
Newton Kowloon	Mongkok	176
Park	Tsimshatsui	430
Prudential	Tsimshatsui	434
Ramada Hotel Kowloon	Tsimshatsui	205
Regal Airport	Kowloon City	400
Regal Riverside	Shatin	830
Royal Park	Shatin	442
Shamrock	Yaumatei	148
South Pacific	Wanchai	293
Stanford	Mongkok	194
Stanford Hillview	Tsimshatsui	163
Warwick	Cheung Chau	70
Wesley	Wanchai	251
Windsor	Tsimshatsui	166

Current room supply 10,866

Current room supply 13,939

Additional room supply due to hotel developments 94/95

Shinechoice Investment (7/94)	Yaumatei	106
L. Hoffman Holdings (12/94)	Causeway Bay	209
Promotal Ltd (1/95)	Hunghom	621
YMCA Hostel Extension (5/95)	Tsimshatsui	156

Reduction in room supply due to reconstruction of hotel into office building 94/95

The Charterhouse	Wanchai	237
Lee Gardens	Causeway Bay	660
Ambassador	Tsimshatsui	313

Reduction in room supply due to reconstruction hotel into office building 94/95

China Harbour View	Wanchai	316
Fortuna	Yaumatei	187
Miramar	Tsimshatsui	500

Total 1995 room supply 9,656

Total 1995 room supply 14,028

Because commercial and residential property development yield a higher return on investment than hotels, it is anticipated that there will be fewer hotel development projects in the next two years. As a result, the growth of rooms supply in the near future should be very limited and possibly unable to satisfy the demand. The impact will be particularly obvious in the supply of luxury hotel rooms which recorded only 1 per cent growth in 1992.

By contrast, the supply of mid-market rooms, which are often part of multi-purpose developments, increased by almost 50 per cent in 1992. Examples of mid-market hotels mainly catering to the less affluent travellers include the Regal Riverside and Royal Park in Shatin, Kowloon Panda in Tsuenwan, and the newly opened Gold Coast at Castle Peak Road.

There are three major driving forces for the development of mid-market hotels in Hong Kong. First, visitor arrivals from China and other Asian countries are increasing rapidly due to their fast economic growth. Tourists from these countries are less willing to spend as much on accommodation as their Western counterparts. Second, high labour cost and labour shortage have been the major barriers hindering the growth of the hotel industry in the last five years. Luxury hotels providing labour-intensive services are particularly hard pressed under the current circumstances to retain good staff members and expand. Third, due to constraints on travel and entertainment budgets, executive travellers seek less expensive and more functional accommodation.

Due to these market conditions and high land prices, it is therefore anticipated that the future trend in Hong Kong will be towards the development of mid-market hotels outside the traditional and expensive locations. Table 6.1 identifies the way in which such developments, especially in tourist class hotels, are taking place.

DETERMINANTS OF COMPETITIVENESS

Hong Kong's competitiveness as a tourist destination concerns its ability to promote or impede hotels and related travel industry businesses by shaping the appropriate context in which corporations can compete. This context, according to Porter's theory on the competitiveness of nations, and confirmed by our own personal observations, is comprised of four main variables:

(a) Factor conditions: the nation's position in factors of production such as skilled labour or infrastructure necessary to compete in a given industry.
(b) Demand conditions: the nature of demand for the industry's product.
(c) Related and supporting industries: the presence or absence in the nation of supplier industries and related industries that are internationally competitive.

(d) Firm strategy, structure and rivalry: the conditions in the nation governing how companies are created, organized, and managed, and the nature of competition (Porter 1990).

Factor conditions

As the hotel business is a business of 'people taking care of people', the lack of well-trained labour represents a very serious problem to Hong Kong's hotel industry. The labour shortage may well have contributed to the postponement of announced new hotel developments and expansions. With Hong Kong residents turning for work to better paying and more prestigious industries, the hotel industry introduced the labour importation scheme in 1993. The scheme was designed to import people from throughout the region and the Philippines in particular, train them and retain them. Though the hotel industry is in acute need of foreign labour, the government has, on average, granted only 12.3 per cent of the hoteliers applications for foreign labour. This has resulted in a considerable under utilization of resources which hoteliers had allocated for the training of foreign workers (HKHA 1993).

Another concern amongst hoteliers is that Hong Kong's infrastructure is no longer adequate to cope with the growing number of tourist arrivals. At Kai Tak, the present airport, the staffing levels at the Immigration Department have not kept pace with the number of tourist arrivals and departures. This has caused delays in the processing time for passengers and affected the on-time performance of air carriers, resulting in late departures and missed slots. The new airport which Hong Kong is building at Chek Lap Kok is also causing concerns. The Government plans to finance Chek Lap Kok through landing charges and an airport departure tax which will be higher than the charges and taxes levied at other airports in the region and increased annually in line with inflation. The airlines will pass on their higher costs to the travellers, the bulk of whom visit Hong Kong for pleasure purposes. It stands to reason that many leisure travellers may reconsider their travel budgets and decide to visit less expensive tourist destinations.

BOX 6.1 HOTEL DEVELOPMENTS ASSOCIATED WITH HONG KONG AIRPORT RAILWAY

The shortage of hotel accommodation may be in part resolved upon the completion of the new airport at Chek Lap Kok. The new airport will be linked, through a 34-kilometre Airport Railway, with Kowloon and Hong Kong Island. The Airport Railway will consist of two services, an Airport Express and the Lantau Line (a domestic mass transit service), which will share running tracks over most of their lengths. The Lantau line will carry on an estimated 266,000 passengers each weekday when services commence in 1997 and 491,000 in 2011. The Airport Express is projected to carry 39,000 passengers per day in 1997 and this is anticipated to increase to 75,000 in 2001. Five sites along the Airport Railway have been marked for property development, including commercial, office and hotel developments. A breakdown of the proposed development sites is shown as follows:

Proposed Property Development for the Hong Kong Airport Railway

Station	Site area (ha)	Residential (sq. metres)	Commercial/office/ hotel (sq. metres)
Hong Kong Central	4.00	nil	415,896
Kowloon	13.96	547,026	543,000
Tai Kok Tsui	16.85	390,000	238,000
Tsing Yi	5.40	245,700	46,170
Tung Chung	21.59	750,120	93,000

Source: Mass Transit Railway Corporation, Hong Kong

In response to past fires in guesthouses the Government introduced the Hotel and Guesthouse Accommodation Ordinance. It was designed to improve fire safety precautions primarily in guesthouses. However, in that the Ordinance also applies to the hotel industry, it has caused many developers to reconsider their plans and develop commercial real estate perceived to generate a higher return and less 'hassles' to the landlords. Hong Kong's hotel industry views the Ordinance demands, which are retroactive, as stringent and unreasonable. It is seeking a review and amendment of the Ordinance. At the same time, the hotel industry has requested the Government to offer developers financial incentives to build hotels rather than office buildings, to avoid a severe shortage of hotel rooms in the imminent future.

The chronic shortage of hotel rooms has already led to conference organizers facing acute problems securing hotel rooms for delegates. If the current hotel room shortage is not remedied, it is likely to result in a significant threat to Hong Kong's hegemony as Asia's leading tourism centre.

Demand conditions

Total visitor arrivals in Hong Kong have grown at 150 per cent over the last eight years, or an annual average of 18.75 per cent. At this growth rate the Territory should exceed the 10 million visitor barrier before 1996.

Taiwan is emerging as the fastest growing and largest market for Hong Kong (see Table 6.2). In 1992, the Taiwan tourist market showed a growth of over 20 per cent over the previous year and accounted for over 23 per cent of visitor arrivals in Hong Kong. The growth of visitor arrivals from Taiwan is expected to continue unabated because of the Republic's growing economic connections with China. However, the impending 'normalization' between Taiwan and China, and particularly the signing of a treaty designed to regulate air travel between the countries, dangles like the proverbial sword of Damocles over the Taiwanese visitation of Hong Kong. Once direct air flights are introduced between Taiwan and China, Taiwanese tourists will no longer be required to pass through Hong Kong. When this occurs, the respective impact on the Hong Kong hotel industry should be quite significant.

However, Martin Barrow, Chairman of the Hong Kong Tourist Association, is of the opinion that despite direct flights between Taiwan and China, circular trips 'taking in both Hong Kong and China will still attract Taiwanese tourists' (SMP 1993).

Japanese visitor arrivals increased rapidly during the late 1980s, while the North American and West European market showed little growth. However, this trend has been reversed since 1990 when the Japanese market began to show little or negative growth and visitor arrivals from North America and West Europe gradually increased.

Looking to the future, it is widely anticipated that the number of visitors from China and South-East Asian countries will increase as the economies in these countries improve, allowing their peoples to satisfy their pent-up desire to travel.

The China market in particular will play a key role in Hong Kong's tourism development due to its proximity and size. Mainland Chinese visitors were for the first time included in the Hong Kong Tourist Association's statistics in 1993. This sector has a market share of 19.8 per cent and showed a growth of 64.7 per cent in the first nine months of 1993 compared with the same period in 1992. 'The growth has only been obvious since March this year [1993], when mainland Chinese were allowed to bring their own money out of China', according to Martin Barrow, chairman of the Hong Kong Tourist Association. 'There are plenty of Hong Kong jewellers who benefit from this and who now accept RMB (the official currency of the People's Republic of China' (SMP 1993). The number of mainland Chinese who will visit Hong Kong was forecast to reach 1.8 million in 1993 (Table 6.2). If the visa procedures for Mainland Chinese

Table 6.2 Visitor arrivals in Hong Kong, by nationality 1985–1993 ('000)

Origin	Actual 1985	1986	1987	1988	1989	1990	1991	1992	Projected 1993
SE Asia	678	711	766	772	693	836	992	1,211	1,215
Japan	626	714	1,018	1,240	1,158	1,318	1,247	1,312	1,270
USA/Canada	741	815	924	915	749	736	750	843	910
W. Europe	571	644	759	780	797	827	868	1,018	1,140
Aus/NZ	278	284	278	303	284	283	263	290	313
Taiwan	168	212	344	1,094	1,117	1,328	1,285	1,625	1,760
Other	308	353	413	485	563	605	626	688	529
China	–	–	–	–	–	–	–	–	1,800
Total	3,370	3,733	4,502	5,589	5,361	5,933	6,031	6,987	8,937

Source: HKTA (1985–1992) *Statistical Review of Tourism in Hong Kong*, Hong Kong Tourist Association

visiting Hong Kong are relaxed and simplified, China tourists may further increase their dominance and replace other countries as the largest tourist market of Hong Kong. Also, Hong Kong's hotel business will continue to benefit from foreign business travellers who pass through Hong Kong to participate in trade and investment opportunities in the rapidly growing economy of China.

As analysis of available data reveals, there is a strong correlation between the length of stay of Hong Kong's visitors and their nationality. For example, visitors from Australia and New Zealand stayed on average more than five nights in 1991 and 1992. Measured over the past eight years this resembles a record and is in sharp contrast with the length of stay of visitors from other major markets, such as Taiwan and Japan, who spent less than three nights in Hong Kong (see Table 6.3).

What brings visitors to Hong Kong? Tourists from the South-East Asia region appear to be attracted by Hong Kong's vibrancy, excitement, food and fashion. Visitors from Europe and the US are more attracted by the Chinese culture and the 'East meets West' phenomenon. Seventy-eight per cent of Hong Kong visitors say they plan to return, and 57 per cent of them do (SMP 1993).

Despite the double-digit inflation rate, shopping remains the key expenditure for visitors during their short stay in Hong Kong. In 1992 the proportion of total expenditure devoted to shopping by visitors was 53 per cent. The highest proportionate spenders on shopping were the Taiwanese who devoted 65 per cent of all their expenditure to this activity, and the lowest were the North Americans with 38 per cent (Table 6.4).

Table 6.3 Average nights spent in Hong Kong, by major market areas 1985–1992

Origin	1985	1986	1987	1988	1989	1990	1991	1992
SE Asia	3.5	3.6	3.6	3.7	4.0	4.0	3.7	3.6
Japan	2.6	2.7	2.8	2.6	3.0	2.9	2.9	2.9
USA/Canada	3.7	3.6	3.7	3.6	3.8	3.9	3.9	3.9
W. Europe	3.8	3.7	3.8	3.8	4.1	4.1	4.1	4.0
Aus/NZ	5.0	5.0	4.9	5.8	5.3	4.8	5.6	5.2
Taiwan	–	–	2.8	2.8	2.3	2.2	2.6	2.9
All visitors	3.6	3.5	3.5	3.4	3.4	3.3	3.5	3.5

Source: HKTA (1985–1992) *Statistical Review of Tourism in Hong Kong*, Hong Kong Tourist Association

Table 6.4 Visitor spending pattern (per cent) 1992

Origin	Shopping	Hotel bills	Meals outside hotels	Tours	Other
SE Asia	55.2	24.1	12.5	2.2	6.1
Japan	57.4	25.3	9.6	2.5	5.2
USA/Canada	38.3	41.6	10.8	2.2	7.1
Western Europe	38.7	39.2	12.2	2.7	7.2
Aus/NZ	44.3	35.9	10.7	3.1	6.0
Taiwan	65.3	17.5	10.1	1.5	5.6
Other	48.7	30.8	11.4	2.0	7.1

Source: HKTA (1992) *Statistical Review of Tourism in Hong Kong*, Hong Kong Tourist Association

On average, Hong Kong's visitors spent about 30 per cent of their expenditure on hotels. North American and West European tourists tend to spend more on accommodation while tourists from South-East Asia, Japan, and Taiwan only spend 25 per cent or less on accommodation. According to Horwath Asia Pacific, over 25 per cent of customers of the mid-market hotels were from China in 1992 while only 1 per cent of customers of luxury hotels were from China. The rapid growth of Taiwanese, Mainland Chinese, and Asian markets have contributed to the development of mid-market hotels in Hong Kong and this trend is expected to continue.

Related and supporting industries

Hong Kong's total land area is only 1,070 square kilometres, which makes it a very compact place. Geographic conditions, especially the close spatial proximity of economic activities, have given rise to mutually beneficial interactions, in particular service providers, through shared use of the infrastructure and specialized services. In this regard, Hong Kong is best defined as the archetype of an agglomeration economy (Price and Blair 1989). In part, because of its geographic heritage, Hong Kong has grown into the Asian headquarters of multinational corporations, including major construction companies and finance and real estate corporations, which through their expertise and by the 'export' of same to countries in the region stimulate the Territory's economy and hotel industry.

Hong Kong ranks as the world's 13th leading service centre in terms of service exports, ahead of South Korea and just below Singapore. It ranks nineteenth with regard to the import of services as Table 6.5 indicates.

There are few places in the world that depend on services as much as Hong Kong. At present, services account for 73 per cent of Hong Kong's GDP. This compares with 63 per cent in the United States. With the service sector contributing 63 per cent to GDP only Singapore comes close to Hong Kong as a major service economy in the region. The 1993 World Competitiveness Report by the Swiss-based International Institute of Management Development ranked Singapore first as measured by eight factors used to rate countries, government, people, infrastructure, domestic economic strength, finance, internationalization, management and

Table 6.5 World trade in commercial services 1991

	Leading world and Asian countries				
Rank	Exporters	Share (%)	Rank	Importers	Share (%)
1	United Sates	16.7	1	United States	11.5
2	France	9.4	2	Germany	11.1
3	Germany	6.7	3	Japan	10.5
4	Italy	6.3	4	France	7.8
5	United Kingdom	5.9	5	Italy	6.3
6	Japan	5.1	6	United Kingdom	4.8
12	Singapore	1.9	13	Taiwan	1.9
13	Hong Kong	1.8	16	Korea	1.5
19	Korea	1.4	19	Hong Kong	1.3
21	Taiwan	1.0	21	Singapore	1.2
22	Thailand	0.9	23	Thailand	0.9

Source: HKCSI (1993) *Service Sector Statistics in Hong Kong*, Hong Kong Coalition of Service Industries

science and technology. Hong Kong beat Singapore in one category – management. The World Competitiveness Report defines management as the extent to which enterprises are managed in an innovative, profitable and responsible manner (WEF 1993).

Some experts argue that Hong Kong is at risk of suffering a dwindling demand as a regional service sector centre, which would include the provision of hotel management contract services, due to its steeply rising costs. However, this argument has been countered by the Political and Economic Risk Consultancy with this persuasive observation:

> The rapid rise in operating costs for companies in almost every country, together with the technology improvements that enable companies to tap service support from increasing remote locations, imply that it will be difficult for Asian countries other than Hong Kong and Singapore to develop a regional role for their service industries, or even bring onshore those functions that are currently performed elsewhere.
>
> (Heath 1993)

The mass industrialization in the region and in China in particular will drive the demand for services and open up great opportunities for Hong Kong because it has a critical mass in service support facilities such as accountancy, financing, law, hotel development, consultancy, and management.

The transportation and travel industries represent the largest sectors in Hong Kong's exports of services (Table 6.6). Hotel management contract services form at present a relatively small component of Hong Kong's trade in services. The impending growth of Hong Kong into a finance, transportation, and multipurpose service depot to support the rapid economic development and hotel development in China over the next decade bodes well for companies that are poised to provide hotel management and franchise expertise that will be geared to the needs of the evolving travel and tourism industry in China.

Given the potential for hotel development in China, the category 'hotel management contract/franchising services' can be expected to become a more substantial component of Hong Kong's trade in services in the near future.

Firm strategy, structure and rivalry

Hong Kong is the international hub in Asia for the regional and head offices of both international and indigenous hotel chains, respectively. Its geographic location has played an important role in turning Hong Kong into Asia's major centre for the provision of hotel management, investment and development expertise. The Territory is home to seven hotel chains that have built a worldwide reputation over the years: The New

World/Ramada International, Shangri-La International, Regal Hotels International, Park Lane Hotels, Mandarin Oriental Hotel Group, Peninsula Group, and Century International Hotels (see Table 6.7).

Table 6.6 Composition of exports of services at market prices of 1991

	US$ million*
Transportation	7,422
Travel	5,199
Insurance	189
Production and distribution of films/programmes	139
Hotel management	46
Advertising and marketing research	96
News transmission	169
Financial assets of dealing and broking	543
Adjustment for import shipment	246
Banking services	398
Expenditure of employees of extra-territorial bodies & dependents	78
Postal services	5
Other services	1,046

Source: HKCSI (1993) *Service Sector Statistics in Hong Kong*, Hong Kong Coalition of Service Industries

Note: *For comparison purposes, 1 US dollar is equivalent to 7.8 HK dollars

Table 6.7 The main indigenous hotel companies in Hong Kong

	No. of hotels	No. of rooms	No. of countries
New World/Ramada International	133	36,520	43
Shangri-La International	21	10,163	21
Regal Hotels International	9	4,687	–
Park Lane Hotels	8	4,450	–
Mandarin Oriental Hotel Group	9	3,899	–
Peninsula Group	6	2,450	4
Century International Hotels	5	1,606	3

Source: *Hotels* (1993) 'Hotels, 325 The world's largest 200 companies', 27(7): 39–41

CORPORATE PRIORITIES AND KEY ISSUES

To gain an understanding of the major corporate priorities and issues, we interviewed senior executives of five hotel chains based in Hong Kong: New World Hotels International; Regal Hotels International Holdings; Park Lane Hotels International; Mandarin Oriental Hotels; and Century International Hotels.

When asked about the location of their head offices, all the companies were unanimous in terms of their policy to remain in Hong Kong after 1997.

Daniel Bong of Regal International Hotels was unequivocal in his reply to the question of head office location: 'It is here and it will stay here!' Mac Ma of New World Hotels International said, 'We will stay in Hong Kong after 1997. Singapore is the only other possible place to establish head-quarters but it has too many rules and regulations. Also, it is far more difficult to qualify for tax benefits in Singapore.' Robert Riley of Mandarin Oriental Hotels was of a similar view 'we fully intend to remain here after 1997 because about 70 per cent of our income is generated in the Territory'. Brian Deeson of Century International sees Hong Kong as a booming location within a similarly booming region, making it an 'ideal position' for their head office. Kenneth Mullins of Park Lane Hotels International explained that whilst Park Lane has a base in San Francisco to oversee its operations in North America, it plans to keep its base for other operations in Hong Kong. Why not, when as he says 'Hong Kong is regarded as the centre of the hotel world, with markets, standards and staffing which are the best in the world.'

The executives were then questioned about the main corporate priority within their companies. Two major issues were raised: the need to maintain profit levels in a secure and healthy market, and the need to find and retain appropriate staff at all levels in the hotels.

Kenneth Mullins pointed out the concern that the market remains healthy, and having got the market being sure to keep that position by constant attention to the available product: 'Park Lane has the market and the money, but must strive to keep the market happy by constantly using financial resources to upgrade the product.' He feels that all indicators are good that there will be stable development in the future, but there is a need to always be aware of the possibility of major global events (such as the oil crisis of the 1970s and more recently the Gulf War) which have a wide-reaching effect.

Daniel Bong stated a similar position, being concerned at a general level with the stability of the marketplace and the way this relates to contributing to the profits of Regal's hotels; linked to this is the availability of funds for expansion, but again he feels that this is market dependent.

Mac Ma echoed this general position: 'New World Hotels' main corporate priority is to maintain good corporate profitability, reasonable growth and constantly eye expansion opportunities.'

Robert Riley listed three priorities within the Mandarin Oriental Group. 'First, we want to completely delight and satisfy our guests. We do this through our second priority of having the right people internally and bringing out the best in them through effective training and personal development. And third, ensure that we plan our business in such a way so that our successes will result in investment returns which are consistently among the best in the hotel industry.'

In this last statement, Robert Riley brings in the people perspective which some of the other executives also discussed.

Daniel Bong told us that at a more practical level, Regal is concerned about the availability of human resources in all positions in the hotels: 'People are not so easy to get or to retain. The company sets up its own training and career development plans, and identifies staff for development. But the training function is in competition with the rest of the business for available funds.'

Kenneth Mullins gave some of the background to labour shortage in Hong Kong, the main reasons being fast expansion in the hotel industry at the same time that service industries in general have been growing – and all in a labour market with virtually full employment.

Brian Deeson placed people, that is staff (or lack of staff) as Century's number one priority. Like Mullins, he points to the fast growth of the industry in Hong Kong and the region as a major reason for staff shortages, plus shortage of training and education throughout the region and the low unemployment rate in Hong Kong coupled with strong competition for employees from other industries. He also refers to general disinterest in jobs in the hotel industry. 'This', he says, 'is more of a problem for the more low-profile hotels like the Century. The Regents, Mandarins and other top-name hotels tend to attract staff because there is prestige attached to the name. Century is trying to overcome this by motivation/ recognition/ training programmes to instil loyalty in its longer term staff. When the hotel first opened it was very aggressive in recruitment, visiting schools and getting staff direct from school. Eighty per cent of initial staff (about 350) started this way two years ago, but only 80 of those are still remaining (and they will be getting extra bonus this year to recognize their loyalty). Century are also trying to provide career paths not just jobs, and we are looking to promote staff within the hotel. Often staff leave to go to other hotels after being trained at the Century, but many leave the industry altogether. At least Hong Kong has the advantage of a high level of general education and a range of hotel-specific qualifications available so that there are ready educated people available. This is not the case in many other of the region's countries where there is a lack of general schooling, especially a lack of people with any language ability, English being the one mainly required. In situations like this employees are constantly stolen from the hotels which do the training and development of staff. Taking Indonesia as an example, it is impossible to get mid-level managers – they just do not exist, and so the movement of Hong Kong managers to these countries as expatriates is increasing all the time. This itself puts more pressure on the Hong Kong situation.'

The interviews then moved to the question of what steps Hong Kong needs to take to sustain its competitiveness. The five executives again shared similar views, but with slightly different priorities.

Brian Deeson featured three main needs: a growth in supply of hotels; a new airport; and the realization that Hong Kong should be seen as part of South China.

Daniel Bong linked business success for hotels with overall economic and business success in Hong Kong. 'To maintain good hotel business, Hong Kong as a whole needs to remain successful in that hotels are a service or support for Hong Kong's business. A good economy equals hotel customers! Hong Kong needs to maintain its attractiveness as a business centre with an awareness of all the things necessary to keep the place attractive to business and business visitors. Hotels can help to add to this attractiveness by the provision of top class services.'

Mac Ma pointed to Hong Kong's blend of staff, products and infra-structure giving it a leading position in the region, but he also counselled against hoteliers becoming too greedy.

Kenneth Mullins was similarly concerned about high prices. He advised, 'Hotels need to beware of outpricing the market, they should keep prices on par and at a competitive level with other cities in the region. Hong Kong hotels are still competitive, but if prices go up dramatically business will move to other cities (such as Bangkok) which are experiencing a downturn in their market and are therefore willing to give very attractive price deals. In the immediate future Hong Kong may become too expensive for tourists at the lower end of the spending structure, but this will be more than compensated by a greater shift to business travellers. The market for the general tourist will come back after a few years, particularly as tourism into China increases at all market levels.'

Robert Riley also points out Hong Kong's desperate need for a new airport, with any delay in its opening adversely affecting the Territory in general but especially its tourism. He also discussed the adverse effects of a combination of high living costs, potential changes to taxation methods and labour costs increasing faster than room rates.

Expansion strategies

Presently, there is excitement in the air throughout Asia from Singapore to Shanghai because the tourism industry in the region can anticipate considerable growth into the twenty-first century. But tourism growth in the Pacific–Asia region will not be uniform, it will differ between destinations and source markets. Within the various source markets the patterns of expansion will differ from one market segment to another. With the rapid expansion of the intra-regional travel market, successful hotel companies will depend on increased market segmentation, in particular the introduction of mid-scale hotel products and more carefully targeted marketing.

Economic growth and advancement in the countries of the Pacific–Asia region has occurred in very short order relative to the economic development of the industrialized countries. The speed at which these changes are occurring is also advancing rapidly. Where will Hong Kong-based hotel companies expand to capitalize on the growth opportunities? Some of the companies we interviewed have very firm plans, others have general intentions, but the one thing they have in common is their very positive view about hotel expansion in this part of the world.

New World Hotels plans to expand primarily in China and throughout Asia, with three-star and four-star products respectively. This development is quite in line with the present and future demand in Asia. Mac Ma said that his company will concentrate on the region so that it will avoid any possible clashes with the other hotel companies in the Corporate New World hotel portfolio. 'Up to now the primary mode of expansion has been through management contracts. In any case we will try not to exceed 25 per cent equity investment participation in any given project. For the future we are looking into franchising opportunities in China. It will become increasingly difficult to renew management contracts in China. On the provincial government level management contracts renewal may not be approved when government officials perceive Chinese staff to have obtained the necessary know-how to operate a hotel by themselves. In the future, growth through franchising will become more important. New World Hotels will introduce a three-star product under a brandname because it will become more important for us to expand the number of our properties to capitalize on opportunities.'

Regal Hotels has general plans for expansion both locally and internationally, but no specific details were available. Daniel Bong saw no problem in raising the necessary funds for expansion, saying that 'financing is available if the proper arguments are presented for the project'. As a public company, Regal can go to the public for funding. They have found this a very good way to get finance because the public (in Hong Kong or USA or anywhere) will respond to a good investment opportunity. Finance can also be raised through institutions and through Regal's own resources as part of Century City Holdings Limited (for example US$125 million was recently raised through a preferred shares issue).

Century International Hotels sees itself as a regional middle market hotel company. The company has immediate intentions for hotels in Shenzen, the Philippines and Jakarta/Indonesia. The biggest single expansion will be in mainland China where Century could develop twenty or more hotels within the next five years. These hotels will not be in the main cities initially, but rather in secondary cities like Dalian and Harbin. Brian Deeson feels that 'it is in these more "inhospitable" locations that a smaller, leaner, more flexible company like Century has an advantage over the large multinationals'. This approach has already worked for Century in Jakarta and Vietnam, and the company will build on these valuable experiences. 'Century is better able to cope with different situations and possibly provide a slightly different product based on available resources, whereas the big boys must stick to their internationally accepted levels of product and service – this is difficult to do in places where there is no basic industry to draw on.' Century is quite firmly a management company. It locates possible situations for hotels and then introduces investors to those situations, using its own performance projections and guarantees (and reputation) to sell the idea to the investors. Investors are institutional not individual, they generally deal with property companies or groups.

Park Lane Hotels International sees itself as an international, five-star hotel company, specializing in large hotels. Park Lane may only have eight or nine hotel properties, but measured in room numbers it is a substantial hotel operator. As a company it often takes out some equity in the hotels it develops and therefore it is quite selective, even conservative, about its expansion targets in Asia. However, in general terms, the company expects to double in size within the next four years. This expansion will almost certainly all be in Asia. The company would like another hotel in Hong Kong, on the Kowloon side of the harbour in the major tourist district. Park Lane currently has two projects under consideration in Indonesia. China is a strong focus for expansion. On the question of expansion methods, Kenneth Mullins told us that, 'Park Lane does everything except franchise.' The company is involved in management contracts, 100 per cent equity and management, and partial equity and management; the common denominator being that it always manages the properties. According to Kenneth Mullins, 'The type of involvement is flexible depending upon the specific situation and circumstances.' He echoed Daniel Bong's sentiments that access to financing can be found if the proper case is presented. 'In the recent past Japanese banks and institutions have provided the main fuel for hotel investment – they are not now so active. Equity funds are now more available from South-East Asia sources in Singapore, Malaysia, Indonesia and Hong Kong itself. Eventually the USA will be back as an investor in hotels.'

Robert Riley told us that Mandarin Oriental have hotels in 11 countries, operating nine of these properties in the Asia–Pacific region. 'Our group is conservative but very interested in expansion. Mandarin Oriental recently agreed to restore the historic Majapahit hotel in Surabaya, Indonesia and to operate on a management contract basis two resorts in Phuket and Koh Samui, Thailand. We plan to open the Mandarin Oriental in Kuala Lumpur in 1997 and are actively looking at opportunities in China.' Some financial analysts have blamed Mandarin's cautious management style on the company's parent, the sprawling Jardine Matheson Holdings. 'That', says Riley, 'is an unfair assessment. I have been looking for a suitable partner with whom to set up a hotel in China. But you have to kiss a lot of frogs to find a prince. Mandarin has good people and a strong balance sheet and will expand accordingly in due course.' Mandarin's approach to expansion is quite flexible. Said Riley, 'To expand I am equally interested in taking an equity interest in a property, signing a management contract, or buying a stake in another company.' One deal that fell through was Mandarin's plan to invest in Amanresorts, which operates seven de luxe resorts in Asia and Europe. Someone else was willing to pay more than Mandarin was.

Information technology

Faced with escalating operating costs and a declining number of workers who are willing to enter the industry, Hong Kong's hotel operators are presented with only one option: to do more with less. Put differently, the hotel industry has to become more innovative and creative to increase its productivity. Hong Kong Polytechnic University's Department of Hotel and Tourism Management is collaborating with the industry, through the application of continuous learning, to raise productivity in hotel operations without reducing quality. Capital cannot substitute the function of labour in full service hotels, and new technology by itself is not the answer. But both are means that can potentially enhance productivity. The application of information technology will become increasingly important to Hong Kong hoteliers who have watched their payroll costs rise and their margins decline dramatically. The application of information technology to enhance productivity requires managers and workers to gain a higher degree of professionalism and knowledge, especially of the appropriate application of information technology in hotels.

To what extent are Hong Kong's hotel companies using information technology (IT) and for what purposes? This was the base of our final question to the executives, and they all expressed views which showed how important they feel it is to utilize new technology.

Daniel Bong sees IT as a factor for communication, being especially important in a large and growing company with properties spread over Asia, North America and Europe.

Brian Deeson told us that when Century opened its Hong Kong hotel it installed state of the art IT equipment at that time with a view to providing the necessary service quality and management information with a minimum of staff. The company is generally moving to reduce the amount of paper generated and replace it with computer terminal information. The hotel now has its own E-mail links and is tied in to SITA to provide airline bookings and information. However, as much as Century wants to duplicate this effort in other countries the 'IT infrastructure' is not available, neither is staff who are competent to use such systems.

'The name of the game in the hotel industry is anticipation', says Mac Ma of New World. 'Computers, especially good databanks, can help us to anticipate what is around the corner. One of the main problems in Hong Kong is that it runs behind in software availability. But even if the software is available that would solve only one quarter of the problem. Computers were only introduced fairly recently in Hong Kong. Many of the senior managers are uncomfortable with computers whilst younger managers dream of applications they cannot turn into reality because their superiors are not interested. This situation has created, to some extent, a gap in organisations and hinders progress.'

Robert Riley thinks that Mandarin is in the top tier of the industry in terms of aggressively applying information technology to the management of people, accounting and marketing functions. He told us, 'The Fidelio system that our Group uses has been an excellent tool in managing the time of our sales staff more productively and effectively. Information technology also has helped in improving processes throughout the Group. When something goes wrong we try to look at it from a process viewpoint rather than blame the people.'

Recognizing that Hong Kong has access to the very latest technology, the Century International Hotel in Hong Kong has a Technical Review Committee which has the job of reviewing what is in use, and what is possible, in all areas of IT and communications technology. It is Century's intention to expand IT developments (and general developments in technology) as much as possible, and such expansion will be pushed even further in the future. 'The prime motive for these developments', according to Kenneth Mullins, 'is to improve productivity as much as possible – by improving quality, improving speed of jobs or by saving resources. A particular objective is to reduce paper work and paper volume, for example by the use of CRTs. Of course improved customer service is also a main objective, and sometimes this is seen as keeping up with competitors – if a competitor hotel offers a particular service (such as in-room fax) then you have to respond with similar facilities. Hong Kong is very fortunate in that the money is generally available for upgrading, and upgrading (in all areas) is a constant process.' Other examples of areas where the hotel is looking to develop IT and related technologies are: satellite technology; voice message systems for staff as well as for guests; and telephone, computer and television systems where replacement times of three to five years are now common compared with a replacement period of ten years until recently. As new technology is developed there is great pressure to have it in hotel rooms just as there is to have it in the domestic situation.

VISION

At the beginning of the Third Millennium, Hong Kong will be an integral part of the future Special Administrative Region (SAR) and the leading economic, cultural, and technological centre of Southern China. The current economic developments and the impending transfer of government in Hong Kong in 1997 are likely to stimulate the emergence of a 'megalopolis', with an impressive infrastructure, and embracing Hong Kong, Shenzhen, Macao, Guangzhou and the urban clusters of the Pearl River Delta (HKU 1992).

Cheap land and labour in southern mainland China have proved attractive to Hong Kong entrepreneurs who have established manufacturing plants across the border, initially in Shenzhen but increasingly further into China. China's Premier Li Peng, in a 1993 address to the National Conference on the Service Industry, said that if China was to achieve an annual growth rate of 11 per cent for the remainder of the decade it had to have a viable and efficient service sector (Wilson 1993).

As manufacturing and service industries move their operations to mainland China, Hong Kong's position as the 'headquarters' for many firms in the region could be seriously threatened.

One of the implications of this development is that Hong Kong shall have to focus on the provision of more advanced, high quality services. It is anticipated that a balanced infrastructure – including the new airport at Chek Lap Kok, the application of high-technology production processes, and the development of quality human resources – will be vital to sustain Hong Kong's competitiveness as a regional service sector centre.

At present work is under way for the building of major transportation infrastructural projects such as airports, railroads, and highways, to cope with the projected increases in freight and passenger movements to and from Hong Kong and China. For example, a 2,400-kilometre highway, connecting Beijing with Hong Kong, will be built by a South Korean conglomerate. The proposed China highway alone will offer enormous business opportunities for companies eager to develop motels along the highway and hotels in cities that will be connected by it.

CONCLUSION

For host communities in the megalopolis and other parts of China to prosper, adequate transportation and hotel accommodation will be essential. The planning, development, management and marketing of a comprehensive tourism system and hotel facilities require professional talent. Universities have embarked on several projects with Hong Kong-based corporations to transfer managerial skills and technology from Hong Kong into China. For example, Hong Kong Polytechnic University and the University of Hong Kong have been involved with local companies in the transfer of hotel and tourism management and transportation infrastruct- ure development expertise to China, respectively.

The vision of Hong Kong into the twenty-first century as Asia's centre of excellence for the export of hotel and tourism management expertise will be realized by Hong Kong's proximity to the vast and rapidly expanding China market and through new levels of cooperation between business and educational institutions.

CASE: HOTEL NIKKO – COMMITTED TO HONG KONG

The environment and tourism are inextricably intertwined. The success of the latter depends to a significant extent and increasingly on a clean environment. The awareness that the environment is an important issue has come rather late to Hong Kong. However, its hotel and tourism industry has been taking a more active role on this issue. Among the industry leaders who are spearheading the drive for environmental protection is Jean-Marie Leclercq, general manager Hotel Nikko Hong Kong. He explains his commitment to the cause as follows. 'I am personally committed to environmental protection for two reasons: the personal responsibility we all bear to leave a better world to the next generation, and the professional responsibility of running the business we have been entrusted with efficiently. My first experience in energy conservation dates back to 1978, when the French government issued a decree to save energy as a result of the oil crisis. At that time I managed the Hotel Nikko de Paris, and along with most other companies started energy saving programmes to take advantage of the French government subsidies of up to 50 per cent designed to save energy. As a thorough energy audit report requires a qualified consultant, the energy consultancies flourished. My experience at the Hotel Nikko de Paris taught me the three basic principles of energy management – namely, to ensure that the staff is closely associated with the programme and is convinced of its usefulness and the need to use equipment appropriately; that all equipment is properly maintained and utilized in an efficient manner; and that the consultant one appoints is fully qualified and committed to produce results.'

The staff of the Hotel Nikko Hong Kong applied these three principles in 1993. The project required only a minimal investment and saved 10 per cent in energy costs or a saving of HK$500,000.

'The good thing about saving energy is that the hotel does not save money for just one year, but for many years thereafter.' As a rule of thumb, investments on energy programmes, following guidelines drawn up by the International Hotel Association, should be paid back in two to three years.

Jean-Marie Leclercq is convinced that government initiatives such as subsidies aimed at energy conservation contribute to the national economy in that they reduce the need for energy and therefore a reliance on costly imported oil. 'Whatever the government policy may be, it does not relieve the hotel industry from its responsibility in protecting the environment. Last but not least, hoteliers should be aware that tourism is very much dependent on the environment as we cannot expect more visitors to come to a city that would establish a reputation of being very polluted.'[1]

READING: STREAMLINING FOR THE FUTURE – PROFITS, SERVICE, PRODUCTIVITY

by Bernd Chorengel, President, Hyatt International Corporation

Let me begin by quoting one of my favourite statesmen. 'The whole map of Europe has been changed. The position of countries has been violently altered. The modes of thought of men, the whole outlook on affairs, the grouping of parties, all have encountered violent and tremendous changes in the deluge of the world . . .'

That quote was written 70 years ago; the eloquent statesman was Winston Churchill. Although it was penned in the aftermath of the First World War, it could be a depiction of our world today in the aftermath of the Cold War. And it does make the point that change is constant.

The pace of change is so swift that we sense history rushing by. There is a relentless shifting in world affairs and in the affairs of business. Business, and our industry in particular, must embrace that change and we must learn to adapt to understand the *process* of change.

Our world and our industry are quite different from what they were only a few years ago. We have come out of the free-wheeling decade of the 1980s into a very changed world of the 1990s. In our business that means shifting market segments, increasing labour costs, and much more demanding investors.

In the past, hoteliers followed trends; we were influenced by what the competition was doing. We moulded services around the expectations of the guests; hired, trained, and developed huge staffs to meet those expectations; and *only* then ensured profitability for owners and investors.

This is what I call a *top*-down approach, build the product, ensure the service, and then worry about profits.

That is no longer a feasible concept in the hotel business today. We should change it. Indeed, we have to turn it upside down. We must now take a *bottom*-up approach to running a hotel. What I mean by that is building profits into our strategic development plan *before* the hotel gets off the ground.

Our people-driven service industry goes beyond guests and tourists. We now 'deliver' services to banks, to investors, to owners. They should be at least of equal priority and our first order of concern. In the future, return on investment will, and must, increasingly drive our industry.

As the world has been redefined, so goes our business. What is service? Who do we serve? How do we serve them?

We must create new partnerships to ensure increased profits and to heighten productivity. We must enlist the understanding of governments and unions if we are to improve our product. In other words we must change our approach. We must work wiser to reduce costs and to increase profits. We must structure management and service to address the financial needs of the investor.

Unlike manufacturers, we in the service industry are less likely to understand cost controls and productivity. It is our duty to learn.

We have to change our way of 'viewing' how we deliver our product. To achieve an equilibrium between owner satisfaction and guest satisfaction, the bottom-up and top-down approaches have to be applied with intelligence, common-sense, and vigour.

Responsibility to investors

The management of hotels has changed from the unrestrained, carefree days of the 1970s and 1980s. Hotel operators, mostly North American at that time, were in a strong negotiating position when it came to dictating terms of management agreements. They held all the cards: skilled and experienced negotiating teams, management expertise, marketing networks, and, for the top development companies, the all-important brand-name recognition.

The owner was usually less sophisticated and more naive when it came to hotel operations. He had less operational leverage.

The owner is now much more sophisticated. He has his own team of experienced lawyers and negotiators. He is more selective and business oriented. Now there are more operators chasing fewer development opportunities and fewer investors.

There is a trend towards shorter management contracts. Profits are tied more closely to bottom-line performance rather than to revenue performance.

Yield and return on investment have become critically important to both the owner *and* the bank and, therefore, should critically concern the operator.

Competition for fewer contracts, heightened sensitivity to foreign exchange, decreasing profits, reduced profit margins. In today's environment, the owner and his bank are insisting on more performance criteria, and they are getting them.

A hotel now has to operate from an owner's perspective, cut costs and achieve a greater return on investment: the owner's investment. In this changing business milieu, we are required to manage wisely and well. Not the mere trappings of our business, but assets, revenues, *and* expenses. And we have to do it with less resources. The owner now wants, demands, greater control over performance. We must satisfy that demand.

The developer knows that he is better off using a well-established and lean management company. That is why a brand-name is important. The owner needs the comfort of well-defined skills in marketing, people management, and high-tech communications. Most of all, he wants profit-oriented management; management that will take that bottom-up approach.

The changing world scene

This new perspective for hotel operators comes in the midst of other new realities. Geopolitical change in just the last couple of years has had a huge impact on how business is viewed, and how it is conducted. That impact was rather eloquently, if somewhat dramatically, noted in a Brussels newspaper, *De Standard.* It said: 'The end of the Soviet Union coincides with the end of the American dream.'

Predicting what repercussions geopolitical change will have on how we 'do' our business is no mean feat. It helps to have vision. The dismantling of the Soviet Union, the shift from Communist authoritarianism to free market capitalism, are having a tremendous impact on world trade. Eastern Europe will gallop towards increasing business opportunities, the potential for domestic tourism will be virtually limitless.

Geopolitical changes bring about some surprising results. One example is the Tumen River which straddles the borders of North Korea, China, and Russia – slap in the middle of former enemy territories. In our post-Cold War world, the UN is sponsoring, in cooperation with North and South Korea, China, Russia, and Mongolia – a US$30 billion plan to develop the sleepy Tumen River basin into a harbour, railway-linked complex.

It is reported that the marshlands and rice fields will be transformed into a 'metropolis of high-tech smart buildings, home to a cosmopolitan population of half a million'. Does this superport-rival to Rotterdam and Hong Kong present tourism opportunities?

The US market for tourism is also changing and shifts in American travel patterns will continue long after their recession has ended. In 1987, 25 per cent of American overseas travellers visited the Far East and Oceania; nearly as many visited the UK. A recent poll shows that in 1992, 70 per cent of American pleasure travellers will not stray from home. Of the

30 per cent who will venture afar, most won't go long distances; most will stay in the Americas.

Of all American tourists in 1992, 11.4 per cent will visit Europe and only 2.4 per cent plan to make it to Asia. In other words, between 1987 and 1992, the percentage of American overseas tourists visiting Asia will drop from 25 per cent to 8 per cent.

So our worldwide market begins to shift.

Changing Asia

The potentially biggest global market, one that will witness the fastest growth, is the Pacific Rim region, home to two-thirds of the world's population.

Four decades ago, at the height of the baby boom in the western world, Asia was considered a backwater; its people condemned to poverty. Today, Asia's vigorous economies have no equal in the history of economic theory. Its peoples are becoming more and more affluent; rising aspirations are reaching new heights.

Four decades ago half of Japan's labour force worked in the fields. The products of its factories were considered shoddy, worthless trinkets.

Taiwan was viewed as a hopeless little island home for the refugees from Mao's Shanghai. Hong Kong, just emerging from Japanese occupation, was a disaster area. Tiny Singapore was nothing more than a busy little port. And Korea, on the brink of a civil war, was more impoverished than Sudan.

At that time, the Asian cities with the most potential to become future players in the world economy would probably have been identified as Rangoon, Saigon, and Manila! How times change. Rangoon and Saigon of the 1990s are economic basket cases and Manila is following fast on their heels.

Meanwhile Japan has recovered from the fortunes of war; it is now a world industrial superpower. Taiwan, Hong Kong, Singapore, and South Korea have emerged as East Asia's four economic 'tigers'. These four countries have forged the fastest industrial revolution the world has ever seen. (Taiwan, for example, will soon have $100 billion in foreign exchange reserves, the biggest of any country in the world.)

Behind the 'tigers' are four other Asian countries on the way to industrial take-off – Thailand, Malaysia, Indonesia, *and*, right next door, China.

This rate of growth, currently two to three times faster than in the developed world, is necessary to continuing economic prosperity. But, it will present challenges and the inevitable change.

If the Asian countries continue at this pace, it is predicted that, by the turn of the century, the average worker in Taiwan will be richer than his counterpart in New Zealand and nearly as rich as his fellow worker in Australia. Workers in Hong Kong will be richer than the average Brit.

Singaporeans will be better off than the Italians. And workers in South Korea will be as rich as the Irish.

If this trend continues, by the middle of the next century, economic power will have shifted from Europe and North America to the western Pacific Rim.

As with other business sectors, the tourism pie will be divided on an intra-regional and intra-continental basis. US business will be aligned across the Americas; Europe will have Europe; and Japan will influence China and Southe-East Asia.

Redefining service in the Pacific Rim

This shifting of economic power is of special significance to us in the hospitality business, especially to those of us operating in the Pacific Rim. Asia, with its low-cost labour, set the standards for luxury and opulent service. In hotels, with staff/guest ratios of up to three to one, there was a revolution of heightened guest expectations. Service was often delivered, mostly to westerners, with all the pomp due an eastern potentate.

With increasing affluence in the area, wages are going up. The aspirations of Asians are fast becoming *expectations*, for travel, for good food and wine, for more lucrative jobs. With booming prosperity, intra-regional tourism is on the upswing. As their income increases, Asians are taking close-to-home holidays just as Europeans and Americans began to do around the turn of the century.

Another trend that reflects the West is demographic patterns. And the evolving patterns are emerging swiftly. What took a century to achieve in the West is occurring in Asian countries, like the four tigers, in just a few decades.

According to a recent *Wall Street Journal*: 'As Asian economies prosper, birth rates fall, people live longer, urbanisation gathers speed as rural workers migrate to higher-paying jobs, and labour costs rise.'

But, as wages go up, our payrolls increase and profits decrease. With the shrinking of the low-cost labour base, and with our investor in mind, we need to redeploy our workforce, rethink skills, re-evaluate and reorganize staffing. And we must define and redefine what is service.

How do we do that? By identifying demographic trends worldwide, and by regions, and by countries. What's happening to our tourist? If he's an American, he's more cost conscious. What impact do ageing baby boomers, our seasoned travellers, have on our industry?

What effect do leisure time versus working time trends have on tourism? What about the shifts from international travel to domestic travel, and vice versa? Are today's travellers more culturally aware, more environmentally sensitive? If so, what impact does that have on our services?

What segments of our markets have a yen for glamour and luxury? What segments are satisfied with, or can only afford, the basics? Should we take a back-to-basics approach? What, indeed, is back to basics? How can it be defined?

For one guest, basic might be a good bed or a large bathroom. For another it might be an in-room computer or a fax machine. Or it might be a cordon bleu menu or a cuisine naturelle meal.

These and other shifting trends must be weighed, and weighed differently, for each region of the world, for each segment of our marketplace. For example, Asians are one of the most brand-conscious consumers in the world. There are more than 60 McDonalds in Hong Kong alone and Mercedes, Volvos, and BMWs are becoming an ever more common sight on the street scene throughout Asia, once a stronghold for Japanese cars.

Needed: A government/union/industry partnership

What is needed is a long-term strategic plan for tourism in the Pacific Rim.

The challenge in Asia is to build diversified economies on the back of tourism. In today's developing world, governments must have a master plan for tourism. They have to work on infrastructure, schools and housing, to plan for future growth of small towns emerging into large cities. Then the governments must let the market do its work.

This means that government and unions should become much more sensitive to, and develop a broader understanding of, issues important to our industry. And we should lead the way to that greater cooperation, to helping to develop long-term goals that will be satisfactory to all sides. We can do that because, traditionally, the travel and tourism industry has always had close ties with governments.

Governments must prepare their workforce for future growth. For the tourism industry that means providing better training *and* development of a broader range of skills. As Confucius wrote: 'If you plan for a year, plant a seed. If for ten years, plant a tree. If for a hundred years, teach the people.'

The unions must also play their part. The rising aspirations of Asians cannot continue unabated. Their dreams can only be satisfied by better education and training. Unions must become more responsive to industry needs and changes. The days of three to one staff/guest ratios are over. It is no longer feasible to support such a huge service staff.

In our industry we need skills training and we need management training. We should encourage governments to use a vocational school track for developing management skills. And we should set the standards for education on both levels.

Asia needs more local tourism and hotel experts because Asians will eventually run the hotels; they will come to rely less and less on expatriates.

For the first time ever, domestic tourism growth will be driven by developing countries. It behoves governments and unions to be ready for the growth and to be prepared for the opportunity. After all, the market for intra-Asian tourism has not yet reached its full potential.

Another current trend deserves a closer look – namely, airline mergers. The major airline players will win the globalization stakes with centres in each of the three major intra-regional markets: Asia, Europe, and the Americas.

Airlines are gearing up for a new era of heated competition. American Airlines and TWA are undertaking a joint promotion effort as part of the frequent flier programme, an unusual step for major domestic competitors.

Three major carriers, BA, KLM, and Northwest, were considering a common carrier. Although the deal fell apart, it is an indication of how the airline industry is moving and changing.

Japan Air, All Nippon, and Singapore Airlines are leading a powerful Asian contingent. Taiwan Aerospace wanted a 40 per cent stake, recently reduced to 25 per cent, in McDonnell Douglas's commercial aircraft business.

Europe is opening her borders to global airlines so it will not be easy to maintain individual country flagships. Europe's state-owned airlines are on a privatization binge: Germany wants to sell its stake in Lufthansa. Greece its share of Olympic Airways. Air France has acquired UTA and Air Inter, and is buying into Czechoslovakia's CSA, and wants a piece of Sabena.

Lufthansa is allied with Japan Air Lines; now it wants a link with US Air. SAS has marketing links with Swissair and Austrian Airlines.

In the end, though, Asia will be the most important market. They are expected to place 60 per cent of all new aircraft orders over the next two decades. As they look to Europe's deregulated skies, the airlines of Asia will be Europe's main rival, not the US.

Conclusion

A shake-out of the travel and tourism industry is overdue. We cannot sit back and blame our current woes on the recession and the Gulf War. Other systemic forces are at work. Our challenges need long-term strategies. We are big business, so we must develop big business problem-solving techniques: rethink our strategies, cut costs, *and* create efficiencies. And this should be achieved without cutting the quality of service. Quite a challenge.

As a result, it is becoming too costly and unprofitable to develop stand-alone hotels. In the future we will see more mixed-use developments encompassing combinations of shops, offices, apartments, convention centres and hotels. This trend is already apparent. Hong Kong has its Convention and Exhibition Centre, with two top-name hotels, and Pacific Place, which includes three hotels. Taipei's World Trade Centre is another example.

We cannot be driven by the past, we must be driven by the future. To do so will take vision to predict the impact of continuing world changes.

It will take courage to change the way we deliver our services, to re-evaluate them, to bring to service delivery a bottom-up/top-down strategic management style. To be bottom-line oriented. But we must do it if we are to streamline for the future.

STUDY QUESTIONS

1   Discuss the key factors of Hong Kong's hotel supply situation.
2   Outline the key points of Porter's theory on the competitiveness of nations.
3   Discuss the application to Hong Kong's hotel industry of Porter's theory on the competitiveness of nations.
4   What makes Hong Kong an attractive location for head offices of major international hotel companies?
5   What problems does Hong Kong need to address in order to sustain its competitive advantage in tourism and related hotel business?
6   Outline the main features of Hotel Nikko's environmental protection activities.
7   Discuss the differences between a 'top-down' and a 'bottom-up' approach to running a hotel.
8   What general economic changes have taken place in Asia over the past few decades, and what impact have these changes had on the hospitality business?
9   What might be the ingredients of a long-term strategic plan for tourism in the Pacific Rim?

Part III

Responses to strategic developments in the global hotel industry

Capitalizing on human resources strategy for competitive advantage*

This chapter presents human resources as a key issue, due to the labour intensive nature of services in the hotel industry, and especially their inseparability and heterogeneity.

The first part of the chapter (Human resources: a key issue) presents the results of a survey conducted on behalf of the International Hotel Association. The survey was designed to gain an understanding of the industry's mindset concerning the strategic importance of human resources and its priority on the management agenda. Despite the limitation of the data on which they are based, some interesting insights into the issue of a discrepancy between the espoused objectives of international hotel corporations and the de-emphasis of human resources practices expected to affect the attainment of these objectives emerge. To that end, the study findings discussed offer guidelines for the development of competitive advantage based on hotel managers' actions which are in line with the corporate notion that the people of a hotel company represent its primary asset.

The second part of the chapter (The use of local versus expatriate managers) is focused on a particular human resource issue which will inevitably face many hotel companies as they expand internationally, especially expansion into locations such as developing countries which do not have a well established supply of local managers. The material is based largely on an M.Phil. thesis by Yu (1994).

The case at the end of this chapter illustrates how Inter-Continental Hotels regards its people as a key resource. The reading features the Ritz-Carlton Hotel Company and the way it incorporates its staff into its overall quality achievement.

HUMAN RESOURCES: A KEY ISSUE

During the 1980s, the international hotel industry exploited market segmentation, product differentiation, corporate diversification and other sources of competitive advantage to the fullest. However, in the early 1990s, conditions have changed significantly because, with across-the-board deregulations, a boom in new technologies, and foreign competition, a company's technological or financial edge can be lost overnight. As a consequence, survival in the international hotel industry today depends upon developing well-qualified, thoroughly-trained staff focused on providing quality service to the customer (Albrecht and Zemke 1985; Normann 1984; Heskett 1986). There are two major factors that intervene in the process of developing a customer-sensitive service staff: (a) the changing demographics of the workforce, and (b) the human resources practices in general.

The results of several studies (Hiemstra 1988; Horwath and Horwath 1988; EIESP 1991; Baum 1993) indicate that by the early 1990s there will be a significant shortage of both semi-skilled and skilled workers. The availability of managers may also decline as, for instance, the British hospitality and tourism industry is 'losing' about 40 per cent of potential supply to other industries (Parsons 1991). In addition, the international hotel industry may continue to experience a defection of its employees (including managers) to other more stable, secure and higher paying industries. As well, Europe's Internal Market will facilitate the free movement of employees 'to engage in their professions throughout the Community' (Reuland et al. 1989: 100).

Labour shortages and migrations in the 1990s will impact all industries, but not to the same extent. They will have the least negative consequences on industries that have effective and advanced approaches to managing human resources. Because these industries are perceived to offer better working conditions, they are likely to be more attractive to employees than the hotel industry.

Traditionally, effective human resource management generally has been one of the lodging industry's primary weaknesses (Geller 1984; IHA 1988) because of the technical orientation of many hotel managers. Although technical expertise remains essential to managing hotel operations, it is, by itself, insufficient to respond to change and complex organizations in a dynamic environment. Yesterday's concepts and practices are being rigorously challenged all over the world, especially in the management of human resources. Within this framework, hotel managers face new legislation and government regulation which in Europe, for example, will lead to the harmonization of labour conditions, a general improvement of social security, and, consequently, an increase of social security costs (Reuland et al. 1989: 103). At the same time, managers will be called upon to lead the way in the improvement of productivity and business performance.

In this dynamic environment, hotel executives can no longer be content to react to corporate developments and external events. Instead, they have to identify issues and respond to them before they threaten the survival of their companies.

There are several *reasons* why the human resources issue represents such a significant challenge to the international hotel industry:

(a) The international hotel industry is plagued by a high staff turnover, which is often the result of ineffective human resources management, and in particular inadequate compensation.
(b) Ill-defined career 'paths' have been an important reason why the hotel industry has encountered great difficulty in attracting well-qualified workers.
(c) The international hotel industry is often perceived in a negative way by prospective employees.
(d) The ageing population in most industrialized countries has resulted in the availability of less young workers who traditionally represented the bulk of the international hotel labour force.
(e) At present, most state-recognized education and training is generally ill-adapted to the needs of the international hotel industry.

The labour issue has at least four major *implications* for international hotel firms:

(a) It poses a significant threat to the future expansion of the international hotel industry in that the lack of sufficiently trained personnel and competent managers may drastically impede the ability of international hotel firms to continue their rapid expansion.
(b) It places international hotel companies in a position where they are required to compete for workers with companies representing many other industries and other countries in order to become the employer of choice.
(c) It may encourage more international hotel firms to acquire other hotel groups that have an experienced staff.
(d) It alludes to the significant role of the availability of trained hotel labour in relation to the host destination's ability to respond to growing business and pleasure travel demand.

Consequently, human resource management has evolved into the most critical issue in the hotel industry.[1] This responsibility has added pressure on hotel executives to discover how leading-edge organizations are managing human resources, and to be proactive to help ensure their organizations' survival in a fiercely competitive environment.

To stay abreast of developments in the human resources field, the International Hotel Association (IHA) holds a Human Resources Forum annually, which aims to examine current problems faced by the international hotel industry in the area of professional training and human resources management. Independent hoteliers, human resources directors of chains, national hotel association executives, and hotel school directors work together to examine and provide solutions to specific issues being raised (Hulton 1992). To the extent that human resources represent a strategic opportunity for international hotel companies, the results of the IHA survey conducted will be examined to provide insights about the policies, practices, and challenges hotel industry executives face when 'crafting' strategies and renewing their corporate structures.

Sample

The sample for the survey consisted of 34 hotels drawn from the list of the 200 largest chain operated and/or owned hotel corporations listed in the July 1991 edition of *Hotels* magazine. This choice of the largest international hotel organizations was made on the assumption that their human resource strategies would reflect more advanced techniques than those of smaller hotels. The general characteristics of this sample are presented below:

(a) The bulk (88.3 per cent) of the hotel groups surveyed were either chain-owned (44.1 per cent), chain-managed (26.5 per cent) or both (17.7 per cent).

(b) The majority of companies surveyed (59.4 per cent) operate in the de luxe category, another 37.5 per cent operate standard category hotels, while 3.1 per cent operate 'budget' category hotel facilities.

(c) The majority of properties (61.8 per cent) operated by the hotel groups surveyed are in city centre locations. The remainder are spread among airport (2.9 per cent), suburban (5.9 per cent), resort (2.9 per cent), locations or a combination thereof.

(d) Business travel comprises the most important market segment at 58.8 per cent; pleasure travel is 14.7 per cent, convention-related travel 11.8 per cent, while business and pleasure was cited as the purpose of stay for 14.7 per cent of the customers who stayed with the hotel companies surveyed.

(e) Fifty per cent of the companies surveyed obtained between 11–20 per cent of their business through a reservation system, while 22 per cent and 19 per cent generated, respectively, less than 10 per cent and between 21 to 40 per cent of their business through reservation systems. And 9.4 per cent of the respondents generated more than 60 per cent of their business in such a way.

(f) Thirty-eight per cent of the respondents had an average room rate which exceeds US$100; 23.5 per cent of the respondents had an average room rate between US$75 and US$99.99; 29.4 per cent of the respondents had an average room rate between US$50 and US$74.99 and 8.8 per cent of the respondents had an average room rate less than US$50.

(g) The majority of respondents (60.6 per cent) operate hotels which average between 100 to 299 rooms; 30.3 per cent of the respondents operate establishments which average more than 300 rooms per property; 6.1 per cent of the respondents operate facilities which average less than 50 rooms per property, while 3 per cent of the respondents operate establishments which average between 50 and 99 rooms per property.

Methodology

In order to provide some insight into the human resource practices and strategies currently being implemented by members of the hotel industry, the following research approach was used. Data were collected by way of an international mail survey conducted from July through October of 1991. This method of collection was determined to be the most appropriate because of the large number of items contained in the questionnaire. The specific factors that were addressed in the survey included (a) organization profile, (b) business strategies, human resource policies and programmes, (c) compensation outlook, and (d) human resource priorities for the next two years.

The questionnaire, along with cover letter and postage-paid return envelope, was dispatched marked for the attention of 'Human Resource Managers, Chief Executive Officer, President or Vice-President in Charge of Operations'. The mail-out, which was administered by the offices of the International Hotel Association in Paris, reached hotel establishments in sixteen countries and one British territory.[2]

A total of 34 usable responses were returned (a response rate of 17 per cent) and used in the analysis of data. This result is quite typical of response rates in the hotel industry (Hiemstra 1990: 208), and we felt that the group of respondents provided a reasonable sample from which to shape preliminary observations regarding the state of the art of human resource management practices in the international hotel industry. The composition of the respondents by location, size, percentage of business booked through reservation systems, and purpose of stay is characteristic of the international hotel industry at large. However, the sample size was too small to effectively apply statistical techniques such as, for example, cluster analysis. Therefore, mainly descriptive statistics were used to analyse the data.

Results

The overall aims and goals that respondents claimed were most important to their organizations are identified in Table 7.1. An understanding of these goals is considered useful because it allows us to develop some sense of the industry's mindset concerning the strategic importance of human resources, and of the priority placed on their management relative to other organizational resources. Perhaps the most striking finding in Table 7.1 is that over 88 per cent of all respondents felt that guest satisfaction ranked as the most important aim of their organization, but that the human resources related goals that would seem to directly further this end, such as developing the best management of people and enhancing employee morale, were identified as most important by only 30 per cent and 36.4 per cent of respondents, respectively. This may indicate that hotel industry participants do not fully appreciate the intimate linkage between the performance and attitude of their employees and customers' perceptions of service quality.

A similar inconsistency was found with respect to the respondents' ratings of critical success factors and the measures that are used to monitor them. Table 7.2 indicates that the price/value perception of customers, superior service, and employee attitudes are considered by the majority of respondents to be the most critical factors behind the success of their organizations. Yet, as Table 7.3 reveals, those indicators that are most relevant to assessing performance on these factors, including rate of repeat business, employee turnover, complaint letters and guest comment cards, were ranked as the consistently least used surveillance tools. While we

Table 7.1 Importance of goals

Goal	Percentage of respondents who indicated goal 'most important'	Mean importance*
Guest satisfaction	88.2	4.77
Profitability/return on investment	61.8	4.50
Brand loyalty among customers	40.6	4.16
Financial stability	40.6	4.16
Employee morale	36.4	4.06
Developing best management people	30.0	3.97
Maximize cash flow	22.6	3.81
Shareholder wealth/value	25.8	3.61
Greatest market share	21.2	3.58
Expansion	18.2	3.33

Note: *Mean importance was calculated from a five-point scale where 1 = 'least important' and 5 = 'most important'

Table 7.2 Importance of critical success factors

Critical success factor	Percentage of respondents who indicated critical success factor 'most critical'	Mean importance*
Superior service	63.6	4.55
Employee attitude	63.6	4.52
Increase customer price/value perception	64.5	4.45
Maximize revenue	53.1	4.44
Cost control	45.5	4.24
Superior location	25.8	3.84
Superior physical plant	22.6	3.65
Achieve market segmentation	15.6	3.50

Note: *Mean importance was calculated from a five-point scale where 1 = 'least critical' and 5 = 'most critical'

Table 7.3 Importance of measures for monitoring critical success factors

Critical success factor	Percentage of respondents who indicated measures 'most important'	Mean importance*
Sales	72.7	4.67
Profit (cash flow)	63.6	4.61
Occupancy percentage	45.5	4.33
Average room rate	48.5	4.21
Rate of repeat business	46.4	4.07
Guest comment cards	21.2	3.67
Complaint letters	23.5	3.65
Employee turnover	12.5	3.50

Note: *Mean importance was calculated from a five-point scale where 1 = 'least important' and 5 = 'most important'

acknowledge the importance of monitoring sales levels and profits, as obviously the respondents do, we suggest that greater attention must be paid to customer and employee feedback if the indicated key success factors are to be properly assessed. This generates directly from the definition of service quality as the degree and direction of discrepancy between customers' perceptions and customers' expectations, and from the service employee's integral involvement in shaping service levels.

Human resource policies and practices

Respondents were asked to describe their perspective concerning the management of human resources, and 42 per cent suggested that it was best represented by the statement that 'Human resource strategies tend to be formulated at the top.' This approach provides a good foundation for a strategic emphasis on human resources management, since it signifies that this function has been accorded an important status within the organization. With a similar emphasis on strategic orientation, 18 per cent of responding organizations expressed agreement with the statement that 'People are viewed primarily as resources to be managed towards the achievement of strategic business goals.' However, 39 per cent of respondents took a very traditional view of human resources management, agreeing with statements that portray this function as providing a supporting role only and being within the exclusive domain of mid-level personnel specialists.

The respondents were asked to provide some insight about their human resources information system and specifically, the data about employees that it readily provides. Overall, the results confirm a very traditional approach to human resources management, with 63 per cent of respondents reporting that information about salary and the employee's history in the company is readily available, while only 3 per cent and 7 per cent, respectively, indicate that information about specific skills, and employee attitude and morale, is accessible. These results are inconsistent with the importance accorded to having superior service and better employee attitudes (Table 7.2), thus indicating another gap between current practices and intended strategies.

Table 7.4 summarizes the strategic policies that respondents indicated were stressed the most in personnel management. Training, the provision of career paths, and the encouragement of employee involvement were rated as important, with high importance ratings accorded to competitive pay, benefits and incentives. This indicates that management is well aware of the need to improve pay scales in order to become more competitive with other industries. Table 7.5 identifies the extent to which various training programmes are used, and, as might be expected, on-the-job training ranked as the most widely employed method. One might conclude from these results that technical training continues to be emphasized possibly at the expense of training designed to improve interpersonal competencies. It is interesting to note, however, that the respondents were somewhat receptive to the notion of sensitivity training, and this may bode well for the future extension of this technique to front-line employees, and thus, for a needed emphasis on training in interpersonal skills.

As far as the methods used to hire hourly workers, Table 7.6 indicates that local newspapers are, at 53 per cent, the preferred medium. At the

Table 7.4 Importance of strategic policies in personnel management

Strategic policy	Percentage of respondents who indicated strategic policy 'most important'	Mean importance*
Formal training or education programme	45.5	4.06
Provide career paths within company	35.3	3.94
Encourage employee involvement	31.3	3.91
Cross-train in related positions	16.1	3.52
Pay relatively high wages	12.1	3.36
Provide job security	18.8	3.31
Provide attractive benefit packages	9.1	3.18
Provide incentive programmes	9.1	3.18

Note: *Mean importance was calculated from a five-point scale where 1 = 'least important' and 5 = 'most important'

Table 7.5 Importance of training activities

Training activity	Percentage of respondents who indicated training activity 'most important'	Mean importance*
On-the-job training	73.5	4.68
Group training and orientation for new employees	57.6	4.21
Handbook of standard operating procedures	26.5	3.68
Guidance on career paths within company	9.1	3.21
Cross training on multiple jobs	3.1	3.13
Sensitivity training for managers	9.1	2.97
Computer training programme	6.3	2.84
Job enrichment seminars	0.0	2.53
Scheduled outside guest speakers	3.0	2.36

Note: *Mean importance was calculated from a five-point scale where 1 = 'least important' and 5 = 'most important'

same time a considerable number of respondents seem to rely on personal recommendations (26 per cent) and flexible staffing (20 per cent) in the hiring of hourly workers.

Table 7.6 Methods used to hire hourly workers

Activity	Percentage of respondents who indicated method 'most often used'	Mean importance*
Advertise in local newspapers	53.1	4.19
Rely on personal recommendations	25.8	3.61
Rely on flexible staffing	20.0	2.93
Affiliate with local high schools	16.1	2.32
Use local employment offices	3.3	2.00

Note: *Mean was calculated from a five-point scale where 1 = 'least often used' and 5 = 'most often used'

Table 7.7 illustrates the sorts of practices that respondents have employed to enhance the motivation and commitment of their staff. It is encouraging to note that at least half of the responding organizations attempted in some manner to implement such tools as empowerment, recognition programmes, and opportunities for advancement within the company. Where employee recognition programmes are concerned, it is important to understand that in order to be effective, they must have challenging standards, acceptance by employees, neither too few nor too many rewards, and longevity.

Respondents were asked to indicate the types of activities that are used to communicate with hourly employees, and, based on the study results, it would appear that the majority of them do understand the importance of keeping the channels of communication open. The challenge now is for these organizations to ensure that they are providing their employees with the right kinds of information, and that they are doing so on a timely and ongoing basis.

Compensation practices and outlook

A hotel company's compensation and reward policies and practices system should be tied directly to quality service performance that engenders customer satisfaction. One key compensation issue is to determine what is needed at each level of the hotel organization to produce organizational performance.

The first step is to identify the appropriate level at which performance can be reliably recognized and measured and to reward it at that level (Lawler 1981). General managers should be evaluated and rewarded based on the performance of their unit – the hotel organization. A supervisor in the housekeeping department, for example, should be evaluated and rewarded for the performance of his/her unit impacting organizational performance. Within this framework, each employee is a participant in a performance unit. Each performance unit can be identified and the hotel organization can clarify for each unit, and the individuals within it, what is important and what will be evaluated.

The survey results indicate, however, that there were no differences between employee categories (i.e., across organizational levels) in the hotel companies examined: all hotel groups reported about the same percentage increase and similar projected percentage increases in compensation, ranging from 26–30 per cent (our range is deliberately kept conservative because of the small sample size). As Figure 7.1 indicates, 37.9 per cent of the respondents pay their employees according to merit; 31 per cent base pay increases on the cost of living factor, while 6.9 per cent give wage increases based on time spent on the job.

Furthermore, the survey (Figure 7.2) shows that 75.8 per cent of the respondents perceive themselves to be paying the same hourly wages as the competition; 24.2 per cent are of the opinion that they are paying their staff more than competitors. In terms of benefit packages (Figure 7.3) most respondents appear to provide their employees with the standard range of

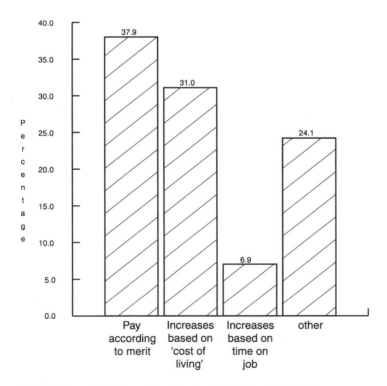

Figure 7.1 Policy regarding pay increases for hourly employees

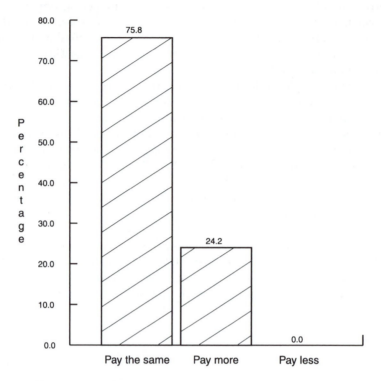

Figure 7.2 Hourly pay compared to that of competitors

benefits. Thus, 67.6 per cent of the respondents provide paid vacations. Health insurance and paid holidays are taken care of by 58.8 per cent of respondents. More than half of all respondents provide some sort of retirement plan and flexible work schedules, while only 23.5 per cent offer employees a profit sharing plan. At the same time, however, the study findings show that most respondents agree that incentives (as opposed to fixed pay and benefits) need to become a more important part of the compensation system (both when the question is posed in a positive and in a negative way as Figure 7.4 shows). Despite this opinion, they demonstrate little if any creativity with regard to the application of incentives in their organizations. As Table 7.7 indicates, the dominant incentive type currently used by respondents is 'money', which may point to a certain lack of creativity and sophistication in the application of incentive schemes at present. Furthermore, there is a limitation to the application of money as an incentive in that below the managers and supervisors levels, *only half* the establishments appear to use this incentive (i.e., about half the companies surveyed do not have any incentive programme at all below these levels). Courses and seminars are also perceived by respondents as a viable incentive

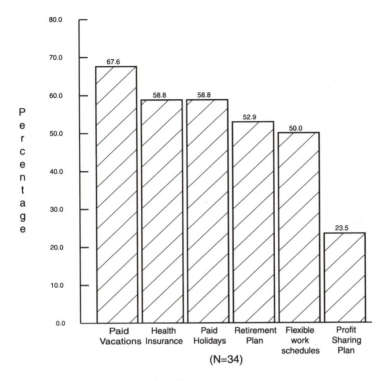

Figure 7.3 Benefit packages for hourly employees

for managers (44 per cent) and supervisors (35 per cent) as Table 7.7 indicates. This is therefore another example of discrepancy between the importance ascribed to incentive plans and the apparent lack of implementation of such plans.

Table 7.7 Motivation of various employee groups (percentage of companies using incentive)

Employee group	Money	Holidays	Presents/ gifts	Courses/ seminars	Other
Managers	88.2	14.7	11.8	44.1	11.8
Supervisors	61.8	11.8	8.8	35.3	8.8
General office staff	47.1	14.7	14.7	29.4	11.8
Maintenance employees	47.1	14.7	20.6	23.5	11.8
Customer services	55.9	14.7	23.5	29.4	14.7
Service employees	58.8	14.7	29.4	26.5	11.8

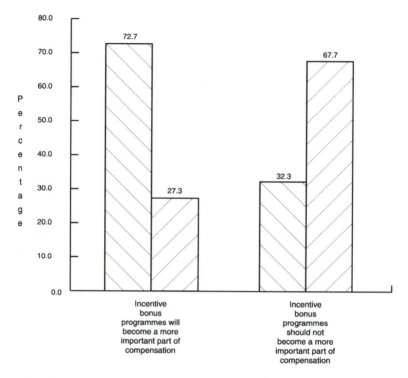

Figure 7.4 Incentive bonus programmes

THE USE OF LOCAL VERSUS EXPATRIATE MANAGERS

The previous section of this chapter has highlighted the anomaly which appears to exist in relation to top managers espousing the need to formulate better human resource policies which are not reflected in actual operating strategies. Whilst that section looked at operating norms such as pay mix, incentive systems and training practices, this section will examine the more general issue of the use of local and expatriate managers in hotels. Such use has more than logistic implications, in that there may be differences in, for example, conditions of employment and attitudes between these two groups which could lead to problems in motivation or even the lack of development of sufficient local managers to satisfy a country's demand for hotel management staff. The use of expatriates in international businesses in general will be examined first before dealing more specifically with the hotel industry. The situations pertaining to Hong Kong and to China will be used to illustrate possible implications.

Use of locals and expatriates in international business

Multinational corporations have various nationality policies with regard to the composition of management in their foreign subsidiaries. Such policies can be of four types: ethnocentric, polycentric, regiocentric, and geo-centric (Heenan and Perlmutter 1979).

Ethnocentrism refers to a preference for putting home-country personnel in key positions of foreign subsidiaries everywhere in the world, in the belief that home-country personnel are more competent and trust-worthy. These home-country personnel are more familiar with the home country's environment and company's strategy. Multinational corpor-ations (MNCs) adopting ethnocentric policy tend to overlook the impact of cultural difference on the performance of management.

Polycentrism refers to a preference for developing local nationals of host countries for key positions in their own countries. Corporations adopt-ing polycentric policy tend to believe that cultures of various countries are quite dissimilar and local nationals in foreign subsidiaries should be left alone as long as their work is profitable. Polycentric policy in MNCs may also be regarded as a localization policy which also aims to put locals into key management positions. However, localization policy is different to polycentric policy in the way that polycentric policy refers to the use of local managers in foreign subsidiaries of MNCs while localization policy refers to the use of local managers in both local business of local firms and foreign subsidiaries of MNCs.

Regiocentric policy tends to recruit and develop managers on a regional basis – that is, regional people are developed for key positions anywhere in the region. This approach has the advantage of considering the political and economic connections between countries in a region and has more flexibility over polycentric policy.

Under geocentric policy, nationality of managers is not considered in the choice of top management. Instead, managers of any nationality can occupy the top managerial positions provided that they are competent and they can optimize the resource allocation of the corporation on a global basis. This personnel policy aims to create a truly international manage-ment who can move around the world.

There is a general tendency during the internationalization of a MNC that its top management nationality policy moves through phases, from ethnocentric to polycentric or regiocentric, and finally to geocentric (Heenan and Perlmutter 1979; Hutton 1988). It is not necessary that all MNCs will follow this trend in their process of internationalization. Some MNCs may reverse the direction from geocentrism to polycentrism because of changing global environment or host country environment.

Researchers suggested that ethnocentric nationality-based companies inevitably run into serious managerial problems when they become multinational corporations because of the basic differences in the various national cultures involved (Hofstede 1980; Hutton 1988). Kuin (1972: 99) concluded in his study: 'No multinational corporation can do without a generous number of nationals in charge of local operations.'

This does not imply an absolute superiority of polycentric policy over other top management nationality policies. Instead, none of these four policies is the best in every circumstance. Ethnocentrism may work better in the initial stage of investment in foreign subsidiaries but polycentric approach may be required with changing national conditions in host countries as well as home countries. For instance, when a MNC faces the problem of high management turnover in its home country because of poor promotion prospects, it may adopt ethnocentric policy in its foreign subsidiaries to alleviate the pressure of more promotion opportunities for home country personnel.

As Kolde (1985) suggested, in the early phases of internationalization MNCs tend to use expatriates in their foreign subsidiaries both to ensure better control and because of the lack of qualified local managers and the simplicity of selection and appointment. Due to the high cost of expatriation and host government pressures, expatriates will seldom be sent abroad unless for senior managerial positions (Tung and Miller 1990). By the time the MNCs approach maturity, local managers in their foreign subsidiaries will have acquired the necessary experience and held the top positions in their particular subsidiaries. Since experienced top management talent is always scarce, the MNCs need to retain these local managers by offering promotion opportunities which are often positions in larger operations of the MNCs in other host countries.

While local managers of developing host countries are seeking more important positions in US and European MNCs, Third World MNCs are also looking for a big share in the global market as they gain experience from subsidiaries of US and European MNCs in their own countries. Developing countries like Hong Kong are no longer only host countries for MNCs, but by becoming also headquarters countries they are competing with MNCs from developed countries in the process of market globalization (Kolde 1985; Fisher 1989; Reynolds 1990). Since these Third World MNCs tend to employ a high proportion of managers from their home country, as their counterparts MNCs from developed countries do in the initial stage of internationalization, there is a high demand for Third World managers. Asian managers provide a good example of how Third World managers become a highly prized commodity and even more valuable than their western counterparts in the world management labour market (Fisher 1989).

Expatriates and locals

Tung (1981) pointed out the advantages of putting more locals in top management. In Tung's survey with 80 multinational corporations, it was found that the advantages of staffing with locals include familiarity with local culture, knowledge of local language, lower costs of compensations to management, and better public relations.

Robinson (1973) presented a comprehensive picture about the advantages of ethnocentric policy or the use of more expatriates. With ethnocentric policy and the use of home country expatriates in top management, MNCs can exercise better control over the local subsidiaries with the assumption that home countries' expatriates are more loyal to the MNCs than locals. Also, expatriates have better knowledge of the multinational firm's global strategies and organizational culture. They can work as a bridge of communication between headquarters and local subsidiaries (Hutton 1988). Control over local managers might be difficult particularly when there is conflict between the benefits of the MNCs and the benefits of the host countries (Kolde 1985; Livingstone 1989). Total absence of expatriates may lead to loss of control over foreign subsidiaries and turn them into closed operations.

Gladwin and Walter (1980: 407) described the dilemma of using local or expatriate managers: 'There is often a trade-off between the ability to operate well in the local environment and the ability to communicate well with executives in corporate headquarters.'

Hutton (1988) shows that in ethnocentric-oriented MNCs, the promotion prospect of local managers will be blocked with the domination of expatriates in top management. This can lead to dissatisfaction and difficulties in retaining local managers:

> In many cases locally recruited managers will simply remain with the multinational enterprise as long as it provides them with training and opportunities not available from local companies. Once these opportunities have been exhausted, local managers will naturally seek new employment elsewhere.
>
> (Hutton 1988: 127)

Cultural difference is the major difficulty faced by expatriate managers. Inability of expatriates in adapting rapidly to the environment of a host country will eventually reflect adversely on their management performance (Hutton, 1988). Black and Porter (1991) found in their study that the managerial behaviours displayed by American expatriates in Hong Kong were ineffective in the environment of Hong Kong. Cultural adjustment is required: in language, in local customs and in organizational culture in foreign subsidiaries. Thus successful expatriates should know the cultural and economic background of the host country, and should possess attitudinal flexibility to accept unfamiliar modes of behaviour and value systems (Tung, 1981).

The use of expatriates can be a source of conflict between host country and MNCs (Gladwin and Walter 1980; Hutton 1988). The tendency of multinationals to rely heavily on expatriates for top management in their foreign subsidiaries would place a ceiling on the aspirations and achievements of local managers. Local managers would see expatriate managers as a barrier to their career advancement, especially when expatriates occupy the most desirable jobs in the host country (Gladwin and Walter 1980) or when the expatriates enjoy a much higher level of compensation compared with locals in similar positions (Hutton 1988). In extreme cases, blocked promotion of local managers by expatriates could lead to legal action (Nash 1977).

The cost of employing expatriates is usually higher than for locals, particularly due to the additional costs of taxation arrangement, accommodation arrangement, children's education, bonus to compensate for being away from home, annual leave with passage, and so on (Hutton 1988; Wyatt 1990). There are also some indirect administrative costs for employing expatriates such as arranging travel, applying for work permits, arranging accommodation, finding schools for their children. To maintain an expatriate manager overseas sometimes costs a MNC twice what it costs to maintain the same individual at the home country. So lower labour cost is often a major consideration for MNCs to adopt a polycentric personnel policy (Gladwin and Walter, 1980).

Localization of management

In most parts of the world, pressure to appoint local managers is increasing (Livingstone 1989). It is also stated in the OECD's declaration in 1992 that MNCs should, to the greatest extent practicable, utilize, train, and prepare for upgrading members of the local labour force (OECD 1992).

Both American and non-American MNCs try to limit the presence of expatriates in their foreign subsidiaries to perhaps general manager and one or two others (Gladwin and Walter 1980; Edstrom and Lorange 1985). MNCs in Japan, like Coca-Cola, Citibank and IBM, attempted to localize the management of their subsidiaries with Japanese. In 1972, Nestlé's in the Ivory Coast tried to fully indigenize the management over a five-year adjustment period, with the number of expatriate managers cut from 11 to five and the number of local managers raised from two to 37.

In the past, MNCs were reluctant to employ local managers in senior management positions in Asia but the track record of Asian managers has proved their competence. There is a strong trend towards localization by MNCs in Asia. MNCs are willing to appoint locals as chief executives, to promote local managers, to train and develop locals as first-line and second-line managers (Fisher 1989).

Progress of localization depends on the availability of trained and experienced local managers. The supply of locals capable of running a complex MNC subsidiary is often very limited. To overcome this problem, many MNCs have established company-run management schools, sent locals for overseas training, and made financial contributions to local educational institutions (Kolde 1985). The actual number of local managers being used is not necessarily a reflection of the commitment of a MNC to localize. Localization does not equal the total exclusion of expatriates (Fisher 1989). Instead, a few local managers can be enough if they hold the key positions and make most decisions (Livingstone 1989). The localization programme of Nestlé's did not simply increase the number of local managers, it put them in the really significant managerial positions including the general manager, marketing manager, and finance manager (Salmans 1977). It seems that American MNCs are more successful than non-American MNCs in putting a higher number of locals into the top management positions of their foreign subsidiaries, partly because it is easier to find locals fluent in English than in German, French, Swedish, or Japanese (Gladwin and Walter 1980). However, local managers in American MNCs' foreign subsidiaries enjoy less decision-making power compared with managers in subsidiaries of non-American MNCs (Negandhi and Baliga 1979). Indeed, increase in localization of management was also recorded in Japanese MNCs (Hanada 1987; Negandhi and Serapio 1991).

United Nations (1982) indicated that there are three major sectors of MNCs in international tourism: hotel sector, airline sector, and tour operations. The growing internationalization of the hotel sector was studied by Dunning and McQueen in 1982. They suggested that the internationalization of hotel corporations is a process to increase their worldwide presence and in turn reinforce their competitive advantages over non-internationalized hotel corporations. There are now a considerable number of hotel corporations working multinationally (Benson 1991). Most of these multinational hotel corporations (MNHCs) were based in the US in the past but there is a growing in importance of Pacific Rim developers including Hong Kong's companies (Litteljohn and Roper 1991). Indeed, Hong Kong is currently home to MNHCs including New World, Omni, Regal, Shangri-La, Park Lane, Mandarin Oriental, Peninsula, and Century International. The biggest one, New World, together with its American subsidiary, Ramada, managed over 150 hotels and 50,000 rooms in the world in 1993 (New World Development Company 1993).

The human factor in technology transfer

In developing countries, one of the most important constraints of economic development is the low availability of skilled management personnel. Farmer and Richman (1970) stressed that management is a primary active ingredient in the productive process of all economic systems. Drucker (1970) noted that there are no underdeveloped countries but only under-managed ones. Management contributes to the growth of economy in the form of advance in knowledge and management technology (Denison 1974). MNCs play a very important role in the transfer of this management technology to developing countries and in the development of the local management capability of these countries (ILO 1973).

Undiandeye (1984) suggested that developing and sustaining industrial growth in developing countries is correlated to the transfer of management technology from Western MNCs. He also found that the diffusion of management skills from MNCs to local firms is through competent local personnel who held managerial positions in these MNCs.

Pine (1991) adopted the technology transfer model of Dahlman and Westphal (1983) and suggested three levels of transfer of management technology in the hotel industry:

Level 1: The capability required to operate a technology, for example, to run a hotel.

Level 2: Investment capability required to create new productive capacity, such as new hotels.

Level 3: Innovation capability to modify and improve methods, products, and services in hotels.

It is relatively easy to achieve Level 1 and Level 2 through management contract and the use of foreign expertise – that is, expatriate personnel. The achievement of Level 3 transfer requires the development of local personnel to the extent that foreign expertise could become redundant. This implies not only an increase in number of local hotel managers but also a local management pool capable of taking full management responsibility at all stages of hotel development; reacting properly to changing local and international business environment; offering internationally acceptable standards of hotel services and maybe even expanding outside its own national boundaries (Pine 1991: 5–6).

In this sense, localization of hotel management capability can be an indicator for the successful transfer of management technology from MNHCs to local personnel and companies. The commitment of MNHCs towards technology transfer can be reflected in the number and proportion of expatriates in hotels in developing countries and the input of these hotels to developing local personnel.

Despite the fact that the number of expatriates should be decreased in the process of technology transfer, technology transfer needs to be achieved through the training offered by expatriate managers (Shelp 1984). Both expatriate personnel and MNHCs are important in providing access to management knowledge and providing training and experience to local people.

Many management contracts of MNHCs in the host country give them little restriction on the employment of expatriates and little formal responsibility of developing local personnel. This may limit the development of the host country's hotel industry and local management capability. Even when there is contractual requirement for MNHCs to develop a certain number of local managers, there is still the threat of over-promoting unqualified locals or insufficient delegation of decision-making power to these local managers compared with their expatriate counterparts (Pine 1991).

The human factor in sustaining competitive advantages

Dunning and McQueen (1982a, 1982b) explained the growing internationalization of the hotel industry through their eclectic theory of multinational enterprise. Dunning and McQueen found that multinational hotel chains have competitive (ownership specific) advantages over local hotels on proprietary knowledge and experience. They have knowledge of foreign markets from experience in tourist-generating countries which are often their home countries (Ascher 1985). This market knowledge enables them to differentiate themselves from local hotels to concentrate on the luxury end of the business traveller market (Cave 1971). Also, they have managerial and organization expertise in the design of hotels, and technically superior methods of production and control.

Western MNHCs tend to use non-equity modes of involvement in their overseas operations. The most popular form of non-equity involvement is management contract (Dunning and McQueen 1982a, 1982b; Reynolds 1990; Meder 1990). In Hong Kong in 1989, only three out of 11 foreign MNHCs' hotels had an equity holding in the actual property itself (Pine *et al.* 1989). Although these MNHCs have little equity involvement in the hotels they managed they are still able to exercise control over resources allocation through management contract, which gives the MNHCs a very high degree of freedom in the daily operation of the hotels. This freedom is important because the MNHCs do need to ensure that the quality of operation in their foreign subsidiaries is up to their international standard. The bargaining power of MNHCs with owners is particularly important when the hotel owners plan to adopt some sort of policies or practices which may be beneficial to the hotel owners only at the expense of quality of service, or to use a hotel manager who is not qualified to manage the hotel effectively. The MNHCs are very serious about protecting their brand image and controlling the quality of operation of the hotel since standardization of quality is often perceived as an important factor for success in these MNHCs (Dunning and McQueen 1982a; Cleverdon and Edwards 1982).

The MNHCs achieve this purpose through the use of expatriates in top management and regular inspection of the hotel by regional directors. This is based on the assumption that expatriate managers are more familiar with the quality standard and operation procedures of the headquarters (Robinson 1973; Kolde 1985), and that they are more strict about quality control (Reynolds 1990). Expatriates are also expected to be more loyal to company headquarters and thus more easily controlled (Kolde 1985; Livingstone 1989).

However, due to the high cost of employing expatriate managers, it is impossible to use expatriate managers in all junior or middle management positions. Instead local managers, who are very familiar with local customs and languages, will be developed to exercise the first-line supervision and may be promoted to higher management later. In order to maintain the quality standard of foreign subsidiaries, MNHCs need to invest a substantial amount of resources to train these local personnel in quality standard and production procedures. Since ownership advantages of MNHCs largely take the form of management knowledge and production procedures (Dunning 1989), these advantages are easily transferred to other hotel firms through turnover of such personnel. As Undiandeye indicated:

> The local nationals learn several things from the American expatriates
> . . . . The acquired skill is transmitted to indigenous firms if the local
> manager terminates his job with MNFs and sets up his own firm or moves
> to a manufacturing or service industry that is locally owned.
>
> (Undiandeye 1984: 10)

The diffusion of proprietary knowledge to local hotel companies and hotel personnel is inevitable unless there is complete refusal to have any local business partner or total exclusion of locals in management. However, total exclusion of locals in management is very disadvantageous to the long-term development of the firm in the local environment (Kuin 1972; Hofstede 1980; Hutton 1988; Livingstone 1989). This kind of diffusion of knowledge can, in the long run, result in loss of competitive advantages in the host country. It should be noted that transfer of management know-how to local personnel and local firms is desirable for many developing regions, but not necessarily desirable for multinational firms.

Some MNHCs protect their proprietary knowledge by reducing the turnover of management personnel, especially locals. Experience of MNHCs shows that stability of management is very important to successful operation (Chorengel and Teare 1992). Many MNCs retain their key managers through better prospects of internal promotion, such as sending them to larger operations or more senior positions in other countries (Kolde 1985). Provided that a MNHC can successfully retain its local management personnel in a host country, investment in the training of local managers can enhance the efficiency of operation in local subsidiaries since local managers are more familiar with local customs, consumer patterns and languages (Tung 1981). It also adds to the ability of the group in adapting to different languages and social environment, by providing a management pool familiar with the regional culture. This kind of cross-cultural ability will be beneficial for the further expansion of the group in other developing countries. For example, in order to operate efficiently in culturally different environments, the management team of Hyatt in its worldwide subsidiaries and corporate office are often composed of managers from different nationalities (Chorengel and Teare 1992).

History of expatriates and MNHCs in Hong Kong

Like most MNCs, MNHCs tend to adopt ethnocentric nationality policy in the top management of their foreign subsidiaries at least in the initial stages of development (Kolde 1985; Reynolds 1990). This can be accounted for by the simplicity of selecting and appointing managers in the home country in lieu of host country. Also, expatriate managers have better knowledge of the parent companies' policies and long-term objectives and are possibly more loyal to the parent companies. They can work as a bridge of communication and help to balance the goals of the subsidiaries and the headquarters (Robinson 1973; Hutton 1988; Livingstone 1989). Perhaps a more important reason for the use of expatriates is the low availability of qualified local talent (Heenan and Perlmutter 1979). Use of expatriates is more favoured in the initial phase of development of a MNC's subsidiaries (Kolde 1985). This is because procedures and policies are not well defined at this stage, and control by home country expatriates is perceived as more important than the later stage.

The domination of expatriates in top managerial positions exists in the whole tourism industry, but the problem is more marked in multinational hotel chains (Calvo 1974; Sany 1977; Ascher 1985). As the tourism industry of a country grows, local personnel will have acquired hotel management knowledge and experience by working in foreign MNCs. The reliance on expatriates will be reduced when there is a sufficient and steady supply of qualified local hotel managers (WTO 1988a).

Use of expatriate managers for top executive posts is very common in the hotel industry of Hong Kong (Reynolds 1990). Despite the fact that a company's commitment to localization should not be merely measured by the number of local managers (Livingstone 1989), the number of expatriates in a MNC's foreign subsidiaries should seldom exceed 10 per cent of the workforce and is typically 1 per cent (Edstrom and Lorange 1985). Expatriates accounted for 16 per cent of management personnel in Hong Kong's companies (Kirkbride and Tang 1989). However, it was found in 1994 that 44.3 per cent of general managers in Hong Kong hotels were expatriates (Yu and Pine 1994). Pine (1991) found that 20 per cent of hotel managers, in Hong Kong were expatriates. These figures show that the proportion of expatriate managers especially general managers in the Hong Kong hotel industry, is higher than the local average (Table 7.8). This implies that there is potential for the Hong Kong hotel industry to further localize its management.

Pine (1991) also found that there was a higher proportion of expatriates at the executive level of management (63.4 per cent) than at other levels of management (14.6 per cent), and very few expatriates at supervisory level (4.6 per cent), as indicated in Table 7.9. This may be correlated to the traditional belief that expatriate personnel are particularly important in the luxury hotel market because they have better international experience and knowledge of foreign customers compared with locals. It should be noted that this traditional belief will be tested in the empirical survey of this study to see if it still persists in Hong Kong.

Changing role of expatriates and MNHCs in Hong Kong

The change in market environment in the Hong Kong hotel industry partly accounts for the changing role of Western and local hotel managers and hotel companies. As the hotel and tourism market in Hong Kong becomes mature, the importance of the luxury hotel market is declining, while the three- or four-star middle market becomes more important (Peartree 1993). Traditionally, Western MNHCs tend to dominate the luxury and business travel market with their competitive advantages in brand-name,

Table 7.8 A comparison of the proportion of expatriates in different situations

Proportion of expatriate hotel general managers among all hotel general managers in Hong Kong (Yu and Pine 1994)	44.3%
Proportion of expatriate hotel managers among all hotel managers in Hong Kong (Pine 1991)	20%
Proportion of expatriate managers among all managers in all industries of Hong Kong (Kirkbride and Tang 1989)	16%

Table 7.9 Proportion of expatriate hotel managers in different levels of management

	Proportion of expatriates (%)	Ratio of locals to expatriates
Executive managers	63.4	0.6
Other managers	14.6	5.8
Supervisors	4.6	20.7

reservation system, and management expertise (United Nations 1982; WTO 1985; Meder 1990; Porter 1990). However, the advantages of multinational hotel chains and expatriates over knowledge of operating luxury hotels is less useful in this mid-level market. In Hong Kong, this market is dominated by local hotels and local management which are more flexible in adapting to the rapidly changing local environment (Reynolds 1990).

Also, Chinese tourism from Taiwan and China as well as from other ASEAN countries is growing into a major source of customers in the hotel market of Hong Kong (HKTA 1990–1992; Yu and Go 1994). Expatriates' knowledge of the traditional European and American markets is becoming less important than, or at best only as important as, the local managers' knowledge of Asian markets (Fisher 1989). Through this knowledge, local hotel chains and local management may develop their competitive advantages over foreign multinationals in penetrating the Asian market.

On the other hand, local hotel managers have acquired knowledge of managing international-oriented hotels by working in local subsidiaries of multinational hotel chains (United Nations 1982). Local hotel groups and local hotel managers have gained the required knowledge by cooperating with MNHCs, or working in a local subsidiary of a MNHC. The more the locals learn, the less will be the competitive advantage of expatriate over local managers, and subsequently of MNHCs over local hotels.

There are also some basic factors which contribute to the growing importance of local hotel managers in Hong Kong. Local managers have an advantage with their knowledge of local customs, local staff, local suppliers and the consumption pattern of local customers. The need for knowledge of local customers is particularly significant in the Food and Beverage sector, as most customers are locals. Proponents of localization also believe that hotels staffed by Hong Kong Chinese managers would be more effective since they speak the language of most employees as well as English. In other words, they can communicate effectively with operational staff and expatriate colleagues, as well as with headquarters management in the United States or Europe. As a result of internationalization, bilingual and bicultural qualifications of Asian managers are highly prized. Many MNCs have come to the conclusion that an English-speaking Asian manager in an Asian setting is better equipped than a Western manager with the same qualifications and experience (Fisher 1989).

The rise of Hong Kong expatriates and Hong-Kong-based MNHCs

There are basically two different groups of Hong Kong expatriate hotel managers. The first group is local hotel managers who have once worked in foreign MNHCs' subsidiaries in Hong Kong, and are then transferred to MNHCs' subsidiaries outside Hong Kong. In such circumstances, these local hotel managers are *third country expatriates* in the host countries.

The second group is locals being trained by Hong-Kong-based MNHCs and managing hotel development projects in developing countries. Since they come from the home country of the Hong-Kong-based MNHCs, they are *home country expatriates.*

As the Hong Kong firms get more experience in hotel management, they become more efficient and thus make more profits. Local hotel groups earned a substantial amount of profits during the rapid tourism growth in the late 1980s (Meder 1990). On the other hand, the profits made by local hotel groups through improving managerial efficiency and tourist growth are limited in comparison with their profits made through property appreciation (Reynolds 1990). As a result, Hong Kong MNHCs became capitally very rich. They grew by expanding to other countries so as to build their international reputation. Expansion of Hong Kong MNHCs was partly achieved through the acquisition of hotel companies and properties in developed countries, as well as the management contracts owned by these companies. This included the acquisition of Ramada by the New World Group in 1989; Aircoa by the Regal Group in 1989; Omni by the Wharf Group in 1988; Southern Pacific Hotel Corporation by the Hale Corporation in 1988.

Indeed, the target for expansion also includes developing countries in the geographically and culturally close Asian countries such as China and Vietnam (Reynolds 1990). For the development of hotels in these developing countries, Hong Kong MNHCs have advantages over their Western competitors in terms of cultural adaptability of management as well as relations with local government. Actually the tourism markets of these countries are growing so rapidly that there are plenty of opportunities for hotel development.

Different from American hotel chains, Hong-Kong-based hotels tend to acquire ownership control over their foreign subsidiaries (Reynolds 1990; Pine 1991). Hong Kong MNHCs' active investment in hotel property investment does not imply their inactiveness in providing management services. Instead, the value of hotel management services being exported from Hong Kong in 1990 and 1991 was 334 and 359 million Hong Kong dollars and the value was growing upwards (HKCSI 1993). A Hong Kong hotel management company, the New World Hotels International, managed over 6,500 hotel rooms of 12 hotels in Hong Kong and China (New World Development Company 1993).

The export of hotel management services is usually related to the export of hotel managers, at least in the initial stage of development. This gives rise to a new group of hotel managers coming from Hong Kong, who either intentionally or unintentionally transfer their hotel management knowledge to hotel personnel in the host country. A typical example is the training offered by Hong Kong hotel managers to hotel staff in China.

Localization policy of MNHCs in China

The pace of localization can be affected by national policy towards the use of expatriates. It is common in many developing countries that they use work permits to regulate the use of expatriates in the tourism sector (WTO 1988b). The actual pace of localization varies from country to country. For instance, Holiday Inn has a formal policy of localization in China (Spearman 1993) but does not necessarily have the same policy in other countries. Indeed, China had the policy that any expatriate member of staff would be 'doubled' with a local member of staff (Pine 1991). For subsidiaries of MNHCs in Korea, Taiwan, and Japan, employment of expatriate staff in management positions is avoided apart from the post of executive chef (Reynolds 1990). Although localization of business management is not a national policy in Hong Kong, the political trend related to 1997 may accelerate the pace of localization in the Hong Kong hotel industry.

In a survey about the subsidiaries of MNHCs in China (HTM 1991), it was found that many MNHCs had problems relating to the use of expatriates. In the hotels owned or managed by the Peninsula group, there was the problem of local staff's resistance to the expatriates who mostly occupied the top positions. In the Hyatt Xian, the lack of local middle management created a communication gap between the top management and the front-line staff. The Shangri-La group also experienced difficulty in communication between expatriate managers and staff in China.

The survey found that several hotel groups had a strong localization policy in their owned or managed hotels in China. The Hilton, the New World, the Sheraton, and the Holiday Inn were trying to promote more local Chinese to managerial positions in their China subsidiaries. As McQueen (1983) and Pine (1991) suggested, both formal education and experience of working in international-oriented hotels are essential in developing hotel personnel who are capable of providing an international standard of hotel service. In order to localize the management effectively, most MNHCs had invested a substantial amount of resources in training. Cross-training by sending local Chinese to Hong Kong for management training and international exposure was common in, for instance, the Lee Gardens, the New World, and the Sheraton.

Indeed, several MNHCs established their own hotel training school in China – for instance, the Palace Hotel School of the Peninsula group in Beijing, the Holiday Inn University of the Holiday Inn group, the Hospitality Management Training Centre of the New World group in Guangzhou. Most of the hotel schools provide training for operational skills, and there are also management development programmes in some of them.

Most MNHCs sent expatriates to China to conduct training programmes to local Chinese. For example, Sheraton group sent senior staff from the regional office to conduct training to local Chinese in China. In the hospitality management training centre of the New World group in Guangzhou, most trainers of the centre were experienced Hong Kong expatriates. Indeed, one expatriate manager of New World's subsidiaries in China was even awarded an honorary citizenship of Guangzhou in 1986 in recognition of his support and contribution to the modernization of China.

The New World group provides a good example of how expatriate managers and MNHCs help the localization of hotel management in developing countries. Indeed, the New World group had a complete plan for the use of local and expatriate managers in China. In the initial stage of development, there was general lack of qualified and experienced Chinese nationals, especially for the managerial posts. Expatriates from Hong Kong and overseas were sent to China to train up the local workers. Although the top management positions were held by expatriates, the use of expatriates was avoided at the middle management and supervisory level. Actually, the group was trying to fully localize the management of their hotels in China as soon as possible. The group had a well planned management succession programme of replacing the Hong Kong expatriate managers with local Chinese managers.

CONCLUSION

The IHA survey data indicate repeatedly that top managers espouse the need to formulate better human resources strategies, yet the operating strategies lag behind. Thus, they rank guest satisfaction as the most important goal, and consider superior service and employee attitude as the most critical factors affecting this goal. At the same time, however, the operating personnel norms seem to lag behind in terms of the pay mix, most notably lack of appropriate incentive systems, as well as training practices. Once again, while managers espouse the view that pay and training are key issues for improving performance, there is evidently a gap between this and operating norms in that regard. Perhaps the major contribution of this study therefore is bringing this gap to light in the hope of stimulating real change. Those hotel corporations committed to bridging the gap will be able to create and sustain a competitive advantage on the basis of their people which will be difficult to match by their competitors.

With regard to the use of local and expatriate managers it is necessary for globalizing companies to appreciate that, in developing country locations particulary, there will sooner or later be a move towards localization of management staff. The degree of localization may be limited or extreme; it may be enacted by the hotel itself for sound business reasons or it may be forced upon the company by prevailing legal and political conditions. Therefore it would be wise to have an understanding of the localization process and potential influences, good or bad, on managers themselves and the hotel business in general. For any specific hotel company and location there will be an optimum blend of local and expatriate managers, and this blend will change with time as the potential of locals increases as appropriate education, training and experience become more readily available. Proper regard for the localization process will enable the transition to be smooth and bring greater success to the hotel company by utilizing the best and most appropriate qualities of both local and expatriate managers.

CASE: INTER-CONTINENTAL HOTELS – PEOPLE ARE A KEY RESOURCE

The hospitality industry is above all a 'people industry'. A guest's impression of any hotel is governed by the attitude and efficiency of its staff. Recognizing people as its greatest resource, Inter-Continental Hotels seek to attract individuals who have worked in many countries and have experienced multicultural business and social problems. Just as there is no single stereotype for a hotel, Inter-Continental advocates an independent management style among its employees, believing in the importance of empowerment. By encouraging management initiative, Inter-Continental is able to attract independent-minded managers capable of solving their own problems to maximize guest satisfaction and run hotels at a profit.

Career development planning is central to Inter-Continental's business. It affects the calibre of the people who are recruited, the level of their performance and ensures that they stay with Inter-Continental. As a result, the company has sophisticated and reliable methods for identifying talent and ensures that potential is fulfilled. A global transfer system successfully places employees at all levels in vacant positions throughout the company, internationally.

As employees rise to positions of greater responsibility, new personnel, recruited from the top training centres and universities around the world, move into entry level positions. Their training begins immediately and continues throughout their career with Inter-Continental. Education and training is an ongoing requirement for all employees and Inter-Continental has developed a range of innovative in-house training programmes, regarded as models for the industry.

The Career 2000 programme gives employees the skills required to fulfil core business objectives and to capitalize upon the opportunities presented by new technology and management techniques. The Corporate Management Development programme or 'Fast Track' is unique in the industry. Combined with an MBA course, it seeks to identify potential General Managers and equip them with the business skills necessary for running a successful hotel operation.

READING: THE RITZ-CARLTON HOTEL COMPANY GOLD STANDARDS

by Patrick Mene, Corporate Director of Quality, The Ritz-Carlton Hotel Company

The Ritz-Carlton Hotel Company aims to succeed in one of the most logistically complex service businesses. Targeting primarily industry executives, meeting and corporate travel planners, and affluent travellers, the Atlanta-based company manages 31 luxury hotels that pursue the distinction of being the very best in each market. It does so on the strength of a comprehensive service quality programme that is integrated into marketing and business objectives.

Hallmarks of the programme include participatory executive leadership, thorough information gathering, coordinated planning and execution, and a trained workforce that is empowered 'to move heaven and earth' to satisfy customers. Of these, committed employees rank as the most essential element. All are schooled in the company's 'Gold Standards', which set out Ritz-Carlton's service credo and basics of premium service. The company's long-term quality goals, six initiatives in work, and process improvement are shown in Box 7.1.

The Ritz-Carlton Hotel Company is a management company that develops and operates luxury hotels for W.B. Johnson Properties Inc., also based in Atlanta. In 1983, W.B. Johnson Properties Inc. acquired exclusive US rights to the Ritz-Carlton trademark, a name associated with luxury hotels for 100 years.

The Ritz-Carlton Hotel Company operates 25 business and resort hotels in the United States and six hotels outside the US, two in Australia and one each in Hong Kong, Spain and Korea. It also has nine international sales offices and employs 14,000 people. Two subsidiary products, restaurants and banquets, are marketed heavily to local residents. The company claims distinctive facilities and environments, highly personalized services, and exceptional food and beverages.

Quality planning begins with President and Chief Operating Officer Horst Schulze and the other 13 senior executives who make up the corporate steering committee. This group, which doubles as the senior quality management team, meets weekly to review the quality of products and services, guest satisfaction, market growth and development, organizational indicators, profits, and competitive status. Each year, executives devote about one-fourth of their time to quality-related matters.

The company's business plan demonstrates the value it places on goals for quality products and services. Quality goals draw heavily on consumer requirements derived from extensive research by the travel industry and the company's customer reaction data, focus groups, and surveys. The plan relies upon a management system designed to avoid the variability of

BOX 7.1 SUMMARY OF RITZ-CARLTON APPROACH TO
SERVICE QUALITY

THE RITZ-CARLTON
HOTEL COMPANY

LONG TERM QUALITY GOALS

100% Customer Retention

100% satisfied customers who loyally use and recommend The Ritz-Carlton Hotel
Company.
Basically, we want to never lose a single customer.

50% Reduction in Cycle-Time

Reducing the total time between determining customer wants
and needs and fulfilling them to the customers total satisfaction.

Six Sigma

A very high level of quality with only 3.4 defects, failure or errors per million units of
product or service.

THE SIX INITIATIVES IN OUR WORK

Customer Needs

All work at The Ritz-Carlton must begin with a focus on customers.

Prevention of Defects

All work is built around Quality to prevent any defect from ever reaching the customer.

Cycle Time Reduction

We want to reduce the duration of time from customer request to delivery of product or
service.

Empowerment

Empowerment is giving employees the authority and resources to solve problems and
achieve results.

Employee Involvement

The participation of employees in making decisions that affect them.

Measurements

Customer requirement measurements involve understanding what customers want most,
and knowing what is worth measuring.

HOW WE WORK TO IMPROVE

PREVENT
DEFECTS
REDUCE CYCLE TIME
RETAIN CUSTOMERS

STRATEGIC
QUALITY
PLANNING

QUALITY
TEAMS

SCIENTIFIC
APPROACH

GOLD STANDARDS

service delivery traditionally associated with hotels. Uniform processes are well defined and documented at all levels of the company.

Key product and service requirements of the travel consumer have been translated into Ritz-Carlton Gold Standards, which include a credo, motto, three steps of service, and 20 'Ritz-Carlton Basics'. Each employee is expected to understand and adhere to these standards, which describe processes for solving problems guests may have as well as detailed grooming, housekeeping, and safety and efficiency standards. Company studies prove that this emphasis is on the mark, paying dividends to customers and, ultimately, to Ritz-Carlton.

The corporate motto is 'ladies and gentlemen serving ladies and gentlemen'. To provide superior service, Ritz-Carlton trains employees with a thorough orientation, followed by on-the-job training, then job certification. Ritz-Carlton values are reinforced continuously by daily 'line ups', frequent recognition for extraordinary achievement, and a performance appraisal based on expectations explained during the orientation, training, and certification processes.

To ensure problems are resolved quickly, workers are required to act at first notice – regardless of the type of problem or customer complaint. All employees are empowered to do whatever it takes to provide 'instant pacification'. No matter what their normal duties are, other employees must assist if aid is requested by a fellow worker who is responding to a guest's complaint or wish.

Much of the responsibility for ensuring high-quality guest services and accommodations rests with employees. Surveyed annually to ascertain their levels of satisfaction and understanding of quality standards, workers are keenly aware that excellence in guest services is a top hotel and personal priority. A full 96 per cent of all employees surveyed in 1991 singled out this priority – even though the company had added 3,000 new employees in the previous three years.

At each level of the company – from corporate leaders to managers and employees in individual work areas – teams are charged with setting objectives and devising action plans, which are reviewed by the corporate steering committee. In addition, each hotel has a 'quality leader', who serves as a resource and advocate as teams and workers develop and implement their quality plans.

Teams and other mechanisms cultivate employee commitment. For example, each work area is covered by three teams responsible for setting quality-certification standards for each position, problem solving, and strategic planning.

The benefits of detailed planning and the hands-on involvement of executives are evident during the seven days leading up to the opening of a new hotel. Rather than opening a hotel in phases, as is the practice in the industry, Ritz-Carlton aims to have everything right when the door opens to the first customer. A 'seven-day countdown control plan' synchronizes all steps leading to the opening. The company president and other senior leaders personally instruct new employees on the 'Gold Standards' and quality management during a two-day orientation, and a specially selected start-up team composed of staff from other hotels around the country ensures all work areas, processes, and equipment are ready.

Daily quality production reports, derived from data submitted from each of the 720 work areas in the hotel system, serve as an early warning system for identifying problems that can impede progress towards meeting quality and customer-satisfaction goals. Combined data from Quality Production Reports and Quarterly Summaries of guest and meeting planner reactions are compared with predetermined customer expectations to improve services.

Among the data gathered and tracked over time are guest room preventive maintenance cycles per year, percentage of check-ins with no queuing, time spent to achieve industry-best clean room appearance, and time to service an occupied guest room.

From automated building and safety systems to computerized reservation systems, Ritz-Carlton uses advanced technology to full advantage. For example, each employee is trained to note guests' likes and dislikes. The data are entered in a computerized guest history profile that pro- vides information on the preferences of 240,000 repeat Ritz-Carlton guests, resulting in more personalized service.

The aim of these and other customer-focused measures is not simply to meet the expectations of guests but to provide them with a 'memorable visit'. According to surveys conducted for Ritz-Carlton by an independent research firm, 92 to 97 per cent of the company's guests leave with that impression. Evidence of the effectiveness of the company's efforts also includes the 121 quality-related awards received in 1991 and industry-best rankings by all three major hotel-rating organizations.

©1992 The Ritz-Carlton is a federally registered trademark of The Ritz-Carlton Hotel Company.

STUDY QUESTIONS

1 Discuss the different conditions in the 1990s compared to the 1980s (and earlier) which now put greater onus on quality of hotel staff.
2 List and explain reasons why human resources issues present a significant challenge to the international hotel industry.
3 Discuss which incentives and motivators appear to be the most significant in the hotel industry.
4 Explain the differences between the following nationality policies: ethnocentric; polycentric; regiocentric; geocentric.
5 Discuss typical phases of nationality policy development a hotel might go through.

6 Compare and contrast the advantages and disadvantages of local and expatriate hotel managers.
7 Attempt to classify Inter-Continental's nationality policy and explain your choice.
8 Explain how Ritz-Carlton attempts to achieve guest satisfaction through its human resources strategy.
9 Discuss the human-resources-related mechanisms employed by Ritz-Carlton to enact its guest satisfaction pledge.
10 What other mechanisms are used by Ritz-Carlton to enhance guest satisfaction?

Chapter 8

Reversing the cycle of failure through organizational renewal

In this chapter we build on the finding that human resources comprise the critical success factor of the hotel industry. The hotel industry has thus far been unable to factor out the human element in providing a quality product, as opposed to, for example, automobile manufacturers who are increasingly producing cars with the input of robots. Since hotel corporations may be classified as a 'people-based' as opposed to an 'equipment based' industry, they have to make a substantial effort to develop their human resources to achieve continuous improvements in order to remain competitive.

The objective of this chapter is to identify the organizational learning process as the major underlying theme in managing change and developing and sustaining competitiveness. As well, transformational leadership is introduced as the catalyst to the renewal process which leads from 'available for service' to 'world class service', and contributes to the creation of competitive advantage. In particular, this chapter emphasizes that hotel corporations should embrace change as an organizational learning opportunity rather than viewing it as a threat.

There are two cases at the end of this chapter. The first features Shangri-La International, highlighting the importance it places on creating a 'proud and enthusiastic attitude' amongst its staff. The second looks at the Mandarin Oriental Hotel Group and describes the challenge of developing an ongoing organizational culture of quality service which draws on the strength of each individual hotel in the Group.

COMPETITIVENESS AND ORGANIZATIONAL LEARNING

The pressure on managers to shift their focus from short-term to long-term results, from operational to strategic activities, and from a domestic to a global market, started in the 1970s. In the 1980s, the environment in which the international hotel industry operated became more turbulent and underwent additional dramatic changes. In particular the decade brought sizeable labour shortages – as the baby boom was being 'replaced by the baby bust'. This shift created a seller's market in human capital. It also placed hoteliers in a position of having to compete for the best people (Naisbitt and Aburdene 1985: 2).

The rapidly expanding hotel corporations are serving niche markets with increasingly specialized products. But the rate of change in the market has clearly outstripped the speed at which conventionally organized hotel corporations can respond, which creates difficult challenges for many operators. Of particular importance is the market shift from customers simply purchasing the goods and services offered to them to customers exercising their buying power on the types of products that are offered for sale. Another significant development is the exponential growth of knowledge. It creates new technology and new technology creates new knowledge (Bardaracco 1991: 26). The vast pool of available knowledge to companies presents a strategic and organizational challenge to managers who have the responsibility to secure, improve and exploit the knowledge base.

The systematic gathering and dissemination of knowledge requires information technology. However, the use of technology in the hotel industry is not widespread and its assimilation is expected to be slow, due to two main barriers:

(a) The gap between management's business needs and technology understanding is the leading reason why the lodging industry is lagging behind others in using technology as a strategic weapon.
(b) Technology buyers [hotels] are uncertain about the effectiveness of technology investments. The proliferation of [technology] alternatives has undermined the confidence [perceived] of many (41 per cent of the hotel executives surveyed) in the effectiveness of their technology investments (AH&MA 1989: 4).

The availability of technology, when properly applied, can enable management to compete more strategically. For now the lack of management's understanding of technology has led 'to dissatisfaction with results and a reluctance to pursue further implementations of technology' (AH&MA 1989: 4). However, given the more fragmented market structure, more demanding customers, and a shrinking labour pool combined with the need to improve productivity, hotel executives will have little choice but to apply technology in a competitive context.

In the 1990s, organizations have to learn to function within an 'information society' and a 'global context' (Handy 1989). In the information society, change is expected to proceed at an even faster rate. Many of the changes that may take place are not readily predictable. And a crucial challenge will be managing paradoxes. Organizations shall have to be very flexible to respond smoothly and quickly to events for which they cannot plan. Therefore, the need for leadership will be greater throughout many organizations.

As a consequence of the accelerating change of pace, the window of opportunity that represents a company's ability to survive continues to narrow, especially for organizations that are not replacing dollar capital with 'human talent' as the strategic resource (Naisbitt and Aburdene 1985: 4). Put differently, corporations will have to be perceived as the preferred employer to attract the best workers available. Furthermore, organizational expansion more and more depends on taking market share from competitors in slow growing markets instead of maintaining share in an expanding market. In the emerging environment, a corporation's competitive advantage will to a great extent depend on one overarching principle: organizational learning. Simply stated,

> Organisational learning is a philosophy that encourages the continuous improvement of the individual and collective capabilities of all the human resources in the business. The principal virtue of this approach is that it fosters a mindset that encourages and seeks change, that champions initiative and that includes a willingness to accept the personal responsibilities associated with change.
>
> (Rugman and D'Cruz 1991: 46)

Increasing competitiveness has triggered the need for change to which organizations must respond by:

(a) Learning, especially by recognizing the need for revitalization;
(b) Creating a new vision based on the enhancement of innovation and continuous improvement; and
(c) Institutionalizing change through employee involvement and transformational leadership.

The learning organization

In today's turbulent business environment, yesterday's managerial concepts and organizational practices are being rigorously challenged. The challenge to traditional methods and organizational formats is particularly relevant to the hotel industry because it lags, for the most part, in managerial sophistication. Kotler (1980b: 57) indicates that 'though environments change, not all industries and companies are exposed to the same rate of change'. Using Kotler's classification which ranges from a fairly 'stable environment' to a 'turbulent environment', the international hotel industry can be considered to operate in the latter environment, in which unpredictable disturbances are the rule.

Within this environment an intelligence system is at a premium. But information in and by itself is insufficient to survive. It is as important to build the capability to adapt to change. The adaptation of an entire corporation to change depends on learning, both individual and collective learning, referred to as 'organizational learning'.

In particular, organizational learning is the process by which an organization obtains and uses new knowledge, tools, behaviours, and values (Bennis and Nanus 1985: 191). As Handy (1989: 225) indicates, organizational learning can mean (a) an organization which learns and/or (b) an organization which encourages learning in its people.

Even as international hotel firms have grown into large-scale businesses, they have not necessarily displayed the leadership throughout the organization, nor have they redesigned their systems to release, rather than smother, initiative. Organizational learning is a major factor in developing and maintaining competitiveness as Porter's analysis of change in organizations indicates:

> [the] imperative of competitive advantage constitutes a mindset that is not present in many companies. Indeed, the actions required to create and sustain advantage are unnatural acts. Stability is valued in most companies not change. Protecting old ideas and techniques becomes the preoccupation, not creating new ones.
>
> (Porter 1990)

But regardless of size, hotel corporations have to provide value-added service if they are to survive in the fiercely competitive business environment in which customers are becoming more and more 'value-oriented'.

Hotel corporations have to understand and adopt customer perspectives to successfully manage service delivery. But the successful design and management of the service delivery interface requires both external (customer) and internal (organizational) perspectives. Put differently, what should the company do 'internally to meet its customers' expectations'. After all, excellent service performance 'derives from processes, decisions, and actions occurring throughout an organization' (Kaplan and Norton 1992: 74).

Hotel managers should focus on critical success factors (CSFs) that enable them to satisfy customer needs. The industry CSF analysis conducted by Geller (1984) identified 'Employee attitude' as leading the list of what (American) executives feel hotels must do right to achieve their goals. However, employee attitude is unlikely to be positively influenced in many international hotel corporations which have organizational charts and job positions that are well-defined.

Discipline is usually enforced through 'top-down' management. Investment in employees is not often a priority. Indeed, 'employers admit that they are not always willing to provide training programmes – or to pay for additional skills required' (EIESP 1991: 9). When offered, training usually focuses on how to teach staff to do their job 'better'.

The validity of this traditional hierarchical organization is crumbling in today's competitive environment because its predictable results include a lack of initiative and personal responsibility among staff members who, even if well trained, do what they are supposed to do within the confines of their task and departments. Due to a turbulent business environment, however, today's task requirements are dramatically different from those of the past. Now, employee tasks and service performance must reflect the concept of adding value to the service chain.

Moreover, in traditionally structured hotel organizations, front-line employees often do not know what to do when the situation and, therefore their task, changes. Traditional hotel organizations are unresponsive to their employees' needs and therefore unlikely to motivate their employees to service excellence. Within such a service system, human resources can be a very weak link in the service chain.

Furthermore, due to generally weak management, a prevailing condition in many hotel corporations, the overriding goal of managers is likely to be profit rather than 'employee morale' or 'guest satisfaction' (Geller 1984: 22).

Organizations that are perceived to pay more attention to profit than people are likely to cultivate a climate dominated by employee frustration and dissatisfaction. Employee dissatisfaction often causes high employee turnover, especially at the front-line employee level.

Since employee turnover is a factor that is measurable and since it can lead to a host of potential problems in the service delivery process, including recruitment difficulties and diminished service quality, turnover should be monitored on a regular basis. The hotel corporations that are unsuccessful in reducing employee turnover to acceptable levels may be considered to be locked in what Schlesinger and Heskett (1991: 74) refer to as a 'cycle of failure', as shown in Figure 8.1.

Figure 8.1 The cycle of failure

Source: Adapted from L.A. Schlesinger and J.L. Heskett as described by P. Sellers, 'What Customers Want', *Fortune*, 121(13), 1990, p. 59

Certainly, retaining skilled and motivated employees is a critical element of successful hotel corporations. Labour turnover hurts hotel companies by decreasing service quality, resulting in higher customer turnover and lower profit margins. Profit is diminished when existing customers and employees are not retained, since it costs companies more to recruit new employees and customers than to retain them. As well, customer dissatisfaction and turnover lessens employee satisfaction, which in turn leads to higher employee turnover. Resulting image problems, coupled with the reality of dwindling labour markets, create an even more dismal situation for companies locked in this 'cycle of failure'. The most consistent finding in the survey, described in Chapter 7 of this study, is the evident gap between what respondents say and what they do. In their landmark work, Argyris and Schou (1978) referred to this as a distinction between 'expressed theory' and 'theory in use'. Many managers possess the knowledge of what needs to be done (i.e., expressed theory), yet do not attempt to implement this knowledge and stick instead to well-established routine (i.e., theory in use). This is so because changing the way things are is a risky business. Yet, such a change is necessary for an organizational change to come about. Argyris and Schou argue that this change requires a double-loop learning, whereby the gap between the operating norms and the desired norms is made evident (i.e., loop 1) and then steps for changing the operating norms themselves are taken (i.e., loop 2). This is the essence of a real organizational change, as opposed to the more frequently witnessed pseudo-change. The major contribution of the survey presented in Chapter 7 is creating an awareness of this gap, thereby stimulating a consistent process of change.

RECOGNIZING THE NEED FOR REVITALIZATION

'The ultimate challenge in organizational learning is to develop the [hotel] firm's competence in innovation' (Rugman and D'Cruz 1991: 48).

Following Schumpeter (1965), the term 'innovation' is used in broad context to encompass 'new combinations' of goods/services, methods of production, markets, sources of raw materials and organizations. Innovation in the hotel industry has been largely limited to 'product innovation'. US hotel firms launched new product lines to cope with the market at the existing level of room rates which in many places was saturated. By launching new product lines, the hotel firms created a new growth vehicle. If the mid-price market in a given location is full, the Choice Hotel corporation can franchise a budget price Comfort Inn, while Marriott which had developed the prime sites for its existing hotel brand could locate its new reduced service Courtyard product in many additional areas (Go and Welch 1991: 98).

Process innovation concerned with enhancing the hotel firm's competitive capabilities like 'improving quality, increasing throughput, lowering costs, and enhancing delivery capability and flexibility' (Rugman and D'Cruz 1991: 48) is a much neglected area in the hotel industry.

The costs of developing and commercializing new facilities and products and delivering tourism services of assured quality are rising. Ohmae (1986: 10) identified three directions in which companies can move to gain from the benefits of integration and cross-fertilization: (a) downstream, to control the interface with the customer; (b) upstream, to acquire new technologies or protect sources of expensive raw materials; and (c) horizontally, to share complementary technologies.

The first two developments have been demonstrated within the tourism sector in terms of travel industry consolidation. The former co-ownership of Inter-Continental Hotels by Scandinavian Airline System's subsidiary and Japan-based Seibu-Saison is one example. Few TNCs in tourism command a distribution network capable of establishing a respectable share of the global market. As a consequence, we have witnessed considerable movement towards cooperative agreements between major national air carriers – for example, those that gave rise to the establishment of global distribution systems (GDS) like Galileo, Amadeus, and Abacus. In this context, process innovation is viewed and should be applied successfully to every aspect of travel including marketing, reservations flow, customer service, and after-sales service.

The hotel firm which devotes resources and maintains relationships with other firms in the integrated tourism network enhances its competitive capability. The hotel firm which does not is bound to fall behind other competitors. The requirement for process innovation as applied to the hotel industry is illustrated by the advent of computerized reservation systems. At present the information-dependent hotel industry continues to depend on the 800-number and the hotel directory for the bulk of its business. But as computerized reservation systems become more sophisticated, they will be a major key to success in operating hotels, independent and chains, in the 1990s, since CRS will provide instant access to numerous travel supply firms around the world.

For instance, the Galileo system initiated by British Airways, KLM, Swissair, and United Airlines will provide a new range of user-friendly services for travel agents, including air fares, hotels, car rentals, and railway information. With the new system, member hotels can receive greater distribution of products and services, especially throughout Europe. More than 90 hotel chains, with 14,500 properties, will be accessible via the new system, including Amfac Hotels & Resorts, Holiday Corporation, Sheraton, and Hilton International. New technology, and the more sophisticated application of existing technology, presents suppliers, governments and destinations with the opportunity to cooperate much closer than before. It will also encourage the furthering of the internationalization of tourism.

As mentioned earlier, the rate of change, caused by information technologies and the internationalization of business, has clearly outstripped the speed at which conventionally managed international hotel companies can respond. Recognizing that yesteryear's structures are being overturned by a convergence of forces makes a compelling case for the revitalization of organizations.

Enhancing innovative competence

Maintaining the status quo is a behaviour typically found in the traditional hotel organization with the boss at the top of the pyramid. In general the 'old' type of organization operates on the basis of what Kanter (1983) coined the 'segmentalism' mode, a type of 'non-systems' approach in which actions, events, and problems are compartmentalized and isolated from their context. Specifically, 'segmentalism inhibits innovation at every step of the solution–search process' as follows:

> The motivation to solve problems declines in segmented systems. Segmentalism discourages people from seeing problems – or if they do see them, from revealing this discovery to anyone else. If people's activities are confined to the letter of their job, if they are required to stay within the fences organisations erect between tasks, then it is much less likely that people will ever think beyond what they are given to do or dream about things they might do if only the right problem came along.
>
> (Kanter 1983: 29–30)

The learning organization embraces change by broadening the search for solutions beyond what the organization already knows. Generally, larger problems are assigned to a team made up of individuals from various departments that can consider the whole before taking action.

Companies operating in an 'integrative mode' try to distribute leadership more broadly within the organizational hierarchy, encouraging entrepreneurial behaviour and employee involvement leading to productive, responsive changes (Kanter 1983: 35). By building linkages, individual initiatives and coalitions of 'teams that represent new and different configurations', the potential is offered for many more people, 'at least in theory, to find a connection with nearly everyone else' (Kanter 1983: 32). The resulting potential for improved creativity, increased understanding of the organization's philosophy, goals, and workings, and enhanced communication among personnel at all organizational levels can help organizations improve their customer orientation.

Hotel corporations can effectively foster positive organizational change by encouraging and rewarding individual and collective initiatives and by minimizing the segmentalism of corporate structures, processes, and systems.

The overriding objective should be to create an environment that is conducive to innovation. Innovation is a crucial skill for hotel corporations, in particular to enhance their productivity. Drucker (1985: 30) refers to innovation as 'the act that endows resources with a new capacity to create wealth', and describes it as 'an economic or social rather than a technical term' (1985: 33).

The volatile environment in which hotel businesses operate provides opportunities to improve the yield of resources through systematic innovation, i.e., 'the purposeful and organised search for changes, and the systematic analysis of the opportunities such changes might offer for economic or social innovation' (Drucker 1985: 35).

To analyse opportunities requires an information base. And in the hospitality and tourism industry such an information base has been described by Ritchie and Goeldner (1987: vii) as 'fragile and, in many cases, simply unreliable'. They go on to provide several reasons for the lack of credible data, such as the diversity of the industry, the nature of the travel experience and the difficulties encountered in understanding consumer behaviour, the decreasing reliability of the data with increasing cost, and the lack of an ample infrastructure required to further systematic research and management information systems.

But innovation is not only dependent on information but also on organizational structure. For instance, Gamble (1991: 18) demonstrates how the introduction of technological innovations in the hotel industry are closely linked to the administrative capabilities of companies and in particular to the choices made by managers based on their perceptions of the situation.

However, once organizations adopt the Schumpeterian (1965) approach to innovation, hotel operators seem able to respond creatively to changes in the environment. Importantly, research by Poon (1988) confirms Gamble's observation that superior performance in the (Caribbean) hotel sector depends on the innovativeness of the management (rather than either their 'foreign' (multinational) or 'local' (indigenous) background). Therefore, innovation seems to offer great opportunities for organizations in Third World and industrialized countries alike.

Hotel managers who examine the 'continuous improvements' of leading manufacturing and service corporations will recognize the heightened importance of innovation to the competitiveness of their organizations. Two aspects of competence in innovation are particularly significant: (a) product innovation and (b) process innovation. Product innovation has been the lifeblood of competitiveness in the international hotel industry. The American hotel industry has set the standard for the rest of the world in this area. It pioneered the motel concept, which Kemmons Wilson in 1952 turned into a worldwide brand-name: Holiday Inn. The introduction of the economy hotel, the 'all-suite' hotel, the conference centre hotel, and the 'fantasy-resort' can be cited as American 'product innovations'.

The realization of economies of scale in the hotel sector used to be nearly impossible due to its fragmented structure and its nature of production which traditionally did not allow for centralized production. However, through the 'industrialization' of hotel services by chain corporations, the hotel chains have been able to perform on a low-cost basis through mass production while offering an assortment of lodging products (through differentiation) to respond to customers' individual needs and expectations (de Jong 1991: 17).

Lately, several innovative lodging products have been launched in Europe. For example, the Center Parcs Company offers a lodging formula that includes a climate-controlled tropical pool, a variety of sports activities, and restaurant and shopping facilities.

ACCOR of France has taken a different approach to developing new one-star motels under the Formule 1 brand. One major result of this new product is the length of time it takes the company to build a Formule 1 property. Because the building is comprised of prefabricated modules, the Formule 1 design allows ACCOR to bring its product more quickly to market at a lower cost (in that the need for interim financing is considerably reduced by the shorter building period and remarkably lower than for the construction of a conventional motel).

Process innovation is concerned with enhancing the corporation's competitive capabilities by 'bringing any new, problem solving idea into use. Ideas for reorganising, cutting costs, putting in new budgeting systems, improving communication, or assembling products in teams' (Kanter 1983: 20). Process innovation tends to be overlooked in the international hotel industry. However, it should be accorded a much greater priority because (a) new hotel products are unlikely to make any corporation a winner in the 1990s and beyond, because new hotel designs can be quickly copied by competitors; (b) slower expansion rates, especially in most industrialized markets, will make it mandatory to enhance growth on the unit level, i.e., to increase the productivity of every unit in the chain; and (c) how effectively corporations deliver service or manufacture goods seems to increasingly dictate who comes out on top.[1]

Hoteliers can learn from the innovative behaviour of leaders in other industries. For example, through profit sharing and numerous ongoing motivational programmes Calgary, Alberta-based travel agent Roger Jarvis has been able to extend the entrepreneurial spirit throughout his company. There are other companies in the service sector that are learning to reverse the cycle of failure by investing in their personnel and the organizational culture by:

(a) Recruiting and selecting desired employees by considering alternative labour markets and offering candidates desirable benefits. For example, the American Express Phoenix, Arizona office gains a more educated workforce by using flexible work hours and richer job content to attract busy mothers who are also college graduates;

(b) Compensating employees on the basis of performance. For example, Au Bon Pain, a Boston based chain of sandwich shops revised its compensation practices so that store managers can earn anywhere from US$50,000 to $165,000, depending on sales and profit performance.

(c) Using technology to support, rather than replace, workers. For example, Taco Bell, a fast-food chain owned by Pepsi Cola, uses computer technology to free its employees from 'detail' work so they can focus on customer interactions. And Avis, a rental car company, developed a self-study, computer-based training package that enables employees to learn at their own pace (Sellers 1990).

Within the 'chain' of service transactions, a hotel corporation has to project a clear vision of its customers and their expectations so that personnel can deliver accordingly. As we have discussed, excellent service depends on management practices that favour an integrative company committed to a customer orientation. Attaining this clear vision is enhanced by continuously scanning its internal and external environments. That is, a company's service capability and performance must be continually assessed, monitored, and adjusted. Scanning also applies to an organization's external environment so that the organization can anticipate and adapt to political, economic, social, and technological conditions – allowing it to successfully maintain or reach its desired home and overseas markets.

CREATING A NEW VISION

The idea of 'Total Quality Control' (TQC) started in America but was first embraced in post-war Japan under the guidance of two Americans, W. Edward Deming and J.M. Juran, who could not find an audience at home. The 'economic miracle' of post-war Japan has received much attention from academics, businessmen, and the media. Their enquiry into the success of Japan has focused on 'unique Japanese' management practices such as quality circles or labour relations rather than 'Kaizen':

> an umbrella concept covering most of those 'uniquely Japanese' practices that have recently achieved such worldwide fame [and] have helped Japanese companies generate a process-oriented way of thinking and develop strategies that assure continuous improvement involving people at all levels of the organisational hierarchy.
>
> (Imai 1986: 4)

The continuous improvement concept has caused 'earthquakes and aftershocks that shattered the complacency of the world's manufacturing companies in the 1980s [and] are now causing tremors in all businesses' (Schonberger 1990: vii).

Due to the fiercely competitive business environment, the quality issue is shaking the very foundation of the hotel industry. Hotel organizations have to be quality conscious if they hope to survive the tremors.

Service quality is a very significant aspect of the customer experience, as is illustrated by the following value equation: the value of a service to a consumer = service quality (both the results realized and the process by which they were achieved) divided by the price and other consumer costs of acquiring the service (Heskett *et al.* 1990: 2). This equation underpins two important aims of every outstanding service organization: achieving desired results and processes (Heskett *et al.* 1990: 6). More specifically, Band (1991) suggests that the desired result of a business transaction is *creating value for the customer.*

This is particularly apt for hotel businesses because transportation and telecommunications offer substitutes that are at times appropriate, convenient, and competitively priced. Furthermore, hotel industry corporations cater to both business travel and pleasure travel markets. Managers therefore have to be price sensitive because recreational travellers have the 'luxury' of comparing destinations before booking a trip. At the same time, to keep business travellers coming back, it is essential to create value for business travellers in a way that is demonstrably superior to that of the competition.

Thus, to add value for customers, service improvements should be based on what customers perceive as important. In this regard the area of customer–employee relations, or relationship marketing, requires significant improvements (Go and Haywood 1990).

Specifically, Schonberger (1990: 14–15) observes that the customer–employee relationship can be easily sidetracked by two factors: (a) functional work demands (e.g., chefs staying in the kitchen and avoiding contact with patrons), and (b) the factions problem (i.e., people following a 'narrow agenda on what to do or how to do it', as opposed to accessing a potential range of knowledge breakthroughs). The challenge in service organizations regarding the former is to cultivate a customer orientation throughout the business functions. The mentality among factions should be geared to using resources for attributes that customers value such as 'higher quality, and quicker, more flexible response at less cost' (Schonberger 1990: 15). Compared to manufacturing industries, these attributes in hotel corporations depend, to a much greater extent, on people.

Continuous improvement

Because the customer is considered the sole judge of service quality, one imperative for service improvement is to focus on customer expectations.[2] Specifically, hotel managers should define their market segments and consumer expectations by finding answers to three questions: (a) Who is being satisfied (what customer segments)?; (b) What is being satisfied (what customer expectations)?; and (c) How are customer needs being satisfied (by what technologies)? (Abell 1980).

Segmentation identifies a company's customers. Research can shed light on their expectations. Consider the tactics that the Marriott Corporation applies to learn more about their guests:

(a) Marriott invests its executives' time in soliciting and understanding guests' comments. In 1988, Chairman Bill Marriott, Jr., personally read 10 per cent of the 8,000 letters and 2 per cent of the 750,000 guest questionnaires the company received each month.
(b) Marriott conducts dozens of well-designed market-research studies. It mails out thousands of minutely detailed survey questionnaires every year. It invites customers to view model hotel rooms; if they don't like the colours, the colours in real hotels will be changed.
(c) Marriott surveys customers to learn how they react to specific features offered by Marriott competitors. If Holiday Inn offers a free continental breakfast, Marriott will know within weeks whether its customers would like one too.
(d) Marriott has analysed its guest population and divided it into segments. For example, Marriott researchers can predict how each kind of traveller will react to a service: how a new policy in staffing the concierge desk will appeal to business people travelling on their own, how it will appeal to people attending business meetings, and how it will appeal to vacationers (Whiteley 1991: 49–50).

Companies that consider customers' needs and expectations have the opportunity to establish market-driven standards against which its efforts can be measured. Companies that can communicate those expectations and demonstrate a passionate belief in them to front-line employees who are eager to exceed those expectations stand an excellent chance of gaining a competitive advantage. The marketing of services is to a great extent managed through subjective customers' feelings, especially perceptions and expectations. Within this context, the importance of managing impressions and setting expectations should be obvious. 'When expectations exceed perceived levels of service, customers are dissatisfied; but when service exceeds expectations, customers are pleasantly surprised and highly satisfied' (Davidow and Uttal 1989: 80). This concept is illustrated by the following example told by Isadore Sharp, Chairman of Four Seasons Hotels and Resorts:

We set the level of expectation through our advertising messages, our promotion programs and sales promises. If we promise more than we deliver, our service will be perceived as poor. Meet customers' expectations and they will perceive it as good; exceed expectations and we are excellent. In our new resorts, for example, we have built in a dozen or so new ideas that we think our resort clients might like. But we do not sell them on more than half a dozen; we let the others be a pleasant surprise. By underselling and overdelivering, we can raise the perception of value.

(Sharp 1991: 17)

As the Four Seasons Hotels and Resorts example reveals, the key to successful positioning of a service is to ensure that expectations are kept just below perceived performance. Keeping expectations at the right level is a constant challenge, because as 'customers gain experience and competition intensifies, expectations invariably seem to rise' (Davidow and Uttal 1989: 82). Training programmes at all levels in hotel organizations will help improve and maintain the quality of service that customers demand. But even the best companies cannot prevent mistakes that are often made in the customers' presence. When the inevitable problems arise, customers are almost always disappointed.

For the 1986–1989 period, customer quality service was perceived to be the most critical issue in US companies. But several polls show that consumers find most service to be mediocre to atrocious. In some instances, customers are of the opinion that service standards are falling.[3]

Why has the service crisis been building throughout the business world? Davidow and Uttal (1989: 6–11) provide several reasons on the macro-level:

(a) Changes in the competitive game rules have thrown entire industries into disarray.
(b) Over the last two decades, business economics theories that advocated cost-cutting and short-term financial gain have influenced managerial thinking and undermined quality service considerations.
(c) The application of technology in service operations has proved to be a double-edged sword, in that it has contributed to labour cost reduction and increased productivity. But simultaneously, technology carries the threat of alienating customers and service personnel in that the complexity of technology has increased much more rapidly than the ability of people to adjust to change.

On the micro-level, within the hotel industry, there are several additional factors that impact negatively on the rendering of quality service in hotels, specifically:

(a) spending on service training in the hotel business is relatively low and often misdirected;
(b) the staff turnover in the hotel business tends to be very high;
(c) hotel companies, even the big hotel chains, transcend mediocrity in terms of caring about customers.[4]

Customer expectations will continue to rise because they learn from experience. Furthermore, due to a growing number of competitors in the hotel business offering similar products, it is easy for travellers to take their business elsewhere.

INSTITUTIONALIZING CHANGE

As the competitive game has fundamentally changed, the corporate success of hotel corporations will increasingly depend on their ability to adapt to an increasingly complex and diverse environment. The hotel firm that is quickest and most effective at anticipating changes in the environment and developing the organizational capability to embrace complexity and dynamism will have a significant advantage. Organizations require direction and time to adapt to change. During the transition period when change is being institutionalized, things are likely to get worse before they get better, because employees have to 'unlearn' old habits and learn new ones. Selected means to build support during the change process include employee involvement and transformational leadership.

Employee involvement

People and profits are inextricably linked in hotel organizations. That is, the front line (personnel) directly influence the bottom line. One of the reasons for this linkage has been described as 'moments of truth'. A moment of truth is that intensely personal experience that occurs when the customer deals with a company for whatever reasons (Carlzon 1987; Albrecht and Zemke 1985: 20–28). Hotel companies must now compete on quality of service as never before and the moment of truth has become the key performance criterion upon which hotel companies will succeed or fail.

In principle, hotel departments should mesh harmoniously to achieve the overall objective of the hotel company: to ensure guest satisfaction. In practice, however, relations among hotel departments are often characterized by rivalries and mis-communications that impede the realization of the hotel company's objective. Due to the nature of hotel operations as service businesses, the problem of the inseparability of the service provider and the service in hotels is as much a marketing problem as it is an operations and human resource management problem.

In order for hotel companies to ensure guest satisfaction, all employees must have a customer orientation and all hotel departments should co-operate to sense, serve, and satisfy the customer (Kotler 1980b: 183). Because of the importance of 'moments of truth' to hotel companies, managers interested in improving the effective delivery of service should learn how and why employee performance occurs before they can effectively manage the service delivery process. This raises the question of what causes hotel personnel to behave or act in a way that leads to successful results (from the hotel's perspective) and satisfactory performance (in the customer's mind) in a service transaction.

To answer this question, hotel operators require an understanding of the factors which influence behaviour and performance. Behaviourial models typically suggest that performance is a function of ability and effort. The two variables operate jointly and neither of the two alone can result in the desired performance. A waiter who is unable to serve a guest because he does not have adequate product knowledge of the menu items the restaurant features, for example, will inevitably fail at his task regardless of the effort put into the job. At the same time, a reservations clerk may have all the information needed to solve a customer's problem but if he/she does not want to make the effort the guest will not be satisfied.

Therefore, managing service delivery should focus on performance results which in turn are dependent on employee behaviour, i.e., actions and decisions taken by an employee. Anticipating customer needs, making a guest feel welcome and eye contact with a customer are all examples of desirable employee behaviour. The behaviour of employees is important because it affects customer satisfaction.

It is significant to distinguish between tasks and performance because though the completion of tasks is of prime concern to hotel managers, the manner by which tasks are performed is under the direct control of the employee. For example, the executive housekeeper who simply advises a room attendant that she has not cleaned the assigned rooms well will probably see little improvement the next time she checks the floor unless (a) the room attendant gets appropriate training, and (b) receives required information which communicates the hotel's standards, or (c) the room attendant in question has been replaced by an employee who has undergone a more rigorous selection process and is able and willing to carry out the required task better than her predecessor.

This view is supported by several studies showing a link between employee satisfaction and customer satisfaction. In their original study, Schneider *et al.* (1980) used 28 branches of a bank and showed that when employees felt they were being rewarded for providing better service, customers reported having received better service (i.e., the two were positively correlated). In a follow-up study, Schneider and Bowen (1985) studied 23 branches of another bank and showed that customer-satisfaction was positively correlated with the following human resource practices: (a) supportive supervision (as opposed to autocratic supervision); (b) training and socialization of new employees; (c) facilitative operating norms (as opposed to inhibitory ones); (d) career development programme; and (e) pride in belonging to the organization. These findings led Schneider (1990) to propose that organizations can create a *climate for service,* and that companies having a high positive climate will provide better service and will be perceived as doing so by their customers. Since the climate for service is a summary measure of supportive human resource practices, this explains the link between employee satisfaction (or stress) and customer satisfaction.

Based on the important role of service employees in the service encounter, it can be argued that the greater the coordination, interplay and equality among the hotel organization's human resources department and its other functional areas, the more likely it is that the hotel company's commercial goal will be met. In short, the hotel organization's human resource department should have a significant input in setting objectives, priorities and policies. Furthermore, the management of human resources on the strategic level is necessary because situational factors such as the organizational structure, the organizational culture, the design of work and reward systems within the company are to a large extent shaped by external forces such as changing demographic patterns, new technology and the nature of competition, as discussed in previous chapters (EIESP 1991; IHA 1988).

The employee–customer encounter and the employee–organization interaction that have been discussed are critical elements in service operations management, human resources and marketing functions. The involvement of various functional areas to 'produce' services in combination with the employee/customer encounter increases the heterogeneity of service delivery. It also provides an impetus for managing the service operations process, comprised of the service concept, service delivery system, and the service levels (Sasser *et al.* 1978: 20).

How can the service operations process in hotels be improved so as to make hotel organizations more competitive?

Chase and Hayes (1991: 16) introduce the notion that 'service firms, like manufacturing firms, can structure their operations according to a four-stage model of competitiveness and they can apply the manufacturing strategy concepts of focus and integration as they move from lower to higher stages' (Table 8.1).

They argue that management needs some classification framework to relate operations activities to the firm's overall service performance in order to:

(a) pinpoint the key elements that must be addressed in the strategy development process;
(b) help position the firm's operations relative to competitors;
(c) provide a current perspective and future vision that can be communicated to the organization's members; and
(d) facilitate answering such important strategic questions as 'where are we now?' and 'where do we want to be?' (Chase and Hayes 1991: 16).

The classification Chase and Hayes (1991: 16) propose 'distinguishes among

Table 8.1 Four stages of service firm competitiveness

Stage	1–Available for service	2–Journeyman	3–Distinctive competence achieved	4–World-class service delivery
	Customers patronize service firm for reasons other than performance	Customers neither seek out nor avoid the firm	Customers seek out the firm based upon its sustained reputation for meeting customer expectations	The company's name is synonymous with service excellence. Its service doesn't just satisfy, it *delights* them, and thereby expands customer expectations to levels its competitors are unable to fulfil
Operations	Operations is reactive, at best	Operations functions in a mediocre, uninspired fashion	Operations continually excels, reinforced by personnel management and systems that support an intense customer focus	Operations is a quick learner and fast innovator; it masters every step of the service delivery process and provides capabilities that are superior to competitors'
Service quality	Is subsidiary to cost, highly variable	Meets some customer expectations, consistent on one or two key dimensions	Exceeds customer expectations, consistent on multiple dimensions	Raises customer expectations and seeks challenges, improves continuously

Back office	Counting room	Contributes to service, plays an important role in the total service, is given attention, but is still a separate role	Is equally valued with front office, plays integral role	Is proactive, develops its own capabilities, and generates opportunities
Customer	Unspecified, to be satisfied at minimum cost	A market segment whose basic needs are understood	A collection of individuals whose variation in needs is understood	A source of stimulation, ideas, and opportunity
Introduction of new technology	When necessary for survival, under duress	When justified by cost savings	When promises to enhance service	Source of first-mover advantages, creating ability to do things your competitors can't do
Workforce	Negative constraint	Efficient resource, disciplined, follows procedures	Permitted to select among alternative procedures	Innovative, creates procedures
First-line management	Controls workforce	Controls the process	Listens to customers, coaches and facilitates workers	Is listened to by top management as a source of new ideas. Mentors workers to enhance their career growth

Source: Richard B. Chase and Robert H. Hayes (1991) 'Beefing Up Operations in Service Firms', Sloan Management Review, 33(1), p. 17

service delivery at different stages of their development'. Specifically, the model relates 'the management practices and attitudes that . . . generally indicate how service firms at each stage deal with key operations issues'. Chase and Hayes point to two major issues that should be considered prior to examining and applying their model:

> First, the stage attained by a firm at any given time is a composite. Every service delivery system embodies a unique set of choices about such factors as service quality, role of the back office, workforce policies, and the like. A company may fall at a different point along the continuum for each category or have some organisational units that are further or less advanced than others. What determines the firm's stage is the overall balance among these different positions – where, in a sense, the firm's centre of gravity lies. In defining this centre of gravity, the model assumes a weighing of each dimension's relative importance. Thus a firm can achieve Stage 3 or possibly Stage 4 status, even if it is not outstanding on all dimensions, providing that it is clearly superior on the critical success factors for its industry.
>
> Second, it is difficult, if not impossible, for a company to skip a stage in its quest for world class status. A company obviously must achieve journeyman performance levels before it achieves distinctive competence, and distinctive competence is a necessary foundation for becoming world class. This does not mean that a company can't pass through a stage in a relatively short time, however.

> (Chase and Hayes 1991: 16–18)

Training is a critical factor in the long-term success of international hotel corporations, because 'well-trained staff enhance the customer experience, add value to the travel and tourism product [which includes international hotel products], improve the image of the corporation, and advance their own career development' (EIESP 1991: 5). However, the emphasis practitioners place on training may reveal very traditional, inward and operational behaviours as was illustrated in a recent study of Irish hoteliers' attitudes, management techniques, and education and training (Baum 1988: 36–40).

As Baum (1988) describes, these attitudes and behaviours illustrate a resistance to change and learning that is most likely to result in a competitive disadvantage rather than a competitive advantage. Unfortunately, this situation too often describes international hotel corporations which have not learned to the extent necessary to align their behaviour more creatively with their environment.

The discussion, up to this point, yields several significant observations:

(a) Providing quality service requires the orchestrated interaction within the service system of customers, employees and the organization.

(b) Important links between and within the main business functions, including operations, administration and marketing, which form a value chain serving both internal and external customers.

(c) A company's ability to meet its external customer needs depends directly on how well it satisfies the needs of the internal customers. Within this framework, every employee should be involved in the production process, taking an active role in gathering and recording data that can be used to improve service delivery processes (Schonberger 1990: 96).

In the quest for creating value-added service as a means of achieving customer satisfaction and repeat business, international hotel organizations should seek interfunctional cooperation rather than traditional adherence to power-based concerns. That is, functional departments, such as operations, human resources, finance and marketing functions, should work as a team to improve service delivery processes and outcomes. These functional areas, including the workers they represent, should also be closely linked to business strategy formulation and implementation processes.

Whereas hotel corporations operating with the traditional model put workers last, the integrative company designs its business functions around its people. The new model, designed by Schlesinger and Heskett (1991) referred to here as the 'cycle of quality service', is likely to be comprised of 'capable workers who are well-trained and fairly compensated, provide better service, require less supervision and more likely to remain on the job. For individual companies, this means enhanced competitiveness' (Schlesinger and Heskett 1991: 72) and higher profit margins as shown in Figure 8.2.

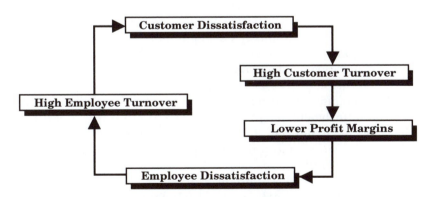

Figure 8.2 The cycle of quality service

Source: Adapted from L.A. Schlesinger and J.L. Heskett, as described by P. Sellers, 'What Customers Want', *Fortune*, 121(13), 1990, p. 59

Corporate renewal through transformational leadership

The model proposed by Chase and Hayes (1991) which suggests that companies move along a continuum from the company that is simply 'available for service' to the firm that delivers world class service, in effect reflects the organizational learning that has to go on, as described earlier in the chapter, in order for a company to build its competitiveness. Waterman (1987: 22) has argued that this developmental process, which he refers to as 'renewal', is an imperative for corporations if they are to remain vital in an increasingly competitive market. Described as a building process, renewal is about leading an organization towards transformation, about leaders 'who go to work in the belief that they can make things somehow better' (Waterman 1987: 22).

The focus of most hotel corporations that aim to become organizations that deliver world class service will be on where they are going and how to improve their performance.[5] They will seldom ask themselves where they come from in spite of the importance of this question. Companies that have to respond to new environmental demands in the context of their existing organizational capabilities may be considered 'captives of their past', in that their internal capabilities developed over a considerable period of time and, ingrained in their organizational culture, cannot be changed overnight (Bartlett and Ghoshal 1989: 35). Thus, the first step for any company in adapting its organization to the emerging changes in the environment is to understand its corporate history, its 'way of doing things' (Bartlett and Ghoshal 1989: 35). The second step involves changing its formal organizational structure to regain fit with the environment and will require the 'unlearning' of certain behaviours and the learning of new ones. However, such changes are extremely difficult to achieve because organizational structure is the product of a firm's unique and ingrained administrative heritage, which represents both an asset and a powerful impediment in the change process (Bartlett and Ghoshal 1989: 54).

Many forces shape a company's configuration of assets, organizational structure, dominant management style and strategic direction, and ingrained organizational values. But leadership seems most influential on corporate norms and priorities (Bartlett and Ghoshal 1989: 41). Until businesses encountered global competition, rapidly changing technologies and the more turbulent economic environment of the 1970s and 1980s, good management sufficed (Kotter 1988). The call for leadership and vision in organizations was a direct response to the unsteady nature of today's business world.

In an age when change is constant, random and discontinuous (Handy 1989), it is essential that hotel corporations break out of traditional ways of thinking in order to use change to their advantage. During an era of greater uncertainty, they have become more responsive to increasing competition, the impact of technology, and the realization that giving workers responsibility and the freedom to exercise initiative enhances their motivation and energy in order to become effective competitors in international markets. Handy captures the situation as follows:

> Today the language is not that of engineering but of politics, with talk of cultures and networks, of teams and coalitions, of influence or power rather than control, of leadership not management. It is as if we suddenly woke up to the fact that organisations are made up of people, after all, not just 'hands' or 'role occupants'.
>
> (Handy 1989)

Leadership is the driving force that enables hotel organizations to adapt and succeed in this changing environment.[6] However, most hotel corporations have depended for their success on a durable advantage in a defined market. Furthermore, and perhaps as a result of their competing in a defined market, they operate on the basis of well-defined organization charts and may be described as 'old guard', because their organizational heritage makes it particularly difficult for them to adapt to the new environmental realities of the 1990s.

In contrast, the 'new organizations' – which Chase and Hayes (1991) referred to as the 'world class service organisations' – try to exceed customer expectations, improve their operations through continuous learning, and view the customer as a 'co-producer' and employees as a potential source of innovation. World class service corporations have a much greater chance of succeeding in today's business environment because they differ from the 'old guard' corporations in terms of structure, processes and vitality and are therefore much better equipped to face the new opportunities and pitfalls. In the new business environment, many 'old guard' hotel corporations will not survive in their present form unless they change. But changing a hotel corporation from 'old guard' to a 'world class service corporation', which is rare in the hotel industry, is a great challenge. To become a world class company requires a complete transformation of organizational structures, decision-making, processes and perhaps most importantly, management mentality. Whereas the 'old guard' hotel organization has well-defined boxes on an organizational chart and everybody is supposed to march in step within their box, the world class service organization invites its people to take the initiative and be innovative. Put differently, the transformation from 'old guard' to 'world class service corporation' requires leaders who can achieve quantum leaps in performance by setting forth an organizational vision, then creating an organizational culture and a way for employees to make that vision a reality. Transformational leaders, 'like architects must redesign outmoded factories for a new use' (Tichy and Devanna 1990: 4), in order to move resources from areas of lesser to greater productivity.

Jan Carlzon, the president of SAS, is a good example of a transformational leader who succeeded in advancing his airline to world class status in one and a half years (Chase and Hayes 1991). He achieved this primarily by focusing:

> not so much on product as on process and organisational structure. In his autobiography, *Moments of Truth*, Carlzon (1987) spells out his organisational blueprint in great detail: it includes making the front-line workers – ticket agents and stewardesses in particular – into managers, giving them the authority to respond to the needs and problems of individual customers. Middle managers are transformed from supervisors into resources for the front-line workers. Carlzon suggests that his organisational blueprint resulted from a number of small insights, discrete moments of inspiration, which he pieced together, bricoleur fashion, to create the whole.
>
> (Westley and Mintzberg 1989: 29)

Transformational leadership is especially important in the hotel industry where front-line employees, like in the airline industry, are frequently considered by customers to be the company they represent. As such, customers expect these employees to have sufficient responsibility, authority, and motivation to fully respond to their service needs.

In response to increased competition, many hotel corporations have differentiated their product and service lines. Or they have segmented their markets and focused their offerings. To effectively manage their businesses, especially across borders, hotel corporations have had to restructure their organizations sometimes into sub-units. Market segmentation, which has been very popular in the hotel industry, requires 'flatter organizations' and a more broadly distributed leadership that is pushed further down the organization. The ACCOR Corporation, for example, has set a goal of becoming the world's largest hotel chain by the end of the century. Since the opening of its first Novotel property near Lille, France in 1967, it has moved into every segment of the hospitality industry and expanded globally. To help cope with its rapid expansion and diversification, ACCOR underwent a large scale reorganization in late 1986. The French corporation is now operated by hotel type from the de luxe Sofitel concept to the one-star Formule 1, each with their own general manager instead of a geographical structure (Leigh 1987: 26–28).

However, decentralization poses a dilemma in that most organizational resources require a minimum critical mass to obtain maximum efficiency and effectiveness. While decentralization enhances focus and responsibilities of lower levels of management, scale economies create pressure for sharing or 'pooling' critical resources.

What is the role of the leader in the organization?

First and foremost, leaders embrace change. They possess insights into how to alter the rules of competition in a particular industry. In most world class service organizations, the leaders interpret the conditions, internal and external to their organizations, to set the overall direction, philosophy and way of thinking on a few major points, so that managers can work within a framework. Leaders shape a vision and strategy to give meaning to the team's work such as involving the 'right' people in developing the team's strategy; standing up for what is important; communicating the strategy of the organization as a whole; and creating a positive picture of the future to the team. This is the important role for the leaders: defining guidelines on values, the way things are handled, and some higher purposes. 'These corporations exist to provide society with the goods and services it needs, to provide employment, and to create a surplus of wealth (profit) with which to improve . . . [the] general standard of living' (O'Toole 1985: 49).

Leaders energize their organizations to meet competitive challenge. They understand that today's business environment is too complex and too competitive for a single hero to succeed. In most world class service organizations, leaders do not create the vision alone. Rather they view their role as articulating from time to time, in a focused way, where the organization is heading so that everyone can see the way forward, and to provide employees with the information so that everyone can assume a leadership role in helping the organization to meet its goals (Tichy and Devanna 1990: 57).

Thus, leaders mobilize individuals by their people orientation, high energy levels, sense of humour, and willingness to span job and company boundaries in search of people with different ideas, information, skills and values around a common mission: communicating expectations clearly, demonstrating care for the team members, letting people know how they are progressing towards the team's goals, appealing to people's hearts and minds to lead them in a new direction. Leaders inspire others to achieve results by promoting development of people's talent, recognizing the contributions of others, empowering others to act like leaders, stimulating others' thinking, building enthusiasm about projects and assignments. They encourage horizontal decision-making by empowering employees to take on the tasks of leadership. The ultimate goal is to enable all team players to take part in the development of a new direction and to understand their role in leading others to achieve it. The characteristics of innovative leaders have been outlined in Table 8.2.

CONCLUSION

The environment strategy structure paradigm suggests that superior performance is rooted in a good 'fit' between corporate strategy and

Table 8.2 Characteristics of innovative leaders

- Ability to juggle many tasks
- High energy levels
- Sense of humour
- People orientation
- Willingness to span job and company boundaries in search of ideas and information

Source: Florence Berger, Dennis H. Ferguson and Robert H. Woods (1989) 'Profiles in Creativity: Companies and Leaders', *The Cornell HRA Quarterly*, 30(2), p. 99. Copyright © Cornell University. Used by permission. All rights reserved

environmental demands and between organizational structure and strategy. The findings in Chapter 7 suggest that there is currently a lack of 'fit' between strategic business practices in the international hotel industry, specifically with regard to the environmental demands of customers and the organizational structure – especially the needs of the employees. It could be implied that hotel corporations could regain the fit by changing the strategy or organizational structure. However, such changes are extremely difficult to achieve due to the unique service nature of the hotel business and its ingrained administrative heritage.

Change in the strategy or organizational structure is rarely effective unless it is accompanied by matching changes in the company's values and management processes. The changing of the company's values requires transformational leadership. In the strategic process, which a hotel firm has to use to achieve the level of world class service corporation, there has to be an equal emphasis on strategy formulation and implementation in order to incorporate the transformational leader's vision.

CASE: SHANGRI-LA INTERNATIONAL – DIVERSE HOTEL PROPERTIES WITH A COMMON IDENTITY

The philosophy and vision of Shangri-La International is to develop and manage de luxe hotels and resorts, at a profit, primarily in the Asia–Pacific region. The Group of Hotels and Resorts is a diverse collection of properties sewn together with a common thread of Shangri-La family identity. In achieving the vision of Shangri-La International, the aim is to be the market leader, while having respect for and blending in with the local colour and flavour of the surrounding community. The name 'Shangri-La' represents the ambience in each hotel property, which is to provide a haven of peace, tranquillity and comfort.

Shangri-La International is a member of the Kuok Brothers Group of Companies.

In 1978 the Kuok Group formed a hotel management company called Kuok Hotels. From this relatively small beginning, managing just five properties in Fiji and Malaysia, there has followed a period of rapid expansion and acquisition. In 1983 the name of the company was changed to Shangri-La International, a name now synonymous with hotel excellence.

From the beginning, the aim of the group was to offer de luxe accommodation coupled with a superior standard of service in a style that is warm and inviting. Those same values still form the culture of the company today.

The group now operates both hotel and resort properties in key city and resort destinations, primarily in the Asia–Pacific region. The hotels offer a unique blend of East and West within a harmonious and hospitable setting. The hotels are renowned for their spacious accommodation, many with extensive conference and meeting facilities. The resorts are situated in exotic destinations and provide a haven of tranquillity, relaxation and comfort while having respect for the local colour and flavour of their own environment.

In order to fulfil its management obligations, Shangri-La International concentrates on five main disciplines, namely: development, marketing, personnel and training, operations and finance.

A proud and enthusiastic attitude exists within the Shangri-La International team. The company pays great attention to the training, development and welfare of its employees so as to provide career advancement and continuity of service. Personnel are exposed to a variety of hotel and resort operations within a multitude of disciplines in order to develop a flexible, adaptable and entrepreneurial spirit.

The Shangri La Group is dedicated to investing in its people, instilling pride, hard work and enthusiasm, which leads to contented customers and therefore a successful business.

CASE: MANDARIN ORIENTAL HOTEL GROUP, WINNING CASE OF THE 1992 HONG KONG MANAGEMENT ASSOCIATION QUALITY AWARD

The company

Established in Hong Kong in 1963, Mandarin Oriental Hotel Group is an international hotel investment and management group operating ten hotels in the Asia–Pacific region. The company manages each of these hotels and has significant ownership interests in all but Mandarin Oriental, San Francisco and the Phuket Yacht Club Hotel and Beach Resort, Thailand.

Mandarin Oriental's overall corporate quality goal is to achieve a level of excellence that sets the Group apart from all of its competitors in the eyes of customers, investors and staff. In order to achieve this level of excellence it strives for total customer satisfaction in its service delivery, and to consistently be a leader in the industry in terms of profitability and the creation of a rewarding working environment for all of its staff.

The Mandarin Oriental Hotel Group has, from its creation, received recognition for providing a level of products and services of the highest quality. While traditions of consistent quality service delivery are practised at each of the hotels, the challenge to the Group is to develop an ongoing corporate culture of quality service drawing upon the strengths of each individual hotel.

At the beginning of 1993, the company introduced a new Group Mission Statement that has been rolled out to every member of staff through personal presentations by the Managing Director at every hotel and corporate office. This Mission Statement has been published in English, Chinese, Thai and Indonesian, and serves as a model in that it conveys guidelines and criteria that can be used by hoteliers who wish to monitor and evaluate their own leadership and quality improvement efforts.

Mission statement

Our company

Mandarin Oriental Hotel Group is a leader in the hotel industry, owning and operating some of the world's finest de luxe and first class hotels.

Our mission

Our mission is to completely delight and satisfy our guests. We are committed to making a difference every day; continually getting better to keep us the best.

Our guiding principles

Delighting our guests

We will strive to understand our client and guest needs by listening to their requirements and responding in a competent, accurate and timely fashion. We will design and deliver our services and products to address their needs. In fact, we are committed to exceeding their expectations by surprising them with our ability to anticipate and fulfil their wishes.

Working together as colleagues

We will emphasize the sharing of responsibility, accountability and recognition through a climate of teamwork. By working together as colleagues and by treating each other with mutual respect and trust, we will all contribute to the Group's overall success more productively than if we worked alone.

Promoting a climate of enthusiasm

We are committed to everyone at Mandarin Oriental by providing a caring, motivating and rewarding environment. As an industry leader, we are committed to bringing out the best in our people through effective training and meaningful career and personal development, and by encouraging individuality and initiative.

Being the best

We will be an innovative leader in the hotel industry and will continually improve our products and services. We will seek from our suppliers the highest quality products and services at the best value.

Delivering shareholder value

We are committed to being a growing company. Our successes will result in investment returns which are consistently among the best in the hotel industry.

Playing by the rules

We will maintain integrity, fairness and honesty in both our internal and external relationships and will consistently live up to our commitments.

Acting with responsibility

We will actively participate in the improvement of the environment, just as we will be responsible members of our communities and industry organizations.

Strategic quality planning and leadership

The executive directors develop the Group's strategic plans through a variety of different processes involving hotel general managers and our marketing and sales team. These processes involve analysis of results of surveys taken to measure our customer's satisfaction, the satisfaction of our competitors' customers and the industry standards as a means of identifying performance requirements and quality product initiatives. Our plans are then implemented at each hotel through redesignated capital projects, staff training, changes in purchasing requirements and through re-evaluation of policy and procedure guidelines. We evaluate and improve our planning process by employing a number of well-recognized and respected outside facilitators from both the academic and consulting fields.

Quality goals and plans

Our quality management programmes and the processes which we developed in our efforts to provide total customer satisfaction have developed towards the goal of provision of service and focus on certain major concepts:

(a) all ranks of management and employees need the right tools, the appropriate training, a willing frame of mind, and support and inspiration from the organization;
(b) substantial research is essential to know what our customers think of our current products and services and what new products and services customers need and expect; and
(c) our quality service delivery systems and employee job satisfaction will be improved substantially through simplifying the communication process.

One of our strategies was to initiate 'Legendary People' in 1989 as the umbrella concept for our renewed commitment to quality service standards. Our Legendary People programme is our effort to continue the many quality service traditions for which the Group has achieved recognition and to successfully improve our quality service delivery systems.

Legendary People was conceived as a result of a series of discussions among the Group executive directors in search of quantifying 'quality' and then creating a programme to maintain it. Our goal was to lead the hotels in developing more process-oriented systems which would help carry forward each hotel's quality values and processes to future generations of management and staff. We also wanted to develop ways to transfer successful processes at one property into the systems and cultures in other Group hotels. Finally, we wanted an overt and ongoing programme focusing on quality service delivery in recognition of the improvement in the competition, the changing expectation of the customer and the evolving needs of our employees.

Our desire was not to introduce a programme that was designed by an outsider, packaged and served to the management and staff at each hotel in a patronizing way. We decided, therefore, to go slowly, to be experimental and to make sure we accommodated the different work ethic and cultures at each hotel. Thus, a period of several months was dedicated by the entire organization to develop and reach agreement on the following principles of our Legendary People programme:

'Legendary People' – Mandarin Oriental service delivery policy

The worldwide reputation of Mandarin Oriental hotels for the delivery of consistent, distinctive, personal service to customers must be maintained and even enhanced in the face of the coming competition in most of our markets. In doing so we must focus upon certain agreed policies and principles, and articulate specific methods for their implementation:

(a) Final responsibility for all aspects of the total performance of each Mandarin Oriental hotel lies with the hotel's general manager.
(b) The satisfaction of customer needs, through delivery of the services of the hotel, and its staff, must be the top priority of responsibility for each hotel's senior management.
(c) The quality, as well as the style, of each hotel's service delivery systems is best communicated to all levels of staff through senior management 'modelling' of service behaviour in a proactive, highly visible and consistent manner.
(d) A positive, motivating management environment is essential in creating the desire in front-line staff to deliver equally positive, warm, and sincere service. A 'Win/Win' discipline philosophy is at the core of Mandarin Oriental's supervision technique.
(e) Daily senior management personal contact and communication with customers and rank and file staff are essential keys to maintenance of quality standards in the consistent delivery of customer services.
(f) Each senior manager's team must be organized such that the hotel's operations support departments and provide the essential customer services to maximize the time devoted to customer service delivery and staff supervision and motivation.
(g) All systems, structures, and policies, both within each hotel and throughout the Group, are designed to strengthen Mandarin Oriental's commitment to these policies and principles.

We are developing Quality Standards under our Legendary People programme as well as our Total Training Concept, an umbrella training programme to organize our training efforts to ensure that staff undertake to delight our guests, with or without supervision.

Customer satisfaction determination

Our market segments are identified through information collected at the time of purchase which is then tracked and compared on a month-to-date and year-to-year basis within each hotel, one Mandarin Oriental hotel to another Mandarin Oriental hotel and each hotel to its own specific competitors.

Market segment information is compared weekly. Information tracked includes geographic source of business, country of residence and breakdowns of the source of booking by industry. This information is then further analysed into more specific segments at the hotel level. Separate corporate accounts are classified into industries and the needs specific to key customer industries are determined by interviewing or surveying our customers in that industry.

Our key customer satisfaction measurement is a guest satisfaction survey taken by Asian Market Intelligence (AMI). This annual survey, printed in English, Chinese and Japanese, gathers information from a minimum of 500 customers from each hotel and seeks the customer's importance rating and satisfaction rating of a broad range of products and services offered. In addition, it obtains certain psychographic and demographic information which we can use together with other research to determine market trends. Through this survey we also seek the customers' views on certain proposed products or services which we are considering introducing.

At the hotel level we track customer complaints through 'Comment Cards'. The format of the cards is such that suggestions can be tracked, as well as comments on existing facilities and services. These are reviewed and acted upon at hotel level daily, compiled into monthly summaries and then tracked against previous months and the previous year.

Surveys and polls taken by the travel trade, as well as various publications' reader opinion surveys soliciting feedback from their customers, have been informal ways of keeping track of the general market opinion on our hotels. We know that the reasons behind the opinions are neither specified nor measured and we do not consider these extremely valid in measuring key customer satisfaction requirements. They are, however, an objective evaluation of customer satisfaction when we are directly compared to our competitors (which is sometimes the case) or ranked as a world-class organization.

Information and analysis

The data and information we select to build our information base is that which measures customers' perceived value for money; customer satisfaction; level of service; the hotels themselves; market information.

The criteria for selecting data to be included in the customer information base includes every aspect of the use of our hotel from the time of arrival at the airport to the moment of departure. We measure each contact with personnel for efficiency, product knowledge and courtesy. We measure all facilities and the range of services offered. We also ask our customers to provide information regarding their potential use of new and alternative products and services. We ask them to rank these items in order of preference to facilitate our prioritizing for future decisions. We also track demographic and market information which we can compare from hotel to hotel to identify our target audiences as well as to assist in our interpretation of variances from the group norm.

Customer satisfaction

Customer satisfaction and results

Our current level for key measures of product and service quality is high. In addition our surveys are providing us with information that indicates in which areas our high quality trends continue and alerts us to specific areas where additional work is necessary. Finally, our comments from our customers have both reflected a positive trend in certain process improvements and alerted us to areas needing improvement.

Customer relationship management

We have determined that the key factors in maintaining and building our relationships with customers are to provide a problem free experience at our hotels and restaurants and to give each customer personal recognition. Our strategies to build these relationships are the same as those employed to build our business, they are tied to each other.

We are currently developing a Group-wide Guest History network whereby the 'history' of a customer of any one hotel can be accessed by any other hotel so that preferences are immediately responded to even if it is the customer's first use of a new hotel. When this is in place, a customer of Mandarin Oriental, Hong Kong who prefers a particular type of beverage will find it waiting for him upon arrival at The Oriental, Bangkok.

We follow up our customers with a personalized written response to every comment card or letter received and recently have begun telephoning customers for follow up. In every case we strive to let the customers know that we appreciate their comments; that their experiences are important to us; that we want to address the specific instance generating the comment; that we want them to be satisfied and, finally, if appropriate, we explain the change that will be made in our processes to assure achievement of better customer satisfaction in the future.

STUDY QUESTIONS

1   Why do hotel companies of the 1990s need to learn how to function in an 'information society' and in a 'global context'?

2 Discuss the concept of 'organizational learning' in relation to hotel companies.
3 Using human resource issues in hotels as an example, discuss the distinctions between 'expressed theory' and 'theory in use'.
4 Discuss the term 'innovation' as it applies to the hotel industry.
5 How can hotel companies enhance their innovative competence?
6 Discuss the application of TQM in hotel businesses.
7 What steps can be taken by companies to institutionalize change?
8 Compare and contrast the features of 'old guard' corporations and those which embrace a 'new organization' form: discuss the importance and style of leaders in new organizations.
9 In your opinion does Shangri-La have the characteristics of a new organization?
10 In your opinion does Mandarin have the characteristics of a new organization?

Chapter 9

Implementing globalization strategies

This chapter presents the changing landscape of competition in the international hotel industry. It chronicles the changing pattern of competition in terms of geographic scope and its implications on competitive benchmarking in relation to strategic management. The potential for globalization in the hotel industry is explored on the basis of market, costs, government regulations, and competitive conditions.

The adaptation of the service management system in internationalization is problematic due to unique local conditions and cultural values, the simultaneous need for critical mass in the network for purposes of scale economies, and differentiated learning.

The case at the end of this chapter features Pan Pacific Hotels and Resorts and looks at some of the key factors regarded by this company as essential for its globalization process. The reading, by Four Seasons' Isadore Sharpe, examines approaches to competing in a global marketplace.

CHANGING PATTERNS OF COMPETITION

The advent of the air transportation industry in the post-war era resulted in the international hotel industry as we know it today. It had its origin with Pan American Airways' creation of subsidiary Inter-Continental Hotels in 1946 to provide its passengers and crews with modern accommodation in Latin America. From these humble beginnings, the hotel group was built into a worldwide 'hotel chain'.

The expansion of international air transportation and jumbo jets carrying greater numbers of passengers created shortages of quality accommodations in a number of locations and accelerated airline involvement in the international hotel industry. For example, in May 1967, Trans World Airlines (TWA) purchased Hilton International Hotels for $17 million, making the airline owner of 42 hotels in 28 countries (Sampson 1984: 164). And in 1970, a merger was negotiated between Westin (then Western International Hotels) and United Airlines (UAL) Inc., with Westin continuing to operate as an autonomous, wholly owned subsidiary.

The implications of the changing patterns of competition in the international hotel industry had a profound effect on the domestic hotel industries of many countries. In particular, traditionally domestic hotel industries which could survive in less competitive times depended for their success on a durable competitive advantage. Furthermore, they operated in a defined, usually local, market wherein competition was restricted.

However, that situation changed when international hotel corporations based in America introduced standardized hotel 'formulas' and modern marketing practices throughout the world. For instance, Tideman (1987: 1) chronicled the significant change in the Dutch hotel industry when the Hilton International hotel in Amsterdam opened in 1962. It was the first foreign-owned and operated hotel in the Netherlands and the forerunner of an 'invasion' of international hotel chains. During the next quarter century, other foreign-owned and operated hotel companies penetrated the Dutch hotel market, despite the resistance and competitive counter measures of Dutch hoteliers.

In 1987, the five largest hotels (measured by rooms count) in the Netherlands were all owned and operated by corporations based in foreign countries. By comparison, the Grand Hotel Krasnapolsky in Amsterdam, with 364 rooms, was the largest domestically owned and operated hotel company in the Netherlands, but ranked only sixth in terms of size.

The invasion of foreign hotel chains resulted in a competitive response by Dutch hoteliers who banded together and, with the help of KLM (Royal Dutch Airlines), established the Golden Tulip Hotels Company. In essence, the Golden Tulip Hotels Company allows independently owned domestic hotels to function more effectively under a brand-name and through a reservations system. The Golden Tulip Hotels brand and referral system has been successful both in the Netherlands and abroad due to a great extent to its link with KLM, the Dutch national air carrier (Tideman 1987: 1, 12).

Since competition in the hotel industry ultimately takes place on the local level, the conduct of the independent hotel and international chain-affiliated hotel will tend to influence to a significant extent the strategic decision process of both.

Independent and, for the most part, local hotel firms will increasingly attempt to become part of a network to benefit from the scale effects brought about by *configuration* to ensure survival. The application of the principle of configuration has been illustrated by, for example, the formation of the Golden Tulip Hotel Chain. Established hotel chains with a large network in place, on the other hand, are likely to focus more and more on system *coordination* to remain competitive by improving communications and cost control.[1]

The matrix depicted in Figure 9.1 draws together the basic ideas of the evolving globalization and industry structure in the hotel sector.

	Local	Global
Independent Hotels	1 Typical small-to-medium sized family owned/operated business	2 Best Western
Chain Hotels	3 A domestic hotel chain, for example	4 Multinational hotel chains such as Hilton International, and Nikko Hotels

Figure 9.1 Globalization of the hotel industry

The vertical axis distinguishes between independently owned hotels and chain-operated hotels. The horizontal axis contrasts the local and global market. Most independent hotels are local in nature and therefore operate in quadrant 1, whereas many of the larger chain-operated hotels are active on the global level in quadrant 4.

The matrix illustrates the need among independent hotels to direct their efforts to become affiliated with a global external network (quadrant 2), or to expand into a corporate chain (quadrant 3).

Despite the ever-present pressure on corporations to localize production and produce local products, a growing number of chain-affiliated hotel firms which operate on a local basis (quadrant 3) are being drawn into the global marketing arena (quadrant 4) for two main reasons. First, the weakening of growth opportunities in their home markets is 'pushing' hotel firms to expand abroad. And second, hotel firms based in Europe, the USA and Japan are being 'pulled' into foreign markets by growing opportunities for their product abroad.

COMPETING INTERNATIONALLY

The pattern of international competition differs from industry to industry. However, international competition in the hotel industry reveals certain generic patterns which are characterized by either local competition or the rivalry that takes places in the hotel industry from country to country, at one end of the spectrum or global competition. Within the local competition scenario hotels may be part of multinational firms, but their competitive advantage tends to be derived domestically and is therefore substantially confined to the local level (Porter 1990: 53).

Only a select number of hotel chains – for example, Sheraton, Hilton International, ACCOR, Holiday Inn Worldwide and Inter-Continental – can be considered to compete on a truly global basis, because of their repre- sentation, in terms of properties, sales and reservation centres in strategic locations worldwide. As their competitive conduct in one nation often impacts on the position of these hotel chains in other domestics markets, and vice versa, they can be considered to compete on the global or geocentric level. The first-tier transnational hotel chains draw on their critical mass to compete on a worldwide basis. In particular, they build on the knowledge and expertise gained over the years in many countries to benefit the entire network. The 'global' hotel players also build on their integrated worldwide business system through resource transfer – in particular, through the transfer of technology, capital, and managerial staff. Furthermore, they tend to benefit from other 'ownership-specific advantages', especially the brand-name and the ability to serve an international client expertly.

Clearly, the famed Dusit Thani hotel group, the leader of Thailand's luxury class hotels, would be unable to compete on the terms of the global operations. Similarly, Four Seasons Hotels and Resorts, the market of which was primarily North American in nature, needed to acquire Regent International Hotels to obtain access to the Asian market and become a global player. In order to leverage both leading brands, the companies have implemented a new identity system. The system consolidates the global marketing of the two brands while maintaining separate images for each brand on a market by market basis.

Though there is no conceptual difference in strategic management for domestic or international hotel firms, managers need a global mindset because the world class service organizations offer a competitive benchmark, whereas traditional service firms of the 'Available for service' and 'Journeyman' types proposed by Chase and Hayes offer little inspiration for building competitiveness.

The contrast in terms of geographic scope within service organizations relative to competitive bench-marking has been reflected on the vertical axis of Figure 9.2. On the horizontal axis, two key concepts of strategic management, respectively strategy and process, have been depicted. To achieve a competitive advantage, hotel executives have to 'craft' an appropriate strategy and then implement this strategy through an effective structural process. The latter stage tends to be the more complex of the two stages in that it requires leadership and skilled and committed workers.

Quadrant 1 of Figure 9.2 is characteristic of the international hotel industry. Many international hotel corporations may be aware of global competitive bench-marks in the formulation of strategy. But as the findings in Chapter 6 have indicated, their organizational structure, required to implement the strategy, leaves much to be desired.

Strategic Management

Competitive Bench-marking	Strategy	Process
Global	1	3
Local	2	4

Figure 9.2 Globalization and competitive bench-marking

Source: A.M. Rugman and J.R. D'Cruz (1991) *Fast Forward: Improving Canada's International Competitiveness*, Toronto: Faculty of Management, University of Toronto (Kodak Canada), p. 26

Quadrant 2 is characteristic of the domestic family-owned and operated hotel sector of many countries. In general, local operators have little, if any, awareness of global standards. Hence, their performance expectation is usually based on local competitive bench-marks.

Ideally, international hotel corporations should be operating in quadrant 3, which is the domain of organizations whose executives think globally and train their staff according to global standards which lead to world class service and excellent performance. Their traditional administrative heritage prevents all but few hotel companies from entering this quadrant. Quadrant 4 is the arena in which most domestic hotel chains in many countries currently compete. Due to fierce competition and limited resources, domestic hotel chains find the 'internationalization' process slow and difficult.

In summary, the analysis reveals that hotel companies that have developed appropriate strategies but lack an internal process, as the research findings presented in Chapter 7 have suggested, cannot expect to make progress towards the world class service organization model. Given the fierce competition in the international hotel industry, managers whose hotel firms operate in quadrant 1 should invest in those means that will help improve their organizational capability and hence the process in their companies, or risk losing the battle.

STRATEGY

In order to achieve a differential competitive advantage hotel corporations employ strategies. A strategy is the pattern of decisions managers make regarding their business and the markets in which they compete. Organizations pursue strategies to set directions, lay out courses of action and elicit cooperation from members around common established guidelines. Hence strategies are both patterns from the past and plans for the future. Consequently the making of strategy requires an understanding of the future, present, and past (Mintzberg 1987: 71).

It is our notion that strategies of hotel corporations find their origin in the home-country culture and are shaped by their subsequent 'learning' in the international areas. The idea of strategy as a plan of action and a deliberate process may be illustrated, for example, by the head of Carlson Hospitality Companies, Juergen Bartels, who epitomizes the 'deliberate' strategist.

> You figure it [the plan] out in a theoretical way. Then you write down how you will do it. Then you execute the plan. Curt [Carlson the owner of Radisson] loves to wheel and deal for real estate. But I like to set a limit and stop. If you love something too much you end up overpaying.
>
> (Anon. 1987)

Deliberate strategy formulation may seem sensible but in practice is somewhat incomplete. Why? Because a chronological review of leading organizations reveals that effective strategies need not be deliberate but can also emerge (Mintzberg 1987: 68). Consider, for example, how Four Seasons Hotels and Resorts founder Isadore Sharp came to adopt a focus strategy.

> My sense of purpose didn't crystallize until 1972 – after 11 years in the hotel business. In partnership with Sheraton, we had built a hotel in Toronto, a huge convention centre downtown. The profit potential looked great; but it wasn't the kind of hotel I wanted. What I wanted was to build a chain of first class luxury hotels, and here I was straddling the market being all things to all people. Managing *ad hoc*. Reacting instead of controlling. So, I sold back our interest to Sheraton.
>
> Our purpose since then has been simple: to only operate medium-sized hotels of exceptional quality, and make them the best wherever they are. A single purpose dictates priorities and that helps keep decisions on track. It's a purpose demanding performance by staff, and one that merits their commitment. It concentrates staff efforts right down the line – employees see that everything you do has just one purpose. I think a person or company that tries to do several things at once usually ends up doing nothing well.
>
> (Sharp 1987)

In the case of Four Seasons, a key to managing strategy was of course Sharp's ability to detect emerging strategies and help them take shape. The foregoing example illustrates how in the 'real world', deliberate and emergent strategies form the end points of a continuum along which strategies are crafted (Mintzberg 1987).

QUANTUM THEORY OF STRATEGIC CHANGE

Most large multinational hotel corporations reveal two distinctly different modes of conduct at different times. They attempt to exploit their strengths through corporate strategies. Simultaneously hotel companies must take full advantage of the evolutionary product development process to make improvements whenever possible to keep up with or get an edge over the competition.

However, from time to time, the evolutionary process of change generally is disturbed by dramatic change in the business environment. Typically, revolutionary change forces firms to alter their established strategic course to keep in 'sync' with their environment.

Research conducted by Miller and Friesen (1984) suggests that large companies, in particular high performing ones, commonly respond to revolutionary changes in the business environment by making a quantum leap in their strategic course. They built a theory around it labelled the 'quantum theory of strategic change'.

One of the basic points this theory makes is that over the long term, strategies tend to change only marginally. Miller and Friesen's theory applies well to the multinational lodging industry and is corroborated by major shifts in strategic orientation among leading US corporations during the past sixty years or so. For example, in a review of major lodging corporations, only two important reorientations in the strategic direction of the Marriott Corporation between 1927 and the present were found; a clear shift after the 1974–1975 recession towards a concentration on hotel expansion, and, a decision to exit the fast food, family restaurant business and In-Flite services in 1989.

Quality International was founded in 1939 as a referral organization of hotel owners in the south-east. Two major changes in orientation at Quality can be detected; in 1980 the company was acquired by Manor Care, and, following a management change in 1981, Quality led the lodging industry with the introduction of brand segmentation. At Sheraton, founded in 1937, the major shift came with the introduction of franchising in 1962; the implementation of this deliberate strategic move became more evident after 1968 when ITT acquired Sheraton, resulting in explosive franchise growth.

Hilton International, a profitable enterprise since 1949, started as a subsidiary of the Hilton Hotels corporation. In May 1967 it became a wholly owned subsidiary of Trans World Airlines, which changed the company little in terms of its strategic direction. However, a significant shift occurred in the late 1970s, when Hilton International decided to expand in the Continental US under the name Vista International.

This pattern of key points of change appears to be common, especially among high performing companies.

In companies where reliance of standardized procedures may be excessive, resistance to strategic reorientation can be great. Consequently, these companies have a hard time when it comes to capitalizing on change (Go 1989a). Holiday Corporation is a case in point. Holiday Inns' franchise strategy made rapid expansion possible and is among the greatest success stories in US business. But the company ignored changes in the market, and by the 1970s the chain was in trouble. The company's obsession with standardization, combined with the psychological momentum of its founder, stifled change. When change came it was fast and furious. It included the launching of two new hotel chains Crowne Plaza and Embassy Suites championed by a new chief executive. In a volatile global economy, domestic and international hotel corporations alike must combine learning with control. Effective strategies require walking on two feet: deliberate strategy formulation and fostering emerging strategies (Mintzberg 1987).

CORPORATE OPTIONS

Globalization increases the complexity of doing business in that hotel companies have to be able to cater to the tastes of foreign guests and manage employees in foreign (host) countries and from diverse cultural backgrounds in the home country. At a strategic level the global market requires hotel companies to redefine their market and the ways of defining and accomplishing work (Moutinho 1989: 139).

Hotel companies that wish to enter the international arena do so either on a multi-domestic basis or on a global basis. With regard to the scope of the business they may decide to (a) concentrate on a single business (hotels); (b) integrate into adjacent businesses (restaurants/catering); or (c) diversify into new business opportunities (Hill and Jones 1989: 143; Beattie 1991). These corporate level strategy options available to hotel companies are diagrammed in Figure 9.3.

Single business

Most international hospitality corporations began as single-business enterprises within the confines of a regional market. For example, Four Seasons Hotels and Resorts, today among the world's leaders in medium-sized hotels of exceptional quality, had a humble beginning. It was founded in 1961 when Isadore Sharp opened its first property, a motor hotel in one of Toronto's less fashionable districts (Go 1986).

Highly successful hotel companies, like Four Seasons, have often achieved an optimal fit between their operating environment and their business strategy (Dev 1989). Although Four Seasons is still a single business enterprise, it has increasingly become involved internationally and is currently in the process of developing properties in Europe, Japan, Mexico and the

Market Scale

		SINGLE BUSINESS	INTEGRATED	DIVERSIFIED
Market Scope	Multi-domestic/ Regional	Journey's End La Quinta	Cardinal Industries	CP Hotels
	Global	Four Seasons Best Western	Marriott	Sheraton Seibu-Saison

Figure 9.3 Corporate-level strategy options

Source: Based on C.W.L. Hill and G.R. Jones, *Strategic Management: An Integrated Approach*, Boston, Houghton Mifflin, 1989, p. 153. Copyright © 1992 by Houghton Mifflin Company. Adapted with permission

Caribbean. In contrast, La Quinta Inns, also highly successful, is 'sticking' to the domestic scene.

Integration

Integrated companies produce their own inputs such as supplies (backward integration) and/or dispose of their own outputs (forward integration). The many hotel and motel corporations selling their rooms through company-operated sales offices and reservation systems illustrates 'forward integration'. Furthermore, the considerable potential for the improvement of productivity through training and recruitment programmes, industrial engineering, and job design, through which costs can be distributed over a broader base, has been exploited by most hotel chains.

For example, the Marriott Corporation was up to recently largely a vertically integrated hotel developer with the expertise and ability to simultaneously site, design and construct large numbers of hotel projects. Marriott's main goal until 1989 continued to be the management of these projects, while largely eliminating its financial commitment. On the other hand, Cardinal Industries, a developer turned lodging operator, is picking the fruits of a vertical integration but has chosen to restrict its operations to the domestic market.

Diversification

Two main factors have contributed to the increasing application of concentric or related diversification strategies in the hotel industry. First, some segments in the lodging sector show over-saturation while new entrants

offering appropriate financial clout are gaining market share. Older properties are forced to lower rates or upgrade facilities to compete with new
entrants. Second, product line extension is fuelled by the fragmentation of
the marketplace causing lodging firms to re-define their products to serve
specific markets (Dev and Olsen 1989: 172).

In the first instance, for example, the Seibu-Saison Group, with annual
sales in excess of £12 billion sterling and one of Japan's leading enterprises,
purchased the Inter-Continental Hotels chain from Grand Metropolitan in
1988. Its interests include real estate, finance and insurance, food manufacturing, wholesale activities, air-transportation, and hotels. The Saison
Group is determined to achieve maximum advantage of its Inter-
Continental Hotels acquisition in selected world markets. Consequently, it
recently sold 40 per cent of Inter-Continental Hotels to SAS International
Hotels (Anon. 1988).

In the second instance, Canadian Pacific Hotels, in late 1987, made the
decision to withdraw from the West German market to concentrate on
Canadian developments instead. This decision was consistent with the
company's strategy to focus on the restoration and expansion of its extensive network of hotels in Canada. Meanwhile, Marriott, who took over the
operation of CP Hotels' 591-room Frankfurt Plaza and the 230-room
Bremen Plaza hotels in 1989, thinks that Germany will play a very central
role in its European operations.

CLASSIC STRATEGIES

As the impact of internationalization picks up speed, more and more
businesses will feel the pressure to rethink their goals, strategy, and
organization. Companies that do not wish to confine their activities to one
nation, as discussed in Chapter 1, have basically three organizational
structures at their disposal. Firms may change from one orientation to
another over time. Each orientation suggests specific organizational goals
and leads to related strategies. The issue is which orientation affords a
company the opportunity to compete more effectively both on a worldwide
basis and a local basis.

The international company

Historically, most hotel companies adopted strategies that were shaped by
their home-country culture and their subsequent internationalization. For
example, Holiday Inns set the standard for quality motel facilities by
including features like air conditioning and ice makers, while keeping
room rates reasonable. These qualities added to Holiday Inns popularity
and Kemmons Wilson's application of franchising made rapid expansion
possible (*Wall Street Journal* 1987: 1). However, Holiday Inns' management

mentality was rooted in the US environment, and, 'exported' abroad, treated overseas operations as appendages to a central domestic corporation. The early franchise operators often had little information about overseas market conditions. Nevertheless they expanded at a rapid pace drawn offshore by pent-up world demand. This category is labelled the 'international company' because operators who used this strategy gave rise to the international product-cycle theory which explains overseas expansion in terms of a company's ability to transfer innovative goods or services from more to less developed markets (Bartlett and Ghoshal 1989). The 'international lodging operator' tends to be opportunistic and transitional in form, as trends and events that it does not anticipate or comprehend affect its success.

The multinational company

Hotel management contract firms like Hilton International and Inter-Continental, during the 1960s and 1970s, may be regarded as multinational lodging operators. Their portfolio consists of multi-domestic companies, each responding to its own operating environment. The organization in this category supplements its international sales and referral capability with much of the decision-making at the local or domestic level. A firm like Hilton International in the 1970s is most accurately characterized as 'multi-domestic', because once managers were selected, and a line-by-line annual budget was approved by the area vice-president, they were expected to make as many decisions as possible at the local level. Under Hilton International President Curt Strand's direction, policy guidelines flew out of the New York head offices, but the problem of adopting hotels to new conditions was the local manager's responsibility (Loving 1978).[2] The management style and sales and marketing techniques of Hilton International changed after the company was acquired by Ladbroke to reflect its new parent company. For example, the present sales and marketing direction concentrates on a broader international market rather than the traditional marketing strategy which, to a large extent, was dependent on Americans travelling abroad.

The global corporation

The emergence of new business centres throughout the world, and the spread of destinations in developing countries with little or no tourism infrastructure and expertise, fuelled the demand for hospitality services and prompted many operators to expand globally.

Global companies treat the world as one single market in order to capture scale economies. The distinguishing feature of a global approach is that competitive strategy is centralized. This move away from adapting services locally to operating as if the world were one large market, by

ignoring superficial regional and national differences, has gained acceptance in some corporate head offices (Levitt 1983a). For example, as part of
the global strategy of the Sheraton Corporation, the company's Europe,
Africa, Middle East and South Asia operations were headquartered in
Boston. Four Regional Management Centres, located in Frankfurt, West
Germany (for Europe); Brussels, Belgium (for Africa); Cairo, Egypt (for
the Middle East); and Karachi, Pakistan (for South Asia) liaise with hotels
in their respective region.

The purpose of the move, according to John Kapioltas, Sheraton's
Chairman, President and Chief Executive Officer, is 'to ensure worldwide
consistency of operations and marketing. To implement our global strategy
effectively, we feel it is important to have a close-knit leadership task force
of corporate and divisional officers at headquarters' (Sheraton 1986).

GLOBAL STRATEGY POTENTIAL

Competition in the hotel industry has internationalized. Hotel chain corporations compete with strategies involving selling worldwide, sourcing
equipment and human resources, especially managers, worldwide, and
locating in many different nations. The globalization of the hotel industry
decouples the individual international hotel corporation from the factor
endowment of a single (home) country. The globalization of industries in
general and the internationalization of hotel companies in particular is
paradoxical. As Porter (1990: 18–19) observes: 'it is tempting to conclude
that the nation has lost its role in the international success of its firms'.
However, 'the leaders in particular industries and segments of industries
tend to be concentrated in a few nations'. For example, a large number of
business travellers within the United States helped American chains learn
to serve this market segment, which enabled them to 'export' their knowledge gained in the domestic market on a global basis (Porter 1990: 258).

'Global strategy is a process of worldwide integration of strategy formulation and implementation. In contrast, a multi-domestic approach allows
the independent development of strategy by country or regional units' (Yip
and Coundouriotis 1991: 6).

'Industry globalization potential, that is, the likelihood that a global
strategy will be effective, depends on a combination of four sets of conditions: market, cost, government regulation, and competition' (Yip and
Coundouriotis 1991: 5), as shown in Figure 9.4.

Cost drivers

Especially noteworthy in the international hotel industry is the dominating
role of the world's largest chains. There is also an obvious trend towards
'consolidation', i.e., the growing concentration of rooms supply and

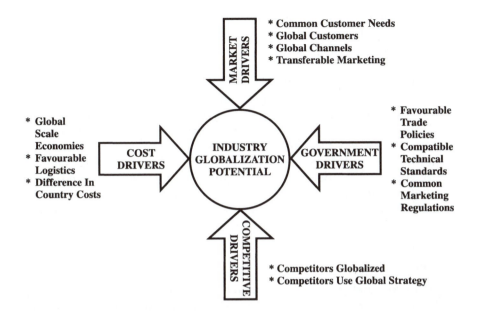

Figure 9.4 Globalization drivers

Source: G.S. Yip and G.A. Coundouriotis, 'Diagnosing Global Strategy Potential: The World Chocolate Confectionery Industry', *Planning Review*, January/February 1991, p. 5. Reprinted with permission from The Planning Forum, The International Society for Strategic Management and Planning

marketing expertise into the hands of relatively few, large organizations, whose international multi-site operations have the capability of achieving economies of scale in order to become the low cost providers in the hotel industry. The recent growth in hotel companies' overall number of rooms has been primarily fuelled by the segmentation trend which gave operators a strategy of choice, i.e., finding a niche to fill. As market segmentation is becoming more important, cost structures are changing and four hotel company types appear to be emerging. Type 1 is the high cost/full service hotel, e.g., the five-star hotel; Type 2 is the low cost/limited service lodging, e.g., the no-frills economy motel; Type 3 is the hybrid lodging offering medium service at low cost, e.g., all-suite hotels; Type 4 is a combination of the aforementioned, e.g., a portfolio of products ranging from budget to de luxe lodging.

Beside the hotel type(s) firms decide to construct, the location determines to a great extent where they build, the customer mix, the direction of the marketing strategy and profitability. Local factor costs, in particular, have a significant effect on hotel demand in that costs of land and labour comprise a large part of hotel capital and operating expenses. International hotels are therefore significantly and most directly influenced in their pricing policy by local factor costs (Lambooy 1988: 79). If land prices are high, such as in major cities like London, then well-sited hotels will all have broadly the same underlying fixed cost structure and will have to set their rates accordingly. Similarly, a selection of hotels offering the same level of service will require roughly the same level of staff per guest to provide that service and therefore their cost structure will be influenced by local labour markets and even by such factors as the host country's immigration policy where local hotel labour is scarce.

In these cases, there is in effect an internationally functioning competitive oligopoly which operates only on the local market concerned. Each hotel of similar type has to watch closely the price/service mix offered by its immediate competitors. To be significantly out of line with the majority is a sure recipe for falling occupancy rates.

Market drivers

Demand for quality hotel accommodation worldwide is being driven by global population growth, increases in the standard of living leading to expansion of leisure and business travel, improved transportation and communications, and the opening up of regions, like Central Europe and the Commonwealth of Independent States, formerly named the Soviet Union, which were heretofore restricted to Western enterprises.

Market changes that might receive the most attention from hotel managers include the key and growing concern among international travellers to get 'value for money' and the move among the working population away from traditional two-week trips, to more mini-trips of three days or less, often taken over the weekend due to time constraints.

Although consumers are expected to continue to play the starring role, there are certain developments in the hotel–client relationship that are worth noting: (a) hotels have become more removed from their clientele; (b) client decisions are largely controlled by more than just the individual user; and (c) the 'gap' between supplier and consumer continually appears to widen (Leven 1982). Channels of distribution in the hotel business refers to the path by which a firm or guests execute a reservation to use a facility. It covers all activities designed to bring the travel product to where the demand is; such activities are generally performed by producing and commercial enterprises. Important features of the travel product, as pointed out earlier, are its complexity – or the variety of services it comprises – and the complementary nature or interdependence existing between the various services that make up the travel product. The features of travel services in combination with the complex nature of travel marketing make it desirable for the hotel firm to use intermediaries or indirect channels.

Direct channels still exist and are chiefly concerned with the sales function at the individual hotel level whereby sales representatives concentrate on (a) maintaining sales contacts with channel intermediaries; (b) maintaining sales contact with community organizations; (c) following leads furnished by other sources. However, indirect channels of distribution have become increasingly important to represent the hotel firm in multiple markets of origin (Kaven 1974: 114–121).

Government drivers

Most governments around the world play a significant role in restricting trade in travel and hospitality services by erecting both financial and legal barriers which contribute to reduced tourist flows. The impediments to international tourism that exist are imposed by governments. They are numerous, complex and include travel allowance restrictions, tariff-type measures, and consumer subsidy type measures (Edgell 1990).

The main features of regulation affecting transnational hotel companies include: (a) controls of entry, establishment and ownership; (b) nationality requirements; (c) policies bearing on the operations and competitive opportunities of foreign affiliates; (d) economic regulations affecting the scope of foreign participation; (e) incentives and performance requirements (UNCTC 1988: 473).

Government drivers have been indirectly significant in that the deregulation of the airline industry in the USA in 1978 brought along a broad choice of airfares and much greater complexity in selecting the most competitive offers. This development required computerized systems capable of handling a vast amount of data and resulted in the changing role of the GDS from an airline information and booking system to a marketing and distribution system. The world of travel, information and reservations started to change in the late 1970s – first in the United States and then gradually throughout the world. Due to deregulation, technology became the key to making the travel trade and hospitality industry function more efficiently and effectively in the new business environment which resulted.

Competitive drivers

At present, there are an estimated 11 million rooms, distributed over hotels and similar establishments around the world. The top 200 hotel chains, as identified by *Hotels*, operate about 2.7 million of these rooms. An estimated 80 per cent of the global lodging inventory is located in Europe and North America. There is a particularly strong presence of Anglo-American owners and operators in the international industry, but recently French, Japanese, and Spanish hotel corporations have stepped up their involvement in international markets (Go and Welch 1991).

With growth opportunities being presented on a worldwide basis and major players in place in the US, Western Europe, and Asia, the international hotel industry has become a 'two-way street', with US companies expanding overseas and offshore companies expanding in the US. Although the international hotel industry is still dominated by American companies, foreign companies are rapidly progressing either through acquisition, joint ventures, or physical expansion. As changes occur in the market, hotel firms have to develop new strategies to maintain market share. Technological developments in information processing and the availability of skilled personnel (or lack thereof) are likely to have a major impact on the policy, planning and strategic direction of hotel corporations.

Competitiveness can be assessed along two dimensions. First, the global dimension measures competitiveness in terms of number of guests attracted, market share, revenues, and expansion. The second dimension focuses on the functions performed in an industry sub-sector and attempts to explain why one sector is more successful than another. When a country's hospitality industry falls behind its competitors in terms of the provision of information, marketing analysis capabilities, and inter-connection among systems and databases, it can have most critical consequences in terms of industry–customer interfacing and affect perceptions and competitiveness most directly (Government of Canada 1988b). The traditional 'competitive strategy' paradigm which focuses on product–market positioning is greatly and increasingly dependent in hotel firms on human resources management which is an integral part of the value-chain (Porter 1980). Therefore, the notion of competitive advantage which provides the means for computing product based advantages at a given point in time (in terms of cost and differentiation) should be complemented with insights into the processes of knowledge acquisition.

The effective acquisition of knowledge will depend on the ability of hotel executives to improve their capacity for the superior execution of activities and programmes within and beyond the system. In their quest for corporate renewal, some companies have embraced the network concept to foster information sharing beyond corporate boundaries. Network transactions for value-adding skill-building purposes will become increasingly critical in the international hotel industry:

(a) to assess marketing opportunities, the cost of sales implications and the difficulties associated with achieving appropriate operating standards in the culturally and economically diverse sectors of the international hotel market;

(b) to acquire more detailed knowledge of local markets;

(c) to create an organizational structure that sees its mission, markets and requirements as both local and global; and

(d) to ensure that international networks including GDS are effectively established and utilized.

Though market drivers, cost drivers and government drivers provide stimuli to globalization in the hotel industry, competitive drivers, especially GDS if effectively utilized, can play a crucial role to contributing to the hotel firm's value chain. As the GDS expands, an increasingly complex hierarchical system of transport and travel networks is evolving which provides important opportunities for gaining competitive advantage by those hotel firms with the necessary competencies and skills to capitalize on the new technology.

The emerging systems based on information technologies will afford hotel firms the opportunity to compete with rivals and complement other travel industry suppliers' services. The idea that the hotel firm is part of a network of economic transactions implies that in order to expand geographically and operate profitably the international hotel firm: (a) must perform its role effectively in the functioning tourism network (this requires cooperation between the hotel firm and 'travel industry partners', such as GDS, rental car, airline and travel agency firms); and (b) should formulate strategies, taking into account the host country's tourism policy and regional development priorities. In this regard, a potential obstacle to effective hotel marketing is the tendency of hotel executives to see problems and solutions in the narrow context of the hotel industry. The latter issue has become more prevalent as a set of global industries, including financial services, (tele)communications, and transportation – especially through their GDS subsidiaries – are affecting the operation and control of hotel firms throughout the world.

Strategy implementation challenges

The requirement for multi-component capability – that is, the hotel corporation's organizational capabilities to respond to global competitiveness, local market needs, and the need for international learning to stimulate innovation – comes to the fore in the challenges managers face as they seek to implement strategies across borders. Specifically and respectively, these challenges deal with the international hotel corporation's ability to simultaneously:

(a) configure and coordinate the transfer of knowledge and expertise to operations worldwide to optimize system-wide performance;
(b) adapt the corporate service management system to new conditions, especially as regards the local human resources and clientele; and
(c) learn from its rivals who, although they may be in the same business and face similar business conditions, are likely to demonstrate a widely different array of strategic and organizational responses due to their corporate history and cultural background.

The most relevant strategy implementation challenges that hotel corporations face are two-pronged. First, hoteliers have to weigh global issues against local conditions. And second they have to be able to meet the changing conditions, caused by internationalization, in their operation. A hotel corporation which operates on a global level, or for that matter a regional or multi-domestic level, has to view any changes to be made in formula against ways and means of international configuration and co-ordination (Porter 1990: 49).

At the broadest level globalization strategy provides insights into issues that are relevant to hoteliers. In areas such as marketing to international clients one of the challenges is to cater to the particular needs and tastes of clients without compromising, where possible, the global corporate system. But at times a formula which has been successful in one market has to be adapted to suit a market in another country. Club Med introduced Americans and Canadians to its all-inclusive vacation concept at the Club's first North American village, Fort Royal, on the island of Guadeloupe in 1968.

Since 1968 a number of changes have been made to the Club's formula to please the North American members, including larger rooms with door keys and security boxes. In two villages there are in-room phones and TVs. The central dining rooms with tables of eight have been supplemented with small speciality restaurants with tables for one, two, seven, or ten guests. All villages in the North American area have at least two speciality restaurants serving menus different from the main dining room. Family-style dining service has been replaced with buffets or waiter service. In addition, the Club introduced flexibility in length of stay. Originally vacationers were required to spend one or more weeks at a village. At present, stays can range from one or two nights to ten or twelve nights, whatever fits one's schedule. The changes form a major departure from the formula the Club offers in Europe.

Though the opportunities for growth and increased market share are considerable in the international market, global expansion is not without its pitfalls. A variety of problems rarely experienced by domestic operators can be encountered in international sites due to political and legal hurdles and different customs and tastes. 'The key to top performance in the international arena lies in gauging which domestic strategies should be transferred directly to foreign markets, which strategies should be modified for export, and which should not be used at all' (Go and Christensen 1989: 77).

Sheraton is one company determined to provide the same high degree of personal, caring service the world over. This implies that employee skills have to be upgraded to precise standards to assure that each given job is done in the same way. To secure the repeat and referral business of satisfied guests, Sheraton employs a 'Customer Rating Index' which invites guests to measure performance results. And the company places major emphasis on recognizing outstanding service – to build and reinforce pride in employees throughout Sheraton's worldwide system.

Though there is a trend towards greater symmetry in the management style of hotel chains based in Europe, North America, and Asia, there are some marked differences in the three major world regions that affect strategy implementation in particular.[3]

(a) In North America, the underlying characteristics of the hotel industry are operated under management contract, franchised hotel and motel chains, and referral hotel and motel chains. Where there remains a substantial measure of private ownership, the perceived necessity is to offer recognizable products within sub-segments of the industry. The customer is not that interested in, and often not aware of, who owns the property. The feature the customer is interested in is what level of facilities and services will be offered from a given hotel type or brand and at what price. Customers typically expect to be able to reserve the hotel of their choice as part of the overall travel arrangements being made. This means by and large that hotel accommodation has to be available for sale at the travel agency retail level along with other travel services.

(b) In Europe, the situation is somewhat different in that, to a greater extent than in North America, the bulk of Europe's hotel room supply remains in the hands of small family businesses. Some of these belong to major referral systems like the 'Logis de France' or 'Best Western' organizations, but most do not. In many cases the very diversity of small properties and their individuality are held up as a unique selling proposition to a sophisticated clientele. The privately owned small hotel is a vital part of European accommodation, but at the same time is an indicator of the market that will find the challenges of new technology, new ways of marketing and the need for professionalization in the service sector due to internationalization and increased competition (Tettero and Viehoff 1990: 6) among the most difficult aspects to cope with. These aspects make it most inevitable that the hotel chain sector consisting of branded products will grow and reflect to some extent the North American experience.

(c) In the Asia–Pacific region, the character of the hotel industry is very different from the situation in North America and Europe. The Asia–Pacific hotel market has experienced explosive growth and is centred upon the more organized and formal side of the travel trade. Both the city centre hotels, whose business is based on the business traveller, and the coastal resort hotels, aimed primarily at the holiday-maker, tend to be large units affiliated to regional or international hotel chains. In the Asia–Pacific region there is less of a tradition of the family operated hotel business, though specific national markets, like

Japan with the *ryokan* system, do have traditional forms of accommodation (Go and Welch 1991: 90).

In addition to differences in the infrastructure of the hotel industry on the various continents, there are cultural, social traditions, economic, and political factors and issues that the managers of international hotel properties must deal with in a manner that will be satisfactory to the local employees, competitors, suppliers and government.

These issues represent strategy implementation challenges for the managers of international hotels that should be analysed on different levels, as defined by Bonoma (1984: 14): action level, programme level, system level, and policy level. Before explaining these levels in greater detail and organizing these four dimensions into a matrix to form a taxonomy for the implementation of hotel development and marketing programmes, it is necessary and instructive to provide examples of issues on each of the four levels.

Specifically, executives of hotel chains which operate properties in foreign countries are likely to face, for example, the following challenges – especially in developing countries:

(a) On the action level an often asked question is: 'How can a hotel manager, whose cultural background differs from that of his local employees, draw them into the hotel company's organizational "climate" to provide culturally sensitive, quality service to a diverse clientele?'

(b) On the programme level, there is the issue of collaboration with local interests versus the cooperation expected from and within the corporate system. For instance: How can a corporate and global marketing strategy be developed so that at the host destination level, a hotel that is part of the worldwide network can implement a localization strategy? It is increasingly desirable that hotels localize their strategies to coincide with the cultural norms in the host community, as the following example illustrates:

Cultural blunders in marketing and customer relations may cost a company dearly in damaged image and lost business. An example is the use of scantily clad men and women on hotel brochures in the Middle East. As a result, hotel corporations are placing more emphasis on cultural sensitivity skills that are so essential to the effective functioning of expatriates in different cultures.

(c) On the system level, there is a similar issue that questions the 'loyalty' of the international hotel manager in relation to the production process. 'How can the international hotel manager balance his interests between the global system – needed to share valuable information required for process innovation purposes – and the growing interests on the host-country level to localize "hospitality" products to reflect the indigenous culture?'

(d) On the policy level, an issue that often arises in relation to managing hotels in a host-country environment is 'How should a foreign owned and operated hotel conduct itself in order to be perceived as a "responsible corporate citizen" by the host country?' From this important issue, several concerns that are likely to be raised include the localization of production, the localization of management, and the localization of profits.

Culturally sensitive, quality service

In today's global economy, which is becoming increasingly multicultural due to increased international travel, the foreign workforce from developing countries being employed in industrialized countries, and the worldwide spread of transnational corporations, it is essential that management practitioners learn about the importance and are aware of the impact of culture in the service delivery process. For example, how many managers of large hotels situated in urban areas of industrialized nations can claim that minorities do not represent a significant proportion of their property's staff and payroll?

In essence TNCs active in hotels, transportation, and tour operation face the challenge of cross-cultural communication on an ongoing basis, not only when expanding overseas but also when catering to travellers whose cultural origin differs from that of the host country. Ziff-Levine (1990: 105–110) suggests the desirability of modifying a global marketing approach by localized elements through embracing cultural values inherent in the target population as an appropriate path to marketing success. It has indeed become critically important (Shames 1986) for decision-makers in tourism TNCs to expand their cross-cultural perspective.

As Shames and Glover (1989) point out, 'service' is not only a business function but also a social experience. They provide a relevant and realistic management framework consisting of elements that address important issues in the service rendering process: business operations strategy, marketing, human resources development, and customer contact. In particular, it is the latter which justifies viewing service as a *human* activity with several universal characteristics, including: (a) the social aspects involving human interaction and communication determined to a large extent by the cultural backgrounds of the interacting individuals; (b) the desirability of meeting customers' expectations, which are shaped by an individual's culture; and (c) the requirement to manage people, both customers and employees, who often bring their own 'cultural baggage' to the same experience.

Some of the leading TNCs in the travel and hotel industries such as, for example, Nikko Hotels International, Hilton International, Sheraton, Delta Airlines, Scandinavian Airlines System, and EPCOT apply cross-cultural service management in a profitable manner. Shames and Glover (1989) cite several benefits gained when TNCs are sensitive to cultural service management aspects, including: 'reduction of operational costs resulting from an ineffectively managed social system; fewer costly early returns of expatriate managers; increased productivity and improved customer relations resulting from a more satisfied staff'.

Bartlett and Ghoshal (1989: 115) refer to the essential requirement for TNCs to constantly learn from host-country cultures and foreign TNC competitors in order to achieve and maintain competitive leadership and innovate. The common superficial character of the TNC headquartered in various countries may be deceiving. For example, despite the 'box-like' similar appearances of hotels around the world the transnational corporations based in various nations that operate them could hardly be more different. One study (Business International 1986) observes how American transnational decision-makers seem to 'lean towards' corporate policy. US sales and marketing skills are portrayed as 'unbeatable' with pricing philosophies of the USA-based and UK-based transnationals leagues apart. American groups are interested for the most part in operating properties under a management contract or granting another firm a licence to operate a hotel on a franchise basis. Many European transnationals, especially those based in the UK, in contrast to American firms are keen on owning and operating properties. The Europeans are best at general management encouraging entrepreneurial management style. Recently, the British have been taking the lead in productivity through performance related bonuses. Japan-based transnationals develop strategies by their well-known consensus approach involving employees to keep and get the most out of talented staff (Business International 1986).

The main concern of the Japanese hotel company is to make employees understand the Japanese concepts of management and service. Japanese hotel companies have been reluctant to expand overseas out of fear that they will not be able to maintain their quality standards with non-Japanese employees. For the most part Japanese investors have left the operating of their newly acquired properties to foreign management companies. The reason for this approach is perhaps best explained by Yasuyuki Miura, president of Nikko Hotels International for USA and Canada, a subsidiary of Japan Air Lines, whose main concern is to communicate Japanese concepts of management and hotel service to (non-Japanese) employees. The entry of Nikko Hotels International posed a number of challenges including the transfer of a corporate culture based on Japanese values to a multicultural workplace; consistent delivery of the highest standards of quality to a highly diverse clientele; and the neutralization of public opinion towards Japanese competition (Miura 1989: 35).

With this understanding of the differences in managerial styles of different nationalities, the need for coordination in a global industry like the hotel industry raises complex problems for any international hotel firm.

In order to build, maintain, and develop their corporate identity multinational organisations need to strive for consistency in their ways of managing people on a worldwide basis. Yet in order to be effective locally, they also need to adapt those ways to the specific cultural requirements of different societies. While the global nature of the business may call for increased consistency, the variety of cultural environments may be calling for differentiation.

(Laurent 1986: 97)

This observation leads us to suggest that in the 1990s the dissemination of traditional management knowledge through tourism research, education, and training will be insufficient and must be augmented by an understanding of cross-cultural management and service quality assurance standards that are international in nature. TNCs operative in the hotel sector that employ better educated personnel will be more likely to gain and maintain a competitive edge than those who are not, because human resources form an integral component of the value chain (Porter 1985).

Implementing a localization strategy

The findings of an earlier study (Go and Welch 1991: 119–120) indicate that the availability of hotel sites will decline in desirable locations during the 1990s. Furthermore, the analysis revealed competitive characteristics which differentiate the hotel industry from most other industries. In particular, on the local market level there is in effect, in some instances, an internationally functioning competitive oligopoly operative. The pricing policy of international hotels is influenced by (a) local factor costs; and (b) by such factors as the host country's immigration policy, where local hotel labour and management expertise may be scarce, necessitating the import of expatriate workers and managers, which increases costs considerably.

The urge among hotel firms to expand on the one hand, and the declining number of available hotel sites in desirable locations on the other, is likely to result in a greater leverage for the host community in negotiations with hotel firms. Specifically, under the circumstances hotel projects are likely to be assessed by the host community in terms of their contribution to the local economy. Accordingly it is suggested that localization strategy for the international hotel industry may be an appropriate means to gain a competitive advantage in the hotel industry of the 1990s. This strategy entails the localization of production, profit and management.

Localization of production

There are essentially two ways to make local production activity optimally effective in the transnational hotel industry. One is to increase the ratio of local content, which gives added impetus to related industries. The other is to increase the value added to local production which not only leaves more profits to the local community but also a greater sense of responsibility and pride in operating their own property.

Establishing local production can take different forms of involvement, because transnational corporations are involved in the international hotel industry to varying degrees. Foreign-associated hotels may be classified into four main categories (Dunning and McQueen 1982a: 78–80): (a) those in which the TNC had an equity interest sufficient to ensure that it had some *de facto* if not *de jure* management control; (b) those in which the TNC operated some kind of leasing arrangement; (c) those in which the TNC operated under some kind of management contract; and (d) those in which the main form of arrangement was a franchise or some form of marketing agreement.

Traditionally, the management contract has been the most predominant means for expansion in the international hotel industry since the 1960s (Dunning and McQueen 1982a: 80). The franchise agreement has been less popular, but offers perhaps even greater advantages than the other alternatives to local businessmen and the host community in that it is easier to apply the latter to downmarket and budget hotel facilities requiring relatively less capital investment.

Localization of profit

In the past, hotel property and buildings were usually owned by individuals or families. Typically, they thought of their hotel in terms of real estate and were not fully aware of how to maximize the hotel's profitability through management techniques. The early hotel chain owners, like Sheraton's Henderson and Conrad Hilton, were also real estate oriented. However, over the past ten to fifteen years, there has been a significant change in the ownership of hotels worldwide (Go and Welch 1991: 34).

It has become more common for hotel management companies to put up a minor percentage of the equity in the properties they manage. Financial involvement in multinational hotel development often takes the form of loans from various sources, including international agencies, international banks, international real estate and development companies and airlines; recently large conglomerates whose main business is not directly connected with the hotel industry have become more prominent (Go and Welch 1991: 81).

The divorce of the ownership and management function in hotel projects has led to a growing number of hotel developments by hotel management firms with the financial assistance of local partners. Local financial partners not only foster the concept of localizing profit (at least in part) but bring their own expertise to bear on the development of the hotel project and on the approach to local authorities and to sometimes complex local situations.

Localizing profit means 'reinvesting as much of the profits as possible in the local market' (Sigiura 1990: 78). International hotel companies investing abroad should regard themselves as a local company and endeavour to prosper together with the host community. 'Reinvestment effectively addresses the concerns that multinationals are interested only in sending profits home and not benefiting the host country' (Sigiura 1990).

Localization of management

The search for 'transnational solutions' in the realm of organization, business–government relationships, human resources and culture (Bartlett and Ghoshal 1989) is likely to result in the balancing of global business strategies on the one hand and strong local/multi-domestic demands on the other. 'Strong local demands and consequently an increasing awareness of diversity in international management relate in particular to quality, customer service and social responsiveness, i.e., the development of employment' (Dijck 1990: 475), and management who have specific local knowledge as part of a worldwide team.

The challenge for international hotel firms in today's environment is to develop hotel managers who understand the local situation, but are able to interface with global clients and a worldwide network of hotels and personnel. International hotel development presents some special problems in meeting management requirements, dealing with local labour laws and regulations, harmonizing tax matters to avoid multiple taxation, and coping with public and government expectations that are not always clear to foreigners.

Christopher Wallis, Senior Vice-President Design and Construction of Four Seasons Hotels and Resorts illustrates the need for the localization of management as follows:

> Moving to different continents and encountering different practices and cultures creates challenges for management. Negotiations must take these differences into account. Similar adjustments need to be made in the construction and operations planning phases. A Four Seasons hotel in Paris is naturally different from one in London or Chicago, but the level of quality and excellence, the sense of welcome and appreciation, the sensitivity to guests' concerns and interests, must be the same. So in Paris, as in other centres where projects are under way, a nucleus of Four Seasons people starts early to assemble a local staff that will embody the attitudes and qualities of Four Seasons and express them in a form adapted to the local culture and style. Literally, the best of both worlds . . .
>
> (Wallis 1991: 10)

The localization of management is a considerable issue, at the time of writing, as Hong Kong moves closer to 1997 and becoming part of China once again. Yu (1994) found that 17.2 per cent of the hotel managers in the Hong Kong hotel industry are expatriate. They are primarily employed to head luxury properties which tend to be, for the most part, either part of a foreign-based hotel group or a subsidiary of a foreign corporation with an interest in the hotel business.

The majority of these expatriates tend to occupy the higher ranks in the management hierarchy. Perhaps not surprisingly the attitude of local Chinese managers, in general, tends to be more positive than their expatriate counterparts, because the former are likely to be promoted when the latter may depart the Territory as a potential consequence of localization policy.

Based on present study findings it could be argued that managing both globalization and localization issues is likely to play a critical role in the 'transnationalization process' of the hotel industry. Hotel firms should therefore develop both in-house expertise and external relations to help overcome the challenge of both localizing and globalizing management simultaneously.

How can hotels best compete internationally?

The formulation of an effective strategy is, of course, essential. But equally important is how to carry out the job when the strategic direction appears to be known among decision-makers. As Ansoff points out:

> Strategy imposes operating requirements: price-cost decisions, timing of output to meet demand, responsiveness to changes in customer needs and technological and process characteristics. The administrative structure must provide the climate for meeting these, e.g., a strategic environment which is characterised by frequent and unpredictable demand fluctuations requires that marketing and manufacturing be closely coupled organisationally for rapid response. . . . In this sense the environment determines the strategic and operating responses of the firm, and these in turn, determine the structure of authority, responsibility, work flows and information flows within the firm.
>
> (Ansoff 1987: 25)

The significance of the host-country environment in relation to strategy implementation and operation affects the international hotel on four levels, as discussed earlier. Therefore, effective implementation is critical to realizing and sustaining a competitive advantage. Put another way, a given strategy is only as effective in practice as its means of implementation. Without effective implementation, hotel marketing strategy may be handicapped, or worse, if strategy is not properly deployed, it is created in vain.

There is a need for the effective implementation of hotel marketing strategy. For reasons identified earlier, the strategy of international hotel corporations, further referred to as hotel strategy, should be analysed on different levels as identified by Bonoma (1984: 14): action level, programme level, system level, and policy level. These four dimensions can be organized in a matrix to form a taxonomy for the implementation of hotel marketing programmes, as shown in Table 9.1.

Bonoma's approach (1984) reverses the order of things, which typically puts strategy first and implementation second. How to operate a hotel in a profitable manner at the operational level is a real and imminent concern as managers struggle with day-to-day realities and face significant challenges in implementing the plans they painstakingly formulated. As a result, practical concerns begin to take precedence over strategy. By focusing on implementation, there may be a chance that in the 'heat of the battle' the manager may begin to lose sight of potential opportunities and threats – especially on the programmes, systems, and policy levels. Therefore, a reasonable balance must be found between the need (a) to effectively implement and (b) to analyse hotel marketing programmes at the local level. The examples found in Table 9.1 may provide some answers on how to strike such balance.

By analysing programme implementation on the actions, programmes, systems, and policy level found on the vertical axis of the matrix, hotel managers – by responding to questions on each level – should progress to more complex problems in hotel marketing (e.g., programmes and then systems/policies). Furthermore, by concentrating on the management skills (arranged along the horizontal axis of Table 9.1) that are required for effective implementation of hotel marketing programmes, managers will 'discover' what it takes to achieve the goals they have set in their devised strategy. In essence, they will learn what is needed to productively implement hotel strategy with regard to interacting, allocating, monitoring and organizing. Based on the analysis of the various levels, effective strategy implementation can be achieved through examining: (a) the interaction among individuals/companies and other groups; (b) resource allocation; (c) organization of responsibilities and tasks; and (d) monitoring of performance.

The travel experience resembles to a certain extent a 'symphony' performed by an orchestra. Both require the firm guidance of an expert conductor who understands the role of all instruments and how they should harmonize to produce the optimal effect on the audience. To blend the varied talents and capabilities of diverse groups, including employees, politicians, financial interests, business, suppliers, and host community groups, whether involved in preservation or sponsorship activities to support the hotel's strategy, represents a real challenge to the manager.

Table 9.1 Marketing taxonomy

Effective implementation can be analysed at the level of:	Effective implementation is achieved through:			
	Interacting	*Allocating*	*Monitoring*	*Organizing*
Actions	How can employees of a service business be sensitized to the different needs, expectations, and attitudes towards the service experience by different segments?	How can hotels, through marketing tactics that seek to change consumer behaviour, increase operational productivity?	How should the service consumption experience be evaluated?	How can front-line service employees become involved in institutionalizing change in the company and get a feeling of ownership in the process?
Programmes	How can customer expectation levels be set so that they are likely to be met and satisfaction will result?	How should a hotel's advertising budget be allocated in the wake of the great wave of change taking place in marketing?	How can the effects of varying service level standard programmes on employee performance be assessed to design jobs and reward systems which direct employee behaviour in pro-customer directions?	How can entrepreneurial individuals be supported so that they will get more people involved in teamwork to bring ideas to innovation?
Systems	How can technological means be incorporated in the service delivery process to free the employees to focus on the customers?	How can a firm devise ways for the effective reward and control of performance relative to customers' needs and satisfaction?	How should the perceptions of employees be evaluated to determine how customer-oriented the senior and middle management and front-line employees are?	How can the tasks for management at all levels be changed so that managers are encouraged to search for better ways to involve the workforce in innovative problem-solving?
Policies	How can marketing and operations in an organization be integrated so that a managerial process is created which focuses on meeting customer needs and ensures market and operating success?	How should dollar and manpower resources be allocated in an international hotel corporation to reap the maximum benefit from the network's marketing efforts?	How can the firm's internal policies be best assessed to determine if they reflect a real commitment to the customer?	How should the organization be redesigned to maximize responsiveness while minimizing organizational conflict at the same time?

Source: T.V. Bonoma (1984) *Managing Marketing*, New York: The Free Press

CONCLUSION

Competition in the international hotel industry takes place on the local level. However, international hotel corporations based in the United States, Europe, and Asia are introducing modern marketing practices and joining the earlier described GDS throughout the world. The introduction of GDS will cause international hotel companies to become more removed from their clientele. As client decisions are largely controlled by more than just the individual user, it is increasingly essential for the hotel firm to build effective and long-term relationships with intermediaries. Furthermore, this chapter identified the need for international hotel corporations to maintain competitive parity in the effective acquisition of knowledge required for value-added skill-building processes. At the same time, and despite the trend towards globalization, this chapter provided reasons why the international hotel industry cannot neglect local issues. A localization strategy imposes requirements which cannot be met by the administrative structure of the international company, the multinational company, or the global corporation.

The uncertain and unpredictable environment requires that marketing and operations be closely aligned organizationally for rapid and effective response. Specifically, this finding points to the need for an organizational configuration that: (a) is dispersed but interdependent; (b) permits differentiated contributions by local units to worldwide operations; and (c) develops and diffuses knowledge jointly and among hotel operations in the global network for purposes of innovation within the system.

CASE: PAN PACIFIC HOTELS AND RESORTS – SPECIALIZING IN THE PACIFIC RIM

California-based Pan Pacific Hotels and Resorts is engaged in management and marketing of hotels and resorts in 12 countries throughout the Pacific Rim.

The hotel group was formed in April 1989 through a consolidation of marketing and operating resources of Tokyu Hotels International and Emerald Management Company. Today, Pan Pacific Hotels and Resorts encompasses 17 hotels (16 managed properties and one marketing affiliate) with more than 6,387 rooms.

Pan Pacific Hotels and Resorts span half the globe, from Jakarta to San Francisco. Some properties, in locales like Palau in Micronesia, Vanuatu off the coast of Australia and Mauna Lani Bay in Hawaii, offer secluded getaways specializing in all the attractions of days devoted to play. Others, like Singapore, Kuala Lumpur and San Diego, stand as striking landmarks in gateway cities catering to a business clientele and excelling in the extra amenities that make international executives most productive.

In a world of formula development and cookie cutter skylines, Pan Pacific Hotels and Resorts reflects a unique standard of individualism. No two Pan Pacific properties are physically alike; rather, consistency is achieved through quality guest services, personnel and amenities.

As a hotelier, Pan Pacific is a company dedicated to providing international travellers with an excellent choice of hotels and services in prime locations throughout the greater Pacific region. But when it comes to travel experiences, Pan Pacific has a more important role. Pan Pacific has made it its mission to ensure that its properties throughout the Pacific Rim embrace the differences of each land and its culture. The company puts forward the philosophy that travel should be a journey into the mystique of a land travellers will long savour and thoroughly enjoy.

The celebration of culture and tradition is infused into almost every facet of the Pan Pacific product, from the experienced staff to the interior designs and dining fare. Each property, through and through, is crafted for its environment and reflects its own personality as well as purpose.

One of the best presentations of culture is found in the culinary delights of each property's dining establishments. Pan Pacific restaurants select the best local spices and specialities, adding signature dishes to menus featuring distinctive Pacific Rim style cuisine.

The belief in cultural travel experiences is reinforced in the careful selection of hotel staff. Pan Pacific strives to attract talented people whose love of their native land is genuine and translates into a willingness to share it with the international clientele. Pan Pacific believes that with good people, good service comes naturally.

As with any successful business, Pan Pacific Hotels and Resorts relies on relationships and long-lasting partnerships, not only with individual business and leisure travellers but also with professional travel planners, to ensure future viability. Consequently, Pan Pacific is constantly evaluating its guest services, travel agent incentive programmes and reservation policies.

As a result, Pan Pacific has recently developed Pacific Reserve, a sophisticated reservations system offering agents up-to-date information and instant confirmation via satellite line to the worldwide Covia network.

The on-line system provides rapid confirmation of hotel bookings, up-to-date room and rate information and easy computer access through Pan Pacific's new two-letter code (PF) to more than 250,000 travel agencies worldwide. Through Covia linkup, reservations for a Pan Pacific Hotel can also be made by calling any one of the hotels or seven sales offices in London, North America, Singapore, Hong Kong, Tokyo, Osaka and Sydney.

Parent company of the hotel group is Tokyu Corporation, a multi-billion dollar conglomerate founded in 1922. It has 351 companies and 92,480 employees in transportation (airlines, railways, and buses); retailing and distribution; development; and recreation and leisure industries.

In Japan, the Tokyu Hotel chain has 18 properties comprising Japan's largest first-class hotel network. In addition, it has Tokyu Inns, a group of 39 urban and resort inns throughout Japan. Tokyu Corporation also has business interests in North America, Australia, New Zealand and Asia including Singapore, Hong Kong, and mainland China.

READING: COMPETING IN A GLOBAL MARKETPLACE

by Isadore Sharp, Chairman, President and CEO, Four Seasons Hotels and Resorts

We've seen a lot of business buzzwords flare and fade in the 1980s, but the two I've been asked to speak about – 'competitiveness' and the 'global marketplace' are not among them. Whole industries are mutating as the battle lines are drawn for what has been called 'the real World War'. That's not a passing phase, that's the corporate world getting ready to test Darwin's theory of survival.

The 1990's have been dubbed – rightly, I think – a white-knuckle decade. The field of struggle for world domination is shifting from the ideological to the economic, and it's going to be the slugfest of the century. We're in one of those rare periods of history that can truly be called transformational. A prospect both alluring and alarming; unparalleled in opportunity and vulnerability. As Dickens put it, 'the best of times and the worst of times' – depending on whose companies and industries survive.

The future of our industry – travel – depends on affluence, according to Lester Thurow, the distinguished economist who addressed the World Travel Roundtable in Paris last April. 'Travel is a luxury, not a necessity', he said, 'so when income per capita goes up or down 1 per cent, spending on pleasure travel goes up or down 3 per cent.' He then noted that during the 1950s and 1960s, the world's GNP grew by 6 per cent a year; during the 1970s by 3 per cent; in the 1980s by about 2 per cent; and that in the 1990s, because of the huge trade deficits in the US and UK, a further slowdown is forecast. The impact on travel, he implies, will be a negative.

I can't fault Dr Thurow's reasoning. But if we look back at 1950, when only 25 million people a year travelled outside their own country, we see that as the world GNP growth rate was falling, the number of people travelling abroad was rising. It's now 325 million, a rise of 1,300 per cent; and an international survey by Horwath & Horwath of London has concluded that growth of 4 per cent a year will continue throughout the 1990s.

Clearly, the travel industry's growth rate can't be predicted on average world economic growth rates – you know what they say about averages: a man with one foot on a hot stove and the other on a block of ice is, on average, very comfortable. Nevertheless, I agree that our future – the future of travel – is keyed to affluence.

Historically, trade creates affluence, and the outlook for trade has never been brighter. The United States and Canada have a trade agreement. American and Canadian consortiums have been formed to invest in Russia. Countries like Mexico and South Korea are easing restrictions on foreign investment. Japan has dropped some of its non-tariff barriers and, along with the four little dragons, the world's fastest developing countries, it's creating a major new market: 200 million people, 92 per cent literate. Consider Asia alone. Over the next 30 years its population will grow by a mind-boggling 1.5 billion people.

Then there's Europe, now being converted from a patchwork of economies into the world's largest unified market. A creation described to the World Travel Roundtable by EC Commissioner Willy deClercq as 'the biggest, most important liberalization and deregulation experience that ever happened in the history of mankind'. And, he added, 'it won't be Fortress Europe because it's twice as dependent on exports as the US.'

The world's corporate leaders see a global market shaping and they're jockeying for position through mergers, buyouts and alliances. Asea of Sweden has merged with Switzerland's Brown Boveri to become the world's largest electrical engineering firm. The giant West German firm of Siemens bought IBM's business telephone division to edge Northern Telecom out of the number one slot in that field. And the same consolidation is taking place in packaging, pharmaceuticals, candies, cars, you name it. Professor Howard Perlmutter of Wharton has identified 136 industrial sectors where it's 'go global or decline'. By the year 2000, he says, we'll see, at most, five majors in each of these sectors.

This isn't bigness for its own sake, this is a reinforcement of core strength. This is business integrating nations with so many interlocking deals that protectionism won't even make short-term sense.

So what does this mean to us? It means growth in foreign trade; more efficient wealth creation; more affluence; more tourism; and more business people trekking abroad to sell, consult, advise, monitor, negotiate, research, cut deals and close them. *The Economist*, in its latest *Travel & Tourism Analyst*, anticipates that in the future West Germany and Japan will outspend the US on international travel. And pollster Daniel Yankelovich says, 'From the business and marketing point of view, the immediate future of the travel industry looks amazingly good.'

Early in 1988 we considered how best to capitalize on these upcoming changes. The majority of our customers are North American business executives. Many already travel abroad and many more seemed about to follow. Our major overseas competitors were coming into our market in strength, and unless we went into theirs and made our name better known abroad, we risked losing market share at home.

We had three of the four requirements for global success: a strong capital base, a top operational capability and rising public awareness of our brand-name. What we didn't have, and what we felt would be needed in the future, is a presence in the three major markets: North America, Europe and the Far East.

We had our pick of offers from financiers and developers. We assessed our capabilities – how much we could develop without compromising standards in our existing hotels. We decided we should lock in, over the next five years, 12 to 15 new properties. Since then we've signed contracts for nine, with three more under final negotiation. We will now have footholds in all major regions.

The hotel industry is positioning itself for the coming global shakeout in the same way as every other sector. Britain's Bass has bought the rest of the Holiday Inns it didn't own to form the world's biggest chain: 1,600 hotels. The British also have Hilton International and Travelodge, the Japanese the Inter-Continental and Westin. Days Inn has teamed up with Cara; Quality International with Alcoa; Radisson with SAS International and Movenpick Hotels of Switzerland. There's a lot of consolidation that will end in more concentration and an estimated 5,000 more hotels within three years.

And our industry, too, is getting down to core businesses. Canadian Hotel & Restaurant ran a story recently about Robert Hazard, president of Quality International. It said he went shopping for jogging shoes in 1981 and found 106 styles to choose from. He came home with a concept of building hotels as tailored to the guest as jogging shoes are to the feet. Then he introduced six separate product lines from luxury to budget and spread the concept of segmentation through the industry.

Personally I would have thought segmentation began long before, with Ritz catering to the rich and Kemmons Wilson to the motorist. Four Seasons, in the mid-1970s, tailored its hotels to top executives and created a quality niche in North American cities. What is really new today is the scale and pace of segmentation. Chains are subdividing like amoebas, offering four to six product lines, each customized for a different class of traveller. And as every chain competes head-on in every market segment, there won't be any more quasi-monopoly niches.

The latest competition, as you know, is in mega-resorts, with everyone trying to out-spectacle each other. We were offered a lucrative contract to put our name on a mega-resort, but we turned it down. We don't believe that's what our customers want. They don't want to line up and take a number for entertainment and food. They don't want groups that can't be controlled partying around them at poolside. They want personal attention, tranquillity, romance. I think George Bernard Shaw spoke for our customers when he said, 'The essence of inhumanity is indifference.'

I think the jury's still out on the final returns from mega-resorts. People travel for change as well as rest, and one Disneyland-type of experience is much like another, whether it's Down Under or in Palm Springs.

The mega-resort is a first-time wonder, but as its numbers increase, how many times will people want the same experience?

The battle of the beds has become the battle of the brand-names. The world is invading the national market, cluttering it with products, and we'll have to be able to set ourselves apart. We'll have to have a brand-name with top-of-the-mind awareness; an image that the customer can relate to. That's going to be tough on the independents, and many are joining forces under a brand-name like Prestige Hotels. But 'whoever loses, it won't be our customer', serves the industry in the long run.

As resorts and hotels proliferate, satisfying the customer will no longer be an option, it will be mandatory. In the 1960s, when we at Four Seasons competed in Canada, we had quite a lot of room for error. In the 1970s, competing in major American and British markets, we had less room for error. In the 1990s the global market will give us no room for error.

Competition is shaping up as a kind of Olympics: we'll be up against the best in the world no matter where we're located, and the winners will be those who are most clearly perceived to make customer satisfaction their number one goal.

I'm sure we're all aware of this. 'Close to the customer' is one of the decade's favourite clichés. The real question is: how fast is a cliché converted into conviction? A study by Peat Marwick McLintock found the industry's number one goal to be profitability, with growth number two. Guest satisfaction was number five. There's the problem. Eyes that are fixed on a dollar sign can't be focused on the customer.

As I say, it's a matter of priority. Our goal is not selling our product. Our purpose is not gaining market share. Our first concern is not beating the competition. Our purpose is gaining customers. Our goal is a satisfied guest. If we make this our first concern, we'll always beat the competition, sell the product and gain market share.

We have two routes to the top in the global market, and both are a climb without plateaux. We have to be always innovating and always improving service. If we think we've reached the point where we can stop and take it easy, that's the point where someone's going to lead the climb right over us.

Innovation anticipates, or responds to, customer needs. When we started Four Seasons in 1961, knowing that business executives like to travel light, we bucked the conventional wisdom and put shampoo in our rooms. We later added, among other things, bathrobes, hairdryers, overnight pressing and shoe shining, and introduced concierge service and mini bars to North America. All useful ideas, but unfortunately, not patentable. Soon all our competitors had them and customers were taking them for granted. Innovation is necessary. It raises industry standards. It keeps us in the race, but it's peripheral.

Service, of course, is primary, but so increasingly costly and difficult that some classes of hotels are moving towards self-service. Others take the opposite approach: the top 100 American resorts now have, on average, 160 employees for 100 rooms.

Service isn't something we can copy. Or standardize, or systemize or automate to any degree. The cartoon of a robot doorman in front of a luxury hotel was drawn by a fantasist, not a futurist. The more high tech in society, the more the upscale customer will appreciate a high touch environment.

We all know the importance of service and the employees who deliver it. Look at the hotel ads in any current magazine. They're all selling a quality service image, all claiming employees are their most valued resource.

But the fact is, according to a recent Horwath & Horwath survey, our image as an employer is not perceived as being attractive. To quote the survey, 'There are other more appealing industries competing for diminishing number.'

Our labour pool is going to shrink in the 1990s. Less than half as many people will enter the labour force every year as entered it in the 1970s. Both the hotel and restaurant sectors will face a semi-skilled labour shortage, and greater labour mobility will aggravate the turnover problem.

I think we've been making some headway in educating hotel colleges and career advisers that hotels can be a worthwhile career. But building a hotel image is not like creating a political image – we're dead if we don't deliver on our promises.

Service will be the battleground of luxury hotels in the 1990s, and finding, keeping and developing employees will be a major preoccupation. But here the Horwath survey points out another problem, and I quote, 'The issue of the more efficient use of existing labour . . . has largely been ignored by the hotel industry. . . . Management has been more concerned with controlling labour than developing it.'

This issue – productivity – can't really be measured in our business except by our rate of return on capital. But it's safe to say that the biggest drag on productivity is service errors – they cost us customers, referrals and reputation.

Service errors are made in two ways: lack of knowledge or lack of attention. Lack of knowledge is a training problem easily spotted and, once recognized, easily rectified. Lack of attention is an attitude problem: how to motivate our front line – bellmen, barmen, waiters – our lowest paid and lowest-level employees.

This is where so many hotel managers go wrong in their efforts to raise service standards. They begin by focusing on this lower level performance.

When I thought about it later it was simple: we had mutual respect and trust. We had worked together by the Golden Rule: treat others as you would want to be treated. I knew that if I could get those values down to the bottom of our pyramid – to all the people who make or break a reputation for service – Four Seasons could compete with the best in the world.

So when we started to spread out – this would be the mid-1970s – I spelled out our goal: to be the best wherever we locate, and backed it with an ethical credo based on the Golden Rule. A behavioural guide that would shape the culture and character of our company.

But I knew it wasn't enough to write it down or talk it up. Eighty per cent of all companies had written credos, and only a tiny fraction have achieved excellence. Most of the others declare every year in their annual report, 'People are our most important resource', then they ignore their people the rest of the year. The only service talk gets you is lip service.

I think it was Andrew Carnegie who said, 'I pay no attention to what men say, I just watch what they do.' People are like my construction crew. They believe only what they see.

I made it policy. At one General Managers' meeting, we showed a slide, just three words: '*facta non verba*' (deeds not words) – I have a rather erudite personnel manager.

The manager is the message, and over the next year or so I discussed our credo with every senior manager in the company. Some thought it was corny, others unnecessary; some agreed, but I felt they didn't mean it. And insincerity doesn't sell trust – ask any politician.

I made cuts at the very top – Head Office Senior Executives, General Managers of hotels – until all those whom others would copy were setting the standard of conduct required.

The message got through and superior service became our competitive edge. To get excellence at the bottom you start at the top. As Napoleon said, 'There are no bad regiments, only bad colonels.' Usually because they're more competent technically than as managers of people.

I think this will be the industry's biggest single future challenge: convincing managers who still believe in the military model that by giving employees responsibility they're not giving up control, they're letting the genie of initiative out of the bottle. We have to have employees who use their heads as well as their hands. Employees who see a guest's problem as a service opportunity. And I don't know how you command or supervise people into thinking.

All we can do is win their trust. Show them we mean what we say in our ads. Every day, in dozens of ways – the decisions we make, how we spend our time – we're sending loud clear signals down through the ranks. We can't expect employees to be committed to front-line service if they see our real concern is only the bottom-line figure. We might as well tell our kids not to drink while we're sipping on a martini.

The key to committed troops on the service front is managerial commitment to values; managerial focus on a goal that employees feel is worth while, that they can take pride in helping to build. It may be simple, it may be motherhood, but it's rare – because it's hard. It means acting out values and purpose day after day, year after year: a never-ending lesson, by example.

Success in the global market will depend on our entrepreneurship and even more on our managerial priorities. It will come from the growth of the industry spearheaded by affluent travellers from the Far East and Europe. In Canada, from our untapped vistas of natural beauty; from clean pleasant cities where people can still walk main streets at night. According to Dr Marvin Cetron, President of Forecasting International, we're the third most stable country for investment in the world, after the US and Australia. If we don't do anything stupid, like taxing ourselves into uncompetitiveness, or closing our doors to immigration, or neglecting our environment, our opportunities will be limited only by enterprise and climate.

But we're also going to face more competition, and the only sure formula for winning that I can give you comes from a highly successful coach who was asked the secret of winning races. 'The thing to do', he said, 'is get out in front at the start and improve your position from there on.'

STUDY QUESTIONS

1 Explain the connection between the advent of high volume air travel and the development of the international hotel industry as it exists today.
2 Discuss the concept of competitive bench-marking in the globalization process of the hotel business.
3 Discuss the various corporate level strategies available to hotel companies which are entering the international arena.
4 With reference to the hotel industry, explain the difference between an international company, a multinational company and a global corporation.
5 Discuss the significance of the four 'globalization drivers' to a company's global strategy potential.
6 Discuss the various challenges faced by hotel corporations in relation to strategy implementation.
7 Explain factors involved in the implementation of a localization strategy by international hotels.
8 Discuss Bonoma's marketing taxonomy as it applies to a hotel's ability to compete internationally.
9 Explain how Pan Pacific blends achievement of international quality standards with individualism of each of its properties.
10 Evaluate the strengths and weaknesses of Four Seasons development since the early 1960s.

Chapter 10

Competing and cooperating in the changing tourism channel system*

This chapter highlights the channel system in tourism in the light of the impact of recent developments in information technology. The changes in the tourism channel system are discussed in terms of demand and supply and how information technology is affecting the marketing distribution channel for tourism producers. The focus of this analysis relates to the pooling of individual energies through and the promotion of cooperation in supplier marketing efforts with compatible partners, so that supplier output is more available and accessible to target markets. Cooperation through networking in the tourism channel system will be the key to gaining competitive edge in the hotel industry.

The case at the end of the chapter features Holiday Inn Worldwide and illustrates the way that this company has improved quality, productivity and competitive advantage by the use of information technology. The reading looks at the use of global distribution systems in the marketing of hotels.

THE TOURISM CHANNEL SYSTEM AND VALUE CHAIN

Tourism comprises businesses engaged in transportation, accommodation, food, beverages, attractions and events, as well as a marketing and distribution network to deliver tourism services to a dispersed and increasingly complex market. Recently, innovations in computer communications technology have found increased application in the tourism sector. The information technology revolution is taking place to varying degrees in most tourism sub-sectors. Some tourism sub-sectors, notably the airlines, through the use of central reservation systems (CRS), are at the leading edge of technological developments and their successful application, but some, such as the hotel industry, may be categorized as 'laggards' since they are 'slow to react to the creative use of communications and information technology' (McGuffie 1990: 30).

The hotel sector can be described as information-intensive because 'the relative importance of time and place utility of tourism services is greater than in the case of goods' (Rathmell 1974: 104). With information technology innovations reshaping the basic structure of society and industry, and consumers' increasing demand for information (Davis and Davidson 1991; Bardaracco 1991), the rates of technological development and diffusion may be anticipated to accelerate in the tourism sector. To be successful in a competitive hotel market it is no longer sufficient to offer more discerning consumers a good product. Increasingly, success in the hotel market, depends on understanding one's customers' expectations, and offering customers a perfect product at a lower cost and faster than the competition by effectively bridging the gap between suppliers and consumers. Information technology is predicted to bridge this gap through the application of computerized reservation systems (CRS) to the travel and hotel industry. Collier claims that 'CRS are providing the route to link the needs of the consumer with the products offered by the travel industry' (Collier 1989: 87).

In the following discussion, the tourism channel system is discussed in respect of some important shifts in tourism demand and changes in the competitive environment which confront suppliers when selecting channel systems. Subsequently, the feasibility of networks and the development of network strategy are analysed with reference to tourism suppliers. The focus of this analysis relates to the pooling of individual energies and the promotion of cooperation in supplier marketing efforts with compatible partners, so that supplier output is more available and accessible to target markets.

The purpose of a tourism channel of distribution is to get sufficient information to the right people at the right time and in the right place, to allow a purchase decision to be made, and to provide a mechanism whereby the consumer can make and pay for the necessary purchase (Mill and Morrison 1985: 399). The channel system is the critical link in the marketing mix between demand and supply, consumer and producer.

The channel system in tourism refers to the path by which a firm or consumer executes a reservation to use a facility (Leven 1982). It covers all activities designed to bring consumers more information and thus closer to the travel product; such activities are generally performed by tourism producers and commercial enterprises. An important feature of the travel product is its complexity – or the variety of services it comprises – and the interdependence which exists between the various services. These features of travel services in combination with the complex nature of travel marketing make it desirable to use intermediaries or indirect channels when getting the message to the market.

Direct channels still exist between buyers and sellers but are chiefly concerned with the sales function at the individual company level, where sales representatives concentrate on (a) maintaining sales contacts with channel intermediaries; (b) maintaining sales contact with local organizations; and (c) following leads furnished by other sources (Kaven 1974: 116).

However, indirect channels of distribution have become increasingly important to represent the tourism supplier in multiple markets of origin (Bitner and Booms 1982). As such, travel agents play an increasingly significant role in distributing travel and hotel products to the consumers. Other intermediaries are the tour packagers and tour wholesalers who generally coordinate and promote the development of package tours. The primary advantage for tourism producers is that these wholesalers tend to purchase services in bulk and, more importantly, in advance, allowing producers to anticipate sales volume. Hotel representatives, such as Utell, comprise another intermediary, acting as sales and reservation agents for a number of non-competing hotels and are frequently used by foreign hotels selling to consumers in the travel generating markets. Other types of intermediaries include association executives, corporate travel offices, and incentive travel firms through which suppliers can attempt to influence when, where and how consumers travel. In other words, they control to some degree how much business an individual airline, cruiseline, or hotel may get (Bitner and Booms 1982). Using intermediaries (i.e. indirect channels in the tourism channel system), means that the hotel firm has third parties playing key roles in contributing to its value chain. The hotel manager must fully understand its relationships with suppliers and intermediaries in relation to customers to ensure that benefits are optimized.

A firm's value chain for competing in the market is embedded in a larger stream of activities known as the 'value system' (Porter 1990: 34). The value system of a typical international hotel corporation includes related travel and business services such as telecommunications, credit card, and banking services, and indirect supplier value chains, like computer reservation systems, brewers, construction firms, real estate, and education and training institutions. The suppliers of related services and manufactured goods provide inputs to the hotel firm's value chain. Within the value chain, the rendering of service by humans, specifically the client–service provider interaction, is the critical success factor in the hotel industry (Geller 1985), as opposed to manufacturing where the producer and consumer may never come into contact. The role of the channel system in tourism is clearly a major factor in the contribution to the value chain of an individual hotel. If a hotel can make its product more accessible and convenient to potential buyers, it has a perceived higher value and should enjoy competitive advantages over other hotels.

Porter's (1985: 34) analysis highlights this importance in respect of product differentiation and subsequent competitive advantage. It must be noted at this stage that the value chain is not a collection of independent activities, but a system of interdependent activities or linkages. These linkages can lead to competitive advantage (Porter 1985: 48). For example, the linkages in the tourism value chain may be illustrated by the newly introduced global distribution systems that connect the information streams of airlines, hotels, car hire companies and travel agents. At each step of the production process, the manager of the travel and tourism corporation has to choose the optimal combination of inputs, such as manpower, physical capital, financial resources, and the channels for the marketing and delivery of services that shall yield the maximum contribution to the value chain of the organization.

In the lodging industry, for example, hotel ownership may be approached as a business activity, separately from the hotel operations management activity, which may be approached separately from the marketing and reservations function through a hotel franchise or referral system. The key factors for the success of each segment (e.g., ownership, operations management contracting, and franchising) are not homogeneous. The key factors for success in gaining market share and profitability shall be elaborated on later in this chapter.

Shifting market demand

On the demand side, the need for reliable travel information is essential. Kaven (1974: 114) describes the customer's need for information and its complex nature as follows: 'the endless combinations and permutations of alternative routes, transportation modes, time, and lodging accommodations make many travel decisions difficult even for the initiated'. Communication through the channel system represents a critical element in the marketing mix, in particular in tourism, since in the complex of service, 'time and place utility appear to be the essence of the product itself' (Rathmell 1974: 105). And also due to the growth of the more discerning independent traveller, 'there is a need for a broader range of information at the point of sale' (Collier 1989: 87).

The fundamental issue of communicating brand-name identity in a 'crowded' channel system is further complicated by several 'unique' features of the tourism product. The intangibility of the tourism product, rendering it experiential in nature, means that the customer is unable to 'touch' and 'experience' the product prior to purchase, in complete contrast to manufactured goods. Furthermore, the distribution process is impacted by virtue of the tourism product's fixed geographic location in a destination area. The fixed nature of the tourism product requires consumers to travel to the destination area to experience what they are buying. Finally, perhaps the most significant aspect of the tourism product is that it is produced by various components that comprise the functioning tourism system (Gunn 1972; Go 1981; Mill and Morrison 1985; Blank 1989) which include the demand (market) side and the supply side.

The role of supply-side components, including attractions, transportation, services and information/promotion, are critically interwoven. Gunn agrees, claiming 'all components of the supply side are essential to a properly functioning tourism system. All must function in a delicate but tightly integrated balance' (Gunn 1988: 67). In order to offer consumers satisfying experiences, the various suppliers require ongoing and excellent communications, shared values, and a customer-driven vision. Unfortunately, the presence of these factors in adequate measure tends to be the exception rather than the rule, often imposing a constraint on a smoothly functioning tourism system. Increased dependency on communication will be critical in the future as the infrastructure of the economy is shifting.

Historically, an economy has relied heavily on a particular kind of infrastructure (Davis and Davidson 1991: 31). Infrastructure is the elementary network on which all activity and especially communication depends. The shift in the infrastructure of today's economy implies a change in travel demand. In the future, suppliers will be much more dependent on the effective functioning of communication within the tourism system than ever before. The railways, and later the highways through to car development, represent those infrastructures upon which regional economies were transformed into a single national economy. The introduction of the jet aircraft resulted in the large-scale expansion of multi-domestic travel and trade. Each time the infrastructure shifted, tourism demand changed, forcing suppliers to adapt their products to new customer demands.

At the core of today's economy, new information technology is causing a shift in the infrastructure of today's economy and is significantly changing tourism demand. In particular, it is altering long-standing relationships in the channel system in tourism, and creating new forms of competition – sometimes overnight. Specifically, the application of micro-electronic technology in general, and the computer in particular, are playing a fundamental role in market shifts that are most vividly demonstrated by:

(a) the decline of the independent travel agent catering to the leisure market, and the growth of agents who have invested in large computerized reservation systems with direct access to flights, accommodation, rental cars, and other services (Hitchins 1991).

(b) the emergence of the global customer. Instant worldwide news reporting through, for example, the Cable News Network (CNN) has resulted in consumers around the world having access to the same information at the same time. The increasing homogenization of customer needs worldwide has spawned a global lifestyle and raised consumer expectations for ever-faster and better information and service delivery. For example, Kendall and Booms (1989) found that information expectations of consumers were rated as more important than physical needs with respect to travel agent facilities.

(c) The current use of CRS in travel businesses have revolutionized operations, improving, facilitating and speeding up all activities including the booking of flights, car rentals, tours, hotel rooms and other tourist services (German Federal Republic 1989).

The bargaining power of buyers has also changed dramatically. Consumers are becoming more experienced and knowledgeable, but at the same time are demanding a better quantity and quality of information about globally dispersed tourism products. Single or independent hotel businesses tend to be especially vulnerable in a climate of intensifying competition. In contrast, hotels operating within a chain or network tend to have better access to the necessary capital, marketing expertise and technology necessary to survive by being able to satisfy these increasing demands.

In the tourism industry, buyers include tour wholesalers, travel agent retailers and consumers. These buyers impact on the hotel industry by forcing down prices, demanding higher quality and greater variety of services, all at the expense of industry profitability. Buyers, sure that they can always find alternative products, have used this knowledge to play one hotel firm against another for example, when meeting planners of a company or association negotiate to hold their conference at a particular hotel.

Wholesalers, travel agencies and tour brokers account for about one-third of the room nights consumed annually in the United States (Brewton 1987: 12). The needs of travel organizations who resell the hotel rooms they buy tend to be different from those of the user. Although consumers are expected to continue to play the starring role, Leven (1982) suggests that tourism suppliers have become more removed from their clientele, that client decisions are largely controlled by more than just the individual user, and that the 'gap' between supplier and consumer will continue to widen.

Shifts in demand are challenging suppliers to make tourism products available and accessible to increasingly demanding customers in often dispersed markets. This issue leads to a reassessment of the tourism channel configuration in relation to the essential and unavoidable activities that are part of the hotel value chain.

Turbulent channel environment

On the supply side, there are significant changes which are causing instability and turbulence in the tourism channel system. The very nature of a competitive environment means that there will be some 'turbulence' and, as Schumpeter (1965) recognized many decades ago, there is no 'equilibrium' in competition. 'Competition is a constantly changing landscape in which new products, new ways of marketing, new production processes, and new market segments emerge' (Porter 1990: 20). Today's dynamic competitive environment is characterized by change and innovation. Kaven (1974: 119) agrees, claiming that 'so long as competitive innovations occur and entrepreneurs seek to implement them in search of survival, growth and profit, these channels of distribution are subject to change'.

In the hotel industry, businesses constantly strive to be identified in the increasingly complex market. The hotel industry is comprised of a relatively small number of large suppliers and a relatively large number of small suppliers. However, both small and the large suppliers face a universal challenge, albeit perhaps to a different extent, which Kaven (1974: 115) refers to as: 'hundreds of thousands of establishments are seeking to gain identity with untold millions of potential customers covering the whole spectrum of incomes, interests, knowledge, sophistication and needs'. However, only the largest suppliers may have the network in place and the resources to establish and sustain their brand identity successfully.

Competitiveness can be assessed along two dimensions. First, the global dimension measures competitiveness in terms of number of customers attracted, market share, revenues, and expansion. The second dimension focuses on the activities performed in an industry sub-sector and attempts to explain why one sector is more successful than another – for example, the airlines in comparison with the accommodation sub-sector. When a country's tourism industry falls behind its competitors in terms of the provision of information, marketing analysis capabilities, and interconnection among systems and databases, it can have most critical consequences in terms of industry–customer interfacing and affect perceptions and competitiveness most directly (Government of Canada 1988a). The traditional 'competitive strategy' paradigm which focuses on product–market positioning is greatly and increasingly dependent in hotel firms on human resources management which is an integral part of the value chain (Porter 1990). Therefore, the notion of competitive advantage which provides the means for developing product based advantages at a given point in time (in terms of cost and differentiation) should be complemented with insights into the processes of knowledge acquisition.

The competitive advantage concept offers another perspective on business strategy that facilitates analysis of the competitive environment. The key factors for success of different industries lie in different production functions 'at different points along the "value chain"' (Porter 1990). The way in which one activity within the value chain is performed affects the cost or effectiveness of other activities. Activities performed in the competition between hotel firms should be designed to contribute to buyer value, and include the following: operations management and in particular managing service delivery, marketing, information technology, human resources, accounting and finance, and administrative functions. Hotel companies that are able to conceive of innovative ways of reconfiguring their activities can, as Holiday Inns did through the intelligent use of information technology, improve quality and productivity, and create competitive advantage.

The introduction of computerized reservation systems (CRS) and global travel distribution practices designed to create transnational links throughout the world have put channel systems at centre stage in the battle for competitive advantage.

The CRS developments have largely arisen through the initiatives of the airline industry. From centralized booking systems, to information providers, to potentially dominant marketing and distribution systems, the CRS role has been critical to airline survival since deregulation in the USA in 1978. Travel agents have adopted links to airline CRS and gained access to an information and booking system which allows them to book (and confirm) seat reservations at the touch of a few keys. Speed, accuracy and reliability of information are just a few of the advantages to the travel agent and ultimately the buyer. At the same time the airlines have instigated an enormous distribution system where travel agents worldwide have access to the marketing and selling information of the airline products.

American Airlines (developers of Sabre) and United Airlines (with its Apollo system) were the early entrants and gained significant competitive advantage over their competitors (Truitt *et al.* 1991: 21). In the USA, the penetration of CRS into travel agencies is virtually complete, and the battle is now on for the global market. Only recently have other tourism subsectors realized the distributive power of the CRS and its ability to allow access to many new global markets. Hotels, car hire companies are now linking up with these CRS and hoping to gain significant competitive advantage. The strategic alliance of Marriott, American Airlines, Hilton hotels and Budget Rent-a-Car for the 'Confirm' project is a good example (Wolfe 1991). Activities vary in their contribution to competitive advantage in different industries, and can vary from segment to segment in a particular industry. The application of communications technology and its level of diffusion in the tourism channel system is, to a large extent, shaped by several dimensions, such as:

(a) the structure of the organizations in a particular sub-sector, e.g., chain-owned, independent, or scheduled versus charter services;
(b) the size of the operation, whether small, medium, or large;
(c) the target markets aimed at, e.g., business, pleasure, or group versus independent business;
(d) the type of service offered, e.g., limited or full service, specialized versus general services (Government of Canada 1988a: 4-5).

Within this context, and to facilitate access to global markets, travel and tourism corporations are reassessing their channel configuration. Hoteliers who wish to reassess the configuration of their distribution channel better realize that the rationale for a channel largely consists of linking customer needs to hotel products through bookings. Increased competition and the rising cost of technology have forced hotel companies, especially multi-national enterprises, to seek out alternative channel configurations.

The effective acquisition of knowledge will depend on the ability of hotel executives to improve their capability for the superior execution of activities and processes within and beyond their value system. Specifically, hotel organizations have to learn how they can share the knowledge required to create and deliver products and processes better, faster, of higher quality, and at a lower cost and risk. In their quest for enhanced communications capability, some companies have embraced the network concept to foster information sharing beyond corporate boundaries.

MOVING TOWARDS COOPERATION – THE NETWORK CONCEPT

A network is a type of cooperation that does not take the form of a merger or a joint venture, but is rather a limited involvement of the parties designed to solve knowledge and information-related problems through the assistance and contribution of organizations which for instance know and understand local markets (Van Rietbergen *et al.* 1990: 214). Thus, each of these service providers in the network contributes specific core competencies to the value chain on a short-term or long-term basis. Following this train of thought, the hotel corporation could be viewed as deriving added value to a lesser extent from traditional functions but to a greater extent from those functions that arrange and maintain transactions in integrated networks (de Jong 1991: 8), a set of partnership, strategic alliances, and joint ventures.

Types of network

Lambooy (1988: 28) distinguishes four traditional network types: (a) the 'growth pole' model; (b) the 'social network'; (c) the '*filière* configuration'; and (d) the 'complex'. The concept of 'social network' dovetails with Pred's theory (1977) and is applicable in the internationalization of services.

(a) The 'growth pole model' is predicated upon the concentration of growth in regions at urban-industrial poles through 'key corporations', i.e., companies that play a significant role in the economy such as, for example, car manufacturers, steel manufacturers, or the producers of computers. Through their transactions with other parties, these manufacturers induce business travel demand. Hotel suppliers could capitalize on such a network existing.

(b) The 'social network' is a concept which recognizes the significance of social relationships among entrepreneurs, employees, and consumers in the decision-making process in addition to the price mechanism.

For example, family connections often influence market relationships. In this regard, Lambooy refers to the example of politicians who 'assist' their family or friends to obtain commissions, in spite of the lower quality and the higher price that may be expected.

(c) The 'branche configuration' complements the company's value chain. It is comprised of a network of relationships that may be likened to the branches of a tree, hence the French term '*filieres*'. Relationships in the branche configuration of the international hotel industry might include, for example, real estate brokers, manufacturers of furniture and electronic equipment, financial institutions, transportation corporations, and travel agents and tour operators.

(d) Large, key businesses are central to the industrial complex. The notion of 'complex' is relevant to networking in the international hotel industry because mega-attractions like, for example, the Disney World amusement park near Orlando, form the focus for hotel developments.

The dynamic network may be defined as 'an organizational architecture that accommodates constant and accelerating change while at the same time stimulating components of the corporate environment to build deep and lasting relationships' (Hickman and Silva 1987: 210).

Why network?

Earlier discussion in this chapter highlighted the external pressures of demand and supply influencing the need for hotel managers to network in the tourism industry. Other synergistic pressures which can be applied to justify networking concern the organization's internal structure. The channel system in tourism will be controlled increasingly through information and communications technologies which tend to be owned by corporations who operate under one or more brand-names (Kaven 1974: 119). Consequently, having and communicating a brand-name is of increasing significance to achieving competitive advantage in international tourism. The earlier mentioned Best Western brand provides the independent hotel with the opportunity to be part of a network of more than 3,500 properties, representing 273,000 guest rooms throughout 48 countries, and to capitalize on the technological advantages the network offers whilst preserving its independence. Best Western, because it saves its network members' hotels between 5 to 8 per cent on fees, as compared to fees charged by franchise companies, can help promote hotels in local economies that have depended on an ever-shrinking agricultural base to tourists who are showing an interest in seeing off-the-beaten-path type locales. For example, in the USA more and more tourists are showing an interest in visiting small towns and Civil War battlegrounds.

Networks share several characteristics that are relevant to hoteliers:

(a) networks raise the cost of entry to a level that few potential competitors can or will pay (Best Western and similar consortia form an exception to the rule); (b) network-oriented services are usually enhanced by expanding the network, the facilities of which tend to be more widely used if the expansion enhances its value to customers; (c) early investment in a network may result in long-term competitive advantage over new entries especially in industries where customer loyalty, switching costs or habit patterns are dominant; (d) once a customer franchise is built through network enhancement, it may be difficult to displace; (e) the greater the need for a multinational network due to the high mobility of consumers the greater the likelihood that a well-established service firm will realize a significant portion of its revenues from foreign activity; (f) the technology of networks is changing so fast that it may transform competition in services such as telecommunications (Heskett 1986: 112, 144). In an increasingly complex and changing environment, hotel corporations cannot effectively compete through channel systems that are unidimensional and static.

While service companies used to have a supporting role in the facilitation of economic transactions in the past, they increasingly tend to take on a transactions determining role (de Jong 1991: 9) and a strategic significance. For instance, the planning and building of commercial accommodation in a tourist destination determines to a great extent the type of tourist market this destination will attract in the future.

Due to the scarcity of required expertise, the high development and operations costs, and the risk factors in the restructuring of the hotel industry, it is becoming more common for hotel companies to seek long-term relationships with suppliers, research and marketing groups around the world. An integrated network of relations between service providers is emerging based on agreements to cooperate with one another by contributing specific knowledge and information that are complementary in nature.

Role of information technology and networking

Another trend which is likely to reinforce the development of the communications network is the concentration of complementary services that together make up systems of services. This development is embodied by the global distribution system (GDS) which comprises vast networks that the major airlines use to communicate the most up-to-date flight and airfare information to travel agents. When linked to the GDS, agents can check schedules, compare fares, make hotel and rental car reservations, as well as order tickets for Broadway shows. What makes GDS so vital to the airlines is its ability to arrange a dizzying permutation of planes, routes and available seats in the most profitable configuration possible (McCarrol 1989: 50).

The implications of GDS are vast because they have become part of a global network connecting many tourism suppliers including airlines, hotels, and car rental companies. The GDS has in effect become an autonomous profit-making organization since tourism producers have to pay for use of the system each time a GDS is used to make a booking. The announcement that Sabre, the GDS division of American Airlines, is more profitable than the airline division, highlights the power and influence of GDS (Hopper 1990). The sophisticated application of new communications technology will present tourism suppliers with the opportunity to cooperate much more closely than before. At the same time, it may result in a greater internationalization of tourism and fiercer competition among travel and host firms.

The GDS, if effectively utilized, can play a crucial role by contributing to the hotel firm's value chain. As the GDS expands, an increasingly complex hierarchical system of transport and travel networks is evolving which provides important opportunities for gaining competitive advantage by those hotel firms with the necessary competencies and skills to capitalize on the new technology.

Information is becoming the critical strategic resource, especially in the travel and hotel sector. The power of information technology is also highlighted by Porter and Millar (1985: 149) since information technology not only transforms the nature of the products but changes the nature of the competition itself. This is especially true for products such as travel which contain a very high information content. The impact of information technology on the travel and hotel industry cannot be ignored. The required investment in information technology may be high, but it can be shared. Hence, in the future, strategic alliances between travel industry and hotel corporations should become the norm to exploit any of the opportunities which arise.

Current networks and the cooperation of tourism producers

Recent developments in the GDS 'industry' highlight a number of strategic alliances, primarily with the airline sector dominant. Some of the major airline GDS have become organizationally more 'cooperative'. For example, Apollo (USA) has developed close links with Galileo (Europe) and Gemini (Canada); Sabre (USA) and Amadeus (Europe) have announced plans to work together; and Worldspan (USA), which also hopes to incorporate System One (USA) in its operations, plans to merge with Abacus (Asia). The result may be a move towards three 'mega' systems which in effect form a powerful 'oligopolistic' market situation (Truitt *et al.* 1991: 27).

Other tourism sectors hope to link with these powerful systems to facilitate their global expansion. The Confirm project outlined earlier is a prime example, with Marriott, Hilton, Budget Rent-a-Car and American

Airlines pooling energies. However, the concern for these other sectors is that the airlines are still dominating tourism distribution channels and plan to remain in this position. As Chervenak (1991: 26) states, 'the thrust of all three global networks is to control the highest percentage of the world's airline, car rental and hotel reservations'.

Developing a network strategy

Strategic information systems offer tourism corporations great opportunities for gaining competitive advantage when organizations implement them appropriately and manage: (a) to take ownership of information technology, i.e., systems should be user driven and add value, rather than complexity and frustration; (b) not to overburden the development process by building too many features into the system; and (c) to understand and implement the strategies behind new systems or risk limited benefits (Anon. 1989: 14).

Since airline deregulation in 1978, the channel system in tourism started to change in a dramatic way, first in the United States and then gradually throughout the world. In particular, because of airline deregulation airfares changed with unprecedented rapidity. And subsequently, travellers demanded more information, faster, from a broader range of suppliers. In the new channel environment which resulted, hotel managers are compelled to rethink how they should access their markets and maintain relationships with their customers.

The ability of hotel corporations to build and manage a strategic channel system may separate the winners from the losers in the marketplace of the 1990s. The future marketplace will be characterized by more demanding customers, aggressive and massive financial accumulation, relatively free-flowing resources, and global brands. In an effort to survive, hotel corporations must respond to a rapidly shifting global marketplace by aligning their channel system and marketing functions with the organizational characteristics of the transnational network. These global opportunities must be exploited, with close, mutually beneficial cooperation, by all tourism producers.

Overcoming threats

It appears that the 'concept of self-interest, the very foundation of a market economy, could be utilised more effectively throughout all parts of tourism' (Gunn 1988: 206). The concept is based on the motivation to achieve and to reap the rewards from such achievement. In the past, this has been directed only internally – within the tourism firm the thinking of managers was guided by best practice. But as Hopper (1990) has suggested, this logic may be actually counter-productive and therefore no longer valid.

In the hotel industry many external factors influence success. Therefore, when viewing the hotel industry from an external perspective it will be seen that its integration with other parts of the travel industry is not only desirable but virtually mandatory. As the travel industry expands, an increasingly complex hierarchical system of transport, tourism and hotel networks is evolving.

Gunn (1988: 207) cites a number of barriers that prevent or constrain the exercise of adequate networking in the tourism system that are relevant to our discussion:

(a) Entrepreneurs often have a misconception of the tourism product. For example, an important part of the hotel product is the travel purpose such as the attractions that brought the traveller to the tourism product in the first place.
(b) Small business and government agencies have difficulty in justifying outreach, in part, because capital and operating expenses are not budgeted for this function.
(c) For competitive reasons in particular 'turf protection' is a major barrier to integration for all businesses and government.
(d) The educational systems tend to foster divisiveness rather than integration.

As observed by Gunn (1988: 207), hotel schools, for example, teach hotel management but seldom are students taught (i.e. in depth) how the hotel industry interrelates to and is dependent upon many other sectors and components of the tourism system. Broader education and training programmes would assist in alerting managers and students regarding networking potential between the various parts of the functioning tourism system. The issue is no longer whether or not one should adapt to the new technological environment. The current generation of computer systems shows that computerization and hence networking is essential to remaining competitive in tourism (Government of Canada 1988a: 2).

Towards an integrated hotel network strategy

There is little doubt that the information technology revolution is reshaping the basic structure of tourism and therefore the hotel industry. Though risky as it may be to interpret what the changes mean and what entrepreneurs, executives and others who have to make decisions should do to prepare for the challenges of the future, there seem to be several emerging patterns that point to the increasing importance and application of integrated network strategy in tourism that will impact the hotel industry and are therefore worth sharing:

(a) Network transactions for value-added skill and knowledge-building purposes will become increasingly critical in the tourism industry: (1) to assess marketing opportunities, the cost of sales implication, and the difficulties associated with achieving appropriate operating standards in the culturally and economically diverse sectors of the tourism market; (2) to acquire more detailed knowledge of local markets; and (3) to create an organizational structure that sees its mission, markets, and requirements as both local and global.

(b) The idea that the hotel firm is part of a network of economic trans-actions implies that in order to expand geographically and operate profitably the tourism corporation must perform its role effectively in the functioning tourism network (this requires cooperation between the tourism firm and 'travel industry partners', such as GDS, rental car, airline and travel agency firms). 'The network avoids the problems of duplication of effort, inefficiency and resistance to change to ideas developed elsewhere by giving subsidiaries the latitude, the encourage-ment, and tools to pursue local business development within the framework of the global strategy' (Czinkota et al. 1989: 609). The main tool for implementing this approach is to develop international teams of managers who meet regularly to develop strategy.

(c) Integrated network strategy should be formulated taking into account the host country's tourism policy and regional development priorities. In this regard, perhaps a potential obstacle to effective tourism market-ing is the tendency of tourism executives to see problems and solutions in the narrow context of the tourism industry as opposed to the services sector. The latter issue has become more prevalent as a set of global industries, including financial services, telecommunications, and transportation – especially through their GDS subsidiaries – are affecting the operation and control of hotel and tourism firms in destinations throughout the world.

(d) The greater importance of information and knowledge transactions in the hotel industry shall require managers to gain greater insight in the use of computer technology to facilitate a change in the management process within organizations and to extend their horizons well beyond the traditional trade channel system. Furthermore, it is essential that executives of tourism corporations learn to bridge the gap between business needs and integrate technology with functional processes to create opportunities and advantages. Or, to paraphrase Hopper (1990: 119), as the possibilities of what computers are capable of changes, hoteliers should change what they do with computers.

(e) In order to function effectively in the integrated network in the fast-moving, competitive market requires an organizational structure which incorporates a much more flexible management mentality than the one which dominates the traditional channel system in tourism. To take advantage of new opportunities and build competitive advantage, the leading hotel corporations are likely to develop the new trans-national model (Bartlett and Ghoshal 1989: 6) which will be discussed in more detail in Chapter 11.

CONCLUSION

The continuing process of change in the tourism market requires hotel managers to reassess their corporations' channel configuration in order to remain competitive. Activities performed in the competition between hotel firms should be designed to contribute to buyer value and competitive advantage. Because a channel system is a method of gaining access to a market, changes brought about by global distribution systems require adjustments in the organizational and managerial logic – namely, the idea that the hotel corporation is part of a dynamic network as opposed to the traditional distribution channel.

Network effects create important opportunities for gaining competitive advantage in the hotel industry in which the basic service consists of linking buyers, sellers and third parties. Networks are designed to build the central competitive advantage of the 1990s. No channel structure, regardless of how de-cluttered or de-layered, can compare with the speed and flexibility of networks to link suppliers, intermediaries, and buyers.

Due to increasing application of information technology the process of change and evolution in the travel and tourism channel system can be expected to continue, perhaps at an even more rapid rate than before. Only those hotel corporations capable of making adjustments to the dynamic characteristics of the travel and tourism market are likely to survive over the long run.

CASE: HOLIDAY INN WORLDWIDE – HARNESSING INFORMATION

The intelligent use of information technology can often lead not only to improved quality and productivity but also to competitive advantage. This is especially true in service businesses when the technology is used to empower employees to better serve customer needs and to empower customers by making the company easier to do business with.

In the lodging industry, few companies have applied technology more intelligently to gain competitive advantage than Holiday Inn Worldwide, the world's largest hotel brand. To help increase that edge, the company is investing more than US$60 million to further enhance its Holidex reservation system by adding a property management capability and the Holiday Inn Reservation Optimisation (HI) system, an industry exclusive that will allow consumers greater access to available rooms and more flexibility in making reservations.

'These changes are not about technology *per se*, but about using technology to change the way we do business and improve our customer service', says Bryan D. Langton, Chairman and Chief Executive Officer of Holiday Inn Worldwide. 'With this latest innovation, we are investing to improve hotel operations, reservations, and customer relations, as well as to bring the most technologically advanced hotel management system to our franchises.'

Already the industry's largest and most sophisticated computerized hotel reservation system, Holidex links the nearly 1,700 Holiday Inn properties in 54 countries around the world with 21 Holiday Inn central reservation offices, more than 60 corporate-implant Holidex terminals, and more than 240,000 airline terminals worldwide. More than 70,000 room nights are booked each day – a total of about 30 million a year – through the system.

Once HI is installed, the company says, Holiday Inn hotels will be able to integrate revenue optimization and customer tracking software to maximize both income for the hotels and options for consumers. In essence, HI is a new method of inventory control, which, by providing more information to both employees and customers, will allow the hotels to book more reservations at the best rates.

'Our strategy is to focus our resources on systems that will increase the gap between Holiday Inn and our competitors', Langton says. 'We believe these innovations will allow us to continue to respond more quickly and efficiently to what our customers want.'

As the Holiday Inn example illustrates, hotel corporations can apply advanced technology intelligently and nowadays have to be linked to their partners in the travel industry to achieve a competitive advantage.[1]

READING: MARKETING HOTELS USING GLOBAL DISTRIBUTION SYSTEMS

by Rita Marie Emmer, Chuck Tauck, Scott Wilkinson, and Richard G. Moore[2]

As recently as five years ago it was not essential for a hotel to be listed in a GDS. Today, however, computer reservation terminals are a travel agent's lifeline, and hotels that want travel agent business must be listed in a GDS. Understanding the electronic reservation process and using various GDS marketing features will allow hoteliers to market their products more effectively through those systems. This reading explains the global distribution network (GDN) and offers specific suggestions that will enable a hotel to increase the marketing effectiveness of its GDS participation.

History and evolution

In the late 1950s, airlines developed computer systems to manage their reservations. The early 1970s saw airline computer-reservation terminals installed in travel agencies to enable agents to book airline seats without using the telephone. Airlines expanded their reservation systems in the late 1970s to encompass hotel bookings and other travel-related services. During the 1980s the hotel reservation function improved so dramatically that the system shifted from merely being a distribution channel to being an effective, efficient marketing tool. Today, 96 per cent of all travel agencies in the United States have computer reservation terminals. In Europe and Asia the percentage of automated travel agencies varies greatly from country to country (see table).

Percentage of travel agencies using computer reservation terminals, 1992

Country	%	Country	%
USA	96	Korea	98
France	85	Australia	91
Italy	85	Japan	85
Scandinavia	61	Hong Kong	65
Spain	53	Singapore	56
Germany	48	Taiwan	50
United Kingdom	23	Malaysia	32
Greece	16	Philippines	32

The number of worldwide hotel reservations booked electronically exceeded 13 million in 1992 and that figure should pass 15.5 million in 1993. This sharp increase in electronic bookings is primarily due to enhancements that allow confirmation numbers to be generated in three to seven seconds. GDS now reach more than 125 countries.

For decades the telephone provided hotels with their primary reservations link. The telephone-based reservations model is familiar to generations of hotel operators. Guests either called a hotel directly or dialled a toll-free number at a central reservations office (C) to book a room. Travel agents typically called the central reservations office unless immediate confirmation was absolutely necessary; for example, at particularly high-demand locations the agent might have called the hotel directly.

Before a reservation is made, the guest or travel agent goes through a selection process to determine which hotel will best suit the guest's needs and budget. For years travel guides and indexes, such as the *Mobil Travel Guide, Fodor's*, the *AAA TourBook, Hotel and Travel Index*, and the OAG (*Official Airline Guide*), have provided information for leisure guests, travel agencies, and corporate travellers. Such published sources effectively provide considerable information about hotels, but details involving rates and room types are intentionally limited since the guides are published relatively infrequently. (Even with *Hotel and Travel Index*'s quarterly schedule, details on prices and room availability can be out of date.) As a result, a search for a hotel room can be concluded only by calling a property to determine rates, room types, and availability before an actual booking is made. This traditional three-step process of searching, calling, and booking is both time-consuming and costly for everyone involved.

As the speed of GDS systems and the accuracy of hotel data have improved, travel agents are less inclined to consult the published guidebooks and indexes. Instead, they favour the fast search-and-selection process made possible by their computers. The behind-the-scenes electronic reservation path between the travel agent and hotel may be more complex than a telephone conversation, but it also reduces human error and is faster. In only a few seconds, information travels between the travel agency and the hotel via (a) the GDS, (b) an electronic or manual switch, and (c) the hotel's central reservations office.

Travel agents are now accustomed to booking airline and car rental reservations electronically through sophisticated and accurate electronic reservation systems. Agencies are increasingly dependent on GDS computers to display hotel selections and reserve rooms instantly in any geographic location worldwide. The airline flight information provided by the GDS has been accurate and dependable for years. Now agents need the same accuracy and dependability from hotel descriptions, especially in room types and rate information.

As computerized hotel reservation processing has evolved over the past 20 years, great strides have been made towards perfecting automated reservation links between guests and travel agents on one side and individual hotels on the other. The most important advancement is the ability of each hotel to list all of its different room types, descriptions, rate categories (including negotiated rates, as described later), policies, and special packages in the GDS. The information is then available to hundreds of thousands of travel agents worldwide, as well as to individual consumers, all of whom are connected to one of several global distribution systems. Each GDS competes for its own network of travel agency subscribers to gain a greater market share. GDS companies continually expand and enhance their travel products and services to make their systems more attractive.

For years hotels struggled to fit their numerous rates, varied room types, and multiple services into the highly standardized computer programs that were designed to process airline reservations. Hoteliers were frustrated that hotel descriptions, rates, and availability took up to 15 days to change and that the response time on a GDS enquiry took 10 to 60 seconds. Hotel marketing managers believed that business travellers were the only market segment reached through GDS. Moreover, the trust between hotels and travel agents deteriorated as availability and room rates in the GDS differed from those quoted by reservationists answering the 800 line. Travel agents felt obligated to double check electronic bookings by phone.

Today, GDS have evolved from narrowly focused airline distribution channels to generic broad-based travel-reservation systems. In 1990, most of the major GDS dramatically improved their hotel programs and introduced the ability to carry negotiated rates, limitless rate categories, and multiple room types. The ability of GDS to give travel agents direct access to hotels' inventories has enabled agents to provide their clients with instant confirmation numbers. The response time for each transaction is normally three to seven seconds for those hotels that are directly connected to a GDS. Interface capabilities are advancing rapidly, and GDS will soon communicate directly with hotel reservation systems (i.e., seamless connectivity), which will eliminate much of the rate and availability discrepancies. Some hotel chains already have seamless connectivity with the GDS, and in the near future those interfaces will be commonplace.

Other integral parts of GDS evolution are visual-imaging programs and GDS applications in personal computers. The current visual imaging programs are Spectrum (Galileo/Apollo) and Jaguar (Sabre Vision). Those user-friendly programs allow hotels to market themselves to travel agents through the display of images and maps on the computer screen. The leisure market is gradually being addressed by global distribution networks. GDS applications in personal computers are enabling consumers to plan their travel and make reservations from their homes and offices, expanding the marketing reach of GDS directly to the consumer.

Call to action

No matter how beneficial global distribution is for all parties involved, reliable and complete information must be accessible to travel agents for GDS to maintain their integrity. Maintaining accurate rates and current availability are key factors in making the entire system work properly. Seamless connectivity will one day give GDS direct access to a hotel's PMS, ensuring complete and accurate 'real time' information for travel agents. It will be several years before connectivity with PMSs is a widespread reality; however, the trend today is seamless connectivity between the C and the GDS. To maximize the marketing effectiveness of GDS, hoteliers will want to update and enhance their electronic brochures just as they would other written collateral.

The following are some ways hotels can maximize bookings from the global distribution network:

- ensure that hotels are indexed by all possible reference points;
- use the availability (status) options to maximize yield;

- keep the hotel description (electronic brochure) current;
- keep packages simple for uncomplicated booking;
- put the hotel's two-letter access code on all advertising;
- use messaging and marketplace news to advertise;
- use the negotiated-rate feature for high-volume agencies and corporations; and
- keep in touch with and work with the central reservation office (CRO) or hotel representative.

Hoteliers must always remember that much of the effectiveness of electronic distribution lies in the hotel's ability to use its GDS as a marketing tool.

STUDY QUESTIONS

1 Explain the difference between direct and indirect channels of distribution in tourism.
2 Discuss the significance of the application of CRS to the travel and hotel industry.
3 What is the value chain of an individual hotel?
4 Explain the contribution of the channel system to the value chain of an individual hotel.
5 Describe the factors which are causing instability and turbulence in the tourism channel system.
6 What types of networks are available to the hotel industry and how are they different from mergers or joint ventures?
7 Discuss the concept of an integrated hotel network strategy.
8 How has Holiday Inn Worldwide used, and gained advantage from the use of, information technology?
9 Discuss the history and evolution of GDS in the hotel system.
10 Identify the key advantages to be gained by all parties utilizing a GDS.

Chapter 11

Evolving towards a business ecosystem

There are three political changes that are most likely to affect travel and tourism in the 1990s, and in turn the hotel industry: the risk of economic protectionism, the current changes in Eastern Europe and the Commonwealth of Independent States, and mounting public concerns about the environment.

The greening of a growing number of companies demonstrates that the hotel industry is taking an active stance with regard to the latter issue. For example, Canadian Pacific Hotels & Resorts undertook the development of an environmental programme for all its hotels in Canada. The objective of the programme is to institute the highest possible standards of environmental responsibility throughout the chain. The programme also aimed to identify areas where environmental improvements can result in lower operating costs.

By the end of 1990, environmental committees were formed at all Canadian Pacific Hotels & Resorts to provide in-house leadership for the chain-wide green programme. In January 1991, Canadian Pacific Hotels & Resorts conducted an environmental audit of all its operating hotels in Canada. The audit was designed to identify areas where it could introduce more nature-friendly products and practices, and to determine the level of support for environmental initiatives among Canadian Pacific Hotels & Resorts employees. It also asked professional environmental consultants for ideas on 'going green'. Most importantly, the company asked its 10,000 employees in Canada how they felt about introducing a green programme. The employees gave the company an overwhelming vote of support (over 90 per cent said they strongly favoured starting a green programme) and they also gave the company lots of great ideas on where to start greening its hotels.

To get the programme started at its 26 locations throughout Canada, the company took an 'environmental roadshow' out to its locations. The roadshow sessions conducted by Canadian Pacific Hotels & Resorts' Director of Environmental Affairs, Ann Checkley, and a team of environmentalists, gave the employees in each hotel practical advice on implementing the 'green plan'. The result: through the waste reduction, energy and water conservation measures outlined in the environmental action programme, Canadian Pacific Hotels & Resorts are afforded the opportunity to simultaneously save money and build a more positive public profile.

The case at the end of this chapter features a European company, Center Parcs, which has been a leader of change in the resort industry, winning various 'green' awards whilst operating a very successful holiday and leisure business. The reading (by Robert Cotter of ITT Sheraton) takes a different perspective in looking at the way that local staff in developing areas need to be respected as a key link in the technology transfer chain so that they can provide the high level of services needed by Sheraton's clients whilst creating an environment for individual growth within the company.

BUSINESS ECOSYSTEM

The notion that hotels are part of a constellation wherein players are attempting to create 'an ever-improving fit between competencies and customers', (Normann and Ramirez 1993: 66) leads to Moore's (1993) observation that the business world may be likened to an ecosystem which is comprised of a wide range of industries. In that hotels depend on a derived demand, the ecosystem concept affords hoteliers an excellent opportunity to frame the constantly changing landscape of competition and the emerging opportunities it creates for new market segments, new products, new ways of marketing, and new production processes.

At a recent annual corporate conference, Juergen Bartels, President and Chief Executive Officer, Carlson Hospitality Group, Inc., used the business ecosystem metaphor 'so that owners and employees could visualize our mission to become the world leader in travel and hospitality by the year 2000 and so they could see how we plan to reach this goal'.

'Every morning in Africa a gazelle wakes up. It knows it must run faster than the fastest lion, or it will be killed. Every morning a lion wakes up. It knows it must outrun the slowest gazelle or it will starve to death. It does not matter if you are a lion or gazelle. When the sun comes up, you'd better be running.'

With his story, Bartels challenged the owners and employees within his Carlson Hospitality Group to 'wake up' to the new realities of global competition, by referring to Charles Darwin's theory of 'survival of the fittest'. Darwin (1859) established an evolutionary view of the world, challenging contemporary beliefs about the fixity of species through his work into the interdependence of species, particularly the ecology of animals and plants.

Bartels' reference to the 'survival of the fittest' theory may mask important parts of the entire picture – that is, the ongoing interdependence of all species which Darwin referred to in his study. In part, Bartels' view of the interdependence of species, reflects the 'head-to-head' type of competition which characterizes the hotel industry's battle for market share. This view implies that as hotel marketers move towards a more strategic orientation, they tend to adopt a militaristic perspective on competition. Such a perspective is likely to be inappropriate for competing in today's marketplace, because potentially it restricts the performance of companies as well as the entire industry in which they operate (Park and Smith 1986). Under an alternative perspective, which is based on inter- as well as intra-industry learning, Park and Smith, for example, suggest that companies use competitive intelligence as input for identifying new products and markets and developing innovative marketing programmes.

All too often hotel managers perceive their product to be a hotel room rather than the whole travel experience. Due to this myopic view, managers of even the largest companies 'can't even comprehend the economic networks in which they operate' (Gardner 1985: 143). The business eco-system presents managers with a framework for the detection of potential strategic alliances with travel industry partners and for potential social innovation through the cooperation with firms in other industries as well.

Companies in unrelated industries may complement the core competencies of hoteliers and therefore may represent the best sources of innovative ideas. Within the broader context of the business eco-system, the competition which Bartels referred to might take on a broader perspective which is loosely based on Crosby's observation of ecology.

The elements of the African plains, its bushes, trees, and animals, are interdependent and vulnerable. Any part of the life cycle that is disrupted or altered affects other parts, rarely for better, usually for worse. Within the ecosystem 'nothing happens without having an affect on something. Sometimes the results will not be discernible for weeks or months, or years' (Crosby 1990: 27). The key to the business ecology, as on the African plains, is relationships. In the hotel business cooperative relationships have to be underpinned by trust to enable hoteliers to build competitiveness and long-term value for shareholders and customers (Sharpe 1990: 100).

The notion of co-evolution, in which interdependent species evolve in an endless reciprocal cycle, in which 'changes in species A set the stage for the natural selection of changes in species B' and vice versa (Moore 1993), further merits its adoption in the hotel industry because it derives its demand substantially from many other industries. For example, to be successful hotels must build core competencies to cater to the specific needs of the business information market, the education/training market, and the entertainment market amongst other sectors. By searching for the optimal fit between organizational competencies within the broader arena which might be labelled 'temporary accommodation' for the 'business', the 'leisure' and the 'learning' markets, hotel companies should be able to broaden their opportunities for survival, not unlike waterfowl in nature manage to use specific feeding strategies to survive.

Many different kinds of waterfowl are able to share the same habitat without undue competition by utilising varying food resources. Geese and widgeons graze the shore vegetation. Dabbling ducks like Teal and Pintail glean food from the water surface but by upending, are also able to obtain plants and small animals from the bottom.

Swans make use of their long necks to secure submerged plants. Diving ducks exploit deeper water to feed on small crustaceans. Shovelers and other surface feeding ducks sift small plants and animals by sweeping the water surface. Greater Flamingos are bottom feeders in shallow water, while the lesser Flamingo is primarily a surface feeder and being able to swim well is able to obtain food far away from the shore.[1]

Though every business should strive to increase its survival capacity, which might seem simple, it should be noted that defining the core skills of a company can be a long term process. For example, it took the Marriott Corporation over a decade to arrive at the conclusion that it had core skills in the operations management of hotels, the construction of hotel facilities, and financial packaging of the real estate involved for sale to investors. Coming to this realization meant the divestiture of Marriott's cruise line business, travel agencies, theme parks and fast food business (Foust 1991).

Among the markets which hotels serve, leisure is particularly interesting because of its direct relationship with recreation and tourism and indirect relationship with travel for business and personal advancement, as illustrated in Figure 11.1. As a result of the constraints of leisure time and discretionary money and the impacts of a myriad of events in society, especially economic trends and fashions, leisure markets are always changing. Resorts, within this context, are part of a business ecosystem that crosses at least four major industries: entertainment, recreational sports, accommodation and foodservice.

The Center Parcs case study later in the chapter tries to illustrate how a company which was traditionally involved in the leisure sportswear and recreation business diversified into the resort industry and is well on its way to capture Europe's leisure market with a unique concept.

Four distinct stages of development

Moore (1993: 76) describes the way that a business ecosystem develops as follows: 'A business ecosystem, like its biological counterpart, gradually moves from a random collection of elements to a more structured community. Every business ecosystem develops in four distinct stages: birth, expansion, leadership, and self-renewal, or if not self-renewal – death.'

Moore lists the types of challenges faced by companies at each of these stages, and makes a distinction between cooperative and competitive

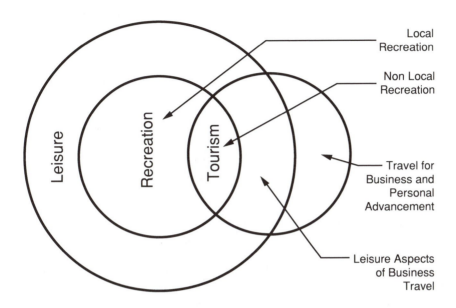

Figure 11.1 The relationship between leisure, recreation and tourism
Source: J.L. Crompton and S.L. Richardson, 'The Tourism Connection', *Parks and Recreation*, October 1986.

challenges. At the birth stage cooperative challenges involve working with customers and suppliers (for example, to define new values and encourage new ideas), whilst competitive challenges would require protecting company ideas from others who might be developing similar ideas. At the expansion stage cooperation might involve working with suppliers to increase supply, and at the same time working to defeat the implementation of similar ideas by competitors. Cooperative leadership could include giving suppliers encouragement to continue their development and improvement of their product, and challenging competitors by maintaining strong bargaining power with suppliers. Self-renewal would be encouraged by cooperating with those who have new ideas to bring to the ecosystem, whilst maintaining high barriers to market entry to stop innovators from creating competitive ecosystems (Moore 1993: 76).

In the paragraphs that follow, an attempt will be made to apply Moore's four stages of evolution to the complex interplay between competitive and cooperative relationships in the hotel industry.

During Stage 1 of a business ecosystem hoteliers focus on defining what customers want, that is, the value of a proposed new product or service, and the best form for delivering it. For example, Kemmons Wilson developed the idea for Holiday Inns because of what he called 'the most miserable vacation trip of my life'. In the 1950s, roadside lodges in the US were of unpredictable quality and price. Together with his mother Wilson opened the first Holiday Inn, near Memphis, Tennessee, featuring large rooms, two double beds, a restaurant and a swimming pool. From the start, Holiday Inns were designed to appeal to families travelling by car. They offered larger rooms than competitors and free television, free ice, and telephone in every room. As a result, Holiday Inns expanded rapidly, outstripping Wilson's ability to raise capital. Consequently, to keep up with demand, Holiday Inns began selling franchises in 1955, and went public in 1957 (CQ 1985: 27).

In Stage 2, business ecosystems expand to conquer broad new territories (Moore 1993: 76). The postwar era witnessed a strong US dollar and American travellers ready to venture overseas, and greatly improved air travel. 'At the same time, many of Europe's hotels had been destroyed, giving U.S. hotel companies an opening for expansion' (CQ 1985: 25). The success of Conrad Hilton can be explained by his meeting two key criteria for Stage 2 expansion. Hilton hotels overseas provided uniform accommodation of consistent quality valued by American travellers. And Conrad Hilton decided to expand internationally by contracting the Hilton name, design, and management expertise to local owners. This gave the Hilton Corporation a significant growth vehicle at virtually no investment. The management contract arrangement was very popular. Hilton International was formed in 1949 as a separate subsidiary of Hilton Corporation with the opening of the Caribe Hilton International. By December 1964 when Hilton International operated 24 hotels in 22 countries, the company was spun off as an independently publicly owned company with its shares traded on the New York Stock Exchange. The agreement governing the spin-off gave Hilton Hotels Corporation the exclusive right to use the name 'Hilton' for hotels in the USA, and Hilton International the exclusive right to control the use of the Hilton name throughout the rest of the world. The one exception is the Kahala Hilton in Honolulu, Hawaii, which is operated as a Hilton International. In May 1967, Hilton International was acquired by Trans World Airlines Inc., and became part of the Transworld Corporation holding company which was created in 1979. In April 1987, Hilton International was acquired by the Allegis Corporation, but after only a matter of months, Allegis decided to sell the hotel company to Ladbroke Group plc. Over the years, Hilton International's growth has been governed by a strict policy of selectivity. In considering a new project, the company must satisfy itself that the prospective hotel will be an asset to the country and community, as well as a profitable enterprise for itself and its owners, and that it will reflect the high standards of its other hotels.

As Moore remarks, 'one of the most important managerial challenges in Stage 2 is to stimulate market demand without greatly exceeding your ability to meet it'. To a large extent, Hilton International's traditional marketing strategy was dependent on Americans travelling abroad. In contrast, the present sales and marketing direction concentrates on providing hotel accommodation to a broader international market. The expansion of the number of sales offices worldwide to 100 with recent openings in Miami, Chicago, Los Angeles, Madrid, Osaka and South Africa, provides opportunities to gain a much larger share of growth markets.

'In general, Stage 2 rewards fast expansion that squeezes competing ecosystems to the margin' (Moore 1993: 80). Currently underway is the most extensive and aggressive development programme in Hilton International's history. Since the acquisition by Ladbroke Group, hotel openings have included such diverse locations as Ponce, Puerto Rico; Beijing, China; Algiers, Algeria; Glasgow, Scotland; Hurghada, Egypt; Oslo, Norway; Cancun, Mexico; and Jeddah, Saudi Arabia. In addition to the company's mainly city centre and airport hotels, Hilton International has set its sights on becoming a major player in the field of prime world resorts.

> In business ecosystems, two conditions contribute to the onset of leadership struggles that are the hallmark of Stage 3. First the ecosystem must have a strong enough growth and profitability to be considered worth fighting over. Second, the structure of the value-adding components and processes that are central to the business ecosystem must become reasonably stable.
>
> (Moore 1993: 80)

During Stage 3 companies become preoccupied with the modular organization and customer relationships, whilst bargaining power is mainly derived from the ability to innovate constantly and create value (Moore 1993: 80).

In recent years, a growing number of hotel companies have developed business relationships with other service providers. This relationship may take the format of a real partnership (see Table 11.1) or be based on out-sourcing. This process of 'out-sourcing' of certain activities through strategic alliances with other companies that have superior capabilities affords international hotel companies the opportunity to develop their own unique core capabilities in selected activities. It also allows companies to avoid investments and inflexibilities that might plague their competitors. For example, San Antonio, Texas-based La Quinta Motor Inns made a conscious decision to be in the motel business. The company views the operation of restaurants and bars on the premises as non-value-added activities. Instead, it leases the real estate adjacent to their motel properties to brand-name foodservice chains that provide around-the-clock foodservice to hotel guests (Anon. 1977). La Quinta's management decision is a rational but nevertheless drastic departure from the hotel industry norm.

Another example demonstrates the greater preoccupation with customer relations in the hotel industry. In an effort to build improved customer

Table 11.1 Five levels of customer relationships

Level	Hotel company action(s)
1 Bare-bones marketing	Employees thank guests for their patronage and attend to the needs of the next guests.
2 Reactive marketing	Employees tend to have a 'wait-and-see' attitude, 'if there is anything I can do, please call', instead of anticipating guests' needs.
3 Accountability marketing	Employees follow up to find out how satisfied guests are. Their attidue is marked by accountability: 'Is there anything about the service that can be improved?'
4 Showing continuing interest	Employees show guests how to get better use of the hotel product (e.g. conference facilities) long after the client's visit.
5 Real partnership	Employees become the client's partner, for example by researching how to mutually gain in the process of cooperating.

Source: T.E. Caruso (1992) 'Kotler: Future marketers will focus on customer database to compete globally', *Marketing News*, 8 June, p. 21. Reprinted with the permission of the American Marketing Association

relationships, Inter-Continental Hotels decided on Project Argonaut, the code name for a research project on a major scale, designed to gain a better understanding of where its Inter-Continental and Forum hotels stand in the perception of frequent travellers relative to the competition. It included almost 4,000 interviews conducted in seven countries, involving over 2,000 frequent international business travellers, 600 travel agency consultants and 90 travel agency managers. One of the purposes of Project Argonaut was to explore possible alternative strategies available in the development and expansion of the business to create competitive advantage. The research revealed many similarities between experienced business travellers around the world: the further they travel and the longer the length of stay, the more the traveller cares about the quality of hotel and services provided. Overall, Project Argonaut indicated that executives view business travel as a positive experience, but one in which the hotel could play a much more substantial role. 'Project Flyright' involved further research aimed at identifying the current and likely future patterns of commercial relationships between hotel chains and the airlines to evaluate the most suitable options for Inter-Continental Hotels. For Project Flyright, a further 60 experts were interviewed plus 1,000 hotel guests all over the world. The research revealed that the offer of certain facilities, provided in conjunction with a number of partner airlines on a non-exclusive basis, could be a very powerful motivating force in hotel selection by international business travellers. It underlined the need for a total travel concept designed to minimize the inconvenience of international travel. In particular, it highlighted the need for the hotel industry to follow the lead of the airlines and embrace the opportunities information technology offers.

Stage 4 of a business ecosystem, according to Moore, occurs when rising new ecosystems and innovations threaten mature business communities. Alternatively, a community might undergo the equivalent of an earthquake: sudden new environmental conditions that include changes in government regulations, customer buying patterns, or micro-economic conditions. Moreover, these two factors reinforce one another.

For example, the physical environment was identified as the core tourism issue of the 1990s. Specifically, the International Tourism Policy Forum held in Washington, DC in 1990 was unanimous in highlighting concern for the environment as the key issue of the decade (Ritchie 1991: 150). Indeed, there is little question that the mounting public concern over the growing threats to our global environment represents a 'new' and significant environmental condition. It has focused attention on the damage caused by the over-development of tourism, from the Spanish Costas to resorts in Thailand and the need to manage limited resources in a more sustainable way.

The hotel industry may be a small-scale polluter but it is widespread. Importantly, it is a part of travel and tourism which is increasingly being perceived as bearing a special responsibility for preserving the environment. Wolfgang Momberger, the president of Steigenberger Hotels, views the responsibility of travel and tourism businesses, including hotels, as follows:

> We move, feed and accommodate hundreds of millions of people around the globe every year. A good environment is at the core of our business. We must ensure that air, water, landscape and heritage are protected. We must make sure that our growth is environmentally compatible. This is not only right, it is sound business.

As Momberger suggests there is an important link between the building of a business strategy and the presentation of the physical environment. This link has become pronounced in Europe. Before long it will become more important in the Americas and Asia as a critical element in every source of competitive advantage, including the economic, technological, marketing, and organizational dimensions. The challenge for hotel corporations is to recognize indicators of environmental 'warnings', both in the urban and resort contexts, to take them seriously, and to act on them in a way that results in an enhanced physical environment and a competitive advantage.

For example, improved resort management and higher standards of environmental engineering, though not the sole responsibility of the international hotel industry, will certainly influence practice in the 1990s and into the twenty-first century. At present, environmental issues and the hotel industry represent a real issue both in resort and urban locations. Investment in environmental management and planning will yield long-term returns in cost-savings, whether it is an energy saving and waste reduction scheme in hotels or cost-savings from unnecessary regulation planning for environmentally compatible development which reduces operating costs. Hotels situated in host communities that demonstrate little or no concern about the environment may see their business dwindle. The Spanish resorts, for example, which have been overdeveloped with cheap accommodation, have attracted a rowdy and anti-social element from major markets such as Great Britain and Germany, with resultant drastic falls in hotel occupancy in 1989 and 1990. This pattern has been seen elsewhere as well. Due to consumers who are growing more environmentally sensitive, the international hotel industry will be obliged to play a much more active role in maintaining and, where necessary, raising environmental standards if hotel occupancy rates are not to suffer.[2]

NEW REALITIES

The globalization of markets offers hotel corporations both challenges and opportunities on which J. Willard Marriott, Chief Executive Officer of the Marriott Corporation, commented as follows:

> Everywhere we look, we see an industry in flux – in some cases the result of de-regulation; in others the result of tax policies that encouraged the construction of facilities that may not have been as well-thought out as they could and should have been. We see consolidation and mergers, we see a consumer who is increasingly discriminating in terms of what he or she wants to buy.
>
> (WP 1989)

Indeed, the 1990s are likely to see a continuing trend towards mergers, acquisitions and take-overs in the hotel industry. Specifically, corporations will continue to seek scale economies in management, technology and in maximizing returns from capital-intensive reservation systems investment. However, the structural shift characterizing the post-industrial economies could have detrimental consequences because it erodes several of the hotel industry's 'golden rules'.

First, the presumption that 'bigger is better'. As the spectacular failures of GM, IBM, and Phillips have demonstrated, big corporations are also vulnerable to changes in their markets. The perceived 'invincibility' of the big hotel chains has therefore become suspect. This implies that owning the largest resource base – that is, the most number of hotel properties to support service activities – does not necessarily have to lead to success. For one, expansion, especially growth across borders, involves new costs.

Furthermore, as they grow, hotel chains often become bureaucratic, inflexible and wasteful. And employees, believing themselves to be mere cogs, tend to become less accountable and harder to motivate.

Second, the assumption that 'moving upmarket' equals success. In an effort to compete in the global business travel market, many hotel corporations are continuing their upmarket move. They have introduced executive floors, upscale extensions of core brands, and sometimes acquired entire hotel chains that had built a reputation as de luxe accommodation operators. Though the global de luxe hotel market is worth US$40 billion and therefore worth competing over, it is also finite. If 'success' in the hotel industry can be equated with 'profitability' and 'growth', hoteliers will have to seek new avenues to fuel their corporate expansion. In the post-Second World War era, new product roll-outs, starting with Kemmons Wilson's Holiday Inns in the 1950s, have contributed importantly to the growth of the hotel business. During the 1970s and 1980s hotel corporations introduced new hotel products, such as the 'no-frills' budget motel, the 'atrium-design' hotel, and the 'all-suite' hotel, designed to 'steal' customers away from the competition. Not surprisingly, many competitors retaliated by cloning the successful new products. Into the twenty-first century, to 'create customers' (Levitt 1983b), growth will have to be derived from the introduction of revolutionary new mass products designed to appeal to a broad market or from specialized products to cater to niche markets. For example, ACCOR has created the Formule 1 format and acquired the Motel 6 to conquer the mass lodging market in Europe and the Americas, respectively. The total budget market is twice as large as all other hotel categories combined. Moreover, it is also growing much faster than traditional motel formats. Importantly, lower-priced basic hotels are 'attracting new customers', amongst young people and retirees who often have the leisure time to travel but lack the budgets to stay in traditional hotels. In Europe, Formule 1's innovative design and state-of the art technology have made it extremely successful. Between 1986 and 1993, ACCOR has opened 250 such units. Despite its sceptics, ACCOR has proved the viability of the basic hotel concept by analysing what travellers really want and value, and then catering to their needs and expectations (Levitt 1983b: 7). ACCOR estimates that it will have 2,000 budget hotels in operation under the Formule 1 and Motel 6 brands by the turn of the century.

Third, a strong product brand is a panacea for the conquering of global markets. There is no question that the branding of hotel products is an idea whose time has come. But hoteliers who are marketing brand-name products should take note of the market changes that are beginning to erode the established brands of giant consumer-product companies such as Philip Morris, Procter and Gamble and Unilever. Will these same changes, sooner or later, affect the hotel brands that are operated globally? Furthermore, the offering of brand products implies an emphasis on a standard line of quality which caters for the customer's short-term, 'bed, board, and bath', needs. To what extent should hoteliers, especially those who operate upscale products, adapt their brands to local conditions?

Fourth, only big chains can afford new technologies. The use of computers, confounding most forecasts, is narrowing economies of scale in hotel operations and marketing. The plummeting price of computers is enabling 'high-tech' know-how to impact on small independent hotels, often described as a low-technology and 'high-touch' industry. For example, a growing number of independent hotels employ the same sophisticated automated payrolls, financial models, and other administrative tasks that were once available only to big hotel chains. Many hotel corporations have also learned that computerized reservation systems and yield management capability allow them to apply sophisticated price discrimination. Hoteliers who are able to apply the new technology effectively have the expertise that enables them to force competitors who may be 'better' hotel operators out of business. This trend within the hotel business resembles developments in other industries. For example, in the personal computer industry, the production of the hardware is considered a low-margin activity, whilst software and service support activities are viewed as creating the greatest value to customers (Quinn *et al.* 1990: 59).

Finally, there is little use in training, compensating, and giving personal attention to employees because, sooner or later, they will leave the company anyway. As discussed earlier, the hotel industry's labour force is not well-trained, nor well-compensated, and suffers from high turnover levels, a poor image, and a lack of career opportunities. The hotel industry has to turn its attention to these challenges. Specifically, hoteliers should develop standards to define acceptable levels of service, and describe the skills and knowledge required to perform selected tasks. There are four categories of skills that may be distinguished when examining the hotel industry's labour force. The technical and social skills required in the traditional 'front-line' hotel jobs such as reception clerk and waiter. The 'back-of the house' technical skills in the kitchen and engineering departments requiring little or no guest contact. Skills, such as accounting, finance, and information technology, that may be required outside the hotel industry but that can be transferred to the hotel industry; and management skills, both technical and social, which may be acquired from within or outside the hotel industry.

At present, many hotel corporations are reviewing their organizational structure at all levels. In certain cases, they are rendering obsolete the category of junior management and department heads and replacing same with a better educated labour force and management utilizing new technology.

Lately, it has become more important to encourage prospective employees to consider the hotel field as a career choice because of the dearth of labour, and hotels are growing more dependent on complex information technology systems. Technological improvements can only enhance the service and convenience of hotel guests when employees are computer literate and understand how to apply their computer skills appropriately. With the increasing use of computers in hotels, the number of employees recruited whose skills have been acquired outside the hotel industry, but who apply those skills within it, are likely to increase. Put differently, competitive advantage shall be more and more derived from greater depth in selected human skills and knowledge bases that lead to demonstrable value for customers (Quinn *et al.* 1990: 60).

SURVIVAL CAPACITY

Rapid technological change, in particular the increased speed and diminishing cost of telecommunications and computerization that have resulted, has created new opportunities for independent hoteliers to compete on a more level playing field. As the advantages of sheer corporate size diminish, many large hotel chains are scrambling to reduce costs, cutting overheads, streamlining organizations and optimizing structures to develop greater synergies among activities. In order to survive, they are trying to become more like their smaller rivals.

In the emerging process of worldwide shakeout, hotel companies that cannot or will not learn the lessons of globalization will not survive. Conversely, the performance of almost any type of accommodation business can be improved by committed individuals who are able to develop an organization through sound growth within the context of globalization.

Presently, with few exceptions, the existing structure and systems appear to dictate what growth opportunities hotel companies see and pursue. Instead of modifying their systems and structure to take advantage of new opportunities, hotel corporations appear too often to respond to opportunities that they can handle with their present organization. However, to respond to structural change by continuing to behave as before will be at best insufficient and at worst counter productive for the capacity of hotel organizations to flourish rather than merely survive (Sharpe 1990: 98).

The creation and delivery of value to customers at a profit, the major theme of this book, is accomplished through strategy (Normann and Ramirez 1993: 65). Within this context, it is essential for hoteliers to understand the underlying strategic logic of change in the hotel industry. In particular, that the rendering of value-adding services in hotel corporations is increasingly less derived from traditional production. Rather, value-adding service is increasingly rooted in two key resources: knowledge and relationships or an organization's competencies and customers (Normann and Ramirez 1993: 65). The effective management of an organization's core competencies allows a hotel product to be delivered to customers at the best price/performance trade-off, and implies that hoteliers should focus on inter-firm competition, as opposed to inter-product competition, and essentially be concerned with the acquisition of skills (Hamel 1991).

The conception of a hotel as a portfolio of core competencies and the growing significance of inter-firm competition suggest that a corporation should not be viewed as a member of a single industry. It also implies that in the rapidly changing global marketplace the logic of value creation is changing, from the conventional value chain to the 'value constellation' (Normann and Ramirez 1993: 65). Indeed, global competition is pressuring hotel corporations to find non-traditional partners – that is, suppliers who were not part of their original value chain. Thus, a hotel corporation's 'value constellation' may range from travel and business services such as telecommunications, credit card, and banking services to public services involving government agencies and educational and training institutions (Mowlana and Smith 1990).

COMMITMENT TO THE ENVIRONMENT

The launching of major environmental initiatives in the hotel industry have been of a recent nature. For example, Inter-Continental Hotels took the first step towards this long-term commitment with the publication of its 220-page *Environmental Reference Manual* in 1990. Through the programme Inter-Continental Hotels aims to implement measures to ensure that each hotel in the group makes a positive contribution to improving the quality of the environment. The *Environmental Reference Manual* was published in Spanish, Arabic and Russian as well as English, and issued to every hotel in the group. In an unprecedented move for the competitive hotel industry, Inter-Continental Hotels gave the manual to its competitors in the summer of 1991 and asked for their assistance in progressing environmental awareness in the hotel community. Under the aegis of the Prince of Wales' Business Leaders' Forum, a non-profit organization which promotes co-operation between international companies, a luncheon was held, hosted by HRH the Prince of Wales and attended by the chief executive officers of seven major hotel companies, to discuss how hotel companies can work together to protect the environment. The result was the formation of The International Hotels Environment Initiative of which 11 leading hotel companies are now members. Their Charter is to develop practical environmental guidelines for hotels, initially based on Inter-Continental's *Environmental Reference Manual*, to collaborate with national and international organizations and generally to upgrade environmental performance in the industry worldwide. This implies that in due course about two million hotel rooms, and later perhaps more, will be run along the environmental protection lines initially developed by Inter-Continental Hotels.

STRATEGIC ALLIANCES

The impact of global competition has caused the need to innovate constantly and create value amongst hotel corporations.

Lately, strategic alliances have become an increasingly important means of conducting business in the hotel industry with one or more partners to create value and innovate. An example of a strategic alliance is that between Choice Hotels and Aircoa, the largest independent US management contract company. Through the agreement, Choice markets Clarion Hotels and Resorts, a collection of 36 four-star hotels in the USA, Canada, Europe and Mexico. Strategic alliances can be defined as 'organisational arrangements and operating policies through which separate organisations share administrative authority, form social links through more open-ended contractual arrangements as opposed to very specific, arm's-length contracts' (Bardaracco 1991). Thus, the difference between a strategic alliance and a joint venture is that the latter requires the formation of a new legal entity, whereas the former enables partners to benefit from the alliance without the creation of a subsidiary.[3]

The aim of the strategic alliance between two companies is to offer each an advantage that one company would be unable to obtain by itself. The main reasons for companies to enter into strategic alliances have been to share risk, to share complementary resources, and to surmount barriers to markets. But rather than seeing them as tools of convenience, Ohmae (1989: 144) views strategic alliances as critical instruments to better serve customers in a global environment.

Most companies cannot meet the value-based needs of customers in the industrialized countries of North America, Europe and Japan, which Ohmae (1989: 146) refers to as the 'Triad', entirely alone. They require the technology and skills of others to meet customer needs. Furthermore, strategic alliances allow corporations to amortize their fixed costs over a larger market base and to be in all important markets simultaneously (Ohmae 1989: 147).

The corollary advantages of strategic alliances which make possible the out-sourcing of selected activities offer international hotel companies several advantages: (a) they allow companies to focus their attention on the areas in which they are able to add the most value per unit of input; (b) they allow companies to compete for the world's best talent in a given activity; (c) they allow companies to make their organizational structure 'leaner' (Quinn et al. 1990: 66).

For example, the establishment of operations abroad essentially allows hotel corporations to 'export' differential advantages and capabilities to other countries where they could prove profitable (Hymer 1976). In order to achieve an advantage by expanding their reach globally despite the dearth of hotel construction sites in prime locations, one likely option for international hotel firms based in different countries or continents is to integrate marketing and/or operational management functions through more or less formalized strategic alliances. For example, Radisson has opted to cooperate with SAS International Hotels based in Oslo, Norway and Movenpick Hotels International of Switzerland, and also has a licensing and marketing agreement with Park Lane Hotels International based in Hong Kong.

An alliance with partners based on different continents allows each individual partner a new logic for management action, in that their focus can switch to maximizing marginal sales contribution to fixed cost. At the same time, the strategic alliance addresses the issue of global marketing because Radisson distributes the Movenpick product in North America, while Movenpick sells the Radisson product in Europe.

Strategic alliances tend to blur the boundaries of corporations and facilitate the transfer of knowledge across corporate boundaries. Collaboration between hotel corporations can help their executives to build value together specifically by, as Sharpe (1990: 100–102) suggests,

(a) educating and encouraging shareholders to develop long term value as opposed to investing in hotels for speculative purposes;
(b) lobbying government, which sets the rules the industry competes by, 'to check its decisions against one overriding gauge: Does the decision strengthen or weaken [the country's] competitive position?';
(c) acting collectively to play a role in preserving the environment and paving 'the way for environmental standards in our business communities', and to become involved on other pressing survival issues including drugs, AIDs, and education;
(d) sharing ideas on how to change the mindsets and attitudes of managers, whose relationships and treatment of employees influence the latter's behaviour regarding, for example, 'corporate loyalty and credibility more missed deadlines and mistakes; and even sabotage'.

The idea of cooperation offers many advantages to hoteliers keen on enhancing their company's competitiveness. However, there is an aspect to any cooperative relationship that cannot be ignored.

Though strategic alliances are key to achieving competitive advantage by providing value-added services to the various publics, they also make firms that have entered into such alliances more vulnerable. Today's ally can easily become tomorrow's adversary, exploiting what it learned from the old relationship (Bardaracco 1991).

GLOBAL REACH/LOCAL ADAPTABILITY

This chapter has placed a significant emphasis on the need in the hotel industry to create value in a broader constellation or eco-business system.

However, hotel corporations have to build the organizational capability to implement their strategic intentions from which a competitive advantage will accrue. In order to maintain market share in the 1990s, it will be essential for hotel companies, both independents and chain-affiliated, to have or gain access to the global market. To tap international demand effectively requires successful access, often through close cooperation with other firms in the travel and tourism network, especially GDS, in source markets. Furthermore, hotel executives should have a global perspective to understand the shifting competitive landscape. The increasing involvement of Asian corporations in the international hotel industry has altered the competitive arena because Asian and Western companies each display different management mentalities shaped by a very different cultural and administrative heritage (Bartlett and Ghoshal 1989: 44).

To compete on the global level, there has been a tendency in the hotel industry to emphasize scale economies in order to achieve a competitive advantage on the basis of low cost leadership. International hotel companies that have opted for a global, low cost strategy are highly standardized to exploit the similar requirements of customers across countries.

While global reach may assist international hotel corporations to deliver customers value for money and achieve competitiveness both worldwide and on a local basis through scale economies, the global corporation's centralized management approach implies that knowledge is developed and retained at the centre. Consequently, the role of overseas operations is limited to implementing parent company strategies, rather than being involved in the innovation process.

The multi-domestic or multinational corporation's strength is in its capacity to sense and exploit local opportunities. The local adaptability of international hotel corporations has become more important, despite – or perhaps because of – the trend towards the globalization of business. There are several reasons for the importance of the local adaptability of international hotel firms.

The recognition of finite limitations to hotel and tourism development has been demonstrated by, for example, the dramatic tourism decline of the Spanish Costas. The limits of hotel development are of course even more pronounced in crowded cities. For example, with many high quality sites occupied by existing hotels, appropriate new sites to build hotels are becoming more difficult to locate. This problem is aggravated by the actions taken on the municipal level.

In London, each borough has taken a different approach to hotel planning, but with the same end result: that of hindering hotel development. The example of the problems hotel developers are encountering in London illustrates that it is no longer sufficient to be consumer-oriented in the international hotel industry. Instead, international hotel firms have to strike a balance between the desires of global customers and the local well-being and values of the host community. At the same time, it is becoming increasingly important for international hotel corporations to learn more about project development in the local tourism planning context because of the rising sentiment that the tourism industry is too important to local communities to be left in the hands of 'outsider' professionals (McNulty and Wafer 1990: 293). Moreover, the growing desire for local partic pation on the part of the host community would suggest that international hotel corporations should examine their options and become more sensitive to the local cultural assets and the potential for the involvement of local workers and entrepreneurs. The latter might include local suppliers, for example.

Furthermore, structural variations between economies represent impediments to globalization that are relevant to the development of hotels. The impediments to the globalization of the hotel industry may vary from destination to destination, but are usually directly related to the importance accorded tourism as an activity and its capacity to develop. Within this context, Wolfson (1964) has identified four main types of host countries in which: (a) tourism is limited and likely to remain so; (b) tourism has limited possibilities; (c) tourism is existing and has the potential to become an important contributor to the national economy; and (d) tourism development is highly advanced and the main problem is how to maintain same.

In summary, the present competitive conditions require hotel corporations to build a market edge by simultaneously capturing global scale efficiency, responding to local market needs, and developing worldwide learning capability that drives continuous innovation.

TRANSNATIONAL MODEL

An analysis by Bartlett and Ghoshal (1989) has shown that the multinational model and global model capture only one of the aforementioned three strategic capabilities, respectively global reach and local adaptability. Both models are ill-geared to reap the benefits of organizational learning needed for continuous innovation.

In an increasingly complex and changing environment, hotel corporations cannot effectively compete through structures that are unidimensional and static. But how can executives develop the organizational structures, processes, and management perspectives to implement the strategic capability to achieve competitive advantage that is broad-based, as opposed to unidimensional?

What model is designed to develop the kind of organization that embraces change and complexity?

Which organizational configuration of assets and resources is optimally responsive to the shifting distribution of roles and relationships and the different set of management skills and capability needed in an environment that demands a sensitivity of managers both on the global and local levels?

In order to function effectively in the integrated network in the fast-moving, competitive market requires an organizational structure such as Bartlett and Ghoshal's (1989) 'transnational model' which incorporates a much more flexible management mentality than the one which dominates the traditional organizational hierarchy which prevails in hotel corporations. To take advantage of new opportunities and build competitive advantage, hotel corporations have to develop three diverse and often conflicting strategic capabilities simultaneously:

(a) the multinational flexibility to respond to diverse, local market needs;
(b) the global competitiveness to capture efficiencies of scale;
(c) the international learning ability that results in worldwide innovation.

As a consequence of these changes, Bartlett and Ghoshal (1989) suggest that a new transnational model relevant to the international hotel company is emerging in the 1990s. This model is characterized by:

(a) the distribution of specialized resources and capabilities through an integrated network;
(b) the coordination of flows of products, resources and information across interdependent units; and
(c) a management mentality which treats worldwide hotel operations as an integrated and interdependent strategic network.

Bartlett and Ghoshal's transnational model shows great potential in enabling hotel corporations to balance global reach and local adaptability.

The transnational network avoids the problems of duplication of effort, inefficiency and resistance to change of ideas developed elsewhere because it affords subsidiaries the latitude, the encouragement, and vehicles to pursue the development of local business within the global strategy framework (Czinkota *et al.* 1989: 609). The main tool for implementing this approach is to develop international teams of managers who meet regularly to develop strategy.

For hotel corporations with the ambition to stay in or join the global arena the central issue of the 1990s is how to organize, integrate and manage their activities to respectively remain or become successful global players. That is particularly true of hotel firms that show overseas expansion potential but are beginning to comprehend that constructing, operating and controlling offshore properties does not necessarily mean they are equipped to compete effectively on a global basis. Increasingly, the issue of global expansion deals with a series of differentiation and integration decisions.

On the one hand, hotel companies have a clear need for a sense of global strategic intent, or for broad-based resource, training and marketing allocation schemes. At the same time the perspective of hotel executives must be 'tuned-in' to local issues. For instance the availability of sites for hotel development in desirable locations or understanding the grievances of a host population which is against hotel development because of its perceived negative impact on their community. Since community demands for active participation in the setting of the tourism agenda and its priorities for tourism development and management cannot be ignored (Ritchie 1991: 151), astute hotel firms should become more sensitive to the local community in which they (wish to) operate and compete. In addition, they must be able to deal effectively with cultural conditions and different behavioural values.

The ability of hotel corporations to build and manage a strategic transnational capability may separate the winners from the losers in the marketplace of the 1990s, which will be characterized by more sophisticated international customers, aggressive and massive financial accumulation, relatively free-flowing resources, and global brands. In an effort to survive, hotel corporations must respond to a rapidly shifting global marketplace by aligning their operations management and marketing functions with the organizational characteristics of the transnational network.

Bartlett and Ghoshal's (1989) transnational model has three main implications that are relevant to the hotel corporation's ability to expand geographically and/or enhance profitability:

(a) It requires a rethinking of relationships between suppliers, competitors and clients. In the network, roles will increasingly become more transitory than permanent and often more negotiated than structural.
(b) It means that the international hotel firm must perform its role effectively in the network. This requires greater cooperation and co-ordination between the hotel firm and its traditional 'partners' – such as travel agencies, rental car firms, airline carriers, and potential new partners like telecommunications corporations, entertainment firms, and institutions of higher education.
(c) The increasing information intensiveness of business offerings means that market power rests with the actor who controls the information flow in the network. Hotel corporations that have not kept in touch with management information systems developments are at the 'mercy' of the channel captain.

The transnational model is especially significant because it allows hotel corporations to balance global reach and local adaptability issues. Moreover, in that the transnational model recognizes the importance of organizational learning, it moves beyond the premise that the people of a hotel company are its most important asset. The transnational model can help hotel executives realize their company's potential for competing on a corporate culture basis in which each team member is keyed into market demands and devoted to the continuous improvement of customer service. The knowledge, skills, and capabilities that are developed and shared worldwide form a competitive advantage that is more difficult for competitors to overcome than, for example, a competitive advantage that is based on either financial resources or technology.

CONCLUSION

As the travel and tourism industry expands, so does an increasingly complex hierarchical system of transport, recreation facilities, and accommodation networks. Though networks may be of a high-cost nature, they are becoming essential as a set of dominant industries – including the financial services sector, and the transportation and telecommunications sectors, which have become involved in travel and tourism activity through the ownership of GDS. The GDS subsidiaries are affecting the operation and control of international hotel corporations throughout the world. A potential obstacle to effective hotel marketing is the tendency of hotel executives to see problems and solutions in the narrow context of the hotel industry rather than in the travel and tourism network.

The idea that the hotel firm is part of a network of economic transactions implies that in order to expand geographically and operate profitably, the international hotel firm: (a) must perform its role effectively in the functioning tourism network, requiring cooperation between the hotel firm and 'travel industry partners' such as GDS, rental car, airline, and travel agency firms; (b) should formulate strategies, taking into account the host country's tourism policy and regional development priorities; and (c) has to think about business in an entirely new way. Forward looking hotel executives will view their companies' services as part of an eco-business system to build a greater interdependence with such 'mega' industries like telecommunications, leisure and recreation, and education and training.

CASE: CENTER PARCS – A UNIQUE CONTRIBUTION TO THE HOLIDAY MARKET

Center Parcs has been leading change in the resort industry since the company opened a group of thirty holiday villas at De Lommerbergen in Holland in 1967. From those simple beginnings, Center Parcs has grown to become a multinational company of seven villages in Holland, two in Belgium, one in France and two in the UK, with a capacity of over 7,000 villas.

In the early 1970s, Center Parcs revolutionized the Dutch holiday market by offering short break holidays on a year round basis, in addition to longer stays during the traditional holiday periods. As the company grew in size, so did its understanding and appreciation of the needs and interests of its guests. In becoming an innovator and trendsetter in the creation of top level leisure facilities, Center Parcs has been acknowledged as setting and achieving new standards in every aspect of its operations.

Since it opened its first UK Holiday Village at Sherwood Forest in July 1987, Center Parcs has had the success of its British venture proved beyond doubt. The unique Center Parcs formula of offering year round short breaks in specially created natural settings was hailed as a revolution for holidays in the UK, and in common with many long awaited revolutions it has succeeded beyond measure.

In bringing its experience, Center Parcs has not only brought pleasure to tens of thousands, but by persuading British guests to take a short break it has certainly been a welcome boost to the economy. Occupancy percentages at all Center Parcs Villages runs in the high 90s, with repeat bookings of 50 per cent. Families, the focus at which Center Parcs is primarily aimed, can always be sure that whatever the weather conditions their stay will not be affected, with a well-thought-out selection of indoor and outdoor activities to appeal to all ages. And with its ability to please both parent and child alike, it is truly a remarkable formula that does work. Center Parcs has created new awareness in the opportunities for holidaying in Britain through the combination of all-weather facilities, superb living accommodation, a wide variety of sporting and leisure activities and an insistence on the creation and maintenance of the highest standards in every facet of its operations.

Its most spectacular area of development has been the introduction of the Subtropical Swimming Paradise. From the first to be opened, in 1981, these magical combinations of water technology, tropical temperatures and foliage have become the central focus of each Center Parcs Village. Under the giant transparent domes of the Subtropical Swimming Paradise, guests can enjoy the wild water rapids, water slides, jacuzzis, wave pools, solaria and children's play pools, all at constant 84 degree temperatures, cocooned in the wonderful atmosphere of luxuriant tropical plants and flowers.

As an early leader in the care of the environment and the maintenance of the ecological balance, Center Parcs always builds its villages on carefully selected inland sites, to take full advantage of the natural surroundings, combining woodland and water to unique effect, managing and developing the existing flora and fauna to add to the overall experience.

Variations on the Center Parcs theme have included the introduction of the Parc Plaza, where all the central facilities are placed under a giant transparent roof to enhance the subtropical experience. In the more traditional Villages, an open square is at the centre of Village life.

The second Center Parcs Village in the UK, at Elveden Forest in Suffolk, is built in the Parc Plaza style, with Sherwood Forest Holiday Village featuring an open square surrounded by the shops and restaurants.

Accommodation at a Center Parcs Village is in stone-built villas which are set amongst the trees and streams, with their own private patios. The villas are furnished to a high standard with fully equipped kitchens and central heating. Sherwood Forest offers a choice from one to four bedrooms (holidays are booked by the villa), while at Elveden Forest one bedroom accommodation is in a fully serviced luxurious apartment. Here, each room has a bathroom, refrigerator, tea-making facilities and a private balcony. The two, three and four bedroom villas also have a baby's cot and high chair. Additional features are colour television with video and satellite channels, optional open fires in all villas, and spa baths in all bathrooms at Elveden Forest and in selected villas at Sherwood Forest.

The restaurants are themed in a selection of eating styles and price ranges from Dutch pancakes, pizzas, French style brasseries, a wine bar, grill, family restaurant and sophisticated French cuisine, which at Elveden Forest is located in a unique revolving restaurant. The retail outlets offer sporting and leisure clothing, gift items and accessories, stylish confectionery shops, a themed children's shop and a well stocked supermarket to cater for every need from the daily papers to a good bottle of wine to enjoy over dinner in the villa. The sports facilities, both indoor and outdoor, offer an unsurpassed variety of activities from roller skating to tennis, archery to badminton, squash to snooker, and windsurfing to pony trekking.

The Country Club at Sherwood Forest has additional squash courts, snooker tables, tennis courts and a unique golf driving range which is one of only two in Europe. Based on a 300-metre diameter circle, it has six grass tees around the circumference to play to marker flags at varying distances. There is a choice of angles and shots, using all clubs, and also a covered driving booth and 18-hole practice putting course.

Always to the fore is health and well-being; this aspect is further enhanced in the trendsetting Aqua Sana health and beauty centres where guests can enjoy the most advanced health and relaxation facial and body treatments, including Thalasso therapy, aromatherapy and reflexology. The Elveden Forest Aqua Sana is located in the £6 million Country Club, which was opened in October 1991, and also offers a computer controlled fitness room, an exercise studio with regular classes, indoor and outdoor children's play areas, and bar and restaurant facilities.

Both Villages have computer controlled bowling alleys and a wide selection of water sports on the lakes, from windsurfing to sailing and canoeing. The Village roads are traffic free, with cars being left in the car park except for arrival and departure periods. Transport is by bicycle, which can be hired at the Village, with adult, children's and BMX bikes, and children's seats for the tiniest guests.

In its five years of operations in Britain, the company has received a number of major national awards reflecting the importance of its contribution to the UK holiday and leisure industry. These include the English Tourist Board's 'England for Excellence' first ever award for 'Green Tourism', now the 'Tourism and the Environment' Award which Center Parcs is currently sponsoring as part of its own responsibility for improving environmental awareness in the UK holiday and leisure industries.

Since 1989, Center Parcs has been part of Scottish & Newcastle plc, with its Head Office remaining in Rotterdam. With daily occupancy percentages that run into the high 90s, Center Parcs holiday villages have proved that it serves the short-break market extremely well. Hoteliers simply cannot ignore the competition of a revolutionary concept such as Center Parcs, because it absorbs leisure market demand. Furthermore, the Center Parcs example provides an excellent illustration of the changes the hotel business ecosystem is currently passing through. Within a climate of intensifying competition it is crucial that hotel executives comprehend, and, more importantly, find ways to direct those changes.

READING: NATURE OF THE GLOBAL CHALLENGE – LOOKING BEYOND THE NUTS AND BOLTS

by Robert Cotter, former President, Asia Division, ITT Sheraton Corporation

The hospitality industry, an integral part of world tourism and the world's second largest industry, is an extremely attractive economic opportunity for the developing communities in the Pacific area.

Hotels of course, become the social centres for much of the business and social entertainment in the communities they serve. For many communities the introduction of the first international hotel is a source of pride, a symbol of the changes and improving conditions in the community.

The first hotel is quickly followed by more: three-, four- and five-star international properties which begin to form the backbone for an emerging labour intense business travel and leisure travel tourism market. In many communities this is just what the doctor ordered as they find traditional agricultural employment no longer adequate to serve their needs and, as important, the new expectations of their community.

Developing nations and communities in the Pacific basin, many if not most with a dense population basis, must find economic growth in industries which accommodate the significant employment requirements of their communities. Additionally, these nations have increasing political motivation to develop self-sufficiency in the new emerging industries of their country. The wealth generated by those industries is wealth that should remain at home to further the development required in the country.

As we work with communities, governments, developers and owners, politics and economics are the drivers of technology transfer to the local community in the hospitality industry.

ITT Sheraton is a hospitality company doing business in 61 countries, or more importantly serving 430-plus communities. Our growth, and in many respects our future, is in the developing communities of the Pacific area, Latin countries, African Nations and Eastern Europe. All of these countries and communities are intensely interested in establishing labour intensive economic development. They are increasingly interested as their development matures in local management of these industries.

For this reason I believe the Human Resources for Tourism Conference to be particularly important to the health of tourism in the Asia–Pacific area. Political motivation and economic motivation are driving technology transfer in the hospitality business in the Pacific.

Consider the following examples: The average wage for Hong Kong hotel employees is US$21,000 per annum. Labour costs in Beijing are rising at 25 per cent to 30 per cent per annum. Australia is suffering from four years of stagnant or negative tourism growth. Hawaii has seen its first drop in tourism in six to eight years.

The 'bubble burst' economy in Japan has left international hotels with average costs per employee at US$38 to US$45K per annum and negative revenue growth.

Gross operating profit performance in Asia remains in the 40 per cent area, while Japan has slipped to the low 30s and high 20s and Australia as well.

Clearly a focus on Human Resources – whether in a developed mature economic market or an emerging destination is a most critical aspect of success in the hospitality business.

I would now like to develop the theory that the focus on human resources is the key local measure of management effectiveness in our business.

There are several key drivers which govern success in the hospitality business. From our perspective they are location – yes its still number one – physical plant, brand awareness and reputation, employee satisfaction, and customer satisfaction.

At ITT Sheraton we focus most directly on employee satisfaction. I will develop at some length why employee satisfaction is so critical to successful performance. Sheraton is a company which is an equity investor with just under US$2 billion in hotel assets. It is also a franchising company with over 200 franchises, mostly in the US. However, Sheraton's core competency is hotel management, which represents the majority of our income and, particularly for our 170-odd international hotels, is the essence of our business. Employee satisfaction is the only one of the five key drivers of success over which local management has complete control and for which local management is solely responsible.

Technology transfer in the hospitality business is involved with the operating systems, training programmes, career development, education, hiring selection criteria and continuity planning which contribute to employee satisfaction. When I speak with the chairmen of our China hotels, a country where we have operated for nearly a decade, they speak with praise about the many Sheraton department heads working not only in our hotels but also in competitive hotels. This is completely consistent with why they were interested in hiring ITT Sheraton in the first place.

Clearly, meeting the global challenge in the hotel industry is understanding the local political and economic motivations of the communities you wish to serve and developing a business strategy which meets these local needs and preserves the global integrity of your product. In 'Looking Beyond the Nuts and Bolts' if you will, our theory of employee satisfaction – at the core of successful human resource development – is both a nuts and bolts topic – but more importantly a strategic imperative for the tourism industry.

For those of us fortunate enough to be doing business in emerging nations, working with local communities such as those in Asia, developing long-term employment in tourism and its related economic development, we derive a great deal of pleasure, excitement and satisfaction from working with the local people to whom many aspects of the hospitality business comes naturally. Treating people with care is a well-known tradition for most countries in this part of the world. Indeed, if this inclination towards warm, friendly human interaction was the sole criteria for success, little else would need concern us. Our ability to operate here with maximum efficiency and profitability would be assured.

Being successful in the hospitality industry is, however, somewhat more complex than this. Proper utilization of even the most positive ingredients involves a somewhat more sophisticated management philosophy. All the warm smiles and friendly greetings in the world cannot offset the effect of a hotel room improperly prepared or a flight reservation gone astray.

The need for technology transfer, as it relates to training and development, is becoming increasingly crucial to improving productivity, efficiency and competitiveness on an international level. A well-trained multi-skilled workforce is essential to the region's continuing emergence as the preferred travel destination and, ultimately, to our economic survival.

There is a myth about operating in the Asia–Pacific region that is an out-of-date carryover from the early days, and it goes like this. The cost of labour in these countries is so low that it is easy to turn a profit here. Well, as we all know, times have changed, and now more than ever, it is important to bring escalating operating costs under control. Effective technology transfer programmes are one very important way to address the problem. The importance of efficiently planned and executed technology transfer is of course, becoming more and more important, as our market expands.

In the past, properties and the representation of international hotel companies were largely concentrated in major centres of Asia. At that time, resident expatriate presence and management was an accepted and reasonably economical method of ensuring that the skills and know-how were available.

Now, however, as we expand into tertiary markets and secondary cities, this is no longer an option that makes economic sense. For example, for us to have ongoing, multi-level expatriate management at each of our 44 properties in the Asia–Pacific region is not practical.

Despite the rather non-human ring to the term 'technology transfer', it is first and foremost a people issue, and thus a key concern for human resource development. Perhaps the most important reason for this is that, above all else, people represent our real products and services. It is impossible to separate them from the business. It is also essential here to recognize a very important fact related to hard, cold, economic reality, which is spelled out quite simply by this basic formula.

Why is employee satisfaction so important?

The answer is simple. A satisfied employee is an efficient employee. I come from a marketing background and tend to see most things in terms of salesmanship. Everyone, absolutely everyone, in your organization is in sales and represents you and your company in his or her own unique way.

The folks down in the laundry room of your hotel turning out crisp clean sheets and the catering supervisor overseeing the loading of meals on your aircraft will be unlikely to meet your customers on a regular basis. But when your tired guest settles into bed or your hungry passenger tucks into a meal, a critical image, good or bad, is being sold. It's up to management to ensure that they understand your key objectives and are well versed with the right skills to create the image you are striving for.

Consider a 400-room hotel property with an annual occupancy level of 75 per cent; that is 109,000 guests per year. Obviously, no general manager will meet every one of these guests. But contact with a certain number of hotel staff is guaranteed: from the doorman, to the front desk personnel, to bellboys, to restaurant and bar staff and the housekeepers. Every guest – all 109,000 – will meet several employees.

Managers must realize that these employees are their front-line representatives or ambassadors, and these are the key people that guests will remember. They and their actions will determine your client's level of satisfaction with not only your own hotel, but with your company as a whole.

Who could be more important to you as a manager? Or put another way, what is your first priority to ensure that these people are projecting the image you are after?

When you are thinking in these terms, issues such as staff initiative become important. For example, the emphasis should be placed on creating an environment where, when something goes wrong, staff are encouraged to fix it. Better this than setting up a bureaucracy which makes them go through several layers of supervisors to handle routine matters. Of course this freedom to act will result in misfires, but with proper training and a good attitude, this incentive to act gives staff confidence.

A mistake should be met, not with a reprimand but with a patient explanation of how to handle the situation next time round. If your staff are satisfied and committed, if they have the tools to do their job, chances are guests are going to be satisfied. The successful drive for guest satisfaction begins with management ensuring that their staff – the 'internal customers' – are content.

How do you go about creating this state of employee satisfaction and, once it is attained, how is it maintained and evaluated on an ongoing basis?

Let me share with you our attempts to effectively deal with this, an area which we consider to be *the* most critical area of human resources development. We call it the Employee Satisfaction Index and with the help of an independent development centre we set out to address a number of different areas, such as company and individual pride, job efficiency, teamwork, leadership, creativity and problem solving, communication, and reward and recognition.

The system was modelled after the Sheraton Guest Satisfaction Survey (SGSS) Programme. The intent in setting up the index system was to create a work climate survey that was comprehensive yet concise. It was aimed at all employees and shaped to be applicable to all our properties.

The Employee Satisfaction Index (ESI) is primarily a communication tool. It is a way for employees to communicate their opinions about their jobs to management, and a way for management to react and respond to these opinions. This communication occurs when the results are shared with the employees and there is dialogue between employees and management.

It is also accomplished within a context of mutual respect, realistic expectations, teamwork, and involvement – recognizing that some problem areas may be beyond the scope of the group due to resource constraints. Our ESI survey is available at present in eight languages, including Chinese, and efforts to add others appropriate to our applications are afoot.

When the survey is administered, about 90 per cent of the employees participate in order that the results represent the collective and individual viewpoints of everyone at that particular hotel. Sheraton wants its employees to be perfectly honest and candid in their opinions, and one way we try to accomplish this is to guarantee that responses to the questionnaire will be anonymous.

Managers encourage their employees to be fair and to tell the truth – that is, do not retaliate to something you are angry about, but do not be afraid of expressing what you think. The resulting report, prepared by the development centre, consists of a statistical summary of the 51 questions plus verbatim comments for five specific questions for all employees and each department with five or more members. Results are presented in percentages and averages so they are easily readable; graphs are also used. Finally, there is a summary of the number of employees in each department and a demographic breakdown of the entire group.

The pattern for working with the results is to pass the report down from the Executive Committee, to department heads, to managers and then to departmental work groups. The purpose of these feedback meetings is to collect specific information about the ratings. For example: when a department gives a low rating about receiving information from their supervisor that affects their jobs, the goal of the feedback meeting is to find out *what information is needed* that they are not getting.

Managers typically facilitate these feedback meetings, but often human resources personnel and GMs co-facilitate. The ESI programme is designed around a continuous improvement process model. To find out if we are making progress on issues that have been identified in the survey, we repeat the process at least every six months. If there has been a significant change, such as a new GM or a property renovation, it might be done again even sooner. Repeating the survey shows employees that you are looking for change, and the results serve as clear documentation about the progress or, occasionally, the regress of a department.

All of this may sound well and good and statistically very interesting, but how does it relate to the bottom line?

We are able to show very clearly that there are distinct relationships between the Employee Satisfaction Index (ESI), the Guest Satisfaction Index (GSI), the so-called Yield Index and the gross operating profit (GOP). A recent survey, based on the analysis of data from a group of Sheraton hotels, highlights some interesting interaction between the figures.

First, the differences in ESI explain 47 per cent of the differences in GSI. The differences in GSI in turn account for 48 per cent of the differences in Yield Performance Indices. Finally, combining the Yield Index with local market REVPAR predicts 64 per cent of the variances in gross operating profit (GOP) per available room. For each one point improvement in ESI, GSI goes up 0.64 points. One point in GSI produces 4 points in Yield.

Finally, every point in Yield Index translates into $0.66 in GOP per available room. ESI changes drive almost 50 per cent of GSI changes. GSI changes drive 50 per cent of revenue changes. Revenue changes obviously drive GOP performance. What management team does not look for gross operating improvement? To have within your total control an issue which affects 45 to 50 per cent of your ability to improve profits is a significant management imperative.

The point I am attempting to make through the use of statistics is to show that there is a real-world, bottom-line, dollars-and-cents relationship between keeping your employees happy and making increased profits. This type of programme works well and in actual practice can lead to some very important employee development programmes. From it can also come significant employee/employer negotiations, which go a long way to satisfying employee concerns over many key issues and cementing company loyalty.

Last year, as a result of such dialogue, Sheraton's properties in Australia successfully entered into an enterprise agreement negotiated between employees, government and industry unions. It encompassed some 30 areas, from occupational health and safety, technological change, sexual harassment and total quality management.

Its key objectives were to establish a profitable and enduring enterprise through the efficient and effective provision of high quality services for the benefit of the employees, the shareholders, the company's customers and the community, and to develop a workforce with the skills to enable the company to provide these services on a consistent basis in order to help expand business opportunities.

The essential factor in achieving these objectives was the development and maintenance of harmonious and productive working relationships between all employees, management and the company so as to ensure that our employees were committed to their jobs and the success of our business. To achieve this all parties agreed to the following platform:

- that employees be involved in the making of decisions in their work areas;
- that employees have the opportunity to achieve their full potential within the context of the business;
- that employees benefit from the success of their efforts;
- that employees willingly accept total flexibility of jobs and duties across the company, subject only to individual skills or abilities to perform particular tasks.

From this agreement our whole approach to multi-skilling was devised. Within Sheraton we have been able to analyse positions within a hotel environment and to show a clear delineation between the level of skill and ability required to perform a number of tasks that make up a particular job function. This enabled us to reduce the layers within our hotels and to provide for a broad banding of skills across each of the similar skill levels.

Technology transfer can also take the form of providing employees with opportunities to upgrade themselves within the organization. This helps them not only to improve their on-the-job effectiveness but also enables them to climb the corporate ladder from within.

By utilizing a consultative management practice we have developed working relationships between employees and management that promote mutual trust, open communication of relevant information and ideas, and, in general, overall cooperation. This has also had the side effect of minimizing differences in conditions of employment between our employees. It also fosters very positive feelings about the company, and is essential to support an environment that carries as its platform a broad banded multi-skilled approach that employees clearly understand in order to achieve their career aspirations through distinctly devised integrated career paths.

As you are well aware, turnover in the hotel industry in the Pacific region is quite high, and is significant not only in terms of cost to the organization but also in the consistency in the delivery of our products and services. An integrated career path that has credibility must be supported by training programmes that enable the employee to move from one level to the next. In Sheraton our proviso is that employees should broad-band their skills across two or three functions at a similar skill level, prior to multi-skilling in a position that sits higher in the integrated career path.

Sheraton has had some wonderful successes with this programme primarily in the Pacific region. However, the company is in the process of implementing the concepts and philosophies in its hotels throughout Asia. It is important to understand that training and development must have a sound educational base. This must also cover all levels of management.

Recently, we launched a Masters in Business Administration (MBA) study programme for our senior executives throughout the Asia–Pacific region. A total of 250 senior executives are eventually expected to take part in the programme – the first group of 60 have completed five subjects with very impressive results.

The two and a half year integrated Learning Programme has been jointly developed with the school of Business at Bond University in Queensland, Australia. Classroom studies are conducted by professors from the University, using Hong Kong and Brisbane as hubs for Asia and the Pacific. The programme allows executives to continue working while studying, although to complete graduation each executive will spend one semester on campus.

About 30 per cent of those currently enrolled are general managers and the rest comprise executives from human resources management, finance, marketing, and operations. Each property in Asia–Pacific nominates two executives and the enrolment numbers are generally an equal combination of those from Asia and the Pacific. In the end, we should have a group of about 250 very well-educated management executives who will transfer their knowledge and expertise to the staff in each of our hotels. The objective is to develop a management team in the Asia–Pacific region that can respond to the complex challenges of the hotel industry through to the end of this century and beyond.

In January 1994, we launched another very important career development programme for our middle management staff in the region. Employee students will pursue a Diploma of Business Management and successful graduates will provide us with 500 middle management employees over the next three years.

The Diploma Course will consist of eight subjects and, as is the case with the MBA programme, will allow the executives to continue working as they pursue their studies. The courses will be held in four different countries, and credits earned can be transferred to any recognized academic institution in the world and count also as credits towards the MBA course.

Focusing on the hospitality industry, the diploma course will deal with marketing, human resources and finance. For example, outlet managers will be equipped with strong skills in human resources, marketing and finance, and will be able to manage their restaurants as if they actually belonged to them. Not only will this lead to increased accountability, it will also promote a higher level of job satisfaction. In order to 'internationalize' managers in the Asia–Pacific region, and to reduce hotel dependency on expatriate staff, the Diploma of Business Management will be supported by a practical application programme tailored to each manager's specific abilities and requirements.

We intend to transfer chosen local managers to one of our properties in the Pacific for a two-year period while they take their Diploma. Upon completion of the course, they will return to positions previously filled by expatriate staff. As well as the obvious benefits of increased efficiency and elevated service levels, the Diploma course will develop strong staff loyalty and commitment – and satisfaction.

The Employee Satisfaction Index, a planned approach to human resources development, and expanding opportunities for staff to upgrade skills and thus job levels, all have a common ultimate objective: to keep your customer happy to maximize revenue. Within the hospitality business, it is important for managers to recognize that in their case their customers include not only the hotel guests, restaurant patrons or airline passengers who ultimately pay the freight, but also their own staff as well.

Just as staff have to listen to customers, so do management have to listen to staff. Only through increased employee satisfaction will we achieve a quality customer experience that increases profitability.

One more point is vital, I think, when it comes to assessing the need for technology transfer in the Asia–Pacific region: in addition to understanding the need for instituting successful technology transfer, it is also very important for emerging countries to understand that this is an ongoing process.

This means that after local staff have received the training and initial supervision, it is not realistic to then think that they can carry on at the required level of efficiency with no further input or supervision from outside sources. Constant upgrading, ongoing exposure to new and improved methods and operating systems, and a continual sharing of ideas through consultative practices – these are the keys to maintaining any operation to international standards. Policy-makers of emerging countries who understand these issues will enjoy the benefits of attracting the right companies to develop the industry within their borders.

STUDY QUESTIONS

1 To what extent do you agree with the 'survival of the fittest' concept being applied to the hotel industry?
2 Apply Moore's four stages of business ecosystem development to the hotel industry.
3 Discuss the challenges and opportunities offered to hotel corporations through the globalization of markets.
4 Describe some of the major environmental initiatives taken within the hotel industry.
5 Discuss the concept of strategic alliances in relation to the hotel industry.
6 Why is local adaptability a desirable characteristic of international hotel corporations?
7 Discuss the advantages available to hotel corporations through the adoption of the 'transnational model' of organizational structure.
8 How does the design of Center Parcs, and the experiences Center Parcs offer to guests, reflect the changing market awareness of 'green' issues?
9 Explain why Sheraton places strong emphasis on employee satisfaction.
10 Describe Sheraton's Employee Satisfaction Index and evaluate its success for that company.

Chapter 12

Charting a new course into the twenty-first century

This exploration of the hotel industry has examined a wide range of ideas, varying from research findings to business practice, and a number of approaches to build and maintain the competitiveness of hotel companies. The discussion commenced in Chapter 1 with an introduction to the idea of globalization at both a general level and as applied to the hotel industry, with Chapter 2 providing an overview of the international hotel industry and its current business environment. Chapter 2 also raises the issue of why the creating of value is a key response to the myriad forces – especially the global market discussed in Chapter 3 – that are causing discontinuous change in the hotel industry and are affecting the competitiveness of both independent and chain hotel companies. Globalization strategy in the hotel industry, which is proposed as a logic to cultivate capabilities which companies need to transform their organizations into sources of competitive advantage by adding more value than rivals, may represent something of a revolution for most hoteliers. However, the 'revolution' is manageable and evolving, to a lesser or greater degree, in many of the progressive companies that are featured in this volume.

Many issues that have been discussed throughout the book suggest that 'managing change', and the complete rethinking of their management philosophy, should be the main concern of hotel organizations. Just making a few 'improvements' will not do. Hoteliers who argue that this is the responsibility of their personnel and training managers may be missing the point. Overall the issue is about improving the competitiveness of hotel companies in a way that is sustainable into the future.

This requires top management, general managers, or independent owner-operators to initiate and encourage the process of creating value-adding service in their organizations. The creation of value-adding service is an imperative for improving competitiveness, and is therefore the responsibility of general managers as opposed to that of personnel directors. In today's turbulent environment, managers at the unit and corporate level, as well as independent owners/operators, need to specify the kind of competitive edge they are seeking and articulate this edge through strategy formulation and implementation. This process requires knowing how to think strategically, making effective strategic decisions, ensuring that those decisions are effectively implemented through 'teamplay'. The idea of cooperation was amplified in Chapter 11 as a powerful means of team-building with partners in industry, education and government, to design and implement better strategies and adapt to new challenges.

What does the future hold?

This chapter summarizes six conditions that have taken on a strategic importance because they are driving the direction and speed of the hotel industry's evolution into the twenty-first century. Its focus then shifts to the imperative to bring about changes in behaviour – specifically management attitudes and how managers think about the hotel business. The chapter concludes with a discussion of globalization strategy and the skills hoteliers need to acquire to enhance their competitiveness and chart a new course into the twenty-first century.

Prospects

When examining the future evolution of the hotel industry, managers have to address the following questions: What trends will cause further struc-tural changes? How will the structure of the hotel industry change? And, will a predominant new management model emerge? These questions are crucial for several reasons.

First, hotel executives have to identify trends and position their com-panies to take advantage of developments. Structural changes often create new markets, new concepts, and new organizational forms. And they often require the adoption of new skills, new technology, new systems, and new product development. Second, hoteliers must be able to pre-empt their competition by formulating optimal strategies and where possible being first to implement them. This implies that managers should be able to anticipate change and chart their company's course towards an intended direction, as opposed to being steered by outside forces. Third, hotel executives need to be able to identify growth arenas and comprehend what specific capabilities will be required to become or remain a major player within these arenas. The ability to envision and articulate how to 'shape' the future can substantially benefit both managers' companies and careers.

There are six major trends that are presently driving the direction and speed of the hotel industry's evolution into the twenty-first century. They are:

(a) The slow growth of demand and the proliferation of 'substitutes' in industrialized countries, and the 'explosive' market expansion in industrializing economies.

(b) The undeniable trend towards 'value-for-money' oriented consumers.
(c) The simultaneous rise of the 'short-break' and 'long-haul' travel market.
(d) The phenomenon of the corporate merger and acquisition leading gradually to greater hotel industry consolidation.
(e) The trend towards the internationalization of the hotel industry, both through geographical expansion and the affiliation of hotels with global distribution systems.
(f) The shortage of (semi) skilled labour in industrialized and developing countries

Obviously, hotel executives will do well to comprehend the background of each of these factors and their implications on the hotel industry, or certain segments thereof, and the manner in which strategies should be 'crafted' and implemented to take their impact into account. Each of the trends that follow are most relevant to hoteliers because they dictate the different, emerging business environment in which companies have to compete and cooperate to achieve a competitive edge, and therefore shall be briefly considered in turn.

First, the slow growth of demand and the proliferation of 'substitutes' in industrialized countries, and the 'explosive' growth in developing economies. Though the number of international tourists reached the half-billion mark in 1993, setting a new record, the overall growth rate dropped to 3.8 per cent from 5.5 per cent in 1992. The World Tourism Organization projects international tourism to grow by 3.2 per cent per year until 1995. Thereafter, it is projected to increase by 4–5 per cent per year.

The main international travel and tourism flows remain highly concentrated in Europe and America with 59.3 per cent and 21.3 per cent of world tourism share in 1993, respectively. In Western Europe, pleasure travel is characterized by a pronounced north–south flow to the Mediterranean Basin countries. About two-thirds of the US travel market travels either to Canada or Mexico, with the other one-third of American travellers visiting overseas destinations. Recently, the Far East has been the beneficiary of the wider dispersal of international business and pleasure travel. The international travel propensity in Asia may be unlikely to reach either the European or the North American level in the foreseeable future because border crossing in Asia implies air travel and the region lacks in airport capacity. Nevertheless, the Pacific–Asian market will experience 'explosive' growth, simply because the travel market is expanding from a narrow base of 68.5 million international visitors in 1993 (compared to Europe's almost 300 million international tourist arrivals that same year). Furthermore, demographic factors combined with growing discretionary income and changing lifestyles are presently creating a geometric progression towards more intra-regional travel. Asia's intra-regional travel market has already overtaken the combined number of inbound tourist arrivals from Europe, North America and other parts of the world.

Accordingly, prospects for the hotel industry in North America and Europe are for continued growth, but at a slower pace. Furthermore, astute hoteliers have begun to realize that the five-star luxury hotel market alone, estimated to be worth over $40 billion annually, will provide very limited scope for expansion. In several corporations there has been a pronounced shift towards penetrating lower income market segments with mid-scale and basic hotel products to stimulate growth and conquer market share.

Second, the undeniable trend towards 'value-for-money' oriented consumers. If there is one overriding global market trend, then it is likely to be the consumers' quest for value-added products and services. The trend towards value-for-money oriented consumers is driven by:

- The most recent economic downturn, which has contributed to long term structural changes and created a climate of uncertainty. At present, preliminary estimates for 1993 indicate that the economic recession in major source markets, such as Germany, France, the UK, Italy, the USA, and Canada, put a 'dent' in the growth of travel and tourism.
- The rising cost of living which has 'nibbled' away on the consumers' disposable income and explains, at least partially, the growing popularity for the purchase of 'do-it-yourself' products and services and substitutes perceived to add similar or greater value. In this context, rather than going on a holiday involving an overnight stay, customers may opt to stay with family or relatives, in a less expensive hotel, stay shorter, or select substitutes such as bungalow parcs, vacation homes, trailers and campers.
- The overcapacity which plagues the hotel industry in Western nations enables buyers to choose the highest possible quality at the lowest price from a large and varied product assortment.
- The proliferation of media use and transportation advances, particularly the development of instant worldwide news reporting such as CNN and an increasingly mobile international workforce, have spawned, as outlined in Chapter 3, a 'global consumer' in the sense that customers around the world, almost without exception, expect faster, better service quality at a lower cost.

Third, the simultaneous rise of the 'short-break' and 'long-haul' travel market. Though the travel market is unified by customers who demand value for their money, it is far from homogeneous. The majority of trips that consumers take are governed by two factors: discretionary income and time. Both factors, which were presented in Chapter 3, show that in contrast to popular belief, many people, especially busy professionals who earn higher incomes, have today, on average, less leisure time. Hence, the market segment with a high level of discretionary income but with little leisure time will demand 'no-hassle' short-break products that offer an appropriate blend of recreation and relaxation. The Center Parcs example, referred to in Chapter 11, provides evidence that the accommodation market is changing in fundamental ways. Consumers want innovative products that are responsive to their specific needs and expectations. In today's environment, time and money matter. Hoteliers should recognize that time and money are two key criteria because they 'set the stage' for making most other market segmentation decisions.

Destinations that fall in the long-haul category tend to be at a competitive disadvantage compared with destinations that are located near major source markets. However, preliminary WTO 1993 data indicate that East Asia and the Pacific have kept their position as preferred long-haul destinations, suggesting that this travel market is sustained by executives who travel on corporate accounts and pleasure travellers who thrive on the phenomenon of 'conspicuous consumption' (Theuns 1993: 6).

The seniors market segment fits in the 'lots of leisure time' category of the 'matter of time and money' model explored in Chapter 3. It has become an increasingly important market segment to the hotel industry, especially in Europe where seniors made 142 million trips domestically and 41 million international trips. As Chapter 5 indicated, Europe's senior population, aged 55 and over, will increase by 10 per cent between 1990 and 2000. But Clech notes that 'the travel industry in Europe has not taken full advantage of the commercial opportunities which it represents . . . and lags behind North America in effective promotional policies' (1993: 136).

Also, greater consumer interest in 'individualism', coupled with the twin demands of 'freedom and independence', has strongly contributed to the fragmentation of the mass market. The trend towards 'customization' has resulted in a much more diverse market, and can also be seen in the holiday market as people turn away from the package tour to choose a holiday more suited to their personal special interests. Special interest travel encompasses a wide range of products from arts, heritage, educational pursuits, ethnic and health tourism, to sports related travel. This phenomenon is driven by structural shifts in consumer buying patterns and is changing the travel industry (Forbes and Forbes 1993: 128). Put provocatively, it can be argued that it is no longer possible for any hotel company to understand the entire travel market. Independent hoteliers are therefore in an excellent position to respond to special travel interests and preferences through 'niche' marketing. The 'uniqueness' independent hoteliers are able to offer tends to be the Achilles' heel of most large hotel chains.

Against the backdrop of these evolving demand trends there are three supply variables that will determine the growth of the international hotel industry in the 1990s.

First, the drive for product standardization shall continue unabated because of the derived scale economies, as Chapter 4 revealed. There are good reasons for the trend towards hotel industry concentration under a brand-name: it helps to bring about a competitive advantage, through consistent service, and fuels growth and profitability. This argument has also caused owners to change brands to take advantage of a name recognition, reservations, and marketing support which they perceive to be better. At the same time, the encroaching consolidation of the hotel industry and an 'invasion' of brand-name hotel corporations has forced many independent hotel companies and smaller second-tier hotel chains to join referral or franchise systems. Consequently, hotel consortia experienced rapid growth between 1991 and 1992.

Second, there is a trend towards the internationalization of hotel operations and ownership. The multinational corporation, discussed in Chapter 1, is the main actor and one of the major drivers in the process towards industry globalization. Slow growth in the industrialized markets has caused expansion opportunities in the 'home' markets of American and European hotel corporations to weaken, and have had a 'push' effect on their foreign expansion. Typically, these companies expand by way of management contracts, franchising, or joint ventures.

Meanwhile, ownership of hotel corporations has become more nationally diversified. For example, during the 1980s Bass breweries acquired Holiday Inns; Ladbroke took over Hilton International, and Seibu-Saison acquired Inter-Continental Hotels. Lately, Asian multinationals from Hong Kong and Taiwan have entered the international hotel industry through foreign direct investment. The injection of Far Eastern investments and the long-term focus of Asian management have heightened the level of competition and changed the 'game rules', respectively.

Last, but by no means least, the labour shortage in industrialized and industrializing countries is affecting the hotel industry to a greater extent than it does many other industries, because the latter had been more proactive to cope with the consequences of the demographic wave, whilst the hotel industry did not take sufficient measures early on. Furthermore, and as explained in Chapter 7, the human resources policies and practices in the international hotel industry are not appropriately aligned with operations and marketing strategies. Since the rendering of value-adding service in international hotels is highly dependent on human resources, the present dearth of trained labour was identified in Chapter 7 – not only as the most critical problem but also as the greatest opportunity to increase hotel service quality and productivity.

Initiating change

Hotel managers are entrusted with the responsibility of ensuring the long-term viability of their companies. To succeed in this task, they need to be aware of the external and internal forces and how these impact their short- and long-term performance. The underlying causes of the hotel industry's present underperformance have their roots, at least partially, in the over-building 'virus' in many markets, and hotel managers cannot be held accountable for this. Nor can they be expected to change the national value system. However, they need to make a series of difficult decisions and significant decisions that would help mobilize their resources towards a sustainable fit with the environment.

First and foremost, executives need to bring about changes in behaviour – especially in the attitudes of managers, whose behaviour in turn affects employee attitude which has been identified as a critical success factor in Chapter 7.

Furthermore, managers can and should change their thinking about the hotel business. In general, the hotel industry is a rather traditional industry. There is always a risk that traditional views may lead to complacency. However, the reality of uninterrupted, rapid-fire change will leave hoteliers who want their businesses to survive with no other option but to look 'outward' through, for example, bench-marking other companies. The process of bench-marking holds the potential to change some of the deeply held, and sometimes outmoded, values in the hotel industry.

Finally, in a turbulent environment, hoteliers need to be able to specify the type of competitive edge they are seeking, and articulate how they intend to achieve their strategy against a backdrop of fundamental change. The hotel industry continues to move gradually away from being a well-defined, traditional, top-down type of industry. But what is it moving towards?

Global opportunities and challenges

The international hotel industry is a recent phenomenon and has its roots in the postwar era when several of today's major transnational hotel chains were established. Since then the political map of the world has changed rapidly, despite forecasts to the contrary. For instance, Terpstra (1985) stated that: 'Our present wall maps will probably be good for the year 2000.' However, in less than one year, the political structure of Eastern Europe was effectively dismantled and the wave of democratic reforms sweeping Eastern Europe opened enormous opportunities for expan- sion to support the growing demand for travel and tourism in the region.

Today's world is beginning to resemble, in many respects, Marshall McLuhan's (1964) 'global village'. Worldwide markets, the spread of information technology and computer networks, and advance transportation have increased the speed of communication and the number of international travellers during this century dramatically, and have significant consequences for the hotel industry. For example, the increasing speed and diminishing cost of telecommunications and global distribution systems have resulted in the creation of world travel markets that overlap domestic frontiers; the impacts of global trends, such as economic stagnation, fluctuating energy prices, terrorism and war, and changing values about work and leisure tend to have an almost immediate impact on the hotel industry.

The globalization of the hotel industry is rooted in and driven by two main variables. First, hotels are an integral component of the transnational infrastructure, are subject to the effects of telecommunications and advance transportation, and are dependent on the patronage of business and leisure travellers for their business. Second, there is another set of dynamics that contribute to further the global nature of the hotel industry, such as foreign direct investments in hotels, joint international financing, the need to compete with foreign rivals either in the international arena or on 'home turf', the involvement in projects of multinational development and management teams, the employment of foreign workers, and the franchising of brand-names (Clark and Arbel 1993: 84).

The opportunities for the global expansion of travel and tourism are staggering. When one considers the following facts it becomes evident that opportunities for hotel development in the future are significant. An estimated 500 million international tourist arrivals were recorded in 1993. Assuming that each traveller would only make one trip per year, this implies that only 8 per cent of the world's population is engaged in international travel, with the remaining 92 per cent of the market remaining constrained, particularly due to a lack of discretionary income and leisure time.

The benefits of international expansion are known and include additional growth and expansion; the opportunity to increase revenues, profits and return on investment; to expand market share, conquering untapped markets and adding to the exposure of a brand identity (Walker 1988). However, hoteliers who have ambitions to compete in the international arena also face many demands. For example, Clark and Arbel (1993: 86) cite several challenges associated with:

- communication difficulties due to inadequate telephone, fax, or computer facilities;
- little control over regulatory, legal and political decisions;
- political instabilities;
- different labour patterns, costs, product supplies, religions, customs, work ethics, and languages;
- fluctuating currency-exchange rates, which have a major impact on profits, costs and project viability;
- expropriations of cash, or regulations restricting the inflows and outflows of funds; and
- lack of codes, planning information, and standards.

To cope with these and other such challenges, according to Clark and Arbel (1993: 86), hoteliers will need:

- more knowledge about international marketing and finance, cultures, and legal and accounting systems;
- a stronger profit orientation (because of stronger competition with players around the world;
- multidimensional performance-evaluation techniques;
- more frequent and flexible goal setting;
- individualized training programmes;
- adjustments to local tests and product preferences; and
- changes in product mix and prices over time and across countries to respond to various economic growth and inflation patterns.

As the trend towards globalization, in the new world order, will continue unabated, hotel companies will have to cultivate managers who can capitalize on the opportunities the global market offers and deal with opportunities and challenges both in 'domestic and global markets' (Clark and Arbel 1993: 86). There appears to be no single 'correct' balance between global and domestic strategies. Therefore, Bartlett and Ghoshal (1989), referred to in Chapter 11, suggest that organizations should abandon the idea that there can be any such thing as a universal 'global' manager and embrace the idea of the more flexible transnational network to deal with the complexities and internal conflicts of balancing global, regional and local requirements.

Unlike companies in manufacturing industries, hotel companies find it harder to come to terms with the fact that the ideal mix varies not only between different regions, nations, and even localities within nations, but also for different brands and even individual properties that operate under the same brand-name. On the organizational side, the key question has been how hotel companies can best alter the roles in the power balance between international hotel managers, domestic hotel managers, and managers at the head office. As far as career paths are concerned, the question is how to breed managers with what has become known in the jargon as a 'global mindset'. Underlying both questions has been the universal need to streamline, or abandon bureaucratic structures. In the multinational model, traditional arrangements slowed decision-making and sustained costly office jobs. In today's competitive international environment, greater speed, leanness, and cost effectiveness are essential.

By building on Bartlett and Ghoshal's ideas and relating them to the hotel business, it is proposed that the present turbulent business environment calls for 'globalization strategists'. The three planks in the suggested 'globalization strategy', which combines the intent for global reach with the need for local adaptability, respectively are:

- the notion that global competition expresses the ease with which the world's best rivals can enter almost any market at any time and leave hoteliers little choice but to compete on worldwide quality and value terms;
- the imperative of adapting to the changing needs of both customers and employees which recognizes that value-adding service hinges on staff attitudes, but that attitude must start at the managerial level;
- the necessity for managers to cultivate the appropriate competencies and capabilities in an intended direction to transform hotel organizations into sources of value creation and sustain their competitive advantage through cooperative transnational partnerships.

Within this context it might be helpful to discuss in broad terms some of the core competencies the globalization strategist shall require in an increasingly demanding market. At the same time it should be pointed out that almost all managers will have a somewhat different perspective on developing growth, depending on the type of business they represent, ranging from the operator who is primarily interested in management opportunities to the real estate investor and franchisor.

Developing a globalization mindset

Amid signs that the future will be more unpredictable and unstable, the number one challenge for managers around the world has become to gain and maintain some degree of control over the direction of their organizations. Furthermore, to achieve success in a turbulent environment, hoteliers need competency in analytical skills and the functional management areas. Finally, to deal with distinctive market demands which range from local and regional to global challenges, nine capabilities stand out as particularly relevant, namely the ability to:

1 Comprehend the shifting context

Globalization strategy abandons the notion that only head office executives should think and act globally and that hotel managers are responsible for meeting customers needs on the local level. It is advocated that globalization strategy as a logic is designed to compete more effectively than the manager with a global and/or domestic mindset. Why? Because the global/domestic approach masks the complex realities of today's world – for instance, the great disparities between the developing countries in terms of their economic progress and cultural composition; the variances between stable and politically chaotic countries; the dichotomy between thriving and 'sick' regions; and communities which have a strong concern for the environment versus places where bad planning has had an adverse affect on tourism.

By getting hotel managers on the local level involved in thinking and asking questions that go beyond their immediate 'jurisdiction', such as: What is the competitive environment like regionally? Who else competes in my segment on a global basis? How is the industry structure and alliance structure in the mid-scale market defined multi-domestically? And, who are its successful players?, hotel companies will be able to:

- build a more flexible management mentality to respond faster to diverse market needs;
- develop organizational learning ability that could result in worldwide innovation; and
- cultivate greater team spirit.

2 Switch gears

As opportunities and actions are constantly shifting in a turbulent business environment, it may no longer be adequate for hoteliers to think strictly in global and domestic terms. Instead, today's hotel industry requires global-ization strategists who seek to achieve growth and excellence along a continuum which ranges from the global level through the regional and multi-domestic level, to the domestic and local level. This challenge may be compared to the analogy of two persons riding their bicycles in moun-tainous terrain. Without doubt, the individual who has the bicycle with five gears will have an advantage over his rival whose bike has only two gears (the domestic and global manager). Similarly, hotel executives have to be able to 'switch gears', to respond more effectively to the changing business 'landscape'. When hotel executives spot an opportunity or threat, they should be able to 'switch gears', along the globalization strategy continuum which is depicted in Figure 12.1, to formulate and implement an appro-priate policy. In an extremely diverse market it will be increasingly essential that hotel strategies 'fit the fabric' and circumstances of specific markets and are sensitive to the issues that are significant on a particular geo-graphic level.

3 Cooperate through transnational networks

One of the main themes throughout the book has been that value creation is derived from the ability to cooperate and learn collectively in a trans-national network. Building the relationship between the hotel corporation and its buyers, suppliers, co-producers and distributors, and using information technology to speed up the information flow, will be the key to maintaining a competitive edge in the face of new entrants and substitutes and there-fore to future success. Not surprisingly, the best teamplay and performance results will occur when partners' goals are compatible and linked to

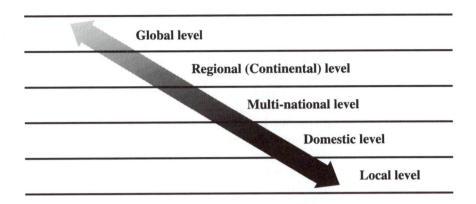

Figure 12.1 'Switching gears' along the globalizing continuum

humanistic values such as integrity, trust, and openness, and business imperatives such as quality, productivity, and a sense of urgency. Globalization strategists demonstrate the ability of deploying policies and programmes with minimal resources because of their active interfacing with an extensive transnational network of professionals. The dual focus and flexibility which globalization strategy affords, enables managers to ask what specific capabilities are required on a particular geographic level and if these capabilities are valuable in competitive terms, before committing to a programme or policy.

4 Think and act 'boundaryless'

Serving guests in a satisfactory manner continues to remain at the core of the hotel business, but in progressive hotel organizations serving guests is viewed as a process integrating all (business) functions ranging from accounting, corporate policy and operations management to marketing, statistics and real estate. The mindset of globalization managers enables them to think and act, to paraphrase GE's Jack Welch, in a 'boundaryless' fashion, not only outside the organization but also within it. This attitude leads to multi-functional and cross-dimensional management, which is characterized by the taking down of departmental or divisional barriers that stand in the way of creating and sustaining value-adding service for all the customers, ranging from suppliers, to buyers, to employees.

5 Demonstrate intercultural sensitivity

The global market has spawned a diverse market. Today's customers are likely to be different from yesterday's in terms of their cultural needs and expectations. It is essential that hoteliers adapt to these changing needs by actively developing markets cross-culturally, by employing multilingual employees, accepting foreign credit cards, providing translation services and language interpreters, currency exchange, and promotional materials in foreign languages.

Hilton International has demonstrated its intercultural sensitivity by changing its service approach both globally and regionally. Regarding the latter, the company introduced, based on comprehensive research, the 'Wa No Kutsurogi', or 'comfort and service, the Japanese way', programme, consisting of special features such as Japanese-speaking staff at participating hotels, safe deposit provision, safety instructions in Japanese, the provision of authentic Japanese cuisine, and the availability of Japanese tea and items such as slippers, bathrobes and Japanese newspapers. It is highly likely that more companies will provide similar programmes aimed to satisfy the specific cultural needs.

6 Influence public policy

Achieving appropriate public policy consideration by lobbying government which sets the rules the hotel industry competes by, is a major consideration to achieve success. An analysis by the World Travel and Tourism Council shows that travel and tourism, of which the hotel industry is an important part, is far from being understood as the leading economic contributor to the world and many nations.

To raise the profile of travel and tourism, hoteliers should cooperate with industry partners and government to:

- create jobs by building the appropriate infrastructure;
- boost exports by aggressively marketing their country's international tourism industry;
- increase the number of tourist arrivals through eased entry and 'open skies';
- tax the industry fairly and 'wisely';
- endorse a national educational campaign to prepare young people for career opportunities in travel and tourism; and
- foster cultural and environmental preservation.[1]

7 Operate in an ethically and environmentally responsible manner

One of today's overwhelming public concerns is the protection of our planet. The environment is a global issue that has particular significance for the hotel business. It is a transnational issue, in that pollution does not cease at national borders, which gets special meaning at the community level where the effects of, for example 'bad tourism planning' become measurable and noticeable. It is imperative that the industry 'move from being simply environmentally conscious to behaving in an environmentally responsible way'[2] as demonstrated by Canadian Pacific Hotels & Resorts and Inter-Continental Hotels in Chapter 11.

Environmentally responsible behaviour is an idea whose time has come, because the introduction of government regulations such as the environmental-impact statement have become a precondition for approval of construction in some jurisdictions (Sherry 1993). More legislation along these lines is almost certain to follow. Furthermore, the marketplace presents another persuasive reason for environmental preservation. According to a recent poll conducted by the Association of British Travel Agents, tourists will look for new destinations if favourite destinations become too polluted. The poll indicates that 63 per cent of the tourists surveyed are concerned about the environmental quality they visit; and 88 per cent are of the opinion they are becoming increasingly environment-conscious.[3]

Environmentally compatible hotel industry growth, as Momberger remarked in Chapter 11, is not only right but also sound business.

8. Preserve a sense of place in communities

At the same time that the world is becoming more uniform, clear-cut differences are likely to remain from country to country. And travellers in Europe, the Americas, and Asia are demonstrating a growing interest in 'heritage' and 'cultural tourism'. Hotel development determines to a great extent the type of tourism that is likely to develop in a destination area. The responsible development of hotels which is sensitive to both quantitative aspects (such as the number of accommodation facilities and the number of hotel rooms to be built) and qualitative dimensions (like the type and architectural style of hotel projects), impacts on the 'sense of place' in the host community. Clearly, today's plural market allows for standardization and specialization in the hotel industry to co-exist and strengthens the existing globalization and localization paradox. In this context there is an opportunity for all types of hotels from de luxe and mid-scale to basic products, to thrive. However, it is hoped that operators in all hotel categories will make a common effort to preserve, where possible, the sense of place in the communities in which they operate.

9 Be involved in enhancing the educational process

The formulation and implementation of a globalization strategy implies the need for creating and sustaining value for consumers, corporate 'stakeholders', and the community. In turn, this may require the upgrading of managers' expertise in some cases, and in other cases the present incumbents may not be capable to meet the challenge globalization strategy poses. Within the value-added context, the cultivation of competencies and capabilities is moving from the realm of corporate philanthropy to the realm of productivity. When that distinction is linked to rising competitive pressures and shortages of skilled labour, the hotel industry should have an incentive to support education, training and research.

Regarding the latter, two suggestions for long-term success are proposed. First, companies should be involved in the efforts of enhancing the educational process, as opposed to just being financial donors (although financial support is of great importance to many educational institutions). And second, companies should make education and training an ongoing agenda rather than an occasional exercise. Hotel companies that cultivate appropriate capabilities and competencies in their organizations will be able to create and sustain the value-adding service the global market demands.

CONCLUSIONS

The rapid expansion of the hotel industry during the past decades has resulted in significant challenges for operators. It has been argued that, through overbuilding, the industry may have grown 'too big'; that the focus has been on adding volume rather than value. To ensure future prosperity, the hotel industry will have to build on productivity and quality gains that flow from value-adding competencies and capabilities – that is, work that employs a higher degree of investment and skills in product and process technology. It is essential that the hotel industry, educational institutions, and government form an effective partnership in order to: (a) raise the standards and skills employers expect from employees, especially those without the basic skills who are unable to reach even the first rung of the value ladder; (b) foster the ability and possibility of lifelong learning for practitioners; (c) turn 'learners into leaders' who try to ensure that the hotel industry will have a positive influence on the economic, social and cultural development of communities and countries; and (d) support leadership initiatives, ranging from the local to the global level, so that resources are most effectively deployed from an environmental viewpoint.

The viewpoints expressed by the leading professionals in the previous chapters lead us to believe that progressive hotel corporations are already in the process of putting into practice many of the principles – such as transformational leadership, creating value through competencies, and cooperative relationships – and other important ideas contained in *Globalization Strategy in the Hotel Industry*.

Notes

1 INTRODUCTION TO GLOBALIZATION

* Parts of this chapter are based on Frank M. Go 'The Multinational Firm' in Khan, M., Olsen, M. and Var, Turgut, *VNR's Encyclopedia of Hospitality and Tourism*, 1993, pp. 354–65.

3 APPRAISING THE GLOBAL COMPETITIVE ENVIRONMENT

1 Normann (1984: 8) refers to a metaphor from bullfighting to explain the moment of truth; it is the encounter between service provider and service consumer, and what happens between them 'can no longer be directly influenced by the company'.
2 The rise of the transnational corporation has led to the globalization of production capability and has made possible much greater product variety and choice for consumers. Furthermore, the utilization of process technology by transnational corporations in particular has resulted in ever-faster service and higher levels of product quality at lower cost.
   The growing product variety, combined with intensive marketing, has raised customer expectation levels considerably and placed great pressures on producers to deliver superior service as a prerequisite to compete.
3 Holography is a new technology which allows reality to interact with an illusion, drastically altering the nature of 'experiencing'. Instead of the viewer being surrounded by a video screen carrying changing images, the three-dimensional images emerge at various points within the room. Holography may eventually permit projecting scenes in which the real person plays one of several characters. The person might choose to be in Napoleon's war room witnessing generals debate whether to attack Russia. The major limitation is that the scenes are 'canned' and cannot be shaped in their interaction with the consumer. Thus, Napoleon and his generals keep talking no matter what the consumer does in the situation. Yet even this limitation may eventually be overcome by interactive programming (Kotler 1984: 13).
4 Cleverdon and O'Brien (1988: 135–139) observe that business travellers account for nearly half of the world's hotel occupants (45 per cent), i.e., 'when attendance at conference events is taken into account. Changes in business travel patterns have been due to the decline of traditional manufacturing industry and the rise of financial services and high technology-related businesses. These new industries tend to locate in secondary cities.'
5 For further information, refer to Buckley *et al.* (1989: 357–383): 'Tourism's

role in internationalizing the economy is forecast [and planned] to increase. In part, this will be a direct function of the increase in leisure time and expenditure which is being demanded. . . . Much of this will be absorbed at home in the rapidly expanding domestic leisure industry but a gradually increasing proportion will be directed to overseas tourism. Negative net tourism balances can thus become an important element in offsetting Japan's surpluses elsewhere.

'During the 1980s, 'the Japanese Ministry of Transport has announced a 'Programme for Doubling' or 'Ten Million Programme' to increase overseas travel and tourism to 10 million visits by 1991 (from 5.52 million in 1986). The programme includes the facilitation of overseas travel procedures, raising the tax exemption limit for travel expenses, establishment of an information network on overseas travel and tax exemptions for employees participating in overseas travel sponsored by employers. For destinations, tourism promotion, exchange of staff, missions and extra services will be undertaken by Japanese agencies. Infrastructural and travel improvements are also under way to cope with the outflow. . . . Our analysis shows that this increase is likely to be skewed toward the US, East Asia and Australia, and coping with this large tourist inflow is likely to pose problems for certain destination countries. This is already the case in Australia where resentment against the Japanese inflow, in particular with regard to land purchase, is widely reported.

'Overall, then, increasing foreign travel and tourism is one part of the structural adjustment of the Japanese economy which is needed to correct the perceived external imbalance.'

6 *Market perspectives for civil jet aircraft*, Blagnac, France: Airbus Industries, 1991, p. 52, defines 'total' trip time as transit from the actual point of origin (i.e., home or office) to the rail station or airport and from the destination station or airport to the actual destination of the traveller.

7 The typical factory worker in Japan may be a robot by the beginning of the twenty-first century. Industrial robots are steadily getting better and cheaper, and the number of such robots in developed nations is growing rapidly. By 1990 (Weil 1982: 179), there will be an estimated 70,000 robots in use in Japan, 60,000 in the US, and 25,000 in Sweden and the UK, followed closely by France.

8 For example, Mexico is stimulating foreign investment by allowing investors 100 per cent ownership in projects. The Mexican government hopes to add 50,000 hotel rooms at a value of US$3 billion and is making available US$312.4 million in loans to boost tourism.

9 The travel markets of the various regions differ significantly. For example, in North America, the domestic market dominates. It contributed more than 82 per cent of the hotel business in 1986. However, in Africa and the Middle East foreign markets are more significant, providing 72.5 per cent of hotel occupancy. Repeat business at 43.2 per cent is greatest in North America, but accounts for only 27.8 per cent in Latin America and the Caribbean, and 36.2 per cent in Europe respectively.

10 Source: 1989 *Golf Digest Almanac* as reported in *Christian Science Monitor*, 24 April 1989, p. 9. In the past fifteen-year period, the number of golfers grew by 231 per cent in Continental Europe, by 140 per cent in Asia, by 123 per cent in Australia, by 87 per cent in North America, and by 33 per cent in the United Kingdom.

11 The intensifying competition will require governments around the world to encourage the travel industry to improve the quality and attractiveness of their product and to research consumer needs.

12 By the year 2000, more than half of the world's population will be living in cities, with a total of 82 cities having a 4 million population or over, two-thirds will be located in today's developing countries. World population will rise by another billion between 1988 and the turn of the century, adding to the present 5 billion and the urban surge past the year 2000. 'The population in all cities of industrial nations will edge upward to 1.2 billion by 2025, while the total population in the cities of today's developing nations will reach 3.9 billion' (Fox 1988: 31). The increase in the population of developing nations will cause, for example, the European Community at the beginning of the next century to have fewer inhabitants than the Muslim countries of the South Mediterranean basin, whilst the population of Brazil and Nigeria combined will be comparable to that of Europe (Godet and Barre 1988).

13 Quoted from *Schweizer Wirt schafts revue*, no. 2, 1982, Zurich, pp. 48–50, in Jost Krippendorf, *The Holiday Makers: Understanding the Impact of Leisure and Travel*, Oxford: Heinemann, 1987, p. 86.

14 The conference entitled: 'Europe's Seaside Resorts and Tomorrow's Tourism', was held in Scheveningen, the Netherlands from 14–16 November 1990 and intended for resort managers, local authority tourism planners, National Tourist Boards, Environment Ministry representatives, tour operators, and the travel industry.

15 Product/market blending has become a reality in the travel and tourism market. More specifically, whereas traditionally the mass market could be differentiated in the business and pleasure travel segments, today the meetings and conventions market has become a significant segment. Furthermore, while vacations during the summer holidays in July and August still form the backbone of the tourist market, short breaks have become more important and have resulted in the 'weekends' and 'mini-vacations' segments. Finally, there is a growing realization that host community residents may be potential consumers of the hotel product, especially its restaurant and conference facilities.

Due to time and cost constraints experienced by many consumers, the blurring between the various segments is likely to continue, in the sense that a busy commercial traveller may combine business with pleasure, by adding a mini-vacation to the business trip he had to make on behalf of his corporation.

Consequently, the changing behaviours of consumers are likely to change when that same person assumes a 'leisure role', after business matters have been conducted.

4 UNDERSTANDING THE STRUCTURAL DYNAMICS OF THE AMERICAN HOTEL INDUSTRY

1 'When Robert Hazard, President and CEO of Quality Inns International went shopping for jogging shoes in 1981 and found 106 styles to choose from, he came home with more than a new pair of runners. Hazard came up with a concept that spread throughout the hotel industry in North America. Why not, he asked himself, build hotels as tailored to the guest as running shoes to the feet? The buzzwords stemming from that idea are "product differentiation" and "market segmentation", and have resulted in Quality International marketing four brands: Sleep, Comfort, Quality and Clarion to the travelling public' (Leitch 1989: 20).

2 Aaker (1991: 8) points to the power of brands, and their 'brand equity' in particular. Because brands are expensive and difficult to establish, an indication of brand equity is what companies are willing to pay for a brand.

Aaker cites the purchase of Kraft at nearly $13 billion and RJR Nabisco at $25 billion; both 'these values are far beyond the worth of any balance sheet item representing bricks and mortar'. Similar examples have occurred in the hotel industry.

3   In *Managing Brand Equity: Capitalizing on the Value of a Brand Name*, David A. Aaker (1991: 234–235) explains the Marriott Corporation's concern about using the Marriott brand-name, especially in product lines like Courtyard which the public would perceive as a 'cut below' conventional Marriott hotels. The Marriott Corporation solved the problem through brand extension.

4   Among the main concerns Chief Executive Officers (CEOs) of major hotel firms have for the years ahead, the top ones are productivity and coping with rapidly changing technology. The application of technologically advanced equipment, like computing and/or production systems generally in combination with skilled management and effective management controls can significantly improve productivity (Bellas 1982: 146). Between 1975 and 1982 there was a 97 per cent increase per service worker in new technology investment, which resulted in many service industries achieving significant productivity improvements, perhaps with the exception of the hotel and motel industry. Technological innovations introduced in the lodging industry since the 1970s ranged from electronic cash registers to the more sophisticated mini-computers. Nevertheless on a comparative basis with other sectors, the hotel industry has registered the lowest productivity gains per annum, respectively 1.6 per cent over the 1960–1983 period and 0.8 per cent over the 1970–1983 period.

In 1987, labour productivity declined about 1.8 per cent. The previous year, output fell 4.8 per cent, the steepest drop of any industry tracked by the Bureau of Labour Statistics, compared to a drop in productivity of 4.5 per cent in 1985. Despite declining productivity, wages rose in 1985 and 1986, before falling 1 per cent in 1987 (Laventhol and Horwath 1988).

New hotels have required the hiring of employees, and a side effect has been reduced productivity – at least statistically. In order to improve productivity managers are striving to break job descriptions into specific tasks and schedule those tasks to correspond more closely to the variations in customer traffic. In addition, the industry is also using more part-timers. The average hotel worker spent 31 hours per week in the first six months of 1988 on the job; compared with an average of 32.5 hours for the service sector (Laventhol and Horwath 1988).

5   In the US hotel industry, average hourly earnings fell well below the average for the total economy between 1958 and 1984. For example, in 1981, the hotel industry's average hourly wage was 67 per cent of the private sector wage, but only 65 per cent in 1984 (*Lodging* 1987: 63). While the number of manufacturing companies that offer incentives grew from 80 per cent in 1981 to 92 per cent in 1987, according to the American Management Association, pay and benefits in the hotel industry were insufficient to attract top people, revealed a recent survey (Laventhol and Horwath 1988). For instance, only 12.6 per cent of hotel companies offered their on-site executives any long-term benefits and fewer than half (44.6 per cent) of hotel companies offered their on-site executives annual performance based incentives.

The industry's failure to offer sufficient benefits was illustrated by the fact that 60.1 per cent of survey respondents listed employee turnover as the top issue. Other main issues were motivation of workforce (46.4 per cent), non-management recruitment (43.6 per cent), individual productivity (42.9 per cent), and organizational productivity (40.8 per cent). In 1988, the wages of salaried hotel workers were expected to rise 6 per cent and 5.5 per cent for hourly workers. Food and beverage directors received the most significant salary increases in 1988, probably because the position is difficult to fill (Laventhol and Horwath 1988).

6 The solution Hiemstra (1988) suggests includes: (a) training the unemployed; (b) reducing the high rate of turnover; (c) becoming more creative in its labour practices; and (d) increasing wage rates to be more competitive with other industries.

7 The turnover rate in the hospitality industry is estimated at 104 per cent, which implies that every position slot must be filled once a year. With the cost to replace each hotel worker at $2,500, turnover is a costly exercise.

5 EXPANDING IN A BARRIER-FREE EUROPE

* This chapter was co-authored by Frank Go, Hong Kong Polytechnic University, and Sarah-Jane Dawson, Pannel Kerr Forster, UK.

1 This interview is reproduced by permission and first appeared in the newsletter of Groupe ESC, Lyon's Graduate School of Business.

2 Reproduced by permission, edited speech given by Michael Hirst, former Chairman and Chief Executive of Hilton International and 1993 Corporate Hotelier of the World at a presentation to Barclays De Zoete Wedd 28 April 1993.

6 SUSTAINING THE COMPETITIVENESS OF HONG KONG'S HOTEL INDUSTRY

* The main text of this chapter was jointly authored by Frank Go, Ray Pine and Ricky Yu and a version of it was originally published in the *Cornell Hotel and Restaurant Administration Quarterly*, October 1994, under the heading of 'Hong Kong: Sustaining Competitive Advantage in Asia's Hotel Industry'.

1 Based on an interview with Jean-Marie Leclercq, 7 February 1994.

7 CAPITALIZING ON HUMAN RESOURCES STRATEGY FOR COMPETITIVE ADVANTAGE

* This chapter was co-authored by Frank Go, Dov Zohar, Ray Pine and Ricky Yu.

1 One of the main findings of a report by the International Hotel Association commissioned in 1988, *Hotels of the Future* (Horwath and Horwath) was the statement: 'Throughout the course of our research it has become apparent to us that human resources are perceived to be the single most important issue facing the industry during the next two decades and beyond.'

'This is perhaps not surprising if one reflects that according to the official data provided by some 50 governments to the International Labour Organisation (ILO) some years ago, some 50,000,000 persons were employed in hotels, restaurants, and similar establishments of the countries which responded. It is estimated that the actual figure probably exceeds 100 million workers worldwide. This underlines that there is a constant need for training and human resource development in the hotel industry' (Hulton 1992).

2 Sixteen countries and one British Territory comprised the geographical distribution of the IHA questionnaire: Australia, Austria, Belgium, Britain, Canada,

Ethiopia, France, Germany, Hong Kong, Hungary, Ireland, Kenya, Singapore, Sweden, Switzerland, Thailand, United States of America.

8 REVERSING THE CYCLE OF FAILURE THROUGH ORGANIZATIONAL RENEWAL

1 Thurow (1992) points to the importance of process technology by referring to examples from several industries. The fax machine and compact disc (CD) player were invented in the United States and the Netherlands respectively. However, both are now 'owned' by Japan, which produces fax machines and CDs most efficiently.

2 Berry *et al.* (1990) emphasize the importance of defining the service role and simultaneously indicate that 'the concept of service is vague and non-credible', generally because service standards somehow fail to 'bring a customer focus into the employee's day-to-day reality of service delivery'. 'Service standards are customer expectations stated in a way that is meaningful to employees.' It is therefore essential to clearly comprehend customer expectations prior to developing effective service standards.

3 In 1985–1986, the Gallup Organization asked 2,575 consumers to rate the quality of service provided by different institutions, from '1' for very poor to '10' for very high. Roughly half the respondents gave scores of '7' or lower to supermarkets, banks, airlines, restaurants, hospitals, and hotels. About three-quarters of them awarded such middling scores to department stores and real estate firms, while half felt that auto repair shops and insurance companies provided service deserving a '5' or worse. Among the biggest customer complaints: failure to do work properly; indifferent, unqualified, or rude personnel; slowness; and high cost. (*The Gallup Poll*, 1986 (March 9), Princeton, New Jersey.)

   The Yankelovich Monitor, an annual survey of 2,500 consumers that tracks social change, includes questions about the perceived quality of service in many industries. Only the quality of supermarkets seems to have improved in recent years. Perceived service levels of restaurants, hotels and department stores have not changed much, while those of airlines, banks and cable TV operators have plunged. Moreover, four years of polls conducted by Gallup for the American Society of Quality Control show that US consumers largely believe that service quality has fallen and will continue to fall (as reported by Davidow and Uttal 1989: 3–4).

4 'Most of the seventeen leading service companies that Citicorp studied spent 1 to 2 per cent of their sales on training front-line employees, managers and executives' (Davidow and Uttal 1989: 125). By deduction this implies that most other service companies spent less than 1 to 2 per cent of their sales. Much of the training in service companies focuses exclusively on employee relations with external customers, ignoring workers' relations with 'internal customers' and the importance of team building, according to Robert L. Desatnick (1987) *Managing to Keep the Customer*, San Francisco: Jossey-Bass, pp. 61, 146–153.

5 Hart *et al.* (1984: 96–98) point out that as organizations descend the learning curve, they tend to reap several advantages over time, including: cost advantages because the firms' 'knowledge grows and the cumulative number of units produced increases; workers become more dextrous and efficient in carrying out their tasks as they accumulate experience (management can accelerate the process through training and motivation); managers become more proficient through experience, and the firm as a whole should accordingly improve its

performance in many areas over time; cumulative experience allows firms to lower their costs not only in the labour area but also through new production processes and improved facility design.'

6 Leadership is about a sense of direction. The word 'lead' is derived from an Anglo-Saxon word, which means a road, a way, the path of a ship at sea (Adair 1983). Leadership has been defined in many different ways and therefore Burns (1978) described it as one of the most observed and least understood management phenomena. While leadership and management are not synonymous, they are both important to organizational success. Effective leadership is grounded in an extensive knowledge of the business environment; an intimate understanding of the industry; relationships within the company and industry; a good track record and reputation in a relatively broad set of activities; a keen mind and interpersonal skills; high integrity and a strong desire to lead (Kotter 1988: 62).

9 IMPLEMENTING GLOBALIZATION STRATEGIES

1 See for instance, S. Medlik, *The Business of Hotels* (2nd edn), Oxford: Heinemann, 1980, p. 156.

2 Multinational hotel firms attempt to exploit the advantages that flow from the paradigm of international production. Specifically they try to achieve their goal by:

- Beating trade problems. Where to locate to attract desirable markets?
- Avoiding political problems. Which location offers a politically stable environment?
- Sidestepping regulatory hurdles. Who to merge with or join to avoid licensing and/or regulatory hassles?
- Balancing costs. Where to shift production to run operations at higher average capacity and keep capital costs down?
- Winning technology breakthrough. Being deployed globally helps to develop localized products at the lowest possible cost (*Business Week* 1990).

3 The international hotel industry has a marked concentration in Europe, which had about 47 per cent of the world's hotel rooms in 1988, and in North America with about 29 per cent. The Asia–Pacific region had slightly less than 13 per cent with the balance spread over Africa, Latin America, and the Caribbean. (Sources: WTO 1989; Go and Welch 1991: 14)

10 COMPETING AND COOPERATING IN THE CHANGING TOURISM CHANNEL SYSTEM

* The main body of text in this chapter is reproduced from F.M. Go and A.P. Williams 'Competing and Cooperating in the Changing Tourism Channel System', *Journal of Travel & Tourism Marketing*, vol. 2, nos. 2/3, 1993, Haworth Press Inc., pp. 229–248.

1 Based on company information.

2 This reading by Rita Marie Emmer, Chuck Tauck, Scott Wilkinson, and Richard G. Moore is an abbreviated version of an article appearing under the same title in *The Cornell HRA Quarterly*, vol. 34, no. 6, pp. 80–89, December, 1993.

11 EVOLVING TOWARDS A BUSINESS ECOSYSTEM

1 Observed on a sign in Kowloon Park, Hong Kong.
2 On 17 September 1991, the World Travel & Tourism Environment Research
  Centre was launched at the Oxford Centre for Travel and Leisure Studies,
  Oxford Polytechnic Institute. The Centre is sponsored by the World Travel
  and Tourism Council and its task is to monitor environmental compatibility in
  the industry and to determine what constitutes good practice in this area.
3 A joint venture can be defined as the creation of a jointly owned, but independent organization by two or more separate parent firms as a means to cope
  with competitive uncertainty.

12 CHARTING A NEW COURSE INTO THE TWENTY-FIRST CENTURY

1 R.H. Ballou 'Opportunities for the travel industry in the new world: Examining
  trends that drive changes', Address to the PATA Conference 'Waves of
  Change', Honolulu, Hawaii, 11 May 1993.
2 According to Glenys Coughlan (1993), PATA's Advisory Council Chairman.
3 From a World Tourism Organization leaflet (undated).

Bibliography

Aaker, D.A. (1991) *Managing Brand Equity: Capitalizing on the Value of a Brand Name*, New York: The Free Press.

Abell, D.F. (1980) *Defining the Business: The Starting Point of Strategic Planning*, Englewood Cliffs, N.J.: Prentice-Hall.

Adair, J. (1983) *Effective Leadership*, London: Gower.

Aderhold, P. (1992) 'Bilanz', *Schweizer Wirt schafts Revenue*, No. 2: 48–50.

AH&MA (1989) *Looking Forward: A Management Perspective of Technology in the Lodging Industry*, Washington, DC: American Hotel & Motel Association and Anderson Consulting.

Airbus Industries (1991) *Market Perspectives for Civil Jet Aircraft*, Blagnac, France: Airbus Industries.

Ajami, R. (1988) 'Strategies for Tourism Transnationals in Belize', *Annals of Tourism Research*, 15(4): 517–530.

Akerhielm, P., Dev, C.S. and Noden, M.A. (1990) 'Europe 1992: Neglecting the tourism opportunity', *The Cornell HRA Quarterly*, 31(1): 104–111.

Albrecht, K. (1990) *Service Within: Solving the Middle Management Leadership Crisis*, Homewood, Illinois: Dow Jones–Irwin.

Albrecht, K. and Zemke, R. (1985) *Service America Doing Business in the New Economy*, Homewood, Illinois, Dow Jones–Irwin.

Anon. (1977) *Annual Report*, San Antonio, Texas: La Quinta Motor Inns, Inc.

—— (1987) 'Juergen Bartels: Risk, Planning and Execution', *The Cornell HRA Quarterly*, 28(3) (Nov): 52–56.

—— (1988) 'Grand Met Sells InterContinental Hotels', *Leisure Management*, 8(10): 25.

—— (1989) *Looking Forward: A Management Perspective of Technology in the Lodging Industry*, Washington, DC: American Hotel & Motel Association and Anderson Consulting.

—— (1991) *WTTC Report The Travel and Tourism Industry: Perceptions of Economic Contribution*, Brussels: World Travel & Tourism Council.

—— (1992a) *The European Quality Award 1992*, Eindhoven: European Foundation for Quality Management.

—— (1992b) *Trends in the Hotel Industry* (1992 international edition), San Francisco: Pannell Kerr Forster.

Ansoff, I. (1987) *Corporate Strategy* (revised edn), London: Penguin Books.

Arbel, A. and Geller, A.N. (1983) 'Foreign Exchange Sensitivity: How a Strong Currency Weakens Hotel Revenues', *The Cornell HRA Quarterly*, 24(3): 64–70.

Arbel, A. and Woods, R.H. (1990) 'Debt Hitch-Hiking: How Hotels Found Low-Cost Capital', *The Cornell HRA Quarterly*, 31(3): 105–110.

Argyris, C. and Schou, D.A. (1978) *Organizational Learning: A Theory of Action Perspective*, Reading, Mass., Addison-Wesley.

Ascher, F. (1985) *Tourism: Transnational Corporations and Cultural Identities*, Paris: United Nations Educational, Scientific and Cultural Organization.

Ashworth, G.J. and Tunbridge, J.E. (1990) *The Tourist-Historic City*, London: Belhaven Press.

Ave, J. (1993) (Chairman) 'Message from the Editorial Committee', in Wiendu Nuryanti (ed.), *Universal Tourism Enriching or Degrading Culture*, Yogyakarta: Gadjah Mada University Press.

Baki, A. (1990) 'Turkey: redeveloping tourism', *The Cornell HRA Quarterly*, 31(2): 60–64.

Ballou, R.H. (1993) 'Opportunities for the travel industry in the new world: Examining trends that drive changes', Address to the PATA Conference 'Waves of Change', Honolulu, Hawaii, 11 May.

Band, W.A. (1991) *Value for Customers Designing and Implementing a Total Corporate Strategy*, Toronto: Wiley & Sons.

Bardaracco, J.L. (1991) *The Knowledge Link: How Firms Compete Through Strategic Alliances*, Boston: Harvard Business School Press.

Barge, P. (1993) 'International management contracts', in P. Jones and A. Pizam (eds), *The International Hospitality Industry Organisational and Operational Issues*, New York: Wiley, pp. 117–125.

Baron, R.R. (1975) *Seasonality in Tourism – A Guide to the Analysis of Seasonality and Trends for Policy Making*, London: The Economist Intelligence Unit.

Bartels, J. (1993) 'Global Hotel Power', *The Cornell HRA Quarterly*, 34(6): 10.

Bartlett, C.A. and Ghoshal, S. (1989) *Managing Across Borders – The Transnational Solution*, Boston: Harvard Business School Press.

Bateson, J.E.G. (1978) 'Do We Need Service Marketing?' in *Marketing Consumer Services: New Insights*, Cambridge: Marketing Science Institute (Report No. 77–177).

—— (1989) *Managing Services Marketing*, Chicago: Dryden.

Baum, T. (1988) 'Toward a New Definition of Hotel Management', *The Cornell HRA Quarterly – Educators' Forum 1988*: 36–40.

—— (ed.) (1993) *Human Resource Issues in International Tourism*, London: Heinemann–Butterworth.

Beattie, R. (1991) 'Hospitality Internationalization: An Empirical Investigation', *International Journal of Contemporary Hospitality Management*, 3(4): 14–20.

Becheri, E. (1991) 'Rimini and Co – The End of a Legend? Dealing with the algae effect', *Tourism Management*, 12(3): 229–235.

Bell, C.A (1992) 'Opening up Eastern Europe: New opportunities and new challenges', *The Cornell HRA Quarterly*, 33(6): 53–63.

Bell, D. (1988) 'The World in 2013', *Dialogue*, 81(3): 3–9.

Bellas, C.J. (1982) 'Improving Productivity in the Operations Function', in A. Pizam, R.C. Lewis and P. Manning (eds), *The Practice of Hospitality Management*, Westport, Conn.: AVI Publishing Company Inc., pp. 146–152.

Bennis, W. and Nanus, B (1985) *Leaders: The Strategies for Taking Charge*, New York: Harper & Row.

Benson, K. (1991) *Quoted Hotel Companies: The World Markets*, London: Kleinwort Benson.

Berger, F., Ferguson, D.H. and Woods, R.H. (1989) 'Profiles in Creativity: Companies and Leaders', *The Cornell HRA Quarterly*, 30(2): 98–105.

Berry, L.L., Zeithaml, V.A. and Parasuraman, A. (1990) 'Five Imperatives for Improving Service Quality', *Sloan Management Review*, 31(4): 29–39.

Bitner, M.J. and Booms, B.H. (1982) 'Trends in Travel and Tourism Marketing:

The Changing Structure of Distribution Channels', *Journal of Travel Research*, 20(4): 39–44.

Black, J.S. and Porter, L.W. (1991) 'The managerial behaviors and job performance: A successful manager in Los Angeles may not succeed in Hong Kong', *Journal of International Business Studies*, 22(1): 99–114.

Blank, U. (1989) *The Community Tourism Industry Imperative: The Necessity, The Opportunities, Its Potential*, State College, Pa.: Venture Publishing Inc.

Bodlender, J.A. (1986) 'Integrated Hotel Development for an Enhanced Environment', Presentation at plenary session International Hotel Association 24th Annual Congress, London: Horwath & Horwath (UK) Ltd, 28 October.

Boniface, B.G. and Cooper, C. (1987) *The Geography of Travel and Tourism*, Oxford: Heinemann Professional Publishing.

Bonoma, T.V. (1984) *Managing Marketing*, New York: The Free Press.

Bosselman, F. (1978) *In the Wake of the Tourist: Managing Special Places in Eight Countries*, Washington, DC: The Conservation Foundation.

Brewton, C. (1987) 'A Model for Analyzing the Lodging Industry', *The Cornell HRA Quarterly*, 28(2): 10–12.

Bringham, E.F. and Gapenski, L.C. (1985) *Financial Management: Theory and Practice*, Chicago: The Dryden Press.

Buckley, P.J. (1987) 'Tourism – An Economic Transactions Analysis', *Tourism Management*, 8(3): 190–194.

Buckley, P.J. and Casson, M. (1985) *The Economic Theory of the Multinational Enterprise*, London: Macmillan.

Buckley, P.J., Mirza, H. and Witt, S.F. (1989) 'Japan's International Tourism in the Context of its International Economic Relations', *The Service Industries Journal*, 9(3): 357–383.

Burkart, A.J. and Medlik, S. (1974) *Tourism: Past, Present and Future*, London: Heinemann.

Burns, J.M. (1978) *Leadership*, New York: Harper & Row.

Business International (1986) *A Guide to Corporate Survival and Growth*, New York: BI Corporation.

Business Week (1990) 'The Stateless Corporation', *Business Week*, no. 3159: 98–104 (14 May).

Byrne, A. (1993) 'International hotel consortia', in P. Jones and A. Pizam (eds) *The International Hospitality Industry Organisational and Operational Issues*, New York: Wiley, pp. 3–24.

Calantone, R. and Johas, J. (1984) 'Seasonal Segmentation of the Tourism Market Using a Benefit Segmentation Framework', *Journal of Travel Research*, 23(2) (Fall): 14–24.

Calvo, D. (1974) *Caribbean Regional Study*, Vol. 6, Washington. [A study showing how West Indians have been excluded from managerial posts.]

Carlzon, J. (1987) *Moments of Truth*, Cambridge, Mass.: Ballinger.

Caruso, T.E. (1992) 'Kotler: Future marketers will focus on customer data base to compete globally', *Marketing News*, 8 June, p. 21.

Casse, P. (1989) 'Managing People's Talents: The Leadership Challenge of the 1990s', *Perspectives for Managers*, no. 5, Lausanne: IMEDE.

Cassee, E.Th. (1983) 'Introduction', in E.Th. Cassee and R. Reuland (eds), *The Management of Hospitality*, Oxford: Pergamon Press.

Cave, R.E. (1971) 'International Corporations: The Industrial Economics of Foreign Investment', *Economia*, February.

Cetron, M. and Davies, O. (1989) *American Renaissance: Our Life at the Turn of the 21st Century*, New York: St. Martin's Press.

Chadwick, R.A. (1987) 'Concepts, Definitions and Measures Used in Travel,

Tourism Research', in J.R.B. Ritchie and C.R. Goeldner (eds), *Travel, Tourism and Hospitality Research: A Handbook for Managers and Researchers*, New York: Wiley.

Chandler, A.D. Jr. (1966) *Strategy and Structure*, New York: Doubleday.

—— (1986) 'Technological and Organizational Underpinnings', in A. Teichova, M. Levy-Leboyer and H. Nussbaum (eds), *Multinational Enterprise in Historical Perspective*, Cambridge: Cambridge University Press.

Charan, R. (1991) 'How Networks Reshape Organizations for Results', *Harvard Business Review*, (Sept–Oct): 104–115.

Chase, R.B. and Hayes, R.H. (1991) 'Beefing Up Operations in Service Firms', *Sloan Management Review*, 33(1): 15–26.

Chervenak, L. (1991) 'CRS, The Past, The Present, The Future', *Lodging*, (June): 25–31.

Chorengel, B. and Teare, R. (1992) 'Developing a responsive global network of Hyatt hotels and resorts', in R. Teare and M. Olsen (eds), *International Hospitality Management*, London: Pitman Publishing.

Christensen-Hughes, J. (1992) 'Cultural diversity: The lesson of Toronto hotels', *The Cornell HRA Quarterly*, 33(2): 78–87.

Clark, J.J. and Arbel, A. (1993) 'Producing Global Managers: The Need for a New Paradigm', *The Cornell HRA Quarterly*, 34(4): 83–89.

Clech, C. (1993) 'The European Senior Travel Market: A Golden Opportunity for the Travel and Tourism Industry', in J.R.B. Ritchie, D.E. Hawkins, F. Go, and D. Frechtling (eds), *World Travel and Tourism Review*, Vol. 3, Wallingford, Oxon, CAB International.

Cleverdon, R. (1992) 'Global Tourism Trends: Influences and Determinants', in D.E. Hawkins, J.R.B. Ritchie, F. Go, and D. Frechtling (eds), *World Travel and Tourism Review Indicators, Trends and Issues*, Vol. 2, Wallingford, Oxon: CAB International.

Cleverdon, R. and Edwards, A. (1982) *International Tourism to 1990*, London: The Economist Intelligence Unit, Special Series 4.

Cleverdon, R. and O'Brien, K. (1988) *International Business Travel 1988*, London: Economist Intelligence Unit.

Cobbs, L. (1991) 'Air Transportation Services and the GATT', in D.E. Hawkins, J.R.B. Ritchie, F. Go and D. Frechtling (eds), *World Travel & Tourism Review Indicators, Trends and Forecasts*, Vol. 1, Wallingford, Oxon: CAB International.

Cohen, E. (1972) 'Toward a Sociology of International Tourism', *Social Research* 39(1) (Spring). Reprinted in R.W. McIntosh, and C.R. Goeldner (1990) *Tourism Principles, Practices and Philosophies* (6th edn), New York: John Wiley & Sons, pp. 197–208.

Collier, D.A. (1989) 'Expansion and Development of CRS', *Tourism Management*, (June): 86–88.

—— (1991) 'New Marketing Mix Stresses Service', *The Journal of Business Strategy*, (March/April): 42–45.

Cook Johnson, G. (1991) 'Working Inside Service Excellence: What is the Difference?', Unpublished article, Toronto: REACON Management Inc.

CQ (1985) 'How they started: The growth of four giants', *The Cornell HRA Quarterly*, 26(1): 22–32.

Crask, M. (1981) 'Segmenting the Vacationer Market: Identifying the Vacation Preferences, Demographics and Magazine Readership of Each Group', *Journal of Travel Research*, (Fall): 29–34.

Crompton, J.L. and Richardson, S.L. (1986) 'The Tourism Connection', *Parks & Recreation*, (October): 38–44, 67.

Crosby, P.B. (1979) *Quality is Free*, New York: New American Library.

—— (1990) *Leading The Art of Becoming an Executive*, New York: McGraw-Hill.

Crouch, G.I. and Shaw, R.N. (1990) 'Determinants of International Tourist Flows: Findings from 30 Years of Empirical Research', Paper presented at the 21st Annual Conference of the Travel & Tourism Research Association, 10–14 June, 1990, New Orleans, Louisiana.

Cullen, T.P. (1981) 'Global Gamesmanship: How the Expatriate Manager Copes with Cultural Differences', *The Cornell HRA Quarterly*, 22(3): 18–24.

Czeptiel, J.A. (1980) *Managing Customer Satisfaction in Consumer Service Businesses*, Cambridge, Mass.: Marketing Science Institute.

Czinkota, M.R., Rivoli, P. and Ronkainen, I.A. (1989) *International Business*, New York: Dryden.

Dahlman, C. and Westphal, L. (1983) 'The transfer of technology – Issues in the acquisition of technological capability of developing countries', *Finance and Development*, December.

D'Amore, L.J. (1985) 'A Third Generation of Tourism Thinking Towards a Creative Conspiracy', *Business Quarterly*, Summer.

Dann, G. (1981) 'Tourist Motivation: An Appraisal', *Annals of Tourism Research*, pp. 187–219.

Darwin, C. (1859) *On the Origin of Species by Means of Natural Selection or the Preservation of Favoured Races in the Struggle for Life*, London: John Murray (reprinted in Penguin Classics 1985).

Davidow, W.H. and Uttal, B. (1989) *Total Customer Service*, New York: Harper & Row.

Davidson, R. (1993) 'European business tourism – changes and prospects', *Tourism Management* 14(3): 167–172.

Davis, S. and Davidson, B. (1991) *2020 Vision; Transform your Business Today to Succeed in Tomorrow's Economy*, New York: Simon & Schuster.

Day, G.S. (1990) *Market Driven Strategy: Processes for Creating Value*, New York: The Free Press.

de Jong, H.W. (1985) *Dynamische Markttheorie* (3rd edn), Leiden: Stenfert Kroese.

de Jong, M.W. (1991) *De Dienstensector transacties in transformatie*, Rede uitgesproken bij de aanvaarding van het ambt van bijzonder hoogleraar economie en ruimtelijke organisatie van de dienstensector aan de Universiteit van Amsterdam, Leiden: Stenfert Kroese (8 maart).

de Kadt, E. (1979) *Tourism Passport to Development*, New York: Oxford University Press.

de Wilde, J. (1991) 'How to Train Managers for Going Global', *Business Quarterly*, 55(3): 41–46.

Denison, E. (1974) *Accounting for United States Economic Growth: 1929 – 1969*, Washington: Brookings Institution.

Desatnick, R.L. (1987) *Managing to Keep the Customer*, San Francisco: Jossey-Bass.

Dev, C.S. (1989) 'Operating Environment and Strategy: The Profitable Connection', *The Cornell HRA Quarterly*, 30(2) (August): 9–13.

Dev, C.S. and Olsen, M.D. (1989) 'Environmental Uncertainty, Business Strategy, and Financial Performance: An Empirical Study of the US Lodging Industry', *Hospitality Education & Research Journal*, 13(3): 172.

Dicken, P. (1986) *Global Shift, Industrial Change in a Turbulent World*, London: Harper & Row Publishers.

Dijck, J.J.J. (1990) 'Transnational Management in an Evolving European Context', *The European Management Journal*, 8(4): 474–479.

Dobyns, L. and Crawford-Mason, C. (1991) *Quality or Else: The Revolution in World Business*, Boston, Mass.: Houghton Mifflin.

Drucker, P.F. (1970) 'Helping the Third World to manage', *International Management*, 25(3): 46–49.

—— (1985) *Innovation and Entrepreneurship*, New York: Harper & Row.

—— (1989) *The New Realities: In Government and Politics/In Economics and Business/In Society and World View*, New York: Harper & Row.

Dunning, J.H. (1970) 'Technology, U.S. Investment and European Economic Growth', in C.P. Kindelberger (ed.), *The International Corporation*, Cambridge, Mass.: MIT Press.

—— (1981) *International Production and the Multinational Enterprise*, London: Allen & Unwin.

—— (1989) 'The Study of International Business: A Plea for A More Inter-disciplinary Approach', *Journal of International Business Studies*, XX(3): 411–436.

Dunning, J.H. and McQueen, M. (1982a) 'Multinational Corporations in the International Hotel Industry', *Annals of Tourism Research*, 9(1): 69–90.

—— and —— (1982b) 'The eclectic theory of the multinational enterprise and the international hotel industry', in A.M. Rugman (ed.) *New Theories of the Multinational Enterprise*, London: Croom Helm.

Edgell, D.L. Sr. (1985) *International Trade in Tourism: A Manual for Managers and Executives*, Washington, DC: US Department of Commerce, US Travel and Tourism Administration.

—— (1990) *International Tourism Policy*, New York: Van Nostrand Reinhold.

Edstrom, A. and Lorange, P. (1985) 'Matching strategy and human resources in multinational corporations', *Journal of International Business Studies*, 16 (Fall): 125–137.

Edwards, A. (1987) *Choosing Holiday Destinations: The Impact of Exchange Rates and Inflation*, London: The Economist Publications Limited.

—— (1988) *International Tourism Forecasts to 1999*, London: The Economist Intelligence Unit (Special Report No. 1142).

EIESP (1991) *Education for Careers in European Travel and Tourism* (Executive Summary), London: European Institute of Education and Social Policy (May).

Elfring, T. (1989) 'The Main Features and Underlying Causes of the Shift to Services', *The Service Industries Journal*, 9(3): 337–356.

Etzel, M. and Woodside, A. (1982) 'Segmenting Vacation Markets: The Case of the Distant and Near-Home Traveller', *Journal of Travel Research*, 20(4) (Spring): 10–14.

Farmer, R.N. and Richman, B. (1970) *Comparative Management and Economic Progress*, Bloomington: Cedarwood Press.

Fedler, A. (1987) 'Are Leisure, Recreation and Tourism Interrelated?', *Annals of Tourism Research*, 14(3).

Feldman, J. (1987) 'CRS in the USA', *Travel and Tourism Analyst*, (September): 3–14.

Fieldhouse, D.K. (1986) 'The Multinational: A Critique of a Concept', in A. Teichova, M. Levy-Leboyer and H. Nussbaum (eds), *Multinational Enterprise in Historical Perspective*, Cambridge: Cambridge University Press, pp. 9–29.

Fisher, A.B. (1991) 'Morale Crisis', *Fortune*, 124(12): 70–80.

Fisher, L.D. (1989) 'Rise of the Asian expatriate', *Far East Business*, 22(8) (August): 43–45.

Forbes, J.R. and Forbes, M.S. (1993) 'Special Interest Travel – Creating Today's Market-Driven Experiences', in D.E. Hawkins, J.R.B. Ritchie, F. Go and D. Frechtling (eds), *World Travel and Tourism Review: Indicators, Trends and Forecasts*, Vol. 3, Oxon.: CAB International, pp. 128–134.

Foster, R. (1986) *Innovation: The Attacker's Advantage*, New York: Summit Press.

Four Seasons Hotels & Resorts (1992) *Impressions*, April, p. 4.

Fourastie, J. (1965) *Moderne techniek en economische ontwikkeling*, Utrecht: Aulaboeken.

Foust (1991) 'Marriott is Smoothing Out the Lumps in its Bed', *Business Week*, (April 1): 74–75.

Fox, R.W. (1988) 'Population Images', *The Futurist*, March–April.

Franck, C. (1990) 'Tourism investment in Central and Eastern Europe – pre-conditions and opportunities', *Tourism Management*, 11(4): 333–338.

The Gallup Poll (1986) 9 March, Princeton, New Jersey.

Gamble, P. (1991) 'Trends in Automation in the Worldwide Hotel Industry', in D.E. Hawkins, J.R.B. Ritchie, F. Go, and D. Frechtling (eds), *World Travel and Tourism Review Indicators, Trends and Forecasts*, Vol. 1, Wallingford, Oxon: CAB International.

Gardner, J.W. (1985) *Excellence Can We Be Equal and Excellent Too?* (revised edn), New York: W.W. Norton & Co.

Gee, C.Y., Makens, J.C. and Choy, D.J.L. (1989) *The Travel Industry* (2nd edn), New York: Van Nostrand Reinhold.

Geller, A.N. (1984) *Executive Information Needs in Hotel Companies*, New York: Peat Marwick Mitchell.

—— (1985) 'Tracking the Critical Success Factors for Hotel Companies', *The Cornell HRA Quarterly*, 25(4): 76–81.

German Federal Republic (1989) Deutscher Verkehrs Verlag GMBH, Neuen Medien, *Ti Geschaftsreise*, 22(20): 14–16.

Gershuny, J. and Miles, I. (1983) *The New Services Economy*, London: Frances Pinter.

Ghoshal, S. (1987) 'Global Strategy: An Organizing Framework', *Strategic Management Journal*, Sept–Oct: 425–440.

Gialloreto, L. (1988) *Strategic Airline Management: The Global War Begins*, London: Pitman.

Gibbs, N. (1989) 'How America Has Run Out of Time', *Time*, 133(17): 48–55.

Gladwin, T.N. and Walter, I. (1980) *Multinationals Under Fire*, John Wiley & Sons.

Go, F. (1981) 'Hospitality and Heritage: A Profitable Partnership', in A. Pizam, R.C. Lewis, and P. Manning (eds), *The Practice of Hospitality Management*, Westport: AVI Publishing.

—— (1986) 'Four Seasons: In Pursuit of Perfection', *Hotels and Restaurant International*, 20(1): 34.

—— (1988) 'Holiday homes in Europe', *Travel and Tourism Analyst*, February, no. 3: 20–33.

—— (1989a) 'International Hotel Industry – Capitalizing on Change', *Tourism Management*, 10(3): 195–200.

—— (1989b) 'Resorts in North America: Problems and Prospects', *Travel & Tourism Analyst*, no. 1, London: The Economist Intelligence Unit.

—— (1991a) 'Human Resources Strategy and Competitive Advantage', A study presented at The International Hotel Association Forum on Human Resources, Strasbourg, 22 November.

—— (1991b) 'The Role of Computerized Reservation Systems in the Hospitality Industry', Address to the delegates of the Tourism and Hospitality Management Conference, University of Surrey, Guildford, UK, 25–27 September.

Go, F. and Christensen, J. (1989) 'Going Global', *The Cornell HRA Quarterly*, 30(3): 72–79.

Go, F. and Dev, C.S. (1990) 'The Internationalization of the Lodging Industry – New Realities of the Nineties', Unpublished paper.

Go, F. and Haywood, K.M. (1990) 'Marketing of the Service Process: State of The Art in Tourism, Recreation, and Hospitality Industries', in C.P. Cooper (ed.), *Progress in Tourism, Recreation and Hospitality Management*, Vol. 2, London: Bellhaven Press.

Go, F. and Ritchie, J.R.B. (1990) 'Introduction' (to a Special Issue on Trans-nationalism and Tourism), *Tourism Management*, 11(4): 287–290.

Go, F., Sung, S.P., Uysal, M. and Mihalik, B.J. (1990) 'Decision criteria for transnational hotel expansion', *Tourism Management*, 11(4): 297–304.

Go, F. and Welch, P. (1991) *Competitive Strategies for the International Hotel Industry*, London: The Economist Intelligence Unit (Special Report No. 1180, March).

Godet, M. and Barre, R. (1988) 'Into the Next Decade: Major Trends and Uncertainties of the 1990s', *Futures*, 20(4) (August): 410–423.

Golf Digest Almanac (1989) *Christian Science Monitor*, 24 April: 9.

Goodall, B. (1989) 'Tourist Accommodation: A Destination Area Perspective', *Built Environment*, 15(2): 78–91.

Government of Canada (1984) *A Profile of the Canadian Lodging Industry from a Tourism Perspective*, Report No. 2 (August), Ottawa: Tourism Canada.

—— (1988a) *Applications of Technology in the Tourism Industry* (Main Report), Ottawa: Tourism Canada.

—— (1988b) *Canadian Tourism Facts* (Research Directorate), Ottawa: Tourism Canada, February.

—— (1988c) *The Challenges in Tourism Product Development*, Ottawa: Tourism Canada, May.

—— (1989a) *Canadian Tourism Industry Performance 1988* (Research Directorate), Ottawa: Tourism Canada, October.

—— (1989b) 'Competition', *Tourism Intelligence Bulletin*, Tourism Canada, May.

—— (1989c) 'Legislation and Government Activity', *Tourism Intelligence Bulletin*, Tourism Canada, April.

Groote, P.D. (1987) *De Belgische hotelsector: een economisch-geografische analyse*, Leuven: Universitaire Pers.

Grosse, R. and Kujawa, D. (1988) *International Business Theory and Managerial Applications*, Homewood, Illinois: Irwin.

—— and —— (1992) *International Business Theory and Managerial Applications* (2nd edn), Boston: Irwin.

Guerrier, Y. and Lockwood, A.J. (1989) 'Managing Flexible Working in Hotels', *The Services Industries Journal*, 9(3): 406–419.

Gunn, C.A. (1972) *Vacationscape Designing Tourist Regions*: Austin, Texas: Bureau of Business Research, The University of Texas.

—— (1988) *Tourism Planning* (2nd edn), New York: Taylor & Francis.

Hall, A. and Braithwait, R. (1990) 'Caribbean Cruise Tourism: A Business of Transnational Partnerships', *Tourism Management*, 11(4) (December): 339–347.

Hall, D. (1994) 'The challenges of international tourism in Eastern Europe', *Tourism Management*, 13(1): 41–44.

Halsey, S. (1976) 'To the Highest Concept of Professionalism for the Travel Industry', Address at the inauguration of the New School for Social Research's graduate degree programme in Tourism and Travel Administration, 1 October.

Hamel, G. (1991) 'Competition for Competence and Interpartner Learning Within Strategic Alliances', *Strategic Management Journal*, 12: 83–103.

Hamilton, J.L. (1972) 'Tourism: Private Benefits Versus Public Cost', *The Cornell HRA Quarterly*, 13(3): 61–64.

Hanada, M. (1987) 'Management themes in the age of globalization – Exploring paths for the globalization of the Japanese corporation', 20(2) (Autumn): 19–26.

Handy, C. (1989) *The Age of Unreason*, Boston: Harvard Business School Press.

Hara, T. and Eyster, J.J. (1990) 'Japanese Hotel Investment: A Matter of Tradition and Reality', *The Cornell HRA Quarterly*, 31(3): 98–104.

Harper, T. (1990) 'Closing the price gap: Mid-range travel takes off', *International Herald Tribune*, March 3/4: 16.

Harris, L. (1987) *Inside America*, New York: Random House.

Hart, C.W.L., Heskett, J.L. and Sasser, W.E. (1990) 'The Profitable Art of Service Recovery', *Harvard Business Review*, (July–August): 148–156.

Hart, C.W., Spizen, G. and Wyckoff, D. (1984) 'Scale Economies and the Experience Curve, Is Bigger, Better for Restaurant Companies', *The Cornell HRA Quarterly*, 25(1): 90–103.

Hassan, S.S. (1986) *Marketing Hotel Operations: An investigation into the Marketing Behaviour of National and International Chain Affiliated Hotels Operating in Egypt*, Glasgow: The University of Strathclyde.

Heape, R. (1987) 'Inclusive Tours – An Untapped Market', *Tourism Management*, 8(2): 169–170.

Heath, R. (1993) 'Hong Kong and Singapore far ahead of rivals in crucial area' *South China Morning Post*, 26 August: 4 (Business).

Hecksher, E. and Ohlin, B. (1933) *Interregional and International Trade*, Cambridge, Mass.: Harvard University Press.

Heenan, D.A. and Perlmutter, H.V. (1979) *Multinational Organization Development*, Addison-Wesley Publishing Company.

Heskett, J.L. (1986) *Managing in the Service Economy*, Boston: Harvard Business School Press.

—— (1987) 'Lessons in The Service Sector', *Harvard Business Review*, No. 2 (March–April): 118–126.

Heskett, J.L., Sasser, W.E. and Hart, C.W.L. (1990) *Service Breakthroughs – Changing the Rules of the Game*, New York: Free Press.

Hickman, C.R. and Silva, M.A. (1987) *The Future 500: Creating Tomorrow's Organizations Today*, New York: Nal Penguin.

Hiemstra, S.J. (1988) *Employment Strategies in the Lodging Industry*. Phase III study conducted for The Hospitality, Lodging and Travel Research Foundation, American Hotel and Motel Association. West Lafayette, Indiana: Purdue University.

—— (1990) 'Employment Policies and Practices in the Lodging Industry', *International Journal of Hospitality Management*, 9(3): 207–221.

Hill, C.W.L. and Jones, G.R. (1989) *Strategic Management: An Integrated Approach*, Boston: Houghton Mifflin Co.

Hirst, M. (1993) Address given by the former Chairman and Chief Executive of Hilton International Co. to Barclays De Zoete Wedd, London on 28 April.

Hitchins, F. (1991) 'The Influence of Technology on UK Travel Agents', *Travel & Tourism Analyst*, 3: 88–105.

HKCSI (1993) *Service Sector Statistics in Hong Kong 1993*, Hong Kong Coalition of Service Industries.

HKHA (1992) *Annual Report 1991/1992*, Hong Kong Hotels Association, p. 5.

—— (1993) Information supplied to the author by Manuel Woo, Executive Director, Hong Kong Hotels Association.

HKTA (1993) *Visitor Arrival Statistics 1992/1993*, Hong Kong Tourist Association.

—— (1985–1992) *Statistical Review of Tourism in Hong Kong 1985–1992*, Hong Kong Tourist Association.

HKU (1992) A forum on the megalopolis, organised by University of Hong Kong, 30 October.

Hodgson, A. (ed.) (1987) *The Travel and Tourism Industry Strategies for the Future*, Oxford: Pergamon Press.

Hofer, C.W. (1976) 'Conceptual Scheme for Formulating a Total Business Strategy' (Harvard Business School Case), Boston, Mass: Harvard Business School.

Hofstede, G. (1980) *Cultures Consequences: International Differences in Work-related Values*, Beverly Hills, Calif.: Sage.

Holloway, J.C. (1989) *The Business of Tourism*, London: Pitman Publishing.

Hopper, M.D. (1990) 'Rattling SABRE – New Ways to Compete on Information', *Harvard Business Review*, (May/June): 118–125.

Horsburgh, S. (1991) 'Resources in the International Hotel Industry: A Framework for Analysis', *International Journal of Contemporary Hospitality Management*, 3(4): 30–36.

Horwath (1993) *The Case for Hotel Management Contracts*, London: Horwath Consulting.

Horwath and Horwath (1987) *Worldwide Hotel Industry*, New York: Horwath and Horwath.

—— and —— (1988) *Worldwide Hotel Industry*. Horwath and Horwath.

Hostage, G.M. (1975) 'Quality Control in a Service Business', *Harvard Business Review*, (July–August): 98–106.

Hotels & Restaurants International (1987) 'H&R's Panel of Experts Explore Strategies for a Successful Management Contract', *Hotels & Restaurants International*, (August): 62–69.

—— (1988) 'Top 200: An Exclusive Report on the World's Largest Hotel Chains', *Hotels & Restaurants International*, July.

—— (1993) 'Hotels, 325 The world's largest 200 companies', 27(7): 39–41.

HTM (1991) A survey about the subsidiaries of MNHCs in China conducted by the students of the Hotel and Tourism Management Department of Hong Kong Polytechnic in 1991 as degree course assignment. Throughout the survey various published literature and company reports were reviewed, and key personnel of hotel corporations were interviewed.

Hugill, P.J. (1985) 'The Rediscovery of America: Elite Automobile Tourism', *Annals of Tourism Research*, 12(3): 435–447.

Hulton, T. (1992) 'Human Resource Development Issues and Initiatives in the Hotel Industry: The IHA Perspective', in D.E. Hawkins, J.R.B. Ritchie, F. Go and D. Frechtling (eds), *World Travel & Tourism Review Indicators, Trends and Issues*, Vol. 2, Wallingford, Oxon: CAB International.

Hutton, J. (1988) *The World of the International Manager*, Oxford: Philip Allan.

Hymer, S.H. (1976) *The International Operations of National Firms: A Study of Direct Foreign Investment*, Cambridge, Mass.: MIT Press.

ICAO (1988) *Civil Aviation Statistics of the World – ICAO Statistical Yearbook 1987*, Montreal: International Civil Aviation Organization.

IHA (1988) *Hotels of the Future: Strategies and Action Plan*, Paris: International Hotel Association.

—— (1993) *The Case for Hotel Management Contract*, Paris: International Hotel Association.

ILO (1973) *Multinational Enterprise and Social Policy*, Geneva: International Labour Office

—— (1989) *General Report, Hotel, Catering and Tourism Committee, First Session Report* Geneva: International Labour Organization.

Imai, M. (1986) *Kaizen: The Key to Japan's Competitive Success*, New York: Random House.

Ishikawa, K. (1985) *What is Total Quality Control? The Japanese Way* (translated by D.J. Lu), Englewood Cliffs, N.J.: Prentice-Hall.

Jafari, J. (1988) 'Introduction to Tourism – A Vital Force for Peace', Address presented at The First Global Peace Conference, Montreal.

Jansen-Verbeke, M. (1988) *Leisure, Recreation and Tourism in Inner Cities: Explorative Case-Studies*, Nijmegen: Katholieke Universiteit – Geografisch en Planologisch Instituut.

Jenkins, C.L. and Henry, B.M. (1982) 'Government Involvement in Tourism in Developing Countries', *Annals of Tourism Research*, 9(4): 499–521.

Jenkins, D. and Frechtling, DC (1990) *World Tourism Model Simulations for West Germany, 1990–93*, Tourism Policy Forum Background Papers, Washington, DC: The George Washington University, Oct 30–Nov 2.

Jobes, P. (1984) 'Old Timers and New Mobile Lifestyles', *Annals of Tourism Research*, pp. 181–189.

Johnson, R. (1991) 'A Strategy for Service – Disney Style', *The Journal of Business Strategy*, (September/October): 38–44.

Johnston, W.B. (1991) 'Global Workforce 2000: The New World Labour Market', *Harvard Business Review.* 115–127.

Jones, C.B. (1993) *Applications of Database Marketing in the Tourism Industry*, PATA Occasional paper series (Paper no. 1), San Francisco: Pacific Asia Travel Association. This paper appears as paper no. 1 in the PATA Occasional Papers series.

Jones, P. and Pizam, A. (eds) (1993) 'International hotel consortia', in *The International Hospitality Industry Organisational and Operational Issues*, New York: Wiley.

Kahler, R. (1983) *International Marketing* (5th edn), Cincinnati: South-Western Publishing Co.

Kaiser, C. Jr. and Helber, L.E. (1978) *Tourism Planning and Development*, Boston: CBI Publishing.

Kanter, R.M. (1983) *The Change Masters Corporate Entrepreneurs at Work*, London: Unwin.

Kaplan, R.S. and Norton, D.P. (1992) 'The Balanced Scorecard – Measures that Drive Performance', *Harvard Business Review*, (Jan–Feb): 71–79.

Katz, D. and Kahn, R.L. (1978) *The Social Psychology of Organizations* (2nd edn), New York: John Wiley & Sons.

Kaven, W.K. (1974) 'Channels of Distribution in the Hotel Industry', in J.M. Rathmell (ed.), *Marketing in the Service Sector*, Cambridge, Mass.: Winthrop Publishers Inc., pp. 114–121.

Keegan, W.J. (1989) *Global Marketing Management* (4th edn), Englewood Cliffs, N.J.: Prentice-Hall.

Kendall, K.W. and Booms, B.H. (1989) 'Consumer Perceptions of Travel Agencies: Communications, Images, Needs, and Expectations', *Journal of Travel Research*, 27(4): 29–37.

Kindleberger, C. (1969) *Direct Investment Abroad*, New Haven, Conn.: Yale University Press.

Kirkbride, P.S. and Tang, S.F.Y. (1989) *The Present State of Personnel Management in Hong Kong*, The Management Development Centre of Hong Kong, Vocational Training Council.

Koepp, S. (1987) 'Pul-eeze, Will Somebody Help Me?', *Time*, 28(34), February 2.

Kogut, B. (1990) 'International Sequential Advantages and Network Flexibility', in C.A. Bartlett, Y. Doz and G. Hedlund (eds), *Managing the Global Firm*, London: Routledge.

Kolde, E.J. (1985) *Environment of International Business* (2nd edn) Boston: Kent Publishing Company.

Kotler, P. (1980a) *Marketing Management*, (4th edn), Englewood Cliffs, N.J.: Prentice-Hall.

—— (1980b) *Principles of Marketing*, Englewood Cliffs, N.J.: Prentice-Hall.

—— (1984) 'Dream Vacations: The Booming Market for Designed Experiences', *The Futurist*, XVIII(5): 7–14.

Kotter, J.P. (1988) *The Leadership Factor*, New York: The Free Press.

Kouzes, J.M. and Posner, B.Z. (1987) *The Leadership Challenge: How to get extraordinary things done in organizations*, San Francisco: Jossey-Bass.

Krippendorf, J. (1987) *The Holiday Makers: Understanding the Impact of Leisure and Travel*, Oxford: Heinemann.

Kuin, P. (1972) 'The magic of multinational management', *Harvard Business Review*, (Nov/Dec): 92–100.

Kurent, H. (1991) 'Tourism in the 1990s: Threats and Opportunities', in D.E. Hawkins, J.R.B. Ritchie, F. Go and D. Frechtling (eds), *World Travel and Tourism Review, Indicators, Trends and Forecasts*, Vol. 1, Wallingford, Oxon: CAB International.

Labich, K. (1990) 'American Takes On The World', *Fortune*, 122(7): 40–48.

Lakatos, P.A.M. and Van Kralingen, R.M. (1985) *Naar 1990 Een Kwestie van Tijd en Geld*, Amsterdam: Elsevier.

Lambooy, J.G. (1988) *Regionale Economische Dynamiek een inleiding in de economische geografie*, Muiderberg: Coutinho.

Lane, H.E. and van Hartesvelt, M. (1983) *Essentials of Hospitality Administration*, Reston, Virginia: Reston Publishing Co., Inc.

Lattin, T.W. (1987) 'Hotel Monopoly', *The Cornell HRA Quarterly*, 27(4): 10–12.

Laurent, A. (1986) 'The Cross-Cultural Puzzle of International Human Resources Management', *Human Resources Management*, 25: 91–102.

Laventhol and Horwath (1987) *US Lodging Industry*, Philadelphia: Laventhol and Horwath.

—— (1988) *US Lodging Industry Compensation Survey*, Philadelphia: Laventhol and Horwath.

Laventhol and Horwath, and The Urban Land Institute, Washington, DC (1984) *Hotel/Motel Development*, Washington, DC, p. 19.

Lawler, E.E. (1981) *Pay and Organizational Development*, Reading, Mass.: Addison-Wesley.

Lecraw, D.J. and Morrison, A.J. (1991) 'Transnational Corporation – Host Country Relations: A Framework for Analysis', in *Essays of International Business*, no. 9 (Sept), Columbia: The University of South Carolina.

Leigh, B. (1987) 'The Two-headed Chairmanship that Keeps Accor Soaring', *International Management*, January.

Leitch, C. (1989) 'Market Segmentation Continues to Drive Today's Lodging Markets', *Canadian Hotel & Restaurant*, 67(3) (March): 20.

Lesure, J.D. (1985) '1910–1985: Years of Economic Impact', *Lodging*, 10(9) (June).

Leven, M.A. (1982) 'The Growing Distance Between the Buyer and the User: Channels of Distribution', in A. Pizam, R.C. Lewis and P. Manning (eds), *The Practice of Hospitality Management*, Westport, Conn.: AVI Publishing Company Inc.

Levitt, T. (1983a) 'The Globalization of Markets', *Harvard Business Review*, (Sept–Oct): 26–28.

—— (1983b) *The Marketing Imagination*, New York: The Free Press.

Lewis, R.C. and Chambers, R.E. (1989) *Marketing Leadership in Hospitality Foundations and Practices*, New York: Van Nostrand Reinhold.

Lewis, R.C. and Pizam, A. (1981) 'Guest Surveys: A Missed Opportunity', *The Cornell HRA Quarterly*, (November): 37–44.

Li, S. (1994) 'They raze hotels, don't they?', *Window*, 28 Jan, p. 57.

Lickorish, L.J. (1987) 'Trends in Industrial Countries', *Tourism Management*, 8(2): 92–95.

Lickorish, L.J. and Kershaw, A.G. (1958) *The Travel Trade*, London: Practical Press.

Litteljohn, D. (1985) 'Towards an economic analysis of trans/multinational hotel companies', *International Journal of Hospitality Management*, 4(4): 157–165.

—— (1993) 'Western Europe', in P. Jones and A. Pizam (eds), *The International Hospitality Industry Organisational and Operational Issues*, New York: Wiley, pp. 3–24.

Litteljohn, D. and Beattie, R. (1991) 'The European hotel industry corporate structures and expansion strategies', Paper presented at the 'Tourism and hospitality management – established disciplines or ten year wonders?', Surrey University Conference 24–27 September 1991, Edinburgh: Napier Polytechnic.

Litteljohn, D. and Roper, A. (1991) 'Changes in international hotel companies' strategies', in R. Teare and A. Boer (eds), *Strategic Hospitality Management*, Cassell Education Limited, pp. 194–212.

Livingstone, J.M. (1989) *The Internationalization of Business*, Oxford: Macmillan.

—— (1992) 'The European hotel industry corporate structures and expansion strategies', *Tourism Management*, 13(1): 27–33.

Lockwood, A. and Guerrier, Y. (1990) 'Labour Shortages in the International Hotel Industry', *Travel & Tourism Analyst*, no. 6: 17–35.

Lodging (1987) The Management Magazine of the American Hotel & Motel Association.

Lodging Hospitality (1988) 'Performance by Hotel Type', *Lodging Hospitality*, August.

Loving, Jr. R. (1978) 'Hilton International Has 75 Palatial Profit Centers', *Fortune*, 28 August, p. 72.

Lum, H.W. and Graham, P. (1984) 'The capital budget analysis of foreign investments', in A. Sweeny and R. Rachlin (eds), *Handbook of International Financial Management*, New York: McGraw-Hill, pp. 1–7, 25.

Mabry, M. (1989) 'Why the Fuss? Just Ask the Japanese', *Newsweek*, 31 July, p. 48.

McArdle, J. (1989) 'Product Branding – The Way Forward', *Tourism Management*, 10(3): 201.

McCarrol, T. (1989) 'Big Eagles and Sitting Ducks', *Time* (15 May).

McDonnell Douglas (1989) *Outlook for Commercial Aircraft 1988–2002*, Long Beach: McDonnell Douglas.

McGuffie, J. (1990) 'Hotels in the UK survey of a buoyant expanding industry', *Travel and Tourism Analyst*, (Sept): 15–32.

McIntosh, R.W. and Goeldner, C.R. (1990) *Tourism Principles, Practices, and Philosophies* (6th edn), New York: John Wiley & Sons.

McLuhan, M. (1964) *Understanding the Media: The Extension of Man*, New York: McGraw-Hill.

McNulty, R. and Wafer, P. (1990) 'Tourism Management: Transnational Corporations and Tourism Issues', *Tourism Management*, 11(4) (December): 291–295.

McQueen, M. (1983) 'Appropriate policies towards multinational hotel corporations in developing countries', *World Development*, 11(2): 141–152.

—— (1989) 'Multinationals in Tourism', in S.F. Witt and L. Moutinho (eds), *Tourism Marketing and Management Handbook*, New York: Prentice-Hall, pp. 285–289.

Makridakis, S.G. (1990) *Forecasting, Planning and Strategy for the 21st Century*, New York: Free Press.

Mansfield, E. (1974) 'Technology and Technological Change', in J.H. Dunning (ed.), *Economic Analysis and the Multinational Enterprise*, London: George Allen & Unwin Ltd.

Marriott Hotels and Resorts (1986) A nationwide survey of 1,513 adult Americans conducted by Audits & Surveys, Inc. between 20 Nov and 3 Dec 1986.

Marriott (1988) *Annual Report* 1988, Bethesda, Maryland: Marriott Corporation.

Mathieson, A. and Wall, G. (1982) *Tourism: Economic, Physical and Social Impacts*, Burnt Mill, Harlow, Essex: Longman Scientific and Technical.

Meder, R. (1990) 'Hong Kong hotels: Americans buy in, local firms buy out', *Hong Kong: Amcham*, 22(5) (May): 15–28.

Meetings and Conventions (1987) *Meetings Market Report* (April).

Middleton, V.T.C. (1988) *Marketing in Travel and Tourism*, Oxford: Heinemann.

Mill, R.C. and Morrison, A. (1985) *The Tourism System: An Introductory Text*, Englewood Cliffs, N.J.: Prentice-Hall.

Miller, D. and Friesen, P.H. (1984) *Organizations: A Quantum View*, Englewood Cliffs, N.J.: Prentice-Hall.

Mintzberg, H. (1987) 'Crafting Strategy', *Harvard Business Review*, 65(4) (July–August): 71.

—— (1989) *Mintzberg on Management: Inside Our Strange World of Organizations*, New York: The Free Press.

—— (1991) 'The Effective Organization: Forces and Forms', *Sloan Management Review*, (Winter): 54–67.

Mintzberg, H. and Quinn, J.B. (1992) 'Strategy Process: Concepts and Contexts', London: Prentice-Hall.

Miura, Y. (1989) 'Success Strategy: Nikko Hotels International Smiles a Hearty Smile', in G.W. Shames and W.G. Glover (eds), *World Class Service*, Yarmouth, Maine: Intercultural Press.

Moore, J.F. (1993) 'Predators and prey: A new ecology of competition', *Harvard Business Review*, (July–Aug): 65–77.

Motel/Hotel Insider (1986) 'Foreign Investors Return for Hotel Investment', *Motel/Hotel Insider*, Weekly Newsletter, 27(29).

Moutinho, L. (1989) 'Hotel Marketing Strategies for 1992: Uniqueness or Me-Too-ism?', *Built Environment*, 15(2): 138–145.

Mowlana, H. and Smith, G. (1990) 'Tourism, Telecommunications, and Trans-national Banking: A Framework for Policy Analysis', *Tourism Management*, 11(4) (December): 315–324.

—— (1992) 'Trends in Telecommunications and the Tourism Industry: Coalitions, Regionalism, and International Welfare Systems', in D.E. Hawkins, J.R.B. Ritchie, F. Go and D. Frechtling (eds), *World Travel and Tourism Review Indicators, Trends and Issues*, Vol. 2, Wallingford, Oxon: CAB International.

Murphy, P.E. (1985) *Tourism: A Community Approach*, London: Routledge.

Naisbitt, J. and Aburdene, P. (1985) *Re-Inventing the Corporation: Transforming Your Job and Your Company for the New Information Society*, New York: Warner Books.

—— and —— (1990) *Ten New Directions for the 1990s Megatrends 2000*, New York: William Morrow.

Nash, N.C. (1977) 'Americans hit Japanese on promotions', *The New York Times*, 31 May, p. 39.

Negandhi, A.R. and Baliga, B.R. (1979) *Quest for Survival and Growth: A Comparative Study of American, European, and Japanese Multinationals*, New York: Praeger Publishers.

Negandhi, A.R. and Serapio, M.G. (1991) 'Management strategies and policies of Japanese multinational companies: A re-examination', *Management Japan*, 24(1) (Spring): 25–32.

New World Development Company (1993) *New World Development Company Annual Report*, Hong Kong.

The New York Times (1988) 'Why All Those People Feel They Never Have Any Time', *The New York Times*, 2 January.

Normann, R. (1984) *Service Management Strategy and Leadership in Service Businesses*, Chichester: John Wiley & Sons.

Normann, R. and Ramirez, R. (1993) 'Form value chain to value constellation', *Harvard Business Review*, (July–Aug): 65–77.

Northern Telecom (1990) 'FibreWorld: Changing the Landscape of Global Telecommunications', *Northern Telecom Limited 1989 Annual Report*, Toronto.

O'Brien, J.G. (1988) 'Is the U.S. Travel Industry Competitive?', *Business America* (15 Feb): 10–12.

O'Toole, J. (1985) *Vanguard Management: Redesigning the Corporate Future*, New York: Doubleday.

OECD (1988) 'The Labour Markets In The Hotel Industries of Member Countries', in *Tourism Policy and International Tourism in OECD Countries*, Paris: Organization for Economic Cooperation and Development.

—— (1989) *National and International Tourism Statistics, 1974–1985*, Paris: Organization for Economic Cooperation and Development.

—— (1992) *The OECD Declaration and Decisions on International Investment and Multinational Enterprise: 1991 Review*, Paris: Organization for Economic Cooperation and Development.

Ohmae, K. (1982) *The Mind of the Strategist: Business Planning for Competitive Advantage*, New York: Penguin.

—— (1986) 'Becoming a Triad Power: The New Global Corporation', *International Marketing Review*, 3(3) (Autumn): 7–20.

—— (1989) 'The global logic of strategic alliances', *Harvard Business Review*, (March–April): 143–154.

Olferman, J. and Robbins, K.L. (1987) 'Standardisation versus differentiation', *European Management Journal*, 5(4): 250–256.

Olsen, M. (1991) 'Environmental Scan: Global Hospitality Industry Trends', in D.E. Hawkins, J.R.B. Ritchie, F. Go and D. Frechtling (eds), *World Travel & Tourism Review, Indicators, Trends and Forecasts*, Vol. 1, Wallingford, Oxon: CAB International, pp. 120–124.

Ostry, S. (1990) 'Governments and Corporations in a Shrinking World: Trade and Innovation Policies in the United States, Europe and Japan', *The Columbia Journal of World Business*, XXV(1/2): 10–16.

Parasuraman, A., Berry, L.L. and Zeithaml, V.A. (1983) 'Service Firms Need Marketing Skills', *Business Horizons*, 26(6) (November/December).

Park, C.W. and Smith, D.C. (1986) *Competitors of Innovative Marketing Strategies*, Cambridge, Mass.: Marketing Science Institute (Report no. 86–109).

Parsons, D. (1991) 'The Making of Managers: Lessons from an International Review of Tourism Management Education Programmes', *Tourism Management*, 12(3): 197–207.

PBC (1990) *Toeristisch Nederland en Europa 1992*, Verslag van het rapport Europa 1992 De Nederlandse toerisme branche, Den Haag: Public Affairs Consultants BV.

Pearce, P. and Caltabiano, M. (1983) 'Inferring Travel Motivation from Traveller Experiences', *Journal of Travel Research*: 16–20.

Peartree, J. (1993) 'Holding the fort at the Hilton', *Asian Hotel and Catering Times*, 16(12) (June).

Pedler, M., Burgoyne, J. and Boydell, T. (1991) *The Learning Company: A Strategy for Sustainable Development*, Berkshire, UK: McGraw Hill.

Peisley, T. (1986) 'Timeshare in Europe: two part review of the industry', *Travel and Tourism Analyst*, (July): 35–44.

Perlmutter, H.J. (1967) 'Social architectural problems of the multinational firms', *Quarterly Journal of AIESEC International*, 3(3) (August).

Peters, T. (1987) *Thriving on Chaos: Handbook for a Management Revolution*, New York: Alfred A. Knopf.

Pfau, B., Detzel, D., and Geller, A. (1991) 'Satisfy Your Internal Customers', *The Journal of Business Strategy*, 12(6): 9–13.

Pine, R.J. (1991) 'Technology Transfer in the Hotel Industry, Ph.D. thesis, The University of Bradford.

Pine, R.J., Boundy, J. Ruddy, J. and Chou, K.L. (1989) 'Hotels in Hong Kong' *Travel and Tourism Analyst*, no. 2, London: Economist Intelligence Unit.

PKF (1990) *Trends in the Hotel Industry* (USA edn), Houston, Texas: PKF Consulting, p. 41.

Poon, A. (1988) 'Innovation and the Future of Caribbean Tourism', *Tourism Management*, 9(3): 213–220.

—— (1989) 'Competitive strategies for a "new tourism" in C.P. Cooper (ed.), *Progress in tourism, recreation and hospitality management*, Vol. 1, London and New York: Belhaven Press.

Porter, M.E. (1980) *Competitive Strategy: Techniques for Analyzing Industries and Competitors*, New York: The Free Press.

—— (1985) *Competitive Advantage: Creating and Sustaining Superior Performance*, New York: The Free Press.

—— (1987) 'Changing Patterns of International Competition', in D.J. Teece (ed.), *The Competitive Challenge Strategies for Industrial Innovation and Renewal*, New York: Harper & Row.

—— (1990) *Competitive Advantage of Nations*, New York: Free Press.

Porter, M.E. and Millar, V.E. (1985) 'How Information Gives You Competitive Advantage', *Harvard Business Review*, (July–Aug): 149–160.

Pred, A.R. (1977) *City Systems in Advanced Economies: Past Growth, Present Process and Future Development Options*, New York: John Wiley.

Price, D.G. and Blair, A.M. (1989) *The Changing Geography of the Service Sector*, London: Belhaven Press.

Quinn, J.B., Doorley, T.L. and Paquette, P.C. (1990) 'Beyond Products: Services Based Strategy', *Harvard Business Review*, (March/April): 58–67.

Raaij, W.F.V. and Francken, D.A. (1984) 'Vacation Decisions, Activities, and Satisfactions', *Annals of Tourism Research*, 11(1): 101–112.

Rapp, S. and Collins, T. (1992) *The Great Marketing Turnaround: The Age of the Individual and How to Profit From It*, New York: Plume/Penguin.

Rathmell, J.M. (1974) *Marketing in the Service Sector*, Cambridge, Mass.: Winthrop.

Reich, R.B. (1990) 'Who Is Us?', *Harvard Business Review*, 9(1): 53–64.

Reichel, A. (1986) 'Competition and Barriers to Entry in Service Industries: The Case of the American Lodging Business', in R.C. Lewis, T.J. Beggs, M. Shaw and S.A. Croffoot (eds), *The Practice of Hospitality Management II*, Westport, Conn.: AVI Publishing Company, Inc., pp. 146–152.

Reuland, R., Choudry, J. and Mortier, W. (1989) *The 1992 Challenge for the Hotel, Restaurant and Cafe Industry*, Paris, France: Confederation of National Hotel and Restaurant Associations in the European Community (HOTREC).

Reynolds, P.C. (1990) 'The Internationalization of the Hotel Companies: Western Theory/Asian Practice', M.Phil. Thesis, Hong Kong Polytechnic.

Rice, F. (1993) 'Marriott know when to change the game', *Fortune*, 127(13) (June): 59–60.

Richter, L.K. (1989) *The Politics of Tourism in Asia*, Honolulu: University of Hawaii Press.

Rietbergen, T.V., Bosman, J., and Smidt, M. de (1990) *Internationalisering van de dienstensector, Nederlandse ondernemingen in modiaal perspectif*, Muiderberg: Dick Coutinho.

Ritchie, J.R.B. (1991) 'Global Tourism Policy Issues: An Agenda for the 1990s', in D.E. Hawkins, J.R.B. Ritchie, F. Go and D. Frechtling (eds), *World Travel and Tourism Review: Indicators, Trends and Forecasts*, Vol. 1, Oxon: CAB International, pp. 149–158.

Ritchie, J.R.B. and Goeldner, C. (eds) (1987) *Travel, Tourism and Hospitality Research: A Handbook for Managers and Researchers*, New York: John Wiley & Sons.

Ritchie, J.R.B. and Yangzhou, J. (1987) 'The Role and Impact of Mega-Events and Attractions on National and Regional Tourism: A Conceptual and Methodological Overview', *Proceedings of the 37th AIEST Congress held in Calgary, Canada (August 23–29)*, Vol. 28, St. Gall, Switzerland: Association of Scientific Experts in Tourism, pp. 17–57.

Robert, M.M. (1991) 'Attack Competitors By Changing the Game Rules', *The Journal of Business Strategy*, (Sept/Oct): 53–56.

Robinson, G. and Mogendorff, D. (1993) 'The European tourism industry ready for the single market?', *International Journal of Hospitality Management*, 12(1): 21–32.

Robinson, R.D. (1973) *International Business Management: A Guide to Decision Making*, Chicago: The Dryden Press.

Rodrigues, C.J. (1987) 'European travel the way ahead', *Tourism Management*, 8(2) June: 134–136.

Rogers, E.M. (1983) *Diffusion of Innovations* (3rd edn), New York: The Free Press.

Rosenfeld, J.P. (1986) 'Demographics on Vacation', *American Demographics*, 8(1): 38–41.

Rounce, J. (1987) 'International Hotel Product Branding: Segmenting the Marketplace', *Travel & Tourism Analyst*, (February): 13–22.

Rubin, B.L. (1991) 'Europeans Value Diversity', *HR Magazine*, 36(1): 38–78.

Rugman, A.M. and D'Cruz, J.R. (1990) *New Visions for Canadian Business Strategies for Competing in the Global Economy*, University of Toronto.

—— and —— (1991) *Fast Forward: Improving Canada's International Competitiveness*, University of Toronto.

Rushmore, S. (1983) *Hotels, Motels, and Restaurants – Valuations and Market Studies*, Chicago, Illinois: American Institute of Real Estate Appraisers.

Salmans, S. (1977) 'Africans get a taste for the top', *International Management*, (October): 39.

Salomon Brothers (1990) *Salomon Brothers Review of Emerging Trends in Hotel Financing*, London: Salomon Brothers International Ltd.

Sampson, A. (1984) *The Politics, Contests and Cartels of World Airlines*, London: Hodder & Stoughton.

Sany, J. (1977) 'Crumbs from the Table, The Workers Share in Tourism', in B.R. Finney and K.A Watson (eds), *A New Kind of Sugar: Tourism in the Pacific*, Hawaii: The East West Center.

Sasser, W.E. and Banks, R.L. (1975) *Financing the Lodging Industry: A Survey of Lender Attitudes*, Philadelphia: Laventhol & Horwath.

Sasser, W.E., Olsen, R.P., and Wyckoff, D.D. (1978) *Management of Service Operations*, Boston: Allyn & Bacon.

Schlesinger, L. and Heskett, J.L. (1991) 'The Service Driven Service Company', *Harvard Business Review*, (Sept–Oct): 71–81.

Schneider, B. (1990) 'The Climate for Service', in B. Schneider (ed.), *Organizational Climate and Culture*, San Francisco: Jossey-Bass, pp. 383–412.

Schneider, B. and Bowen, D.E. (1985) 'Employee and Customer Perceptions of Service in Banks: Replication and Extension', *Journal of Applied Psychology*, 70: 423–433.

Schneider, B., Parkington, J. and Bxtou, V. (1980) 'Employee and Customer Perception of Service in Banks', *Administrative Science Quarterly*, 25: 252–267.

Schonberger, R.J. (1990) *Building a Chain of Customers Linking Business Functions to Create the World Class Company*, New York: The Free Press.

Schumpeter, J.A. (1965) *The Theory of Economic Development: An Inquiry into Profit, Credit, Interest, and the Business Cycle* (4th edn), Oxford: Oxford University Press.

SCMP (1993) 'Hong Kong and Singapore far ahead of rivals in crucial area', *South China Morning Post*, Business Section, 26 August.

Segal, G. (1988) *The Stoddart Guide to the World Today*, Toronto: Stoddart Publishing Co. Ltd.

Sellers, P. (1990) 'What Customers Want', *Fortune*, 121(13): 58–68.

Shafer, E.L. (1989) 'Future Encounters with Science and Technology', *Journal of Travel Research*, XXVII(4) (Spring): 2–7.

Shames, G. (1986) 'Training for the Multicultural Workplace', *The Cornell HRA Quarterly*, 26(4): 25–31.

Shames, G.W. and Glover, W.G. (1989) *World Class Service*, Yarmouth, Maine: Intercultural Press.

Shapiro, A.C. (1982) *Multinational Financial Management*, Boston: Allyn & Bacon.

Sharp, I. (1987) 'In Search of Success', Address to The Harvard Business Club of Toronto, 27 October.

—— (1991) 'Managing for Global Market Leadership', *Business Quarterly*, (Summer): 16–19.

Sharpe, J.I. (1990) 'Directions for the 90s: Lessons from Japan', *The Cornell HRA Quarterly*, 31(1): 98–103.

Shelp, R.K. (1984) 'The role of service technology in development', in R.K. Shelp, *et al.* (eds) *Service Industries and Economic Development – Case Studies in Technology Transfer* New York: Praeger.

Sheraton (1986) *The Employee Magazine of the Sheraton Corporation*, 2: 32.

Sherry, J.E.H. (1993) 'The Legal Status of Bed-and-Breakfast Operations', *The Cornell HRA Quarterly*, April: 12–13.

Sigiura, H. (1990) 'How Honda Localizes Its Global Strategy', *Sloan Management Review*, (Fall): 77–82.

Slattery, P. (1991) 'Hotel branding in the 1990s', *Travel and Tourism Analyst*, no. 1 (Sept): 23–35.

Slattery, P. and Johnson, S. (1990) *Quoted Hotel Companies: The World Markets*, London: Kleinwort Benson Securities.

Slattery, P. and Olsen, M. (1984) 'Hospitality Organisations and Their Environment', *International Journal of Hospitality Management*, 3(2): 55–61.

Smith, G. (1991) 'Tourism, Telecommunications, and Transnational Banking: A Study in International Interactions', Doctoral dissertation, Washington, DC: International Communications Program, School of International Service, The American University.

Smith, S.M. and Beik, L.L. (1982) 'Market Segmentation for Fund Raisers', *Journal of the Academy of Marketing Science*, (Summer): 208–216.

SMP (1993) 'Industry fuels growth', *Sunday Morning Post*, 5 December.

Snepenger, D. (1987) 'Segmenting the Vacation Market by Novelty-Seeking Role', *Journal of Travel Research*, XXVI(2): 8–14.

Sonnenberg, F.K. (1991) 'A Strategic Approach to Employee Motivation', *The Journal of Business Strategy*, (May/June): 41–43.

—— (1991) 'Internal Communications: Turning Talk into Action', *The Journal of Business Strategy*, 12(6): 52–55.

Spearman, R. (1993) 'Interview with regional vice-president of human resources of Holiday Inn Worldwide, Mr. Robin Spearman, talking about the new Holiday Inn University in China', *Asian Hotel and Catering Times*, 6(12) (June): 34.

Steene, A. (1991) 'Personal Network as a Business Strategy', *Annals of Tourism Research*, 18(4): 666–668.

Stephens, T., Surprenant, C., English, M. and Gillett, T. (1987) 'Customers Speak Out About Value', *Add Value to Your Service*, 6th Annual Services Marketing Conference Proceedings, Chicago: American Marketing Association.

Stewart, H.B. (1989) *Recollecting the Future: A View of Business, Technology and Innovation in the Next 30 Years*, Homewood, Illinois: Dow Jones–Irwin.

Stigler, G.J. (1965) *Essays in the History of Economics*, Chicago.

Sullivan, S. (1989) 'The New Supertrains', *Newsweek*, 31 July: 46–48.

Teichova, A. (1986) 'Multinationals in Perspective', in A. Teichova, M. Levy-Leboyer and H. Nussbaum (eds), *Multinational Enterprise in Historical Perspective*, Cambridge: Cambridge University Press, pp. 362–375.

Terpstra, V. (1985) 'The Changing Environment of International Marketing', *International Marketing Review*, 2(3): 7–16.

Tettero, J.H.J.P. and Viehoff, J.H.R.M. (1990) *Marketing voor dienstverlenende organisaties*, Beleid & uitvoering, Deventer: Kluwer.

Theuns, H.L. (1985) 'Onstaan en ontwikkeling van het massatoerisme naar de derde wereld', *Economisch Statistische Berichten*, 70(3516): 752–759.

—— (1988) *Toerisme in Ontwikkelingslanden*, Tilburg, The Netherlands: Tilburg University Press.

—— (1993) 'Matching Regional Products with Demand – The Case of Mountain and City Tourism, Warsaw', Paper for the Conference on Development of the Tourism Product in the Malopolska Region, Krynica, October 13–16.

Thomas, D.R.E. (1978) 'Strategy is Different in Service Businesses', *Harvard Business Review*, (July–August): 158–165.

Thurow, L.C. (1992) 'Lesson for Success Skilled Workers are Tomorrow's Only Real Asset', *Challenges*, 5(1): 8–14.

Tichy, N.M. and Devanna, M.A. (1990) *The Transformational Leader*, New York: Wiley.

Tideman Dr, M.C. (1987) '25 Jaar Hotellerie in Nederland', Farewell lecture presented at the Hotelschool, the Hague (June).

Towner, J. (1985) 'The Grand Tour: A Key Phase in the History of Tourism', *Annals of Tourism Research*, 12(3): 298–326.

Townsend, B. (1990) 'Hotels of the Future, An Interview with Adam M. Aron', *American Demographics*, 12(1): 46–47.

Transport (1991) *Scala*, 6 (December): 9.

Truitt, L.J., Teye, V.B. and Farris, M.T. (1991) 'The Role of Computer Reservation Systems: International Implications for the Travel Industry', *Tourism Management*, (March): 21–35.

Tung, R.L. (1981) 'Selection and training for personnel for overseas assignments', *Columbia Journal of Business*, (Spring): 68–78.

Tung, R.L. and Miller, E.L. (1990) 'Managing in the twenty-first century: The need for global orientation', *Management International Review*, 30(1): 5–19.

Turner, L. and Ash, J. (1975) *The Golden Hordes: International Tourism and the Pleasure Periphery*, London: Constable.

Turner, S.M. (1990) 'Introduction', *EuroCity Survey*, London: Pannell Kerr Forster Associates.

ULI (1984) *Hotel/Motel Development*, Washington, DC: The Urban Land Institute.

—— (1987) *Development Trends*, Washington, DC: The Urban Land Institute.

UNCTC (1988) *Transnational Corporations in World Development Trends and Prospects*, New York: United Nations Centre on Transnational Corporations.

Undiandeye, L. (1984) *The Role of Multinational Corporations in the Transfer of Management Technology to Nigeria*, University Microfilms International.

United Nations (1982) *Transnational Corporations in International Tourism*, New York: United Nations Centre for Transnational Corporations (UNCTC).

Van Doren, C.S. (1981) 'Outdoor Recreation Trends in the 1980s, Implications for Society', *Journal of Travel Research*, 19(3) (Winter).

—— (1990) *A History of Knowledge – The Pivotal Events People, and Achievements of World History*, New York: Ballantine.

Van Doren, C.S. and Lollar, S. (1985) 'The Consequences of Tourism Growth', *Annals of Tourism Research*, 12(3): 467–489.

Van Rietbergen, T., Bosman, J., and de Smidt, M. (1990) *Internationalisering van de dienstensector. Nederlandse ondernemingen in modiaal perspectief*, Muiderberg: Dick Coutinho.

Vernon, R. (1966) 'International Investment and International Trade in the Product Cycle', *Quarterly Journal of Economics*, 80 (May): 190–207.

Viant, A. (1993) 'Enticing the elderly to travel', *Tourism Management*, (February): 52–60.

Walker, B. (1988) 'A comparison of international versus domestic expansion by US franchise systems', Tempe, Arizona: International Franchise Association. Cited in F. Go and J. Christensen (1989) 'Going Global', *The Cornell HRA Quarterly*, 30(3): 72–79.

Wall Street Journal (1987) 'The Holiday Inns Trip: A Breeze For Decades, Bumpy Ride in the 1980s', *The Wall Street Journal*, 11 Feb.: 1.

Wallis, C. (1991) 'Remarks in 1990 Operations Review', *Four Seasons Hotels and Resorts 1990 Annual Report*, Toronto: Four Seasons Hotels and Resorts.

Walsh, J. (1994) 'Will the jobs ever come back?', *Time*, 143(6): 32–38.

Wardell, D. (1987) 'Airline Reservation Systems in the U.S.A.', *Travel & Tourism Analyst*, (January): 45–56.

Washington Post (1989) *The Washington Post*, 2 January.

Wasmer, D.J. and Bruner II, G.C. (1991) 'Using Organizational Culture to Design Internal Marketing Strategies', *The Journal of Services Marketing*, 5(1): 35–46.

Waterman, R.H. Jr. (1987) *The Renewal Factor, How the Best Get and Keep the Competitive Edge*, New York: Bantam Books.

Waterman, R.H. Jr., Peters, T.J. and Phillips, J.R. (1980) 'Structure is Not Organization', *Business Horizons*, (June): 14–26.

Watson, W.G. (1988) *National Pastimes – Economics of Canadian Leisure*, Vancouver: Fraser Institute.

Weekly, J.K. and Aggarwal, R. (1987) *International Business Operating in the Global Economy*, New York: The Dryden Press.

WEF (1993) *The 1993 World Competitiveness Report*, Lausanne, Switzerland: World Economic Forum, IMD International.

WEFA (n.d.) *The Contribution of the World Travel and Tourism Industry to the Global Economy*, New York: American Express Travel Related Services Co. Ltd.

Weil, R. (ed.) (1982) *The OMNI Future Almanac*, New York: World Almanac Publications.

West, J.J. and Olsen, M.D. (1989) 'Competitive tactics in foodservice: are high performers different?', *The Cornell HRA Quarterly*, 30(1): 68–76.

Westley, F. and Mintzberg, H. (1989) 'Visionary Leadership and Strategic Management', *Strategic Management Journal*, 10: 17–32.

Wheatcroft, S. (1990) 'Towards Transnational Airlines', *Tourism Management*, (December).

Whiteley, R.C. (1991) *The Customer Driven Company: Moving from Talk to Action*, Reading, Mass.: Addison-Wesley.

Williams, A.V. and Zelinsky, W. (1970) 'On Some Patterns in International Tourist Flows', *Economic Geography*, 46(4): 549–567.

Williams, A. and Shaw, G. (eds) (1988) *Tourism and Economic Development Western European Experiences*, London: Belhaven Press.

Wilson, K. (1993) 'Guangdong gears up for service revolution', *Sunday Morning Post*, 29 Nov, p. 2 (Money).

Wind, Y., Douglas, S.P. and Perlmutter, H.V. (1973) 'Guidelines for Developing International Marketing Strategies', *Journal of Marketing*, 37 (April): 14–23.

Withiam, G. (1985) 'The evolution of the hospitality industry', *The Cornell HRA Quarterly*, 26(1): 36–68.

Witt, S.F., Brooke, M.Z. and Buckley, P.J. (1991) *The Management of International Tourism*, London: Unwin Hyman.

Wolfe. C. (1991) 'Talking Tech With Marriott', *Lodging Hospitality*, (June): 39–42.

Wolfson, M. (1964) 'Government's Role in Tourism Development', *Development Digest*, 5: 50–56.

WP (1989) Interview with J.W. Marriott Jr, Chairman and CEO of the Marriott Corporation, *Washington Post*, 2 Jan, p. 1 (Business).

Wright, R.W. (1990) 'Networking Japanese Style', *Inside Guide*, 4(4): 58–62.

WTO (1983) *International Tourism in Europe 1970–1992*, Madrid: World Tourism Organization.

—— (1985) *The Role of Transnational Tourism: Enterprises in the Development of Tourism*, Madrid: World Tourism Organization.

—— (1987) Seminar on the development of international tourism in Europe by Madrid, Spain, World Tourism Organization, 2–4 June (26 pages).

—— (1988a) *Guidelines for the Transfer of New Technologies in the Field of Tourism*, Madrid: World Tourism Organization.

—— (1988b) *The Problems of Protectionism and Measures to Reduce Obstacles to International Trade in Tourism Services*, Madrid: World Tourism Organization.

—— (1989) *Compendium of Tourism Statistics*, Madrid: World Tourism Organization.

—— (1990) *Message of the Secretary General* (August), Madrid: World Tourism Organization.

—— (1993) *International Tourism in Europe 1970–1992*, Madrid: World Tourism Organization (January).

WTTC Report (1991) *Travel and Tourism in the World Economy*, Brussels: The World Travel & Tourism Council.

Wyatt (1990) *Survey of Compensation Benefits in the Hotel Industry of Hong Kong*, Hong Kong: Wyatt Company.

Wyckoff, D.D. and Sasser, W.E. (1981) *The U.S. Lodging Industry*, Lexington, Mass.: Lexington Books.

Yip, G.S. (1989) 'Global Strategy . . . In a World of Nations?', *Sloan Management Review*, (Fall): 29–41.

Yip, G.S. and Coundouriotis, G.A. (1991) 'Diagnosing Global Strategy Potential: The World Chocolate Confectionary Industry', *Planning Review*, (Jan/Feb): 4–14.

Yu, R.W.Y. (1994) 'The Use of Local and Expatriate Hotel Managers in International Tourism Development: Policy and Attitude in Hong Kong', M.Phil. Thesis, Hong Kong Polytechnic.

Yu, R.W.Y. and Go, F. (1994) 'Hong Kong's hotel industry and international competitiveness', Proceedings for the First South China International Business Symposium, Vol. 1, pp. 241–243.

Yu, R.W.Y. and Pine, R.J. (1994) 'Localization of management in Hong Kong hotel industry', *The Hong Kong Manager*, (May/June).

Zall, M. (1989) 'Public International Law Trends in Tourism: Current Developments', *Tourism Policy Forum Brief*, 1(3): 1–4.

Ziff-Levine, W. (1990) 'The Cultural Logic Gap: A Japanese Tourism Research Experience', *Tourism Management*, (June): 105–110.

Zimolzak, C.E. and Stansfield, C.A. Jr. (1983) *The Human Landscape, Geography and Culture* (2nd edn), Columbus, Ohio: Charles E. Merrill.

Index

Aaker, D.A. 103, 377–8
Abacus 317
Aburdene, P. 68
ACCOR 337; brands 150–1, 153–5, 155; Europe 138, 146, 151, 153; Formule 1 244; global scale business 162–4, 258, 272
acquisitions 9, 336, 362; Europe 150; global competition 300, 301; Hong Kong MNCs 226; USA 98–9
actions, implementation challenges 288, 295–6
adaptability, local 342–4, 346, 368–9
added value see value chain
Aderhold, P. 75
Adriatic Sea 75
affiliation costs 40–1
ageing population 71–2
Aggarwal, R. 7–8
Airbus Industries 64, 376
Aircoa 226, 341
air travel 62–3, 63
airline industry: accommodation 78, 81; GDS and hotel reservation systems 65–6, 313, 322–3; impact of US dereg– ulation 283; mergers 196
airport locations 107–8
Alcoa 301
Allegis Corporation 332
alliances, strategic 127, 329, 341–2
American Airlines 313, 317, 317–18
American Express 244–5
American hotel industry see United States of America
American Hotel and Motel Association (AH&MA) 113
Amsterdam 142, 157
Ansoff, I. 110, 294

Apollo 317, 325
Arbel, A. 29–30, 367–8
Arctia 143
Argyris, C. 240
Asea 300
Asia 24, 225, 300; see also Pacific Rim
Association of South East Asian Nations (ASEAN) 130
AT&T 91
Athens 134, 147–8
Au Bon Pain 245
Austria 144
automation: global competitive environment 66, 376; marketing 46–7; see also computerized reservation systems, database marketing, global distribution systems
automobiles 62
Avis 245

bargaining power: buyers' 111–12, 311; suppliers' 113–18
barriers to entry 100–10
Barrow, Martin 175
Bartels, Juergen 125, 274, 328–9
Bartlett, C.A. 18, 344–5, 346
Bass plc 99–100, 150, 301, 365
Becheri, E. 75
bedrooms 31; see also rooms
Belgium 142–3
bench-marking 14, 272–3
benefit segmentation 80
benefit packages 211–12, 213
Berlin 138–9
Best Western International 39–40, 40, 315
Birmingham 137

birth stage 330, 331, 331–2
Bitner, M.J. 112
Bloomer, Lucius 22
Bong, Daniel 181–7 *passim*
Bonoma, T.V. 288–9, 295, 296
booking agents, hotel 115
Booms, B.H. 112
Borel (Jacques) International 150, 162
'boundaryless' thought/action 371
'branch configuration' 315
brands/brand-names 337–8; ACCOR
    150–1, 153–5, 155; brand equity
    377–8; entry barriers 103; Europe
    152–4; global products 68; multi-tier
    branding 152–3; networks 315
Bretton Woods agreement 51
Brown Boveri 300
Brussels 142–3, 157
Buckley, P.J. 59, 375–6
Budapest 146, 158
Budget Rent-a-Car 313, 317–18
Bundesbank 139
business ecosystem 327–59; Center
    Parcs 347–50; commitment to the
    environment 340; global
    reach/local adaptability 342–4;
    industry in flux 336–9; Sheraton
    and nature of global challenge
    350–9; stages of development
    330–6; strategic alliances 341–2;
    survival capacity 339–40;
    transnational model 344–7
business environment analysis 155–6
business formats 36–41; *see also under
    individual names*
business travel 58, 77–8, 375
buyers' bargaining power 110–12, 311

Canada 305
Canadian Pacific Hotels and Resorts
    278, 327–8, 373
capacity, hotels' 135, 136
capital intensity 27
capital requirements 104–6
Cara 301
Cardinal Industries 277
Caribbean cruise business 89
Carlson Hospitality Group 124–5
Carlzon, Jan 258
cash flow analysis 160–1
casinos 85
Cathay Pacific Airways 87
Center Parcs 244, 328, 330, 347–50, 364

Central Europe 12
Century International Hotels 180,
    181–8 *passim*
chain hotels *see* hotel chains
change: geopolitical 192–3; initiation
    by managers 365–6;
    institutionalizing 249–60; quantum
    theory of strategic change 275–6
channel system *see* distribution
    channels
Channel Tunnel 140
Chase, R.B. 251–4
Chek Lap Kok airport 173–4
China 168, 175, 175–6, 188;
    localization policy of MNHCs 227–8
Choice Hotels International 42–3,
    104, 240, 341
Citibank 218
cities, European 134–49
city centre locations 107
Clark, J.J. 367–8
climate for service 250–1
Club Méditerranée (Club Med) 153,
    286
Coca-Cola 218
Collins, T. 52
commercial accommodation 26
communication with employees 210
compact disc (CD) 380
Compagnie des Wagons-Lits 162, 163
compensation/reward practices
    210–14
competition 27; business ecosystem
    328–9, 330–1, 339–40; changing
    patterns 269–71; and cooperation
    in distribution channels 306–26; in
    global marketplace 299–305;
    inter-firm 173, 179–80, 339–40;
    international 271–3; strategies for
    international 294–6; USA 97–9
competitive environment, global
    50–93; automation 66; database
    marketing 85–92; economics of
    substitution 55–60; end of mass
    marketing 50–5; fragmentation of
    travel market 70–6; globalization of
    travel market 67–9; implications of
    shifting demand 76–84; quality
    69–70; technological environment
    60–6
competitiveness 84, 312; determinants
    in Hong Kong 172–80; globalization
    drivers 283–5; human factor 221–3;

international hotel industry 34–41; and organizational learning 235–40
'complex' (industrial/international hotel networks) 315
computerized reservation systems (CRS) 241, 306, 310–11, 313, 322–3; *see also* global distribution systems
concentration: hotel industry 364–5; Europe room stock in 151, 154; USA room stock in 98–9, 112
conference business travel 78, 81
conference rooms 32
configuration 270
'Confirm' project 313, 317–18
Conrad Hotels 143, 148
consolidation 33, 122–3, 362, 364–5; *see also* acquisitions, mergers
consortia 39–41
construction costs 104–6
consumer preferences 58
context, shifting 369–70
contingent lease 166
continuous improvement 245–6, 246–9
conversion of buildings 152
Cook (Thomas) & Son 62
cooperation: business ecosystem 329, 330–1; and competition in distribution channels 306–26; through transnational networks 314–21, 370–1; *see also* strategic alliances
cooperative agreements 241
coordination, system 270
core skills 329–30
corporate priorities 181–3
corporate travel market 77–8, 81
cost, as globalization driver 280–2
Cotter, Bob 88
credit cards 91
Crest Hotels 41, 100
Critical Success Factors (CSFs) 119–21, 206–7, 238
cruise line business 89, 112
culture: expatriate and local managers 217–18; implementing globalization strategies 288, 289–91; intercultural sensitivity 371–2
customer: database marketing 90–1; 'global' 54, 310, 363; internal 52–3; 'value-for-money' oriented 362, 363
customer expectations 36, 37, 246–9, 380
customer relationships 246; business

ecosystem 333–4; end of mass marketing 52; Mandarin Oriental 267
customer satisfaction 250–1, 265–7, 302
'customization' 364
'cycle of failure' 239–40
'cycle of quality' 255
Czech Republic 147

D'Amore, L.J. 78–9, 79
Danubius Hotel and Spa Company 146
Darwin, Charles 328
database marketing 52; accommodations 87–8; applications to tourism industry 85–92; Harrah's casinos 85
Day, G.S. 83
Days Inns 88, 301
D'Cruz, J.R. 237
debt costs 29–30
Deeson, Brian 181–7 *passim*
Delta Airlines 289
demand: distribution channels 309–11; fluctuations 27; future trends 361–2, 362–4; Hong Kong hotel industry 172, 175–7; shifting in travel market 53–5, 76–84; travel in Europe 133
demographic change 70–2, 194–5
developing countries: development of tourism 7; foreign direct investment 12; local and expatriate managers 216; Sheraton and Pacific region 350–9
differentiation, product 80, 102–4, 155; *see also* brands/brand names
direct distribution channels 307
direct marketing 52, 85–6; *see also* customer relationships, database marketing
direct reservations 69
discretionary income 72–5, 363–4
Disney Productions 9–10
Disney World 315
distribution channels 306–26; buyers' bargaining power 111–12; database marketing 89; GDS *see* global distribution systems; globalization drivers 282–3; Holiday Inn Worldwide 321–2; network concept 314–21; shifting demand 309–11; turbulent environment 311–14; and

value chain 306–14
diversification 277–8
Drucker, P.F. 243
Dubrule, Paul 162
Dunning, J.H. 221
Dusit Thani group 272
Duta Anggada 127

Eastern Europe 12, 157, 192, 366;
    cities 146–7
eclectic theory of MNCs 221
economies of scale 9, 100–2, 244
Econo Lodges 42
ecosystem *see* business ecosystem
Edinburgh 137–8
education 122; enhancing educational
    process 373–4; *see also* human
    resources strategy
educational institutions 374
Edwards, A. 59–60
effectiveness, global 13–17
'elderly' travel market 71, 71–2, 364
Elfring, T. 58
Emerald Management Company 297
employee attitude 119–20, 238
employee involvement 249–55, 303–4
employee performance 249–50
employee recognition programmes
    210, 212–13, 214
employee satisfaction 250–1; ITT
    Sheraton 351–8
entrants, threat of new 100–10
entry barriers 100–10
entry strategies 149–61
environment: commitment to 327–8,
    335–6, 340; operating responsibly
    372–3; rising concern for 54, 75–6
environmental scanning 245
EPCOT 289
Estonia 145
ethically responsible operations 372–3
ethnocentrism (home-country
    orientation) 4, 6, 215–16, 217
Europe 129–67, 290, 364, 381; ACCOR
    162–4; business environment
    analysis 155–6; Eastern Europe
    146–7; entry and expansion
    strategies 149–61; fore-casting sales
    159; hotel trends in major cities
    134–5; market potential 156–8;
    overview of cities 135–49;
    prospective profitability vs risk
    159–61, 164–7; Scandinavia 144–6;

Southern Europe 147–9; strategy
    implementation challenges 287;
    and tourism 59, 60, 129–34;
    Western Europe 136–44
European Commission 142
European Community (EC): GNP 67;
    population growth 70, 377; Single
    Market 132, 133, 155, 300
European Economic Area (EEA)
    129–30
European Institute of Education and
    Social Policy (EIESP) 118
European Monetary System 133
'Europe's Seaside Resorts and
    Tomorrow's Tourism' conference
    75–6, 377
Exchange Rate Mechanism 133
exchange rates 60
expansion: business ecosystem 330,
    331, 332–3; strategies 27–8, 30–2
    (comparison 41–3; in Europe
    149–61; in Hong Kong 183–6)
expatriate managers 214–28
experience-curve effects 109
'expressed theory' 240

factors of production 172, 173–4; *see
    also under individual names*
'failure, cycle of' 239–40
family vacation market 71
fax machine 380
Fiat 147
Fieldhouse, D.K. 5–7
'*filiere* configuration' 315
finance 32–3; entry barrier 104–6;
    localization strategy 292–3; origins
    of oversupply 29–30; prospective
    profitability vs risk 165–7; *see also*
    investment
finance lease 166
Finland 144–5
foreign direct investment (FDI) 12,
    106
formats, business 36–41; *see also under
    individual names*
Forte Hotels 41–2, 43, 153, 153–4
Forum Hotels International 21, 22, 23
Four Seasons Hotels and Resorts 301,
    302; customer expectations 36, 37,
    247–8; Europe 139, 141;
    globalization strategy 272, 274,
    276–7
fragmentation, market 54–5, 70–6; *see*

also segmentation
France 62, 134, 140–1
franchising 38–9, 166–7, 278–9, 292
Franck, C. 12
Frankfurt 139, 157
Friendship Inns 42
Friesen, P.H. 275
Fuller, Edwin 125

Gardner Merchant 41
Geller, A.N. 119–21
Galileo 241, 317, 325
Gemini 317
General Agreement on Tariffs and
    Trade (GATT) 67
General Agreement on Trade in
    Services (GATS) 67
General Motors (GM) 336
Geneva 143
geocentrism (global orientation) 5, 6,
    215
geographic segmentation 80
geopolitical change 192–3
Germany 64, 132, 134, 278; cities
    138–40
Ghoshal, S. 18, 344–5, 346
Gladwin, T.N. 217
global brands 68
global competitive environment *see*
    competitive environment
global corporation 13, 279–80
'global customer' 54, 310, 363
global distribution systems (GDS)
    14–15, 241, 283, 285; airline
    industry 65, 65–6, 322–3;
    concentration of demand 50, 53;
    history and evolution 322–5;
    marketing hotels using 322–6;
    networking 316–17, 317–18;
    suppliers' bargaining power
    114–16, 123; value chain 308–9
global opportunities/challenges 366–9
global reach 342–4, 348–9
'global village' 366–7
globalization 3–24; effectiveness
    13–17; orientations 4–5, 6; rise of
    MNCs 5–12; trend towards 362, 365
globalization drivers 280–5
'globalization mindset' 368, 369–74
globalization strategies 16–17, 368–9;
    classic 278–80; competing
    internationally 294–6, 299–305;
    corporate options 276–8; cultural

sensitivity 289–91; drivers 280–5;
    implementation challenges 285–9;
    implementing 269–305; localization
    291–4; Pan Pacific 297–9; potential
    280–96; taxonomy of
    implementation 295–6
Glover, W.G. 289–90
Go, F. 26
goals, organizational 205–6, 206
Gold Bond Stamp Company 123–4
Golden Tulip Hotels Company 270
Goldfarb Consultants 36
golf 69, 376
governments: globalization drivers
    283; influencing public policy 372;
    partnership with hotel industry and
    educational institutions 374;
    partnership with hotel industry and
    unions 195–6; and tourism 3
Grand Metropolitan 9, 21–2
Greece 147–8, 159
gross domestic product (GDP) 57–8,
    58, 134
gross national product (GNP) 299
group business travel 78, 81
growth *see* expansion
'growth pole model' 314
Guertin, M.K. 39–40
Gulf War 27
Gunn, C.A. 319

Hale Corporation 226
Handy, C. 256, 257
Harrah's Casinos 85
Harris, L. 72–3
Hayes, R.H. 251–4
Hazard, Robert 102, 301, 377
health centres 32
Helsinki 144–5
Henderson Hotels 106, 292
Heskett, J.L. 239, 255
Hiemstra, S.J. 117, 379
high-speed railways 63–4, 140
highway locations 108
Hilton, Conrad 292, 332
Hilton Corporation 332
Hilton International 272, 289, 301;
    China 227; 'Confirm' project 313,
    317–18; Europe 149, 150, 151, 153,
    270; expansion strategy 332–3;
    Hong Kong 169; intercultural
    sensitivity 372; MNC 279; take-over
    by Ladbroke 9, 150, 279, 332, 365;

take-over by TWA 269, 275, 332
hiring methods 208–9, 210
Holiday Corporation/Holiday Inns
    243, 272, 312; Bass plc 99, 301, 365;
    birth and expansion 331–2; China
    227; Europe 143, 149, 150, 151, 157;
    information technology (Holidex
    reservation system) 331–2;
    international company 278–9;
    resistance to change 276
holography 55, 375
Hong Kong 168–97, 219, 221;
    corporate priorities and key issues
    181–8; deter– minants of
    competitiveness 172–80; expansion
    strategies 183–6; Hotel and
    Guesthouse Accommodation
    Ordinance 174; Hotel Nikko
    189–90; hotel supply overview
    168–72; IT 186–8; local and
    expatriate managers 223–6, 294;
    streamlining for the future 190–7;
    vision 188
Hong Kong Airport Railway 173–4
Hong Kong Hotel Association
    (HKHA) 169
Horwath and Horwath 103, 117, 122–3
hotel booking agents 115
hotel chains: reason for growth 33;
    response to globalization 270–1;
    trends towards 101–2, 122–3;
    vulnerability and expansion 336–7;
    see also consolidation
hotel industry, international 25–49;
    changing structure 122–3;
    comparison of growth strategies
    41–3; competitive advantage 34–41;
    growth strategies 30–3; nature 44–5;
    origins of oversupply 29–30;
    prospects for future 361–5;
    research's role 43–9; strategy 27–9
hotel management services 179, 226
household size 72
human resources strategy 201–34,
    238–9; pay/reward practices and
    outlook 210–14; IHA survey 201,
    204–14; Inter-Continental Hotels
    229; key issue 201–3, 379; local vs
    expatriate managers 214–28;
    policies and practices 208–10;
    Ritz-Carlton Hotel Company 'Gold
    Standards' 230–3; Sheraton 351–9
Human Resources for Tourism

Conference 351
Hungary 146
Hutchison Whampoa 169
Hutton, J. 217
Hyatt Hotels Corporation 39; Europe
    141, 148; improving service 121–2;
    local and expatriate managers 223,
    227; mega-resorts 10; separation of
    real estate from operations 106

IBM 218, 336
Imai, M. 245
implementation of globalization
    strategies see globalization strategies
incentives 210, 212–13, 214
income, discretionary 72–5, 363–4
independent hotels 101; survival
    options 15–16, 270–1
indirect distribution channels 308
individualism 364
industrial market segment 78
Industrial Revolution 61–2
information: innovation and 243;
    travel 309
information technology (IT):
    competitiveness 236, 284–5, 338;
    distribution channels 306–7,
    310–11; global competitive
    environment 50, 53–4, 60–1, 64–6;
    marketing automation 46–7; Hong
    Kong 186–8; and networking
    316–17, 319–21; see also
    computerized reservation systems,
    database marketing, global
    distribution systems
infrastructure, transportation 158,
    173–4, 188, 310
innovation 302, 311–12; enhancing
    competence 242–5; organizational
    renewal 240–5
institutionalization of change 249–60
integration 277
integrative mode 242
Inter-Continental Hotels 241, 269,
    272, 301, 373; business ecosystem
    333–5; Environmental Reference
    Manual 340; Europe 23, 138, 149,
    150, 152, 157; globalization process
    4, 21–4; human resources strategy
    229; multinational company 279;
    Project Argonaut 333–4; Project
    Flyright 334–5; take-over by Grand
    Metropolitan 9, 21–2; take-over by

Seibu-Saison 9, 22, 24, 278, 365
InterHotels AG 138
internal customer 52-3
internal rate of return (IRR) 160
internalization advantages 11
'international company' 278-9
International Hotel Association (IHA)
    203-4; *Hotels of the Future* 31, 32-3,
    38, 379; survey on human resources
    201, 204-14
international hotel industry *see* hotel
    industry
International Hotels Environment
    Initiative 340
internationalization *see* globalization
investment: foreign direct (FDI) 12,
    106; international investment
    analysis 159-61, 164-7;
    responsibility to investors 191-3; *see
    also* finance
Istanbul 134, 148
Italy 134, 141-2
ITT *see* Sheraton

Jafari, J. 7
Jaguar 325
Japan 16, 193, 300; GDP growth 57;
    high-speed rail 64; investment in
    USA 106; localization of
    management 218, 219; promotion
    of tourism 376; quality revolution
    70, 245; tourism expenditures 59,
    59-60; tourism market in Hong
    Kong 175; transnationals and
    management style 290
Japan Travel Bureau 86
Jarvis, Roger 244
Johnson (W.B.) Properties 230
joint ventures 341, 382

Kanter, R.M. 242
Kapioltas, John 149-50, 280
Kaven, W.K. 112
KLM 270
Knott Hotels Corporation 41
Korea 193, 194
Kotler, P. 237
Kraft 378
Kuok Brothers Group 261

La Quinta Motor Inns 277, 333
labour: Hong Kong hotel industry
    shortage 173, 182-3; pay *see* pay;

shortage trends 202, 303, 362, 365;
    skills and competitive advantage
    338-9; turnover 239-40, 378-9, 379;
    US hotel industry 116-18, 122, 123,
    378-9; *see also* employee attitude,
    employee involvement, employee
    performance, employee satisfaction,
    human resources strategy, training
Ladbroke Group plc 9, 150, 279, 332,
    365
Lakatos, P.A.M. 74
Lambooy, J.G. 314-15
Langton, Bryan D. 322
Laurent, A. 291
leadership 381; business ecosystem
    330, 331, 333-5; transformational
    256-60
Leading Hotels of the World 40
learning, organizational 235-40
leases 166
Leclercq, Jean-Marie 15, 16, 189-90
Lee Gardens (hotel) 227
legislation 109-10
leisure: income and time for 72-5,
    363-4; recreation, tourism and 330,
    331
leisure travel segment 80-2
length of stay 176, 177
Leven, M.A. 111
Levitt, T. 5, 118
Li Ka-shing 169
Li Peng 188
life expectancy 72
lifecare centre concept 72
limited partnerships 105
Lisbon 148-9, 157-8
Liverpool and Manchester Railway
    61-2
local adaptability 342-4, 346, 368-9
localization 291-4; management
    214-28, 293-4; MNHCs in China
    227-8; production 291-2; profit
    292-3
location 107-8, 165; location-specific
    advantages 10-11
London 136-7, 157, 343-4
'long-haul' travel market 362, 363-4
Lyons (J) & Company 41

Ma, Mac 181-7 *passim*
Mabry, M. 64
Madrid 149, 157-8
management: localization 214-28,

293–4; national styles 290–1

management contracts 292; hotel ownership vs 37–8; management technology transfer 220, 221; multinational company 279; prospective profitability vs risk 166

managers: implementation of globalization strategy 295–6; initiation of change 365–6; local vs expatriate 214–28

Manchester 138

Mandarin Oriental Hotel Group 180, 235, 261–7; customer satisfaction 265–7; Guest History network 267; Legendary People programme 264–5; mission statement 262–3; priorities and key issues 181–7 *passim*; strategic quality planning and leadership 263–7

Manor Care 42, 275

Maritim Hotels 138, 140

market: fragmentation 54–5, 70–6; globalization 14; globalization drivers 282–3; penetration 28; potential 156–8; segmentation *see* segmentation; travel market *see* travel market

marketing: automation 46–7; database marketing *see* database marketing; using GDS 322–6; mass 50–5, 92; new environment 86–7; orientation 57; productivity 90; relationship marketing *see* customer relations

Marriott, J.W. 336

Marriott Corporation 378; 'Confirm' project 313, 317–18; continuous improvement 247; core skills 330; Demand Forecasting System (DFS) 126; Europe 141, 146; expansion through partnerships 125–7; franchising 39; Germany 278; Honored Guest Awards (HGA) program 87, 126–7; integration 277; MARSHA reservation system 126; product innovation 240; Residence Inn 31; strategic reorientations 275; value 35; weekend pleasure travel 82

mass marketing 92; end of 50–5

McQueen, M. 221

media, private 89

mega-resorts 10, 301

mergers 9, 336, 362; global competition 300, 301

Meridien group 143

Mexico 376

migration 61, 67–8

Milan 141

Miller, D. 275

Miura, Yasuyuki 290

Momberger, Wolfgang 335

'moments of truth' 249

Moore, J.F. 330–3

Motel 6 162, 163, 337

motivation 210, 212–13, 214

Mount Charlotte 151

Movenpick Hotels International 143, 148, 301, 342

Mullins, Kenneth 181–8 *passim*

multinational corporations (MNCs) 5–12, 365, 375; character 7–8; cultural sensitivity 290–1; FDI 12; globalization strategies 279, 381; internalization advantages 11; local vs expatriate managers 214–28; location-specific advantages 10–11; ownership-specific advantages 8–10; travel infrastructure 3–4

multi-skilling 356–7

Munich 140

Nabisco (RJR) 378

Naisbitt, J. 68

Nestlé's 218, 219

net present value (NPV) 160

Netherlands 142, 270

networks 314–21, 368; barriers to 319; characteristics relevant to hoteliers 315–16; competitive globalization drivers 284–5; cooperation 314–21, 370–1; IT and 316–17, 319–21; types of 314–15; *see also* global distribution systems

new entrants, threat of 100–10

'New Tourism' 50

New World Hotels International 179–80, 219, 226, 227, 228; priorities and key issues 181–8 *passim*

nights spent abroad 59–60

Nikko Hotels International 189–90, 289, 290

North America 23–4, 287, 381; *see also* Canada, United States

North American Free Trade Area (NAFTA) 129–30

Norway 145

Novotel SIE 150, 162

ocean liner travel 63
Ohmae, K. 241, 341
'old guard' hotel corporations 257–8
'Old Tourism' 50
Olympics 145
Omni 226
One Stop Sweden 146
Organization for Economic
  Cooperation and Development
  (OECD) 58
organizational learning 235–40
organizational renewal 235–68;
  competitiveness and organizational
  learning 235–40; continuous
  improvement 245–6, 246–9;
  employee involvement 249–55;
  institutionalizing change 249–60;
  Mandarin Oriental Hotel Group
  261–7; recognizing need for
  revitalization 240–5; Shangri-La
  International 260–1;
  transformational leadership 256–60
organizational goals 205–6, 206
organizational structure 173, 179–80
orientations to globalization 4–5, 6
Oslo 145
oversupply 29–30
ownership: vs management contracts
  37–8; ownership-specific advantages
  8–10

Pacific Rim 54, 381; market trends
  and tourism 193–6, 362–3; Pan
  Pacific 297–9; Sheraton 350–9;
  strategy implementation challenges
  287–8
Pan American Airways 21, 22, 269
Pan Pacific Hotels and Resorts 297–9
Pannell Kerr Forster Associates'
  EuroCity Survey 134, 136–49
Pannonia Hotel and Catering
  Company 146
Parasuraman, A. 57
Paris 140–1, 157
Park Lane Hotels International 180,
  181–8 passim, 342
pay: practices and outlook 210–14; US
  hotel industry 116, 378–9
Pélisson, Gérard 162–4
Peninsula Group 227
performance: compensation and
  reward policies 210–11; employee
  249–50

personal computer industry 338
Phillips 336
Pine, R.J. 220, 224
'place, sense of' 373
planning 47–9
pleasure travel 78–9, 81, 377; weekend
  80–2, 83
Poland 147
policies: implementation challenges
  289, 295–6; influencing public
  policy 372
polycentrism (host-country
  orientation) 4, 6, 215–16
Poon, A. 50
population growth 70–1, 377
Porter, M.E. 100, 107, 110, 280;
  competitiveness 172–3, 238;
  structural model 97, 98
Portugal 148–9
positioning themes 84
Prague 147, 158
Preferred Hotels Worldwide 40
prices: competition 135; relative price
  changes 60
Prince of Wales' Business Leaders'
  Forum 340
private media 89
process: bench-marking and 272–3;
  design and output problems 121
process innovation 240–1, 244–5, 380
product differentiation 80, 102–4, 155
product growth strategies 31–2
product innovation 240, 243–4, 337
product/market blending 78–9, 79, 377
production, localization of 291–2
productivity: declining labour
  productivity 378; marketing 90;
  streamlining for the future 190–7
products, substitute 112–13
profit, localization of 292–3
profitability 302; prospective vs risk
  159–61, 164–7; strategy and 27–8;
  streamlining for the future 190–7
programmes, implementation
  challenges and 288, 295–6
property lease 166
prospects for the hotel industry 361–5
Prudential Realty 37
public policy, influencing 372

quality: cultural sensitivity and 289–91;
  cycle of quality service 255; fall in
  service quality 380; global

competitive environment 69–70; Mandarin Oriental 264–5; organizational renewal 245–9; Total Quality Control (TQC) 245; Total Quality Management (TQM) 127
Quality Inns International 102, 275, 301, 377
quantum theory of strategic change 275–6
Quinta (La) Motor Inns 277, 333

Radisson 125, 301, 342
railways 61–2, 63–4, 140
Ramada 88, 98, 141, 179–80, 219, 226; *see also* New World Hotels International
Rapp, S. 52
reach, global 342–4, 368–9
real estate 104–6
real estate investment trusts (REITs) 104–5
recreation 330, 331
Regal Hotels International Holdings 180, 181–7 *passim*, 226
Regent International Hotels 272
regiocentrism (regional orientation) 4–5, 6, 215
Relais and Chateaux 40
related/supporting industries 172, 178–9
relationship marketing *see* customer relations
renewal *see* organizational renewal
research 43–9
reservation systems, computerized (CRS) 241, 306, 310–11, 313, 322–3; *see also* global distribution systems
reservations, direct 69
Residence Inn 31
resort locations 108–9
restaurants 32
Riley, Robert 181–7 *passim*
risk, prospective profitability vs 159–61, 164–7
Ritz-Carlton Hotel Company 'Gold Standards' 230–3
Roach, Lynn 87
Robinson, R.D. 217
robotics 66, 376
Rodeway Inns 42, 98
Rome 141–2
rooms: concentration in EC 154; Hong Kong 169–72, 174; product

strategies 31, 32; revenue in European cities 134–5; total stock 27; *see also* supply
Rugman, A.M. 237
Rushmore, S. 40–1

Sabre 317, 325
Saison Group 9, 22, 24, 278, 365
sales forecasting 159
SAS International Hotels 278, 301, 342
scale economies 9, 100–2, 244
Scandic 151
Scandinavia 144–6
Scandinavian Airlines System 289
Schlesinger, L. 239, 255
Schneider, B. 250
Schou, D.A. 240
Scottish and Newcastle plc 350
Scott's Hospitality Inc. 99
Scott's Hotels 127
segmentalism mode 242
segmentation, market 32, 281, 301; Europe 152–4; global competitive environment 79–82, 83–4; product differentiation 80, 102–4, 155; US hotel industry 102–4; *see also* fragmentation
Seibu-Saison Group 9, 22, 24, 278, 365
self-renewal 330, 331, 335–6
'sell through' techniques 114–15
seniors market segment 71, 71–2, 364
'sense of place' 373
service: climate for 250–1; competing in global marketplace 302–4; cultural sensitivity and quality 289–91; profits, productivity and 190–7; quality 245–9, 380
service sector: growth 51–2; Hong Kong's dependence on 178–9, 180; hotel management services 179, 226; 'old guard' and 'world class' organizations 257–8; performance classification for firms 251–4; typology 56–7; Uruguay Round 12
Shames, G.W. 289–90
Shangri-La International 227, 235, 260–1
Sharp, Isadore 247–8, 274, 276
Sharpe, J.I. 342
Sheraton 106, 272, 289, 292, 351–9; database marketing 87–8, 88, 89; Employee Satisfaction Index (ESI) 354, 355; Europe 149–50;

franchising 275; global corporation
280; gross operating profit (GOP)
355; Guest Satisfaction Index (GSI)
286–7, 355; human resources
strategy 351–9; localization in
China 227, 227–8; Sheraton Club
International (SCI) 89; Yield Index
355
'short-break' travel market 362, 363–4
Siemens 300
Singapore 178–9, 193, 194
single business strategy 276–7
skills: competitive advantage and
338–9; core skills 329–30;
multi-skilling 356–7; *see also* human
resources strategy, training
Slovakia 147
'social networks' 314–15
Sol Group 151, 153
Sony 139
Southern Pacific Hotel Corporation
226
Spain 3, 149, 336, 343
Special Administrative Region (SAR)
188
Spectrum 325
Speed Travel Destination
Management Company 66
spending patterns 58–60, 157; Hong
Kong 176–7
Standard Life 137–8
steamers 62
Steigenberger Reservation Service
(SRS) 66
Stockholm 146
Strand hotels 41
strategic alliances 127, 329, 341–2
strategic change, quantum theory of
275–6
strategic choices 83–4
strategy 27–9, 273–4; bench-marking
and 272–3; competitiveness in
Hong Kong 173, 179–80;
globalization *see* globalization
strategies
substitutes: economics of substitution
55–60; threat of substitute products
112–13
suburban locations 108
supplementary accommodation 26
suppliers' bargaining power 113–18
supply: European tourism trends
133–4; Hong Kong's hotel supply

168–72; origins of oversupply
29–30; prospects for the future 362,
364–5
supporting/related industries 172, 178–9
survival capacity 339–40
Sweden 146
SwissAir 143
'switching gears' 370, 371
Switzerland 143–4
System One 317
systems, implementation challenges
and 288, 295–6

Taco Bell 245
Taiwan 175, 193
take-overs *see* acquisitions
technology 122, 378; barriers to use of
236; global environment 60–6;
suppliers' bargaining power
113–15, 123; *see also* automation,
information technology
technology transfer: human factor
219–21; Sheraton 352–3, 356–8
telecommunications 64–6; *see also*
information technology, technology
Tettero, J.H.J.P. 55–7
TGV (high-speed rail) 63–4, 140
'theory in use' 240
Thurow, Lester 299
time, leisure 72–5, 363–4
Tokyu Corporation 298–9
Tokyu Hotels International 297
Total Quality Control (TQC) 245
Total Quality Management (TQM) 127
tourism: arrivals 130–1; dynamic and
static elements 26; Europe 59, 60,
129–34; expenditures 58–60, 157,
176–7; government, unions and
industry partnership in Pacific Rim
195–6; Hong Kong 168; host
countries and 344; and national
economies 12; 'old' and 'new' 50;
prospects for 362–3; receipts 51,
130–1; recreation, leisure and 330,
331; *see also* travel market
Townsend, B. 121
trade 299–300
trade barriers 67
training 26–7, 122, 239, 254, 374, 380;
ACCOR 164; IHA survey 208, 209;
Inter-Continental 229; local and
expatriate managers 222–3, 227–8;
see also human resources strategy

Trans World Airlines (TWA) 269, 275, 332

Transworld Corporation 332

transformational leadership 256–60

transnational corporations *see* multinational corporations

transnational model/networks 344–7, 368, 370–1

transportation: infrastructure158, 173–4, 188, 310; revolutions 61–4

travel allowance restrictions 67

travel information 309

travel market: fragmentation 70–6; globalization 67–9; product/market blending 78–9, 79, 377; prospects for 362–3, 363–4; shifting demand 53–5, 76–84

Travelodge International 41

'Triad' 67

Trusthouse Forte 41, 100, 151

'truth, moments of' 249

Tumen River basin 192

Tung, R.L. 217

Turkey 3, 148

turnover, labour 239–40, 378–9, 379

Undiandeye, L. 220, 222

unemployment 132, 134

unions 195–6

United Airlines (UAL) 269, 313

United Kingdom 59, 134, 136–8

United States of America (USA) 97–128; buyers' bargaining power 110–12; Carlson Hospitality Group 123–5; changes in tourism market 192–3; Economic Recovery Tax Act (1981) 110; impact of automobiles 62; impact of deregulation of airline industry 283; industry rivalry 97–9; leisure time and income 72–3; Marriott 125–7; MNCs and localization of management 218, 219; MNCs' operating styles 290; strategic opportunities for improvement 118–23; suppliers' bargaining power 113–18; Tax

Reform Act (1986) 110; threat of new entrants 100–10; threat of substitute products 112–13; tourism expenditure 59; weekend pleasure trips 80–2

Universal Studios 10

Uruguay Round 12

value chain 120–1; competitive advantage 34–6, 37; distribution channels and 306–14; service quality 246; survival capacity 339–40; value-added processes 18, 19

'value constellation' 340

'value-for-money' oriented consumers 362, 363

Van der Valk hotels 151

Van Kralingen, R.M. 74

Viehoff, J.H.R.M. 55–7

Vienna 144, 158

vision 259

visual-imaging programmes 325

VMS Management Companies 37

Wallis, Christopher 293

Walter, I. 217

Warsaw 147

Waterman, R.H. 256

weekend pleasure travel 80–2, 83

Weekly, J.K. 7–8

Welch, P. 26

Westin 88, 269, 301

Wharf Group 226

Wilson, Kemmons 243, 278, 331–2

Woods, R.H. 29–30

world class service organizations 257–8

World Competitiveness Report 178–9

World Tourism Organization 130–2

World Travel and Tourism Environment Research Centre 382

Worldspan 317

young professional travellers 71

Yugoslavia, former 155

Zurich 143–4